Exam 70-623: *Supporting and Trou Applications on a Windows Vista* (Consumer Support Technicians

CW00405477

Objective

INSTALL AND UPGRADE WINDOWS VISTA		
Evaluate potential upgrade environments.	1	1, 2
Prepare to install Windows Vista.	2	1, 2
Troubleshoot and resolve installation issues.	2	3
Troubleshoot and resolve post-installation issues.	2	3
POST-INSTALLATION: CUSTOMIZE AND CONFIGURE SETTINGS		
Configure Sidebar.	3	2
Configure Windows Aero.	3	1
Customize and configure user accounts.	6	1
Evaluate user requirements and recommend, set up, and configure appropriate applications.	4	1, 2
Evaluate user's system and recommend appropriate settings to optimize performance.	5	1, 2
CONFIGURE WINDOWS VISTA SECURITY		
Configure Windows Security Center.	7	1
Configure Firewalls.	10	2
Configure Windows Updates.	7	1
Configure Windows Defender.	5 7 12	2 1 2
Configure Parental Controls.	8	1
Configure Internet Explorer 7+.	8	2
Configure User Account Control.	6	2
Protect data.	13	1, 2
CONFIGURE, TROUBLESHOOT, AND REPAIR NETWORKING		
Configure and troubleshoot network protocols.	9	1
Configure and troubleshoot network services at the client.	9	1
Configure and troubleshoot Windows Vista by using the Network and Sharing Center.	9 10	1 1
Configure and troubleshoot wireless networking.	9	2
Troubleshoot file and print sharing.	10	2
Configure Media Center.	4	2
INSTALL, CONFIGURE, AND TROUBLESHOOT DEVICES		
Connect peripherals to Windows Vista.	11	1, 2
Install, configure, and troubleshoot mobile devices.	11	2
Install, configure, and troubleshoot digital cameras and camcorders.	11	1
Install, configure, and troubleshoot media devices.	11	1
Install, configure, and troubleshoot printers, fax machines, and copy devices.	11	1
TROUBLESHOOT AND REPAIR WINDOWS VISTA		
Diagnose a specified issue.	12	1
Repair a corrupted operating system.	13	1, 2
Remove malware from a client system.	12	2

Note: Exam objectives are subject to change at any time without prior notice and at Microsoft's sole discretion. Please visit the Microsoft Learning Certification Web site (*www.microsoft.com/learning/mcp/*) for the most current listing of exam objectives.

MCITP Self-Paced Training Kit (Exam 70-623): Supporting and Troubleshooting Applications on a Windows Vista® Client for Consumer Support Technicians

Anil Desai

PUBLISHED BY
Microsoft Press
A Division of Microsoft Corporation
One Microsoft Way
Redmond, Washington 98052-6399

Library of Congress Control Number: 2007934737

Printed and bound in the United States of America.

1 2 3 4 5 6 7 8 9 QWT 2 1 0 9 8 7

Distributed in Canada by H.B. Fenn and Company Ltd.

A CIP catalogue record for this book is available from the British Library.

Microsoft Press books are available through booksellers and distributors worldwide. For further information about international editions, contact your local Microsoft Corporation office or contact Microsoft Press International directly at fax (425) 936-7329. Visit our Web site at www.microsoft.com/mspress. Send comments to tkinput@microsoft.com.

Acquisitions Editor: Ken Jones
Developmental Editor: Jenny Moss Benson
Project Editor: Laura Sackerman
Editorial Production: nSight, Inc.

Body Part No. X14-02699

About the Author

Anil Desai, MCITP, MCSE, MCSD, MCDBA, is an independent consultant and writer based in Austin, Texas. He specializes in implementing and managing solutions based on a wide range of Microsoft technologies. He has worked extensively with Microsoft's server products and the Microsoft .NET development platform and has managed environments that support thousands of virtual machines. He is also a Microsoft Most Valuable Professional (MVP).

Anil is the author of numerous technical books focusing on the Windows Server platform, virtualization technology, Microsoft Active Directory, Microsoft SQL Server, and IT management best practices. He has made dozens of conference presentations and is also a frequent contributor to online and print publications. When he's not busy with IT-related projects, Anil enjoys cycling in and around Austin, playing electric guitar and drums, and playing video games. For more information, please visit his personal Web site at *http://AnilDesai.net.*

Contents at a Glance

Table of Contents

What do you think of this book? We want to hear from you!

Microsoft is interested in hearing your feedback so we can continually improve our books and learning resources for you. To participate in a brief online survey, please visit:

www.microsoft.com/learning/booksurvey/

What do you think of this book? We want to hear from you!

Microsoft is interested in hearing your feedback so we can continually improve our books and learning resources for you. To participate in a brief online survey, please visit:

www.microsoft.com/learning/booksurvey/

Introduction

This training kit is designed for Consumer Support Technicians (CSTs) who support Windows Vista users in home and small business environments. It also covers all of the required objectives for Exam 70-623, Pro: Microsoft Desktop Support – CONSUMER. Candidates who pass this exam receive the Microsoft Certified IT Professional: Consumer Support Technician certification. To make the most of the content of this training kit, you should be familiar with the Microsoft Windows client operating system and using the Internet. Experience in supporting home, small business, and retail consumers is also helpful.

This training kit covers a wide variety of topics related to working with the Windows Vista operating system. Specifically, you will learn how to do the following:

- Select and recommend the most appropriate edition of Windows Vista based on customers' requirements
- Install Windows Vista and upgrade to Windows Vista from Microsoft Windows XP
- Perform postinstallation configuration and troubleshooting tasks
- Configure the many built-in media and communications applications of Windows Vista
- Optimize performance of Windows Vista
- Configure Windows security
- Enable and configure Parental Controls
- Configure wired and wireless network connections and set up network sharing
- Manage and troubleshoot hardware and device driver issues
- Troubleshoot and resolve Windows Vista operating system issues

Hardware Requirements

To follow along with the lessons and exercises in this book, you should have access to at least one computer that is running Windows Vista. Some practice exercises involve making changes to operating system configuration settings. Therefore, you should use a computer that is not relied on by specific users and that can be reconfigured for test purposes.

You can complete the majority of the practice exercises in this training kit using Windows Vista Home Premium or Windows Vista Ultimate. You can install the operating system on a desktop or notebook computer that meets the minimum system requirements for the edition of Windows Vista you are planning to use. For more information on hardware requirements, see Chapter 1, "Preparing to Install Windows Vista." If you are unfamiliar with installing the operating system, you will learn about the steps involved in Chapter 2, "Installing Windows Vista." Additional hardware and system configuration requirements are described in the introductory text for each practice exercise.

As an alternative to running Windows Vista on a physical computer, you can use a product such as Microsoft Virtual PC 2007 to install Windows Vista within a virtual machine. For more information about Virtual PC, see *http://www.microsoft.com/windows/products/winfamily/virtualpc /default.mspx*. Although you can successfully complete most exercises from within a virtual machine, you should be aware that there are additional hardware requirements on the physical computer that is running Windows Vista. Your computer should meet (at a minimum) the following hardware specifications:

- Personal computer with a 1-GHz or faster processor.
- 512 MB of RAM (1.5 GB if you plan to use virtual machine software).
- 40 GB of available hard disk space (80 GB if you plan to use virtual machine software).
- DVD-ROM drive.
- DirectX-capable graphics card with a Windows Display Driver Model (WDDM) driver, Hardware Pixel Shader 2.0 support, and a minimum of 128 MB of graphics memory. Graphics cards with lower specifications might work, but it will not be possible to use Windows Aero.
- Keyboard and Microsoft mouse or compatible pointing device.

If you do not yet have a copy of Windows Vista, or you would like to download an evaluation version of the product, you can use Microsoft's Virtual Hard Disk (VHD) download Web site (*http://www.microsoft.com/technet/try/vhd/default.mspx*). At the time of this writing, a Windows Vista Enterprise 30-Day Edition VHD is available for download. Windows Vista Enterprise is not a consumer-focused edition of Windows Vista and is not directly covered in the lesson contents. However, this edition does include the majority of features that are required in the practice exercises.

Software Requirements

The following software is required to complete the practice exercises:

- Windows Vista Ultimate (preferred) or Windows Vista Home Premium

Using the CD

A companion CD is included with this training kit. It contains the following:

- **Practice tests** You can reinforce your understanding of how to configure Windows Vista by using electronic practice tests you customize to meet your needs from the pool of Lesson Review questions in this book. Or you can practice for the 70-623 certification exam by using tests created from a pool of 200 realistic exam questions, which give you many practice exams to ensure that you are prepared.

■ **An eBook**   An electronic version (eBook) of this book is included for when you do not want to carry the printed book with you. The eBook is in Portable Document Format (PDF), and you can view it by using Adobe Acrobat or Adobe Reader.

How to Install the Practice Tests

To install the practice test software from the companion CD to your hard disk, do the following:

1. Insert the companion CD in your CD drive and accept the license agreement. A CD menu appears.

> **NOTE   If the CD menu does not appear**
>
> If the CD menu or the license agreement does not appear, AutoRun might be disabled on your computer. Refer to the Readme.txt file on the CD-ROM for alternate installation instructions.

2. Click Practice Tests and follow the instructions on the screen.

How to Use the Practice Tests

To start the practice test software, follow these steps:

1. Click Start, All Programs, and then Microsoft Press Training Kit Exam Prep. A window appears that shows all the Microsoft Press training kit exam prep suites installed on your computer.

2. Double-click the lesson review or practice test you want to use.

> **NOTE   Lesson reviews vs. practice tests**
>
> Select the (70-623) Supporting and Troubleshooting Applications on a Windows Vista Client for Consumer Support Technicians lesson review to use the questions from the "Lesson Review" sections of this book. Select the (70-623) Supporting and Troubleshooting Applications on a Windows Vista Client for Consumer Support Technicians practice test to use a pool of 200 questions similar to those that appear on the 70-623 certification exam.

Lesson Review Options

When you start a lesson review, the Custom Mode dialog box appears so that you can configure your test. You can click OK to accept the defaults, or you can customize the number of questions you want, how the practice test software works, which exam objectives you want the questions to relate to, and whether you want your lesson review to be timed. If you are retaking a test, you can select whether you want to see all the questions again or only the questions you missed or did not answer.

After you click OK, your lesson review starts.

- To take the test, answer the questions and use the Next, Previous, and Go To buttons to move from question to question.
- After you answer an individual question, if you want to see which answers are correct—along with an explanation of each correct answer—click Explanation.
- If you prefer to wait until the end of the test to see how you did, answer all the questions, and then click Score Test. You will see a summary of the exam objectives you chose and the percentage of questions you got right overall and per objective. You can print a copy of your test, review your answers, or retake the test.

Practice Test Options

When you start a practice test, you choose whether to take the test in Certification Mode, Study Mode, or Custom Mode:

- **Certification Mode**   Closely resembles the experience of taking a certification exam. The test has a set number of questions. It is timed, and you cannot pause and restart the timer.
- **Study Mode**   Creates an untimed test in which you can review the correct answers and the explanations after you answer each question.
- **Custom Mode**   Gives you full control over the test options so that you can customize them as you like.

In all modes the user interface when you are taking the test is basically the same but with different options enabled or disabled depending on the mode. The main options are discussed in the previous section, "Lesson Review Options."

When you review your answer to an individual practice test question, a "References" section is provided that lists where in the training kit you can find the information that relates to that question and provides links to other sources of information. After you click Test Results to score your entire practice test, you can click the Learning Plan tab to see a list of references for every objective.

How to Uninstall the Practice Tests

To uninstall the practice test software for a training kit, use the Add Or Remove Programs option (Windows XP) or the Program And Features option (Windows Vista) in Windows Control Panel.

Microsoft Certified Professional Program

The Microsoft certifications provide the best method to prove your command of current Microsoft products and technologies. The exams and corresponding certifications are developed to validate your mastery of critical competencies as you design and develop, or implement and support, solutions with Microsoft products and technologies. Computer professionals who become Microsoft-certified are recognized as experts and are sought after industry-wide. Certification brings a variety of benefits to the individual and to employers and organizations.

MORE INFO All the Microsoft certifications

For a full list of Microsoft certifications, go to *www.microsoft.com/learning/mcp/default.asp.*

Technical Support

Every effort has been made to ensure the accuracy of this book and the contents of the companion CD. If you have comments, questions, or ideas regarding this book or the companion CD, please send them to Microsoft Press by using either of the following methods:

E-mail: tkinput@microsoft.com

Postal Mail:

Microsoft Press
Attn: MCITP Self-Paced Training Kit (Exam 70-623): Supporting and Troubleshooting Applications on a Windows Vista Client for Consumer Support Technicians, *Editor*
One Microsoft Way
Redmond, WA 98052–6399

For additional support information regarding this book and the CD-ROM (including answers to commonly asked questions about installation and use), visit the Microsoft Press Technical Support Web site at *www.microsoft.com/learning/support/books/.* To connect directly to the Microsoft Knowledge Base and enter a query, visit *http://support.microsoft.com/search/.* For support information regarding Microsoft software, connect to *http://support.microsoft.com.*

Chapter 1
Preparing to Install Windows Vista

Exam 70-623 focuses on many aspects of working with Windows Vista. The technical focus is on providing assistance, guidance, and troubleshooting services while working as a Consumer Support Technician. If you already work in a retail environment, you probably know that this is a rather tall order: You can get questions ranging from how to plug in a keyboard to how to set up media sharing for three computers and an Xbox 360. Of course, this range of responsibilities is often what makes the job interesting.

Perhaps one of the most important aspects of your job is ensuring that you install the version of the operating system that best suits your customers' needs. This chapter focuses on determining which version of Windows Vista is most appropriate for various audiences. That might include yourself, a friend, a family member, a customer, or anyone else who might ask for your advice.

One of the most important skills you can learn as an IT professional is the ability to collect and analyze requirements and translate them into the right technology solution. Whether you're doing this for a single customer in a retail store or for thousands of desktops spread across a multinational business organization, the basic steps are the same. First, you should determine the customer's priorities: What is the primary purpose of the computer, and which features are the customer most interested in? Then, you need to prioritize these requirements: Which are "must-haves" and which are "nice-to-haves?" When this information is combined, the best option often becomes obvious.

This chapter begins with details about the editions of Windows Vista. Each edition has various features and benefits, and less technical people will expect you to know and understand them. Exam 70-623 tests this knowledge by making you determine the most appropriate edition to use for a particular set of requirements. The chapter also covers the information you need to know before you can install Windows Vista. You'll gain a solid understanding of the technical hardware requirements, and you can use that information to advise users whether a particular computer can be upgraded to Windows Vista. You'll also learn about the various certifications that can help ensure consumers that new computers, applications, and hardware are compatible with this operating system.

Exam objectives in this chapter:
- Evaluate potential upgrade environments.

Lessons in this chapter:

Before You Begin

For this chapter, it will be helpful to have a basic understanding of the purpose and function of an operating system, along with an idea of common questions that consumers might ask.

Lesson 1: Comparing Windows Vista Editions

Suppose you were given the challenge of designing the perfect operating system for everybody. What approach would you take? Would you add as many features as possible, making sure that all of the needs of the power user were met? Or would you opt for simplicity, providing only the core features that the majority of users would need? Coming up with a single answer is not always easy, especially when you add in the factor of pricing and supporting both business and home environments.

Microsoft has taken the approach of providing several editions of the Windows Vista platform. The goal is to provide the right balance of features, functionality, and cost for a particular subsets of users. Although this can make it a little more difficult to determine which edition is right for a particular situation, the result is that customers can get the features and functionality that are most appropriate for their needs. This lesson covers which features are included in which versions.

After this lesson, you will be able to:

- Describe the intended user type for each edition of the Windows Vista platform.
- Identify which features are present in each consumer-focused edition of Windows Vista.
- Recommend the most appropriate edition of Windows Vista based on customers' requirements.

Estimated lesson time: 30 minutes

Understanding Windows Vista Editions

The Windows Vista operating system comes in several versions known as editions. Each edition includes a certain set of features and is targeted toward a particular type of user. When purchasing a new computer or planning to upgrade an existing one, consumers must decide which edition is most appropriate for them.

Editions that include more features can provide more functionality but are more expensive and might be too complicated for some users. Editions that contain a subset of features might lack some functionality but might provide the best balance of cost, complexity, and options for a particular usage scenario. Before you look at the differences in each edition of Windows Vista, let's start with the similarities.

Features Common to all Editions

Although the number of editions of Windows Vista might make you think that these are all completely different platforms, the core components of the operating system are alike in all of them. The following features and functionality are common to all editions of Windows Vista:

MORE INFO   Product features

If you're unfamiliar with some of the products and features mentioned here, you'll learn about them in depth in later chapters.

- **Base operating system**   The heart of the Windows platform is known as the kernel. This core portion of the operating system is responsible for interacting with hardware and is relied on by applications and services. The Windows Vista kernel is identical in all versions of the platform, as are various supporting services.

- **Hardware support**   In general, all versions of the Windows Vista platform are able to support a very large number of hardware devices. Device drivers that were written for Windows Vista should work properly on all editions without any modifications. There are, however, some exceptions. For example, to record programs using a TV tuner card, you will either need to use a third-party application or the Windows Vista Media Center feature.

- **Integrated Search**   A key usability enhancement in the Windows Vista platform is the ability to search for content quickly and easily. These features are included in all editions of Windows Vista.

- **Security**   Security is an important concern for all users, ranging from home users to people that work in multinational organizations. All versions of Windows Vista were designed with core security features integrated into the operating system. These core security features include additional security features such as Windows Defender and Windows Firewall.

- **Parental controls**   All editions allow parents to monitor and limit their family members' use of features such as Internet access, playing games, instant messages, and other activities.

- **Software compatibility**   Software that has been designed for Windows Vista will generally run on any edition of the platform because the core operating system services are the same. Later in this chapter, you'll learn about software certification logos. In some cases, specific features that are available only in certain editions (such as Media Center) might be required. Also, keep in mind that some software applications might have hardware requirements that are greater than the minimum system requirements for a particular edition.

Overall, when comparing editions of Windows Vista, the primary differences are which features are included. Performance, reliability, and compatibility remain largely the same.

Comparing Consumer Editions of Windows Vista

In this section, you'll first look at each consumer-focused edition of Windows Vista independently. If you're new to Windows Vista, the most important point to keep in mind is the intended user type or situation for each edition. This will help give you a general idea of the intended audience for each set of features.

If you're supporting consumers, there's a good chance that you'll be quizzed regularly on whether a particular feature is available in a specific Windows Vista edition. Because the focus of this Training Kit is on supporting this audience, you'll start with the most appropriate options for people who will be purchasing Windows Vista from a retail channel (such as a physical retail store or an online Web site). To bring it all together, this section also provides a summary to compare specific features that are available in each edition of Windows Vista.

MORE INFO   Getting up-to-date information

It's no secret that technology changes quickly, but it's also important to keep in mind that pricing and availability details can change over time. For example, at the time of this writing, Microsoft is offering a Windows Anytime Upgrade program that allows customers who have purchased certain editions of Windows Vista to upgrade to another edition at a special price. A special discount offer is also available for users who would like to run Windows Vista on multiple computers within the same home. To get the latest pricing and availability information for Windows Vista, start at *http:// www.microsoft.com/.*

Windows Vista Home Basic   Many home users need only a subset of the many features that are available within Windows Vista. They use their computers for relatively simple tasks like creating documents, sending and receiving e-mail, and visiting Web sites. Windows Vista Home Basic was designed for those customers and provides all of the core features of the platform.

Home users can benefit from search capabilities and operating system security features. Windows Vista Home Basic also offers the advantage of being the lowest-priced version available to consumers.

Windows Vista Home Premium   As its name implies, Windows Vista Home Premium provides more operating system features than Windows Vista Home Basic. It supports the Windows Aero user interface, which allows for using advanced 3-D features for managing and working with applications. Windows Vista Home Premium also offers several advantages for users who have mobile devices such as notebook computers or Tablet PCs. For example, the Windows SideShow feature allows these devices to show important information even when the system is in a low-power state (assuming, of course, that the hardware was designed to take advantage of this feature). Additionally, features for simplifying wireless networks and file sharing are included in this edition.

It's common for home users to want an easy way to manage files such as photos, video, and music. Windows Vista Home Premium includes the Media Center feature, which allows users to view and record television programs (if they have the appropriate hardware), and to share photos and video with other computers and devices such as an Xbox 360. It also includes features for better organizing these content files and for burning them to DVD media.

Overall, Windows Vista Home Premium is targeted toward those home users who rely on their computers for more than just basic Internet access and productivity applications. Although this edition costs more than Windows Vista Home Basic, it provides numerous additional features for those users who need them.

Windows Vista Business   The needs of business users and organizations differ in some important ways from those of consumers. Microsoft designed Windows Vista Business for small business users. This might include independent consultants, store owners, or others who work in environments that probably do not have full-time, dedicated IT staff. The primary goals for these users tend to be productivity, data protection, and manageability. Windows Vista Business includes many of the features of other editions, including the Windows Aero user interface and security features such as Windows Defender and Windows Firewall. It does not include features that are not commonly useful in business environments, such as Windows Media Center, newer games, and tools such as Windows DVD Maker.

To allow IT departments to more easily support Windows Vista, solutions for quickly and easily deploying the operating system are also available. Windows Vista Business also supports the ability to join Active Directory directory service domains to take advantage of centralized security and management features. One other major advantage of Windows Vista Business is that it allows users to perform an in-place upgrade of an existing Microsoft Windows XP installation. This allows small business users who have existing applications installed on their Windows XP systems to easily move to Windows Vista.

Customers and businesses can purchase Windows Vista Business through retail channels or directly from Microsoft.

Windows Vista Ultimate   There's a certain subset of computer users who rely on technology in practically all areas of their lives. They're often known as power users and can benefit from as many operating system features as are available. Windows Vista Ultimate was designed for these users. It includes all of the features of Windows Vista Home Premium, along with some useful additions.

Users who will be using their computers to connect to business networks can benefit from several networking-related features. Windows Vista Ultimate allows users to connect to a domain-based environment, such as a company that uses Active Directory. This is often important for employees and consultants who might use their computers in a variety of different environments. Apart from these security-related features, the Remote Desktop component allows users to easily connect to other computers and for other computers to connect to theirs.

Security is also enhanced in Windows Vista with the addition of a feature called Windows Bit-Locker Drive Encryption. BitLocker technology provides the ability to encrypt the entire contents of a hard disk at a system level. It prevents the usability of data in the case that a hard disk or a notebook computer is lost or stolen. Like Windows Vista Business, Windows Vista Ultimate allows for in-place upgrades from Windows XP.

Finally, Windows Vista Ultimate includes a feature called Windows Ultimate Extras that allows users of this edition to download new programs and to add functionality to Windows Vista as Microsoft makes them available. Although not all users will be interested in these additional features, Windows Vista Ultimate provides a complete set of the operating system's available technology.

Summary of Consumer Edition Features   From the standpoint of supporting consumers, it's important to keep track of the major differences between the Home Basic, Home Premium, Business, and Ultimate editions of Windows Vista. Table 1-1 provides a summary that compares the major features that are available in each version.

Table 1-1   Comparing features in consumer editions of Windows Vista

Features	Windows Vista Home Basic	Windows Vista Home Premium	Windows Vista Business	Windows Vista Ultimate
Integrated Search capabilities	X	X	X	X
Windows Aero desktop experience		X	X	X
Windows Mobility Center and TabletPC support		X	X	X
Collaboration features (Windows Meeting Space)		X	X	X
Windows Media Center		X		X
Windows DVD Maker		X		X
Advanced backup options (complete PC backup and restore and scheduled backups)			X	X
Business networking features and Remote Desktop			X	X
Windows BitLocker Drive Encryption				X
Supports in-place upgrade from Windows XP			X	X

MORE INFO   Exam Tip

Exam 70-623 tests your ability to determine the most appropriate edition of Windows Vista based on a set of feature requirements. For example, a customer might want to use Windows Aero and Windows Media Center features at the lowest possible cost. Rather than memorizing the entire list of available features for each edition of Windows Vista, focus on the target audience (or user scenario) for each edition. For example, would most Windows Vista Business users need Windows Media Center? Probably not. Would most home users appreciate this feature? The answer is yes. Overall, keeping the main focus of each edition in mind can help you determine which features are available in which edition.

Evaluating Users' Needs

One of the challenges related to choosing the most appropriate Windows Vista edition for particular consumers is evaluating their particular needs. Some customers might already have done some research into the various features of Windows Vista. They're likely to quickly understand the benefits of a feature like Windows Media Center.

Many consumers are more likely to be unaware of all of the technical details. For example, many users will have no idea what features like BitLocker Drive Encryption mean to them. Your goal should be to help them determine the best option for their particular requirements.

There are several questions you can ask users and customers to get a better idea of their intended use for their computer, including these:

- **What is the primary purpose of your computer?**   Customers who are mainly interested in sending e-mail and accessing the Internet Web sites might be satisfied with Windows Vista Home Basic. If users are interested in sharing photos and video with other devices, advanced security, and collaborating with other users, Windows Vista Home Premium or Windows Vista Ultimate might be most appropriate.

- **How would you prioritize your requirements?**   There are many different reasons to upgrade to a new operating system such as Windows Vista. The complete list of features is very long, and users might be tempted to state that they require everything. However, from a daily usage basis, it's important to judge which features and functionality are most important, and which are just nice to have because they might be valuable in the future. Often, you'll be able to discover a user's true priorities by asking these questions.

- **Would you consider yourself a "power user?"**   Often, you'll be able to quickly determine the level of knowledge of a particular customer or user. Customers who are aware of advantages of additional features will likely be happier with a higher end edition. For those users, features such as Windows Media Center and the Windows Aero user interface might be must-haves.

- **Are you planning to perform an in-place upgrade?**   In some cases, customers might prefer to perform an in-place upgrade of Windows Vista. The benefits include an automatic transfer of operating system settings and applications to the new installation. Certain editions of Windows Vista allow for in-place upgrades from Windows XP, whereas others do not (more details are covered in Chapter 2, "Installing Windows Vista").

- **What are your hardware limitations?**   When helping customers who are planning to upgrade their current computers to Windows Vista, it's important to ask them about any hardware limitations with which they might be working. In general, the older the computer, the less likely it is that the computer will be able to meet all of the requirements for Windows Vista's advanced features. In some cases, users might be willing to upgrade their computers, but in others, they might find it not to be worth the cost. Keep these limitations in mind when deciding which editions are most appropriate.

- **How important is cost?**   Versions of Windows Vista that include more features carry a higher price tag. In the case of a new computer purchase, the user might be able to upgrade to a higher edition for an additional charge. When buying a retail copy, customers must choose which edition provides the right balance of cost versus benefits. Some customers might be satisfied with basic operating system functionality if they can reduce the cost of the product. Others might be willing to pay a premium for additional features and functionality.

Asking the right questions and interpreting the responses is an important aspect of determining the best technical solution. This additional research can greatly help you provide the best advice for a particular customer.

Other Editions of Windows Vista

So far, you've focused on details related to consumer editions of Windows Vista. These editions will likely cover the needs of most retail customers, but there are also other available editions of the operating system. In this section, you'll look at features of Windows Vista editions that are designed for specialized audiences. Although you're less likely to run into them when supporting consumers, it will be helpful to know some basic information about editions of Windows Vista that users might have in their workplace.

Windows Vista Enterprise

Windows Vista Enterprise is designed for medium- to large-sized organizations and includes all of the features that are a part of Windows Vista Business. These organizations tend to have dedicated IT staff and are faced with the challenge of supporting hundreds or even thousands of desktop computers. The primary requirements for these organizations are simplified deployment, enhanced manageability, and centralized security.

For example, Windows Vista Enterprise includes support for BitLocker Drive Encryption, a feature that can be extremely important to organizations that support hundreds of mobile and remote users. Windows Vista Enterprise also includes features that allow for interoperability with UNIX-based systems and the ability to use virtual machine technology. IT departments can obtain the Microsoft Desktop Optimization Pack for Software Assurance, which provides many advanced features for better managing large numbers of computers. Companies that are interested in obtaining this edition must subscribe to Microsoft's Software Assurance subscription program.

MORE INFO   Windows Vista for medium- to large-sized businesses

It might seem like a challenge to manage a few home computers, but the technical issues faced by IT organizations can be significantly more complex. Important tasks include deploying and upgrading hundreds of computers, ensuring that business rules are being followed, and keeping systems up to date. For more details on the business-focused features of Windows Vista, see *http://www.microsoft.com/windowsvista/businesses/*. Learning about these problems (and their related solutions) can also help you move toward a career in IT.

Windows Vista Starter

The primary goal of Windows Vista Starter is to provide a product for markets in which cost and compatibility are primary concerns. In many developing nations, standard computers are less capable than those in other areas of the world. Individuals and organizations might be willing to purchase only the most basic functionality of an operating system if it is more affordable and compatible. The base operating system of Windows Vista Starter is identical to that of the other editions of the platform. The primary difference lies in the additional features and components that are available. Specifically, the Windows Aero user interface (which has higher graphics adapter requirements) is not available. This edition is also appropriate for users that are newcomers to working with PCs, as the user experience is focused toward providing more help and guidance.

It is important to note that Microsoft has intended Windows Vista Starter for emerging markets that are very sensitive to pricing. This edition is not available in high-income markets, such as the United States and nations in the European Union. Details related to pricing and availability will be determined based on the country of sale. For these reasons, we won't focus further on details about Windows Vista Starter in this chapter.

Quick Check

1. Which consumer-focused editions of Windows Vista support the Windows Aero user interface?
2. Which edition of Windows Vista is most appropriate for a customer who is willing to choose fewer features for the lowest price?

Quick Check Answers

1. Windows Vista Home Premium, Windows Vista Business, and Windows Vista Ultimate
2. Windows Vista Home Basic

Practice: Evaluating Upgrade Requirements

In the following practice exercises, you apply the information you learned about the various consumer-focused editions of Windows Vista. Specifically, you will determine the best edition of Windows Vista based on users' requirements.

▶ **Practice 1: Choosing an Edition of Windows Vista**

Ask several friends, coworkers, and family members about how they use their computers and determine which features would be most important to them. Based on these requirements, decide which consumer-focused edition of Windows Vista would be most appropriate. Options include Home Basic, Home Premium, Business, and Ultimate. Sample questions you might ask include the following:

1. What are the primary ways in which you use your computer?
2. What would you like to improve about your current operating system?
3. Would you like to upgrade your current computer? If so, what are its technical specifications? You will need to assist the user in determining those details. Also, determine any upgrades that might be required.
4. Which features of Windows Vista would you be most interested in using? Practice describing the features briefly for users who are unfamiliar with them.

▶ **Practice 2: Understanding Users' Preferences**

Develop a hypothetical scenario for a typical user of each consumer-focused edition of Windows Vista. For example, describe the requirements for a customer who would be most likely to purchase Windows Vista Business and compare these requirements with those of a purchaser of Windows Vista Home Premium. Some possible considerations include the following:

1. What are the target user types for Windows Vista Business and Windows Vista Home Premium?
2. Which features are available in Windows Vista Home Premium and not in Windows Vista Business?
3. What are some reasons that a customer might prefer to purchase Windows Vista Business for use by employees in a small office environment?

Lesson Summary

- All versions of Windows Vista offer the same core operating system features, including software support, hardware support, and security.
- Windows Vista Home Basic is targeted toward consumers that are looking for basic operating system functionality.
- Windows Vista Home Premium includes the Windows Aero user interface along with additional multimedia features.
- Windows Vista Ultimate includes a complete set of features that are available for the operating system platform.
- Windows Vista Business is targeted toward small-business users and includes productivity and data protection features.
- Windows Vista Enterprise is designed for larger organizations and is available as part of Microsoft's Software Assurance program.

Lesson Review

You can use the following questions to test your knowledge of the information in Lesson 1, "Comparing Windows Vista Editions." The questions are also available on the companion CD if you prefer to review them in electronic form.

NOTE   Answers

Answers to these questions and explanations of why each answer choice is correct or incorrect are located in the "Answers" section at the end of the book.

1. Which of the following Windows Vista features are available in Windows Vista Home Premium? (Choose all that apply.)
   A. Windows Aero
   B. Windows Media Center
   C. BitLocker Drive Encryption
   D. Advanced backup features

2. While talking to a customer, you have determined that he is not interested in using the Windows Aero user interface, but he would like to be able to watch and record TV shows on his computer. Which of the following editions of Windows Vista will meet these requirements? (Choose all that apply.)

   A. Windows Vista Home Basic

   B. Windows Vista Home Premium

   C. Windows Vista Ultimate

   D. Windows Vista Business

Lesson 2: Preparing to Upgrade to Windows Vista

With all of the new features that are available in the Windows Vista operating system, you're likely to face many questions related to compatibility. Some customers will want to know whether they should upgrade their existing computers to Windows Vista and also whether they might run into any problems. There are several important considerations that must be taken into account when deciding to upgrade. The first consideration is related to the hardware specifications of the current computer. Does it already meet the requirements for Windows Vista, or will hardware upgrades be required? If upgrades will be required, you should consider the costs of the hardware, as well as the expertise necessary to install it. The same considerations apply to software. Upgrading will always take time and effort, but for many customers, the cost savings over buying a new computer will make it worthwhile.

Other customers will be interested in purchasing a new computer and will want to make sure that it is compatible with Windows Vista. They often prefer to start with a clean slate and with a system that has been designed with Windows Vista in mind. In this lesson, you'll learn how you can answer these questions and provide guidance on moving to the Windows Vista operating system.

After this lesson, you will be able to:

- Determine whether a particular computer is compatible with Windows Vista.
- Specify the CPU, memory, hard disk, and other hardware requirements for various editions of the Windows Vista operating system.
- Identify hardware requirements for enabling Windows Aero user interface features.
- Determine whether software and hardware devices are compatible with Windows Vista.
- Use the Windows Vista Upgrade Advisor to determine whether a computer can be upgraded to Windows Vista.

Estimated lesson time: 45 minutes

Verifying Windows Vista System Compatibility

Modern computers are complex pieces of machinery with many different components. Although the computer industry has tried to remove some of this complexity, it's still important to understand various components such as CPUs, memory, hard disks, and related pieces of hardware. This is especially true when it comes to understanding the requirements for a new operating system. In general, Windows Vista places higher requirements on users' computers when compared to earlier operating systems.

Many computers were sold to customers during the time period between the introduction of the Windows Vista operating system and its general availability. Hardware vendors needed a way to assure customers that the systems they purchased could be upgraded to the latest operating system when it was released. In this section, you'll look at two logos that provide information about upgradability.

Windows Vista Capable

The base Windows Vista operating system has been designed to run on a wide variety of existing computers. To ease the transition to this version, Microsoft has provided requirements that must be met for a computer to be called "Windows Vista Capable." As the name implies, this label ensures users that the system meets the minimum hardware requirements to install and run Windows Vista.

With respect to supporting a new operating system, the most important components that must be evaluated are the CPU speed, amount of memory (RAM), and available hard disk space. For Windows Vista, minimal system requirements are as follows:

- CPU: 800Mhz or faster
- Memory: 512 MB of RAM or greater
- Hard disk: 20 GB hard disk with at least 15 GB of free space

Although these requirements might not seem steep for most modern computers, it is important to keep in mind that these are only minimum requirements. Customers should also factor in additional disk space and hardware requirements that might be necessary to use certain applications. For example, a customer who plans to store a large number of digital photos on her computer will likely need a larger hard disk. Users who want to make the most of all of the features of Windows Vista will benefit from exceeding these minimum specifications.

Windows Vista Premium Ready

In addition to the basic features of most operating systems, Windows Vista includes additional functionality that is available for users who need it. These features can raise the system requirements for a computer beyond the bare minimum specifications on which the operating system will run. Specifically, the primary requirements are as follows:

- CPU: 1.0 GHz or faster
- Memory: 1.0 GB (1024 MB) of RAM or greater
- Hard disk: 40 GB hard disk

Systems that meet or exceed these specifications will include the "Windows Vista Premium Ready" logo and are ready to provide support for the Windows Aero user interface and other advanced options. As with all system requirements, customers should consider the specific applications they plan to install and use. For example, customers who plan to use Windows Media Center for recording television shows will likely benefit from additional hard disk space.

Recognizing the Windows Vista compatibility logos can make the process of determining whether a system is compatible with the operating system quick and easy.

Windows Aero Requirements

One of the easiest ways to recognize the Windows Vista operating system is by looking at new features in the user interface. The ability to "flip" through windows and to use transparency features can help productivity and improve the look and feel of the system. These features do place a burden on graphics adapters, however.

There are several hardware requirements that a computer must meet to be able to support the advanced user interface features included in Windows Aero (for more information on configuring Windows Aero, see Chapter 3, "Configuring and Customizing the Windows Vista Desktop"). To qualify for the Windows Vista Premium Ready logo, the system must include a video adapter that meets the following specifications:

- **Memory**   128 MB of video memory is required. When running at higher monitor resolutions or with multiple monitors, performance can be significantly improved through additional video memory. Some video adapter chips are designed to use the computer's primary physical memory for at least a portion of the stated total amount of RAM on the graphics adapter. This is often referred to as *shared system memory* and is most commonly seen in video adapters that are embedded on the computer's motherboard. Although this method can lower costs, it can also decrease overall graphics performance. In general, dedicated memory for the video adapter will provide the best Windows Aero experience. If you have already installed Windows Vista, you can find more details on the amount of shared and dedicated memory by accessing the Advanced properties of the Display Settings dialog box (see Figure 1-1).

Figure 1-1   Viewing details about video adapter memory

- **Windows Display Driver Model (WDDM) support**   The WDDM specification is Microsoft's newest standard for display adapter drivers. Apart from performance benefits, WDDM drivers provide design specifications to improve reliability and for performing a secure installation. To ensure compatibility with Windows Aero, the manufacturer of the display adapter must provide drivers that meet these requirements.
- **Hardware Pixel Shader 2.0 support**   Transparent glass and other features of the Windows Aero user interface rely on pixel shading techniques to perform rendering tasks. The responsiveness of the operating system will be based on the graphics adapter's ability to perform these calculations. Therefore, hardware-based Pixel Shader 2.0 support is a requirement.
- **Color depth**   The video adapter must be able to support 32 bits per pixel. The number of bits specifies the total number of colors that is possible for each pixel on the display. Generally, any video card that meets the video memory specifications will also be able to handle this. There might be exceptions in situations where multiple monitors are being used or when the adapter resolution is set extremely high.

Most new computers ship with video adapters that support these requirements, but it is important to keep the specific details in mind to help customers who are planning to upgrade existing hardware. In addition, the minimum requirements given here can vary based on the required display resolution. For example, if customers are using multiple monitors, are running at higher resolutions, or want to use a higher color depth, more video memory might be required.

Windows Media Center Requirements

Windows Media Center is another component of the Windows Vista operating system that has specific hardware requirements. Customers have two different options when evaluating systems. The first is to select a new computer that specifically states that it supports Windows Media Center. Such systems will generally have a TV tuner card and will meet CPU and memory requirements for this feature. When deciding to upgrade an existing system, customers should verify whether Windows Vista is a supported platform for their TV tuner card.

Summary of Windows Vista Upgrade Requirements

Table 1-2 provides a summary of the specific hardware requirements for Windows Vista. It is important to keep in mind that these are minimum system requirements and that additional hardware might be required to support other applications.

Table 1-2   Minimum system requirements for Windows Vista Capable and Windows Vista Premium Ready logos

Component	Windows Vista Capable Requirements	Windows Vista Premium Ready Requirements
Processor (CPU)	800 MHz or faster	1.0 GHz 32-bit CPU or 64-bit CPU.
Memory (RAM)	512 MB	1.0 GB (1024 MB).
Video adapter	DirectX 9 support	Support for Windows Aero requires DirectX 9 support, a WDDM driver, hardware Pixel Shader 2.0 support, 32 bits per pixel, and 128 MB of graphics memory (more memory might be required based on resolution, number of displays, and color depth).
Hard disk space	20 GB hard disk (15 GB available)	40 GB available disk space.
Optical drive	Might be required for installation	DVD-ROM drive.
Audio output capability	Not required	Required.
Ability to access the Internet	Not required	Required.

Windows Vista and Windows Vista Basic Logos

So far, you have focused on specific requirements that are related to computers that were designed to be upgraded to Windows Vista. Now that the operating system has been released, many computers will ship with it preinstalled. Hardware manufacturers are responsible for ensuring that the specifications of new computers meet these requirements. There are two different levels of compatibility with Windows Vista, each of which has its own logo.

The lower level is called "Windows Vista Basic," and it ensures customers that the system meets the minimum hardware requirements for running the operating system. This allows users to get up and running with basic system functionality.

The other logo, which simply shows "Windows Vista," indicates that the computer ships with a hardware configuration that is fully compatible with the complete Windows Vista feature set. This includes desktop and mobile computers that meet or exceed the requirements to enable features such as the Windows Aero user interface. Additionally, the computer contains compatible audio hardware and support for network connectivity (using wired features, wireless features, or both). All of the components of the computer should have full device driver support for Windows Vista. Figure 1-2 shows the two logos.

Figure 1-2   The Windows Vista and Windows Vista Basic logos

Evaluating Software and Hardware Compatibility

The primary purpose of an operating system is to provide support for the hardware and software a user wants to run. This can range from productivity applications (such as Microsoft Office) to specialized hardware devices (such as a scanner, an advanced 3-D graphics adapter, or a TV tuner card). One of the primary strengths of the Windows platform is its broad compatibility with a large array of hardware and software. Windows Vista includes a number of internal changes that can cause compatibility issues with customers' existing software.

In developing a new operating system, there are two primary goals that are fundamentally at odds with each other. The first is to ensure compatibility with as many existing applications as possible. Customers should be able to use current versions of their products. The other goal is to provide for core improvements within the platform. In some cases, these improvements can result in changes that might prevent older technologies from running properly.

Because consumers typically have a limited knowledge of application requirements, it's up to technical professionals and hardware and software vendors to determine compatibility. In this section, you'll look at various ways in which you can evaluate whether a product is compatible with Windows Vista.

Hardware Device Compatibility

There are several important requirements for computer hardware to work properly with an operating system. The first is related to hardware compatibility and concerns whether the device is compatible with the system. Assuming that it is compatible, appropriate device drivers must be available for the operating system that is installed. Windows Vista ships with thousands of built-in drivers for the most popular hardware. Still, it's possible that some devices might not have the appropriate drivers.

The "Works with Windows Vista" logo has been designed to designate hardware devices that have been tested based on Microsoft's requirements. It ensures that minimum compatibility and reliability standards have been met and that the device will function within the Windows Vista operating system.

Whenever possible, customers should look for the "Certified for Windows Vista" logo on new hardware purchases. In addition to meeting basic operating system compatibility requirements, the certified drivers for this hardware have undergone extensive and rigorous testing by Microsoft. This ensures that the devices follow the latest design guidelines for the operating system and that they take advantage of new features whenever appropriate. For example, a wireless network interface card that carries the Certified for Windows Vista logo should be easy to install and configure using the operating system's built-in wireless network tools. Figure 1-3 shows the Certified for Windows Vista and Works with Windows Vista logos.

Figure 1-3   Comparing Windows Vista hardware and device certification logos

Software Compatibility

Modern software applications can have many components that rely on a variety of different operating system components. For these reasons, older applications might not work properly on newer operating systems. In some cases, the differences might be minor—perhaps some graphical user elements appear different, or there's a change in how a task is accomplished. In other cases, critical functionality might be completely broken, and users will be unable to accomplish tasks using the software. Microsoft has developed several logos that can help technical professionals and customers determine whether or not a program is compatible with Windows Vista.

The most basic level of compatibility is defined by the "Works with Windows Vista" logo. This logo specifies that the software vendor has tested the product on Windows Vista and will provide technical support if the application is run on this platform.

As with hardware products, the "Certified for Windows Vista" logo provides a higher level of assurance of the compatibility of the product. In addition to meeting basic requirements for installation, applications eligible for this designation must complete a third-party certification process. Tests for reliability and security ensure that the application takes advantage of improvements in the Windows Vista platform. Wherever possible, customers should look for the Certified for Windows Vista logo on new applications.

One final area of software is important to many users: games. In the past, the process of installing, configuring, and playing games could be difficult. First, customers would have to determine whether their systems met the minimum or recommended system requirements for the game. Then, the installation process might involve numerous steps. Finally, graphics, sound, controller, and other options had to be configured. Compared to the process of launching a game on a gaming console (such as the Xbox 360), this experience leaves much to be desired. The "Games for Windows" logo is designed to help customers determine whether or not entertainment software is designed for and compatible with Windows Vista. In addition to ensuring compatibility, certification provides numerous benefits, including the following:

- A simple installation process that shows the software's icon in the Games Explorer.
- Support for reporting ratings and the ability to be restricted using Windows Vista's Parental Controls feature.
- Support for the Xbox 360 controller (where appropriate). A common issue with some PC games was the hassle of mapping buttons and other controls to the requirements of a game. Providing support for this standard helps resolve this issue because game developers can expect a standard controller layout.

When combined, these features can help potential gamers launch and enjoy entertainment software as quickly and painlessly as possible.

Real World

Anil Desai

A major source of difficulty and confusion for retail customers (especially those that are not computer savvy) is in dealing with compatibility issues. When these consumers plug in a new hardware device or install new software, they just expect it to work. When things go wrong, they often don't have the time or expertise to perform troubleshooting. Microsoft has realized that ensuring compatibility can be challenging, both for product vendors and for users. That's the primary reason for developing certification and logo programs. Companies that are willing to update their products, testing processes, and support agreements for Windows Vista should be able to clearly state this in their packaging and marketing materials.

But what if a product isn't certified? What if it doesn't even claim compatibility with Windows Vista? From a technical standpoint, some of us might be tempted to make it work. We know how to dig up older drivers, search support forums, and look for third-party assistance. Often, there's no strong technical reason for the product not to work properly; it just might not have been tested. So should you recommend using uncertified products to customers?

As a Consumer Support Technician, customers and end users will depend on your advice to run their systems optimally. In general, you should recommend only those hardware devices and software packages that are compatible with Windows Vista. This helps assure you and your customers that they can obtain support from the vendor if problems do arise. Considering the alternative—that you will personally have to support the device or software if it doesn't work properly—this is a good trade-off. In other cases, you might suggest to knowledgeable users that an application might work properly, but be sure that they understand the risks. Overall, strongly recommend certified products, and warn users about potential support issues with uncertified ones.

MORE INFO Logos

In this lesson, you've learned about numerous different logo types that are related to computers, hardware, and software. It's often easiest to keep these logos in mind by visualizing them. You can find an up-to-date list of logos (and their meanings) on the Microsoft Windows Vista Web site at *http://www.microsoft.com/windows/products/windowsvista/buyorupgrade/default.mspx.*

Understanding CPU Options

CPU technology is clearly a moving target, with significant new features and capabilities being introduced every few years. When evaluating and purchasing computers, customers must be able to select the most appropriate balance of performance and cost.

Comparing 32-Bit and 64-Bit Options

The majority of computers in service at the time of release of Windows Vista are running 32-bit CPUs. The overwhelming majority of applications and operating systems that are currently available have been written with 32-bit processors in mind. Although the 32-bit platform has generally shown that it is scalable and has met the needs of users for many years, it does have its limitations. One such limitation is related to the ability to support larger amounts of memory. Despite methods of increasing the overall memory address space, systems are limited to using only a few gigabytes of RAM.

The 64-bit CPUs are intended to help increase these limits and to improve overall system performance. Although there are potential gains that can be realized using 64-bit CPUs, there are also possible incompatibilities. Applications must either be designed to run on 64-bit architectures or they must be run in a special compatibility mode. Users who choose to upgrade to 64-bit editions of Windows Vista need to ensure that their hardware supports the operating system, and 64-bit drivers will also be required. New computers that contain 64-bit CPUs and that ship with Windows Vista will include all of the necessary drivers.

In general, unless users have a specific requirement for a 64-bit computer (or they want to purchase a system that has been designed with 64-bit Windows Vista in mind), they might prefer to stay with 32-bit versions to maximize compatibility.

Multiple CPUs and Cores

All versions of Windows Vista support either a single or dual CPU configuration. Multiple physical CPUs can help increase performance in certain applications or when multitasking.

A popular option on modern PCs is multicore technology. CPU chips with multiple cores have two or more physical cores on the same physical chip. They can offer performance improvements that are similar to having two separate physical processors but with lower power consumption and reduced heat generation. For licensing purposes, Windows Vista considers only the number of physical CPUs that are installed in the system. Therefore, when evaluating desktop and notebook computers, power users can often get more value for their money by purchasing systems that use multiple processor cores.

Evaluating an Upgrade to Windows Vista

One of the major advantages of working with the Windows platform is that there is a wide array of options to choose from when purchasing hardware. There are many different options that allow customers the freedom to choose from among a wide variety of complete computer systems. Additionally, numerous hardware vendors offer a broad array of components and upgrades. These types of devices include hard disks, video adapters, wired and wireless network interface cards, and memory. In addition, there are many available external products such as scanners, digital cameras, printers, game controllers, and other devices. The ability to choose from such a large array of products can help customers choose the best solution for their needs, but it can also make the decision process significantly more complicated.

Some consumers might be interested in purchasing a new computer for use with Windows Vista, but many will prefer to upgrade their current system with the new operating system. As a general rule, it's important to ensure that older devices are compatible with a newer operating system. Microsoft's goal with Windows Vista is to support the majority of computers that were built within two years of the official release of the operating system. However, system specifications for existing computers can vary widely, so more information is needed to make a definite determination.

As a consumer support specialist, it's important to be able to give advice related to operating system compatibility. The primary issue is generally related to device driver support. It's likely that many newer devices will support Windows Vista, but it's not uncommon to find older hardware and peripherals that will not support it. In this section, you'll look at some ways in which you can determine compatibility.

Upgrade Methods

There are two main ways in which an existing computer can be upgraded to Windows Vista. The first approach is to perform a clean installation on the computer. This generally involves either creating a new operating system installation alongside the current one (in what is known as a dual-boot or multiboot configuration). The benefits are that the installation process can be very quick, and there's less of a chance of incompatibility because existing applications are not automatically upgraded. The Windows Easy Transfer program can be used to make the process of migrating applications and operating system settings easier.

The other method is to perform an in-place upgrade. In this process, the Windows Vista installation process attempts to keep all installed programs and relevant operating system settings intact. Users might be required to install operating system updates on their Windows XP computers and will need to ensure compatibility of software and hardware before the process can begin. The major advantage of performing an in-place upgrade is that users can move to Windows Vista without reinstalling and reconfiguring all of their applications.

MORE INFO   Which versions of Windows Vista support in-place upgrades

For more information on which versions of Windows Vista support in-place upgrades, see Table 1-1, earlier in this chapter. Additional details related to these two upgrade methods are provided in Chapter 2.

Understanding the Windows Vista Upgrade Advisor

One of the most common questions that consumers have when deciding whether to upgrade to Windows Vista is whether their current hardware will be supported on the new operating system. One way of making this determination is to take a manual inventory of every device and then verify support details with each manufacturer. Most users, however, are not familiar enough with the components of their computer to be able to make this determination.

The Windows Vista Upgrade Advisor is a free utility created by Microsoft to provide users with the information they need to determine whether or not they can upgrade their systems to the new operating system. The tool is designed to run on computers running either Windows XP or Windows Vista. Users will most commonly run the program on computers running Windows XP to test whether their hardware will be supported by Windows Vista and to identify any potential issues that must be resolved prior to the upgrade. For example, certain versions of software programs might prevent the upgrade process from being performed. In those cases, either a newer version of the program must be installed, or it must be removed from the system entirely. Users who are already running Windows Vista can also run the Windows Vista Upgrade Advisor to test compatibility of their hardware and to verify compatibility with other editions of the platform. Figure 1-4 shows an example of a summary of the results from a scan.

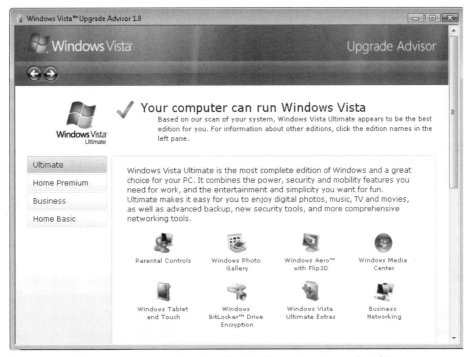

Figure 1-4 Viewing overall results using the Windows Vista Upgrade Advisor

Using the Windows Vista Upgrade Advisor

The first step in using the Windows Vista Upgrade Advisor is to download the program from the Microsoft Web site. The easiest way to find the download is to search for "Vista Upgrade Advisor" on the Microsoft.com home page (*http://www.microsoft.com*). After you have downloaded it, you can quickly and easily install the software on any computer running Windows XP or Windows Vista.

When you first run the Upgrade Advisor, it will connect to Microsoft's servers over the Internet for any updates that might help improve the accuracy of the scanning process. The introduction screen for the Upgrade Advisor provides details about the purpose of the program (see Figure 1-5). It is important to plug in any peripherals or devices that you might want to test. For example, if you routinely use a USB-based scanner, make sure that the device is plugged in and turned on. To begin the process, simply click Start Scan.

Figure 1-5   Running a scan with the Windows Vista Upgrade Advisor

The scanning process will likely take several minutes. After it completes, you can click See Details to get an overall report. Figure 1-6 shows another example of some sample results. The top of the screen will show an overall evaluation for the selected edition of Windows Vista. By clicking the buttons on the left, you can find out which of the editions of Windows Vista are supported by the hardware.

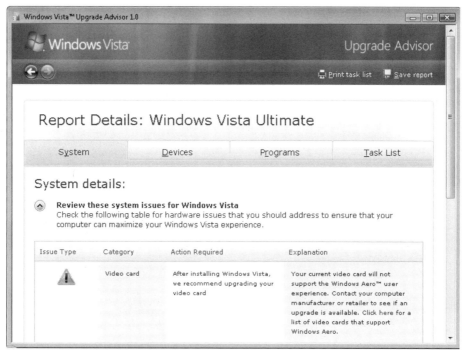

Figure 1-6   Viewing a System report in the Windows Vista Upgrade Advisor

Additional details are also available. There are three different sections that provide more compatibility data when you click the associated See Details button. Figure 1-7 shows an example of the types of details that are provided in the Devices report.

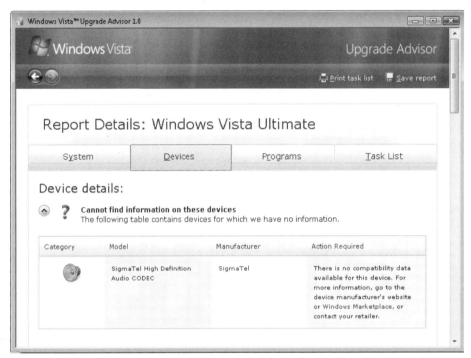

Figure 1-7 Viewing a Devices report in the Windows Vista Upgrade Advisor

The report details are divided into four sections:

- **System** A summary of the overall hardware components that are part of the computer, along with any actions that might be required before an upgrade is performed.
- **Devices** A list of all of the devices that were detected by the Upgrade Advisor during the scanning process. Any devices for which information could not be found are also listed. If any actions are required before performing an upgrade, they are listed here.
- **Programs** This section lists any currently installed programs that might either be incompatible with Windows Vista or might require updates. If any action is required (such as visiting a vendor's Web site to obtain an update), that will also be specified.

■ **Task List**   The final section provides a summary of the results of the scan, along with a list of steps that might be required before starting the upgrade process. Figure 1-8 shows some of the types of tasks that might be returned.

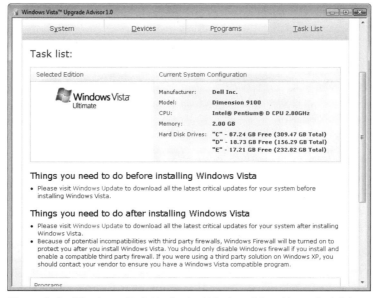

Figure 1-8   Viewing a Task List in the Windows Vista Upgrade Advisor

Overall, the Windows Vista Upgrade Advisor provides a quick and easy way to analyze a system for potential incompatibilities when planning for an upgrade.

NOTE   **Keeping up with changes to the Upgrade Advisor**

When supporting consumers who are considering an upgrade to Windows Vista, you'll likely find yourself recommending that they download and install the Upgrade Advisor. Note that some of the details of this utility are likely to change over time, so if you haven't downloaded and run it recently, it can be helpful to run the latest version to regain familiarity with it.

Installing Updates

Before starting the process of upgrading from Windows XP to Windows Vista, you should download and install any available updates for Windows XP. You can do this by using the Windows Update feature in Windows XP (see Windows XP's Help and Support Center for more details).

Quick Check

1. A customer is comparing several different notebook computers. She wants to be able to take advantage of all of the features of the Windows Vista operating system. Which logo or certification should she look for?

2. On which operating systems can a customer run the Windows Vista Upgrade Advisor utility?

Quick Check Answers

1. The Certified for Windows Vista logo is designed to indicate that a new computer meets the hardware and software requirements for compatibility with the operating system.

2. The Windows Vista Upgrade Advisor will run on Windows XP and Windows Vista operating systems.

Practice: Testing for Windows Vista Compatibility

Select several Windows XP computers that might be candidates for upgrading to Windows Vista. Download and install the Windows Vista Upgrade Advisor on these computers and run it to assess whether or not the systems are compatible. Make notes of what steps might be required to resolve potential incompatibilities. Details might include software and hardware updates or the removal of some programs. The general steps you'll perform for each computer include the following:

1. Download the Windows Vista Upgrade Advisor from the Microsoft Windows Vista Web site (*http://www.windowsvista.com*).

2. Install the Upgrade Advisor on the computer.

3. Start the Upgrade Advisor and begin a scan of the system.

4. View the overall reports that are generated.

5. Determine which hardware and software components, if any, will prevent upgrading to Windows Vista.

6. Determine which hardware and software components are listed as warnings and might not work properly after the upgrade to Windows Vista.

7. Save a copy of the Upgrade Advisor report by clicking Save Report. Open and view the report file to see the types of information that are recorded.

8. When finished, close the Windows Vista Upgrade Advisor.

Lesson Summary

- When planning to migrate to Windows Vista, it is important to understand the hardware and software requirements of the operating system.

- The Windows Vista Capable and Windows Vista Premium Ready logos specify that a computer that shipped with an earlier operating system will be compatible with Windows Vista.

- The Windows Vista Premium Ready logo specifies that a computer meets the hardware requirements to take advantage of all of the features of the Windows Vista platform.

- Windows Aero requires several features to be present on a computer's graphics adapter.

- Customers will need a TV tuner card and additional disk space to use Windows Media Center.

- The Windows Vista Upgrade Advisor is a free utility that allows customers to evaluate whether their current computer will support Windows Vista.

- The Windows Vista Upgrade Advisor reports on any actions that might prevent a successful upgrade to Windows Vista, including potential software or hardware incompatibilities.

Lesson Review

You can use the following questions to test your knowledge of the information in Lesson 2, "Preparing to Upgrade to Windows Vista." The questions are also available on the companion CD if you prefer to review them in electronic form.

NOTE Answers

Answers to these questions and explanations of why each answer choice is correct or incorrect are located in the "Answers" section at the end of the book.

---

1. A customer would like to upgrade his current computer to Windows Vista to use the new Windows Aero user interface. He is evaluating the purchase of a new graphics adapter and is comparing specifications. Which of the following features do NOT meet the minimum requirements for enabling the Windows Aero user interface? (Choose all that apply.)

    A. 64 MB video memory

    B. 32-bit color depth

    C. Available WDDM drivers

    D. Support for DirectX 9

2. A customer purchased a new computer several months before the release of Windows Vista. She would like to know whether she can upgrade the computer to Windows Vista. She would also like to take advantage of new features such as the Windows Aero user interface and Windows Media Center. Which logo specifies that the computer meets these requirements?

   A. Windows Vista Capable

   B. Windows Vista Premium Ready

   C. Certified for Windows Vista

   D. Works with Windows Vista

3. A customer would like to upgrade his current computer to Windows Vista but is not sure whether his current hardware and software are compatible. Which of the following is the quickest and easiest method for him to determine whether or not he can upgrade the system?

   A. Look for the Works with Windows Vista logo on the existing computer system.

   B. Contact hardware manufacturers for details related to Windows Vista compatibility.

   C. Run the Windows Vista Upgrade Advisor on another computer that is running Windows Vista and compare the results with the current computer.

   D. Run the Windows Vista Upgrade Advisor on Windows XP to evaluate current hardware.

Chapter Review

To further practice and reinforce the skills you learned in this chapter, you can perform the following tasks:

- Review the chapter summary.
- Review the list of key terms introduced in this chapter.
- Complete the case scenarios. These scenarios set up real-world situations involving the topics of this chapter and ask you to create a solution.
- Complete the suggested practices.
- Take a practice test.

Chapter Summary

- The consumer-focused editions of Windows Vista include Windows Vista Home Basic, Windows Vista Home Premium, Windows Vista Business, and Windows Vista Ultimate.
- The Windows Vista Capable and Windows Vista Premium Ready logos are designed to indicate whether a computer has been designed to be upgraded to Windows Vista.
- There are several logos that customers and technical support professionals should look for to verify whether a hardware or software product is compatible with the Windows Vista operating system.
- Customers can evaluate the Windows Vista software and hardware compatibility of an existing computer by using the Windows Vista Upgrade Advisor.

Key Terms

Do you know what these key terms mean? You can check your answers by looking up the terms in the glossary at the end of the book.

- Windows Aero
- Windows Device Driver Model (WDDM)
- Windows Media Center
- Windows Vista editions
- Windows Vista Upgrade Advisor

Case Scenarios

In the following case scenarios, you will apply what you've learned about preparing to install or upgrade to Windows Vista. You can find answers to these questions in the "Answers" section at the end of this book.

Case Scenario 1: Evaluating Windows Vista Upgrade Options

You are working as a consumer support technician for a local computer store. A customer has decided that he would like to upgrade his current computer to Windows Vista, but he is unsure of the technical requirements. He purchased his computer approximately three months prior to the release of Windows Vista, and it came preinstalled with Windows XP Professional. The customer would like to use Windows Media Center, the Windows Aero user interface, and the BitLocker Drive Encryption features.

Answer the following questions:

1. Which consumer-focused edition(s) of Windows Vista would meet the customer's feature requirements?

2. Which system compatibility logo(s) would help you determine whether his computer is compatible with Windows Vista?

3. The customer has installed numerous third-party applications and several hardware devices (including a printer and a scanner) after purchasing the computer. How can he most easily determine whether these devices are compatible with Windows Vista?

Case Scenario 2: Verifying Hardware and Software Compatibility

You are working as a consumer support technician for a local computer store. A customer has recently upgraded her computer from Windows XP Professional to Windows Vista Home Premium. She is now planning to purchase several items to upgrade her computer. The first is a new graphics adapter that will allow her to play current games. The second is new entertainment software. She also plans to purchase a new accounting software package to support her home-based business. The customer's primary concern is ensuring that the products she purchases will work with Windows Vista.

Answer the following questions:

1. Which logo should the customer look for when evaluating graphics adapters that will work with Windows Vista and that have been optimized to take advantage of new operating system features?

2. Which logo will indicate that the accounting package she is considering has been extensively tested for compatibility with Windows Vista?

3. Which logo should she look for to ensure that an entertainment software title takes full advantage of Windows Vista's new gaming features?

Suggested Practices

To help you successfully master the exam objectives presented in this chapter, complete the following tasks.

Planning to Upgrade to Windows Vista

- **Practice 1: Evaluating Hardware Configurations**   Choose three different computers running Windows XP and manually evaluate them for an upgrade to Windows Vista. Specifically, make sure you take into account the following system specifications:
    - CPU
    - Memory
    - Hard disk (total and available space)
    - Video adapter (whether or not it will support Windows Vista)
    - Other hardware, such as scanners, printers, and digital cameras

    In some cases, you might need to access third-party vendors' Web sites to determine whether a particular device or component is compatible with Windows Vista.

- **Practice 2: Using the Windows Vista Upgrade Advisor**   Using the same three computers that you manually evaluated in Practice 1, download, install, and run the Windows Vista Upgrade Advisor on each system. Compare the requirements and recommendations with your earlier assessment. In addition, pay attention to any software or device driver issues that might prevent a successful upgrade.

Take a Practice Test

The practice tests on this book's companion CD offer many options. For example, you can test yourself on just one exam objective, or you can test yourself on all of the 70-623 certification exam content. You can set up the test so that it closely simulates the experience of taking a certification exam, or you can set it up in study mode so that you can look at the correct answers and explanations after you answer each question.

MORE INFO   Practice tests

For details about all the practice test options available, see the "How to Use the Practice Tests" section in this book's Introduction.

Chapter 2

Installing Windows Vista

For many customers, the most important step in getting started with a new operating system is installing the product itself. Users perform this task relatively rarely, and they might be intimidated by the process. For example, consider a small-business owner who is upgrading his or her primary work computer over the weekend or a home user who is anxious to get up and running with some of the new multimedia features in Windows Vista. These types of users tend to rely on your expertise to guide them through the installation process and to provide assistance if issues arise. Therefore, as a Consumer Support Technician, it's important for you to understand the Windows Vista installation process completely.

In Chapter 1, "Preparing to Install Windows Vista," you learned which features are included with each edition of Windows Vista as well as what version of Windows Vista might be appropriate to install based on the capabilities of a particular computer. In this chapter, you will learn how to select an installation type based on specific conditions such as the current state of the computer or the user's desire to retain existing data. In many cases, users will have the ability to perform clean installations of Windows Vista or to perform an in-place upgrade from Microsoft Windows XP. You will also learn to identify the supported upgrade paths from previous versions of Windows. The practice exercises walk you through the process of performing an installation of Windows Vista, both in the case of an upgrade and in the case of a new installation.

Exam objectives in this chapter:

- Install and Upgrade Windows Vista.
    - ❑ Prepare to install Windows Vista.
    - ❑ Troubleshoot and resolve installation issues.
    - ❑ Troubleshoot and resolve post-installation issues.

Lessons in this chapter:

Before You Begin

To complete the lessons in this chapter, you need a computer capable of running Windows Vista as well as a Windows Vista product installation DVD. This chapter covers several of the steps involved in installing and troubleshooting an operating system, so a basic working knowledge of computers, including basic input/output system (BIOS) settings, hard disk partitioning, and basic troubleshooting skills are required. In addition, recent experience with the following tasks will be helpful in getting the most out of the chapter lessons:

- Configuring the BIOS, specifically the device boot order
- Starting a CD-based or DVD-based installation of Windows
- Partitioning and formatting a hard disk

Lesson 1: Preparing a System for Installation

In this lesson, you learn about the considerations you should take into account prior to installing Windows Vista. Although installing an operating system might represent only a fraction of the overall PC life cycle, how you install it can have a lasting effect on the performance and resiliency of a PC. For example, if a computer has been through several operating system upgrades, performing a clean installation of Windows Vista rather than an in-place upgrade might result in a more robust computing experience in the end. Overall, your goal as a Consumer Support Technician should be to provide the customers you support with information about their options. They rely on you to make recommendations based on their specific needs.

After this lesson, you will be able to:
- Determine which installation types are supported by different editions of Windows Vista.
- Recommend the appropriate edition of Windows Vista based on an existing installation of Windows.

Estimated lesson time: 20 minutes

Understanding Windows Vista Installation Types

There are several installation options available in Windows Vista. The installation type you choose will probably be based primarily on whether the customer wants to preserve existing applications and settings. For example, if the user's existing PC is running Windows XP and he or she has several applications for which he or she cannot locate the original installation media, an in-place upgrade might be the best choice. However, if the customer likes the idea of starting fresh, a clean installation of Windows Vista might be the way to go.

In terms of licensing, you can upgrade Windows 2000 and Windows XP to a corresponding or better edition of Windows Vista by purchasing and installing an upgrade copy of Windows Vista. In general, if the edition of Windows Vista you plan to install will result in a loss of functionality over the current version of Windows, you need to perform a clean install or install Windows Vista to a new partition.

You can use Table 2-1 to determine which installation type is supported based on the existing Windows installation and desired version of Windows Vista. The rows in the table specify the current operating system that a customer might be using, and the columns specify the supported installation types for each consumer-focused edition of Windows Vista.

Table 2-1   Windows Vista–Supported Installation Types

	Windows Vista Home Basic	Windows Vista Home Premium	Windows Vista Business	Windows Vista Ultimate
Windows 2000	C	C	C	C
Windows XP Home	U	U	U	U
Windows XP Media Center	C	U	C	U
Windows XP Professional	C	C	U	U
Windows XP Tablet PC	C	C	U	U

Note. C = Clean installation; U = Upgrade in place

Understanding Clean Installations

The first installation option is to perform a clean installation of Windows Vista. This process is similar to installing an operating system on a new computer. A clean installation automatically replaces the current version of Windows, including all of the related operating system files, configuration settings, and applications. You perform a new or *clean* installation when:

- You want to replace the current operating system. Most home and small-business users are accustomed to using only a single operating system on their computers. If they plan to move to Windows from an operating system other than Windows XP, it is likely that they will want to replace their current operating system.

- You want to install Windows on a separate partition, and an existing operating system is on the computer. For example, you might want to configure the computer to enable you to boot into either Windows XP or Windows Vista when the system is started. This is sometimes useful for situations in which you need to keep an earlier operating system available for testing purposes or for backward compatibility.

- The computer has no operating system currently installed. Customers who have recently purchased new computers that did not come with an operating system preinstalled can choose to start a clean installation process. Experienced home users and hobbyists often choose to build their own computers by purchasing parts separately. A clean installation enables them to get up and running with Windows Vista, even when starting with a blank hard disk. As you'll learn later in this chapter, the Windows Vista setup process provides features for partitioning and formatting the hard disk.

For users who currently have an operating system installed, the biggest drawback of performing a clean installation is the work that is required to copy data files and to reinstall applications. You can always back up files and settings prior to a clean install, but you also must manually reinstall the programs and restore all of the backed-up files when the installation is complete.

Using Windows Easy Transfer

When upgrading to Windows Vista with a clean install, you can use Windows Easy Transfer to copy all the user data files and program settings automatically to a separate hard disk or other storage device prior to installing Windows Vista. Windows Easy Transfer supports Windows XP–based computers. You can launch Windows Easy Transfer directly by running the application from the menu that appears when you insert the Windows Vista installation media into a computer that is running Windows XP. The process for transferring these settings includes the following steps:

1. Run Windows Easy Transfer on the source computer (for example, Windows XP) prior to starting the installation process.

2. Follow the steps presented in the utility to back up all of the relevant applications and settings to another hard disk drive or storage location.

   It is important to choose a hard disk location that is separate from the one in which you plan to install the Windows Vista operating system because you might want to format that partition during the installation process. If the environment has multiple computers, you can copy the resulting files over the network to another computer.

3. Perform a clean installation of Windows Vista.

4. Run Windows Easy Transfer again and choose to restore applications, settings, and other information from the backup that you created in step 2.

NOTE   Specific installation scenarios

If the customer is using Windows 2000 Professional, he or she is eligible for an upgrade copy to a corresponding or better edition of Windows Vista, but a clean install is required. Upgrade copies are not available for versions of Windows earlier than Windows 2000. These earlier versions of Windows require you to install a full copy of Windows Vista.

In addition to assisting customers with the process of performing a clean installation, Windows Easy Transfer can also make the process of upgrading to a new computer easier. In this situation, you can run Windows Easy Transfer on the old computer, and then restore the resulting backup on the new computer. The result is a transfer of the most important operating system settings, applications, and data files.

Understanding In-Place Upgrades

If customers are running a supported operating system version, they can choose to perform an in-place upgrade. An in-place upgrade to Windows Vista retains the programs, files, and settings from the current version of Windows. The primary benefit is that users generally do not need to reinstall and reconfigure their applications. The upgrade process also attempts to migrate relevant operating system settings wherever possible. For example, user accounts, desktop settings, and other details are generally preserved after you complete the upgrade process.

Although performing an in-place upgrade is the fastest way to get back up and running, the end result is somewhat related to the condition of the previous Windows installation. For instance, if the computer has gone through several generations of in-place upgrades, it might have accumulated a large number of unnecessary files and applications. Over time, this additional overhead can reduce system performance and reliability. For that reason, users might prefer to perform a clean installation to give Windows Vista the best foundation with which to work.

In general, if the current version of Windows and applications are working properly and the customer needs to be back up and running in the shortest amount of time, an in-place upgrade is a good choice. Alternatively, if the customer does not mind spending some time reinstalling and reconfiguring applications and settings, a clean installation can often provide the best experience. Before choosing to start a clean installation, however, instruct customers to ensure that they have made backups of their important data. They also need to have copies of the installation media for the programs that they plan to run on the new operating systems.

NOTE   Verifying hardware and software compatibility

In some cases, certain applications or hardware devices might have known issues with Windows Vista. It is helpful to test a computer's current hardware and software configuration prior to performing an in-place upgrade to Windows Vista. The Windows Vista Upgrade Advisor provides a method for scanning the computer for potential problems that might prevent a successful upgrade. For more information on using the Upgrade Advisor, see Chapter 1.

Quick Check

1. Which edition(s) of Windows Vista support an in-place upgrade from Windows XP Media Center Edition?
2. Which method should you use if you want to install Windows Vista in a partition separate from an existing installation of Windows?

Quick Check Answers

1. Windows Vista Home Premium and Windows Vista Ultimate support in-place upgrades from Windows XP Media Center Edition.
2. You should perform a clean installation of Windows Vista.

Creating a Multiboot Installation

When you install Windows Vista, you can keep an older version of Windows on the computer. This is often called a dual-boot configuration (if there are two operating systems), or a multiboot configuration (if there are more than two). To perform a multiboot installation, Windows Vista needs its own partition on the hard disk. If the computer has another installed operating system, you might need to repartition the hard disk or add additional storage to the computer. You can also use disk partitioning software available from various manufacturers to preserve the existing operating system while creating space for Windows Vista.

In general, multiboot configurations work by presenting the customer with a choice of operating systems to load when a user starts the computer. The specific details depend on which operating systems are installed on the computer.

MORE INFO Virtual machines versus multiboot

Although configuring a computer with multiple operating systems can be useful, one of the potential drawbacks is that customers need to reboot the computer to access each one. Users who would like to run multiple operating systems concurrently can look into the use of virtual machines to enable more than one operating system to run concurrently on the computer. As long as the computer's hardware configuration meets the system requirements, this can be a much simpler configuration to set up. Microsoft Virtual PC is a free product that enables the creation of virtual machines within Windows Vista. For more information, see the Virtual PC Web site at *http://www.microsoft.com/windows/products/winfamily/virtualpc/default.mspx*.

Repairing and Reinstalling Windows Vista

In some cases, users might need to reinstall Windows Vista due to a configuration issue or to recover from a hardware failure. The Windows Vista setup process provides the ability either to reinstall the operating system or to perform various repair functions. You'll learn more about reinstalling Windows Vista in Lesson 3, "Troubleshooting Installation Issues." For more information on troubleshooting and repairing Windows Vista, see Chapter 12, "Troubleshooting Windows Vista," and Chapter 13, "Protecting Data and Repairing Windows Vista."

Partitioning the Hard Disk

For the majority of installations, using the default hard disk options presented by Windows Setup is the best practice. However, there might be cases in which it would be a good idea to validate where Windows is going to be installed. This is especially true for computers with several partitions or several hard disks. Users have the option of placing the operating system on any available partition that does not currently contain an operating system.

Many computer manufacturers create a special reserved partition (sometimes called an original equipment manufacturer [OEM] partition) that contains a local recovery solution. This is typically used for disaster recovery if the system becomes unbootable. When you install Windows Vista, it might be important to the customer to retain the OEM partition so that he or she can restore the computer back to the factory load if required. To determine where Windows Vista will be installed on the hard disk, review the advanced disk options during setup. Because deleting or modifying partitions is usually a process that you cannot easily undo, make sure you fully understand the customer's usability and technical requirements before advising him or her to make modifications.

Practice: Evaluating Upgrade Options

In this practice exercise, you apply the information that you have learned to develop recommendations for upgrade options.

▶ **Practice: Analyzing Computers' Upgrade Options**

Assume that you would like to upgrade one or more available computers to Windows Vista. Using any available computers, determine the options that you might have for performing an upgrade. Questions to ask include the following:

1. What is the primary purpose of the computer?
2. Is an in-place upgrade supported from this operating system?
3. Does the computer meet the system requirements for running Windows Vista?
4. How can you back up system settings and data files before performing a new upgrade?
5. What are the partitioning options for the new operating system?
6. Can you set up a multiboot configuration on this computer?

Based on these details, develop a recommendation for migrating the computer to Windows Vista.

Lesson Summary

- A clean installation of Windows Vista involves deploying a new operating system, using all default settings. It does not migrate existing applications or settings automatically.
- An in-place upgrade to Windows Vista preserves existing applications, settings, and user data by replacing the current operating system.

- You can use Windows Easy Transfer to create a backup of applications, configuration settings, and user data for restoring on Windows Vista.
- You can set up a computer to dual-boot Windows Vista and another operating system.
- You must perform a clean installation when installing Windows Vista on a computer that is currently running Windows 2000.
- Users can choose to repair or reinstall Windows Vista to resolve various technical issues. For more information on these topics, see Chapter 12 and Chapter 13.

Lesson Review

You can use the following questions to test your knowledge of the information in Lesson 1, "Preparing a System for Installation." The questions are also available on the companion CD if you prefer to review them in electronic form.

NOTE Answers

Answers to these questions and explanations of why each answer choice is correct or incorrect are located in the "Answers" section at the end of the book.

---

1. Which of the following editions of Windows Vista support an in-place upgrade from Windows XP Professional? (Choose all that apply.)
    A. Windows Vista Home Basic
    B. Windows Vista Home Premium
    C. Windows Vista Business
    D. Windows Vista Ultimate

2. Which of the following types of installations will result in a loss of operating system settings and installed applications that are present in the current version of Windows?
    A. Clean installation
    B. In-place upgrade
    C. Multiboot installation

Lesson 2: Installing Windows Vista

In this lesson, you learn how to perform a Windows Vista installation, using the different methods covered in the previous lesson. The setup process itself has been significantly simplified from that of previous versions of Windows. Most end users should be able to walk through the basic installation steps without much assistance. However, as a Consumer Support Technician, you need to understand completely the details of what is occurring during the Windows Vista setup process. Specifically, in this lesson, you learn how to perform both a clean installation and an in-place upgrade.

Installing the base operating system is generally only the first step in getting the computer up and running based on users' requirements. An important second step involves ensuring that additional hardware is configured to work properly. Generally, that means installing additional device drivers on the computer. In this lesson, you'll learn how to install device drivers that are required by the computer hardware but that are not included with the Windows Vista operating system.

After this lesson, you will be able to:

- Install Windows Vista on a computer with no operating system.
- Replace a previous version of Windows, using a clean installation.
- Upgrade a previous version of Windows, using an in-place upgrade.
- Install device drivers that are not included with Windows Vista.

Estimated lesson time: 120 minutes

Starting a Clean Installation

As discussed earlier in the chapter, there are several reasons to perform a clean installation of Windows Vista. The primary benefit of performing a clean installation is that it brings no additional difficulties along with it. Because the installation begins with a new default configuration for operating system settings, this approach can provide the best foundation for Windows, programs, and device drivers. If a previous version of Windows exists, it is replaced, and all programs, documents, and settings are lost.

NOTE   Verifying upgrade edition requirements

You cannot install an upgrade copy of Windows Vista on a partition unless a copy of Windows 2000 or Windows XP is already installed on that partition. As a Consumer Support Technician, you should advise your customers to verify the details and requirements of an edition of Windows Vista before they purchase it.

Microsoft designed the Windows Vista installation discs to be bootable, and you can use them to start the installation process. Booting from the installation disc also enables you to perform various troubleshooting tasks (a topic that is covered in Chapter 13). Perhaps the most notable difference between a clean installation and an in-place upgrade is the act of booting the computer by using the product media.

The first step in a clean installation is to turn on the computer and insert the Windows Vista installation disc. Many computers are configured by default to search the computer's CD/DVD-ROM devices for bootable media during the boot process. If you do not see a prompt that asks you to press any key to boot from the media, you need to consult the computer manufacturer's documentation. Generally, you should look for information about accessing a special computer boot menu or information about accessing the computer's BIOS settings to make boot order preference changes.

NOTE Troubleshooting CD/DVD boot issues

If the Install Windows page does not appear and you're not asked to press a key to start from DVD or CD, you might need to specify that the computer should use its DVD or CD drive as the startup device. This means that you need to set the DVD or CD drive to the first startup device in the BIOS. (Some computers might use the term CMOS Setup instead.) After you have selected the DVD or CD drive as the startup device, restart the computer, and then start Windows from the installation DVD or CD as previously described.

After you press a key when prompted to boot using the Windows Vista installation media, the computer automatically loads the Windows Vista installation screen. During the installation of Windows Vista, you are prompted for common information such as regional and network settings. You will learn about the specific steps later in this lesson. When performing a clean installation, you can select an existing disk partition onto which you want to install Windows Vista. The setup process also provides the ability to create, delete, and format partitions before the installation of Windows Vista begins.

Starting an In-Place Upgrade

When you perform an in-place upgrade to Windows Vista, the files, settings, and programs are retained from the currently installed version of Windows XP. As with previous versions of Windows, check the compatibility of the hardware prior to performing the upgrade. Microsoft has provided a new automated tool called the Windows Upgrade Advisor that evaluates a system's ability to run Windows Vista. You can launch the Windows Vista Upgrade Advisor from the Microsoft Web site or simply run it during the upgrade by clicking Check Compatibility Online in the Install Windows window. For more information on using the Windows Vista Upgrade Advisor, see Chapter 1.

NOTE   **Starting the upgrade installation process**

If you have an upgrade copy of the 32-bit version of Windows Vista, you must start the Windows Vista installation while running the existing version of Windows.

To start the in-place upgrade process, insert the Windows Vista installation media into the computer while your original operating system is running. For example, if you plan to perform an in-place upgrade from Windows XP Professional to Windows Vista Ultimate, first boot the computer into Windows XP. When you insert the Windows Vista upgrade media, the Auto-Play settings should automatically load a menu that gives you the option to start the installation process. If it does not appear, you can run the Setup.exe program manually from the root of the media.

Quick Check

1. What type of installation retains the existing data and settings?
2. What installation type provides the best foundation for Windows Vista?

Quick Check Answers

1. An in-place upgrade retains existing data and settings.
2. A clean installation results in a default collection of operating system settings and other details when installing Windows Vista.

Performing a Windows Vista Installation

So far, you have learned how to start the process of installing Windows Vista. In this section, you learn about the various steps that you can perform during the installation. The general steps in the process are identical regardless of whether you're performing an in-place upgrade or a clean installation. The primary difference is that, when you are performing an upgrade installation, disk partitioning options are not available.

Overall, the process begins with collecting various pieces of information that are required to determine how and where the operating system should be installed. For the purpose of this section, you learn about walking through a new installation of Windows Vista.

Real World

Anil Desai

As a Consumer Support Technician, you generally have knowledge, insight, and experience in installing and configuring operating systems. Many computer users, on the other hand, do not. To them, some of the configuration options might seem strange, and they might feel forced to make an educated guess. Microsoft is certainly aware of this, and the Windows Vista installation process is dramatically easier and more accessible than that in previous versions of Windows. Gone are the intimidating text-based screens that use highly technical language. They're replaced with a graphical environment that looks much more like the familiar Windows user interface. Customers can use the mouse to make their selections, and plain-language help is usually available.

When assisting customers in installing operating systems, one reassuring thought seems to help significantly: with few exceptions, it's unlikely that a user will make a "wrong" decision. You can modify just about every setting and option available during the setup process after the installation completes. Often, when customers know that they can't completely ruin their computers, they're more willing to guess on various settings, and they're less likely to give up on the installation process.

Another very valuable piece of advice is to familiarize users with the types of information they'll need to provide during installation. For example, if you're working in a retail environment, you might help customers decide certain settings before they start the installation process. With respect to Windows Vista, considerations include the following:

- The edition of Windows Vista that is to be installed
- The name of the computer
- The name of the primary user of the computer
- Network security requirements

Overall, through the use of reassurance and planning, you can make a potentially scary process much easier for the customers you support.

Starting the Installation Process

When you begin a clean installation by booting the computer, using the Windows Vista installation media, the first page you see is shown in Figure 2-1.

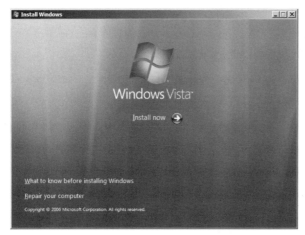

Figure 2-1   The initial Windows Vista installation page

The most common option is to begin the setup process by clicking Install Now. Other options include the ability to click What To Know Before Installing Windows. This command launches a Help and Support window that provides information about the entire upgrade process. Users who are new to the operating system installation process might want to read through the details. Another option is Repair Your Computer. The troubleshooting and repair process is covered in more detail in Lesson 3 of this chapter and in Chapters 12 and 13.

One important note related to the Windows Vista installation process is that it uses a limited operating environment. Because a full operating system is not yet available on the computer, you are limited in the types of operations you can perform. For example, there is no way to run other programs, copy or paste text, or perform operations such as printing the help file. Although this does place some limitations on functionality, it also simplifies the information collection process. Customers should be reassured that they can modify many different system settings after they complete the operating system installation.

Choosing Language and Preference Settings

Microsoft designed Windows Vista to run on a broad range of hardware that is available throughout the world. Because users might want to perform the installation by using different settings that are unique to their environment, the setup process initially prompts for these details. Figure 2-2 shows the available options. They include the following:

Figure 2-2   Choosing Windows Vista setup language and preference settings

- **Language To Install**   Some versions of Windows Vista enable you to change the language that is used during the setup process and for the installed operating system. This feature is usually available in countries in which multiple languages are commonly spoken.
- **Time And Currency Format**   Different regions of the world use different conventions for displaying time and currency. This drop-down list enables you to select the most appropriate option.
- **Keyboard Or Input Method**   Hardware that is produced to support different languages might include a variety of different keyboards or other input devices. The user can choose the type of device and its layout from this drop-down menu.

After you have selected the appropriate options, click Next.

Providing the Product Key

To protect against software piracy and to ensure that users install a legitimate copy of their operating systems, Windows Vista requires an activation process. There are two main steps to the activation process itself. The first involves providing a product key. Figure 2-3 shows the installation process step that requests this information.

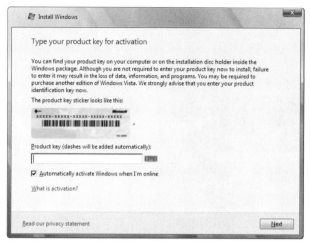

Figure 2-3   Providing product key information

Most commonly, users can find their product key sticker located in one of several places:

- **In the Windows Vista product packaging**   For customers who have purchased a retail copy of Windows Vista, the product key should be located inside the Windows Vista packaging. The page shows an example of what the sticker should look like.

- **In additional computer documentation**   If a computer shipped with Windows Vista pre-installed, the manufacturer might have included the product key information on a certificate or other document that shipped with the computer.

- **On a sticker attached to the computer**   New computers that shipped with the Windows Vista operating system might include a sticker that includes the product key. You can often find the sticker on the bottom of the computer (in the case of a notebook computer), or affixed to the back of the computer.

- **In an electronic format**   Customers can purchase Windows Vista online. In these situations, they might have received the necessary product key information from a Web site or in an e-mail message.

The product key information is automatically validated against a mathematical algorithm. This validation helps reduce the likelihood of entering an invalid product key. It is important to note, however, that just because a product key is accepted does not mean that the operating system will be successfully activated. Activation is performed after the operating system installation is complete. Users have different options for performing activation. The most commonly used method is to activate Windows Vista automatically over the Internet. You can use the check box on this page to select that option.

It is highly recommended that customers provide their product key during the installation process, but it is not required. When you provide a product key, the setup process is able to determine automatically the correct edition of Windows Vista to install. When you click Next without providing the product key, you must manually specify which edition of Windows Vista you wish to install (see Figure 2-4).

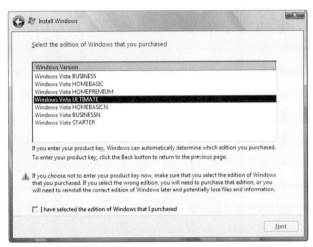

Figure 2-4   Choosing an installation type when the product key is not provided

The Windows Vista installation media includes the ability to install a variety of different editions of the operating system. Typically, the product key is used to determine which edition to install. Users must manually specify the edition that they have purchased when they do not provide a product key. The specific list of options might vary based on the type of installation media that is used. This is a very important option because you cannot easily modify it after you make a selection. The warning messages state that, if an incorrect edition is selected, users might need to reinstall their entire operating system.

Accepting the License Terms

The next step of the installation process involves reviewing the software license terms for the selected edition of Windows Vista (see Figure 2-5).

Customers must accept the terms of the license agreement to continue with the setup process. If a customer does not want to agree to the terms, he or she should contact the product vendor for options related to returning the software.

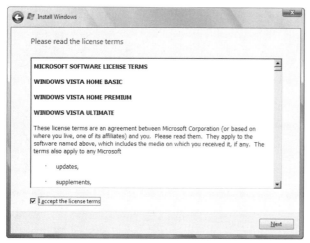

Figure 2-5   Reviewing the Windows Vista license terms

Choosing an Installation Type

When performing a new installation of Windows Vista, users might have the option of upgrading an existing installation of Windows Vista or performing a custom installation. Figure 2-6 shows the available options.

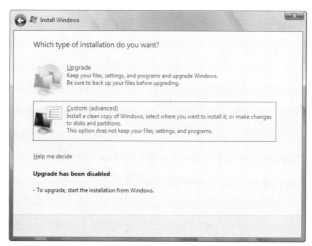

Figure 2-6   Choosing an installation type

If you launch the setup process by using Windows Vista installation media, the only available option is to perform a custom (advanced) installation. This is the same as performing a clean installation. If users would prefer to perform an in-place upgrade, they must reboot the computer into their current operating system and then begin the installation process from there. The next steps in this section assume that you are performing a clean installation.

Choosing the Installation Location

Some computers are configured with multiple hard disks and partitions. In these cases, users can choose the specific partition to which they want to install Windows Vista. This is often helpful if you want to configure the computer to provide multiple boot options. Figure 2-7 shows the installation location options along with advanced options that are available.

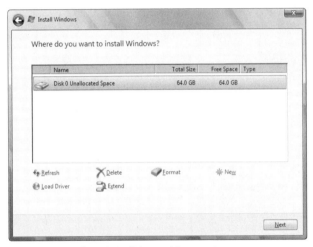

Figure 2-7   Choosing disk partition options

In addition to selecting the appropriate partition, users can also perform other helpful tasks. For example, they can create new partitions on the available hard disks. They can also delete existing partitions, extend partitions (if free space is available), and format partitions. Typically, it is not necessary to format a partition manually because the installation process does this automatically.

Another option that might be required on some computers is the Load Driver command. By default, the Windows Vista installation process provides support for the most common types of storage controllers and devices. Some computers might require users to provide custom drivers to access other types of storage. When you click Load Driver, you are prompted either to browse for or scan media on the computer (see Figure 2-8). Most commonly, you need to insert a floppy disk or CD/DVD-ROM media to provide the necessary drivers. Alternatively, the drivers might already be stored on another local hard disk partition that is accessible by browsing the computer.

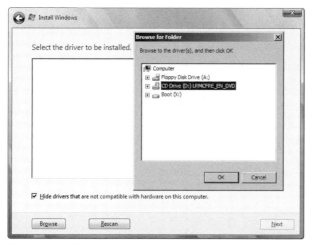

Figure 2-8   Providing a custom storage driver during the installation process

Monitoring Installation Progress

After you have selected the appropriate installation location, the Windows Vista setup process has all of the information it needs to continue. The next steps involve an automatic process that generally does not require any user intervention. Figure 2-9 shows the progress screen.

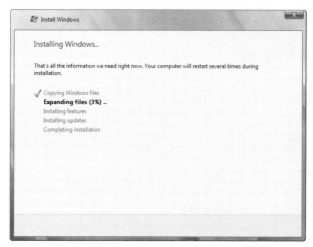

Figure 2-9   Viewing the progress of a Windows Vista installation

The steps in this installation process include the following:

1. Copying Windows files
2. Expanding files
3. Installing features

4. Installing updates
5. Completing installation

The actual amount of time it takes to complete the installation varies based on the hardware specifications of the computer. On most computers that are compatible with Windows Vista, the entire process should take less than an hour. During this time, setup needs to restart the computer automatically. The system is configured to resume the setup process after it performs a reboot, so there is usually no need to for a user to be involved.

Performing Postinstallation Configuration

After the installation process is complete, users can perform various setup and configuration tasks. At this point, the base operating system has been installed. This includes the process of enumerating attached hardware devices and installing the appropriate drivers (if available). In this section, you'll learn about the various required choices.

Providing User Name Information

The first setup prompt asks the user to provide the name of a user account to create on the computer. Although it is not required, the user can also provide a password to use when logging on to the computer with this user account. Additionally, you can select a picture to help users (especially children) easily identify accounts on the logon screen. Figure 2-10 shows the available options.

Figure 2-10 Providing user name information during the setup process

Users can also create additional accounts after this portion of the setup process is complete.

Configuring the Computer Name and Desktop Background

This step (shown in Figure 2-11) enables customers to provide a name for the local computer and choose a default desktop background. You primarily use the computer name when working with multiple computers in a network environment. It is recommended that you choose a name that is descriptive of the purpose and function of the machine. For more information on configuring the network name, see Chapter 9, "Configuring Windows Vista Networking."

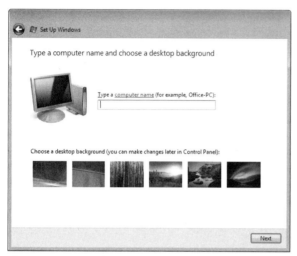

Figure 2-11   Configuring the computer name and choosing a desktop background

As with most of the setup options, the desktop background is a convenience-related feature. As you'll learn in Chapter 3, "Configuring and Customizing the Windows Vista Desktop," you can easily change the setting at any time.

Configuring Windows Update Settings

An important aspect of keeping Windows Vista secure is downloading and installing new updates on the computer. Because this is an important consideration that should be configured during the setup process, users can select the initial settings for Windows Update (see Figure 2-12). For most users, Use Recommended Settings is the best option. Assuming that an Internet connection is available, this instructs the operating system to download and install available updates on the computer automatically. For more information about configuring Windows Update settings, see Chapter 7, "Using Windows Security Center."

Figure 2-12 Configuring Windows Update settings during the setup process

Reviewing Time and Date Settings

Although most computers are already configured with the correct date and time, customers who have purchased new computers might need to change their time zone settings. Figure 2-13 shows the available options for setting the current date and time and for selecting the appropriate time zone.

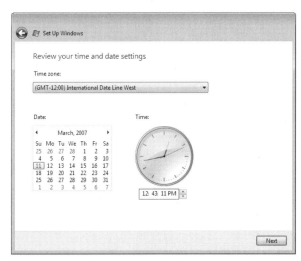

Figure 2-13 Selecting date, time, and time zone settings during setup

For time zones that include automatic seasonal adjustments (such as Daylight Savings Time in the United States), there is an option for the adjustments to be made automatically.

Selecting the Computer's Location

Security is an important part of installing and configuring Windows Vista. From the moment you install the operating system, numerous network-related configuration recommendations are based on the current location of the computer. Figure 2-14 shows the following available options:

- **Home**   This option is most relevant to computers that are running in a private location. It enables the computer to be discovered by other computers on the network and enables sharing-related features.
- **Work**   The effective settings here are similar to those defined for the Home setting. It is assumed that work environments are relatively secure and that only authorized computers are allowed on the network.
- **Public Location**   From a security standpoint, public locations such as restaurants, hotels, and airports enable a wide variety of computers to connect to an installation of Windows Vista. When the Public Location option is selected, the computer is configured so that it is not easily discoverable by other users on the network.

Figure 2-14   Specifying computer location information

For more information about configuring network location details, see Chapter 9.

Completing the Configuration Process

After users have finished the postinstallation configuration process, they'll see a simple Thank You screen, as shown in Figure 2-15. After clicking Start, users are able to begin working with Windows Vista.

Figure 2-15 Completing the postinstallation configuration process

Figure 2-16 shows the default Windows Vista desktop for a clean installation of the product. At this point, customers typically click the Start menu to access configuration options and other settings on their computers.

Figure 2-16 The initial Windows Vista desktop

Installing Device Drivers

The Windows Vista installation disc includes most of the device drivers required for the most typical hardware platforms. Over time, however, there will be a need to add support for newer computers and peripherals. Fortunately, there's Windows Update. When you install Windows Vista and determine that an additional or updated driver is required to support the hardware fully, it might be available through Windows Update. When you check Windows Update, click View Available Updates to determine whether a driver is available for the device. For more information, see Chapter 11, "Managing and Troubleshooting Devices."

Practice: Installing Windows Vista

In these practice exercises, you walk through the process of installing Windows Vista. The steps include performing an in-place upgrade and performing a clean installation.

Practice 1: Performing an In-Place Upgrade

To complete the steps in this exercise, you need a Windows Vista–capable computer running Windows XP and an edition of Windows Vista that supports an in-place upgrade from your current version of Windows XP.

1. Insert the Windows installation disc into the computer's CD/DVD drive.
2. On the Install Windows page, click Install now.
3. On the Get Important Updates For Installation page, use the default selection and click Next. This option enables Windows Vista Setup to retrieve any critical updates during installation rather than as a postinstallation task.
4. On the Type Your Product Key For Activation page, type the 25-character product key. Click Next.
5. On the Please Read The License Terms page, if you accept the license terms, click I Accept The License Terms.
6. On the Installation Type page, click Upgrade to begin the upgrade. You might see a compatibility report. This report contains useful troubleshooting information in the event you run into issues during or after the setup of Windows Vista.

Practice 2: Performing a Clean Installation

In this practice exercise, you perform a clean installation of Windows Vista. The ideal configuration is a new computer that includes a single hard disk partition. The steps assume that you are using this method. However, you can also use a computer that has an existing operating system and choose to install to a different partition. You need Windows Vista installation media for an edition of the operating system that allows for clean installations. For more details on the various steps and options, see the associated text in the "Performing a Windows Vista Installation" section earlier in this chapter.

1. Turn on the computer and insert the Windows Vista installation media. If necessary, choose the Boot The Computer From This Device And Media option.

2. On the initial setup screen, click Install Now to begin the setup process.

3. Select the appropriate options for your language, time and currency format, and keyboard or input method. For most installations, the default options should be correct.

4. On the Product Key For Activation screen, enter the product key if you have one available. If you do not plan to activate this copy of Windows Vista, you can click Next and then select the edition you want to install. If you are performing this installation for testing and practice purposes only, it is recommended that you not provide a product key. Note, however, that you need to provide activation information to continue to use the operating system after 30 days.

5. Choose to accept the license terms to continue the installation process.

6. Select the Custom (Advanced) installation option.

7. Select the partition to which you want to install Windows Vista. If necessary, you can choose to create, delete, or extend partitions. Note that some of these operations could result in permanent data loss on the computer.

8. Click Next to begin the installation process. Note the steps that are being performed and that the computer will likely be rebooted several times.

9. When finished, complete the configuration process, as described in the text.

Lesson Summary

- You can perform a clean installation on a computer with no operating system installed as well as on a computer with Windows XP.
- To perform an in-place upgrade, you must start the Windows installation from within the existing version of Windows.
- If you purchase an upgrade version of Windows Vista, you must start the installation from within the existing version of Windows.
- To boot the computer to the Windows installation disc, you might need to configure the device boot order within the BIOS.

Lesson Review

You can use the following questions to test your knowledge of the information in Lesson 2, "Installing Windows Vista." The questions are also available on the companion CD if you prefer to review them in electronic form.

NOTE   Answers

Answers to these questions and explanations of why each answer choice is correct or incorrect are located in the "Answers" section at the end of the book.

---

1. If a customer is unable to locate the installation source for some of his or her existing software programs and he or she wants to install Windows Vista, what type of installation should you perform?

   A. Clean installation

   B. In-place upgrade

   C. Multiboot installation

Lesson 3: Troubleshooting Installation Issues

Although the vast majority of Windows Vista installations should complete without any additional user effort, there are situations in which troubleshooting might be required. Microsoft has made significant efforts to ensure that a large subset of device drivers and applications are compatible with Windows Vista. In some cases, however, hardware devices or software programs might stop working after you install the new operating system. You can avoid many of these issues by taking advantage of tools such as the Windows Vista Upgrade Advisor as well as by visiting the vendor Web sites of the applications for up-to-date information about operating system compatibility.

As a Consumer Support Technician, you need to support users who experience issues after installing Windows Vista. In this lesson, you'll learn about ways in which you can troubleshoot potential problems.

> **After this lesson, you will be able to:**
> - Troubleshoot hardware issues that might occur after installing Windows Vista.
> - Resolve program compatibility issues.
> - Configure device drivers.
>
> **Estimated lesson time: 20 minutes**

Troubleshooting Hardware Compatibility Issues

Diagnosing hardware compatibility issues related to installing Windows Vista can be done in steps. A good first step is to verify whether a particular hardware device is supported. You can do this by using the Windows Vista Upgrade Advisor, as described in Chapter 1. This program contains the information that was previously published as the Windows Hardware Compatibility List (HCL). The information you find can generally tell you whether a particular device is supported in Windows Vista. In some cases, you will need to download and install updated drivers manually after you install Windows Vista. In this section, you'll learn how to troubleshoot hardware compatibility issues. For more information about working with device drivers, see Chapter 11.

Updating Device Drivers

One of the most common troubleshooting steps for Windows Vista installation issues is updating or replacing drivers. This is often necessary to address hardware that might have stopped working after the installation of the operating system. For example, you might be supporting a customer who has a universal serial bus (USB) scanner that is no longer accessible after upgrading to Windows Vista.

MORE INFO   Practice tests

One of the benefits of performing an in-place upgrade to Windows Vista is that many existing device drivers can be used automatically. Potential conflicts or issues are highlighted in the Windows Vista Upgrade Advisor, as described in Chapter 1. More information about performing an in-place upgrade is presented in Lesson 1, "Preparing a System for Installation," and Lesson 2 of this chapter.

In the past, finding the correct device drivers for a particular hardware component could be a long and frustrating process. Customers often needed to visit their computer manufacturer's Web site, the hardware vendor's Web site, or the Microsoft Web site. Windows Vista includes several features designed to simplify the process of locating, downloading, and installing device drivers.

After installing Windows Vista, users should access the Windows Update feature. Although most users might think of Windows Update as a feature for downloading and installing security updates, it is also able to find relevant device drivers automatically that might have updates by scanning the system for attached hardware devices (whether they are functioning properly or not), and looking for newer versions of the required software and driver components. When hardware-related updates are found, they can either be downloaded directly (like other types of updates), or a link is provided to obtain more information.

Obtaining Device Drivers

When you are supporting customers who are experiencing hardware-related issues, using the Internet is one of the most efficient methods of supplying device drivers. What should you do, however, if the customer does not have Internet access (or if the problem is with a network adapter or modem)? One option is to use any manufacturer-supplied installation media (such as a CD-ROM that contains drivers). Computer manufacturers and third-party vendors generally include this media with new hardware. It is important to note, however, that the drivers found on this media are often not the latest available versions. Still, they might allow a device to work well enough to allow for downloading updates.

Another method of obtaining necessary drivers is using another computer that is able to access the Internet. The general process is to download (but not install) device drivers from manufacturers' Web sites. You can then place them on removable media such as a USB memory device or a CD-ROM or DVD-ROM. You can then copy the files to the computer that is experiencing the problem.

After you have obtained the necessary device drivers, you can install them by using Device Manager. To open Device Manager, click Start, choose Control Panel, click System And Maintenance, and then select Device Manager. Figure 2-17 shows the default view, which displays a list of hardware devices organized by device type.

Figure 2-17   Using the Windows Vista Device Manager

For more information about installing and managing drivers, see Chapter 11.

Quick Check

1. How can you determine whether a particular hardware device is compatible with Windows Vista?

2. What is a potential drawback of using device drivers that were included with a hardware product versus downloading device driver files using the Internet?

Quick Check Answers

1. You can get up-to-date hardware compatibility information for Windows Vista by running the Windows Vista Upgrade Advisor application on a potential upgrade candidate computer. For more information, see the Windows Vista Upgrade Advisor Web site at *http://www.microsoft.com/windows/products/windowsvista/buyorupgrade/upgradeadvisor.mspx.*

2. It is always best practice to check Windows Update first, then the manufacturer's Web site, and then, as a last resort, to locate the original installation media and see whether the driver works.

Troubleshooting Application Compatibility Issues

Perhaps the most common problem after upgrading to a new operating system is that a previously installed program no longer works, or it behaves differently. To resolve this issue, a common troubleshooting approach is to verify compatibility with Windows Vista by visiting the software manufacturer's Web site. In some cases, known workarounds might be listed, or software-based updates might be required to run under the new operating system.

Whenever possible, advise customers to select software that is designed to work with Windows Vista. Most programs written for Windows XP also work in Windows Vista, but some older programs might run poorly or not at all. Potential reasons for incompatibilities include the enhanced visual interface in Windows Vista.

Using the Program Compatibility Wizard

The Program Compatibility Wizard enables you to run older programs in an environment that simulates earlier versions of Windows. To start the Program Compatibility Wizard, in Control Panel, click Programs. Click Use An Older Program With This Version Of Windows to start the wizard. Figure 2-18 shows the first step.

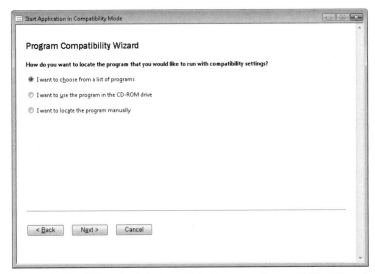

Figure 2-18   Using the Windows Vista Program Compatibility Wizard

---

NOTE   Troubleshooting driver issues

Hardware device drivers might cause some program compatibility problems. If an older driver is causing problems, you'll need to update it, using the steps outlined in the beginning of this lesson.

The wizard walks you through several steps, including the following:

■ **Locating or selecting the program**   The program itself will most likely be located within the Program Files folder on the System drive. In some cases, however, it might be located on removable media (such as a CD-ROM or DVD-ROM) or on a USB memory device. If the program has already been installed, you can select an option to view a list of installed programs.

- **Selecting a compatibility mode** Microsoft designed compatibility mode settings to emulate various settings from previous versions of the Windows platform. These options can be helpful when troubleshooting an application that does not run on Windows Vista because the version of the operating system is unsupported. The default option, however, is to not apply a compatibility mode. Included operating system versions are the following:
  - ❑ Microsoft Windows 95
  - ❑ Microsoft Windows NT 4.0 (Service Pack 5)
  - ❑ Microsoft Windows 98/Windows Me
  - ❑ Microsoft Windows 2000
  - ❑ Microsoft Windows XP (Service Pack 2)
- **Selecting display settings** This step enables you to disable or modify the standard desktop elements of Windows Vista. For more information about the Windows Aero user interface, see Chapter 3. The specific options include the following:
  - ❑ 256 Colors
  - ❑ 640 x 480 Screen Resolution
  - ❑ Disable Visual Themes
  - ❑ Disable Desktop Composition
  - ❑ Disable Display Scaling On High DPI Settings
- **Security settings** To provide increased security, Windows Vista includes numerous features that are designed to make programs run with a limited set of permissions. In some cases, these issues might prevent a program from running properly. In this step, you can choose to run a program always using Administrator credentials. For more information about configuring security in Windows Vista, see Chapter 6, "Configuring Windows Vista Security."

After you have selected the relevant options, the Program Compatibility Wizard gives you the option of testing the settings by running the program. If the settings do not resolve the problem, customers should contact their software vendors for more details.

Using Software Compatibility Modes

The Program Compatibility Wizard provides users with a guided method of locating programs and providing appropriate compatibility settings. This is a good method for users who are new to Windows Vista, but it can take several minutes to walk through the steps. Fortunately, there's a quicker alternative to accessing the same settings that are available through the wizard.

You can view and modify compatibility settings for a program manually by accessing the Compatibility tab of a program's Properties dialog box. Figure 2-19 shows the options that are available. Table 2-2 provides additional details related to the settings and their purpose.

Figure 2-19   Viewing settings on an application's Compatibility tab

Table 2-2   Description of the Compatibility Tab Settings

Setting	Description
Compatibility Mode	Runs the program using settings from a previous version of Windows. Try this setting if you know the program is designed for (or worked in) a specific previous version of Windows.
Run In 256 colors	Uses a limited set of colors in the program. Some older programs are designed to use fewer colors.
Run In 640 × 480 Screen Resolution	Runs the program in a smaller window. Try this setting if the graphical user interface appears jagged or is rendered improperly.
Disable Visual Themes	Disables themes on the program. Try this setting if you notice problems with the menus or buttons on the title bar of the program.
Disable Desktop Composition	Turns off transparency and other advanced display features. Choose this setting if window movement appears erratic or you notice other display problems.
Disable Display Scaling On High DPI Settings	Turns off automatic resizing of programs if large-scale font size is in use. Try this setting if large-scale fonts are interfering with the appearance of the program.
Privilege Level	Runs the program as Administrator. Some programs require Administrator privileges to run properly. If you are not currently logged on as an Administrator, this option is not available.

Table 2-2   Description of the Compatibility Tab Settings

Setting	Description
Show Settings For All Users	Enables you to choose settings that apply to all users on this computer.

Reinstalling Windows Vista

Windows Vista includes numerous tools and features for troubleshooting a wide variety of potential installation issues. In some cases, however, customers might choose to reinstall the operating system. This should generally be considered a last resort because it can result in the loss of all operating systems and installed applications. For more information about troubleshooting Windows Vista (including boot-related problems), see Chapter 12.

Before starting the reinstallation process, it is very important to create a backup of important data files. Tools such as the Backup and Restore Center (covered in Chapter 13) and Windows Easy Transfer can help make the process easier. To reinstall Windows Vista, start by booting the computer from the installation media. Several different repair-related operations are also available for managing the most common issues.

Getting Additional Troubleshooting Assistance

So far, you have learned about several different ways to obtain updated information about hardware and software compatibility for a device or program. Over time, and as new products are created and updated, details related to compatibility issues might change. Additionally, you might encounter various error messages or other issues that can prevent the system from working optimally.

Microsoft has provided a central starting point that can assist customers and Consumer Support Technicians with resolving the most common types of issues they are likely to encounter. You can find the Windows Vista Solution Center at *http://support.microsoft.com/windowsvista*. The site includes groups for various types of issues, such as these:

- Installing and upgrading
- Hardware
- Configuring and maintaining
- Networking
- Security and privacy

Each section includes steps that can help resolve the problem or that can provide more details about the issue.

Practice: Troubleshooting Installation Problems

In these practice exercises, you walk through some ways in which you can troubleshoot common Windows Vista installation problems. Although true troubleshooting requires an actual problem, you can simulate several ways to resolve issues by using these steps.

Practice 1: Configuring Application Compatibility Settings

In this practice exercise, you use the Program Compatibility Wizard to configure an application to run with application compatibility settings. Before you begin, choose a particular program that you want to test in this way. The steps in this exercise assume that you are using a program that has already been installed on the computer. If you prefer, you can use an executable file from another program instead.

1. To start the Program Compatibility Wizard, open Control Panel and click Programs. In the Programs And Features section, click Use An Older Program With This Version Of Windows.

2. Click Next to start the process of configuring application compatibility.

3. From the list of options, select I Want To Choose From A List Of Programs, and then click Next. (If you'd prefer to use a specific executable file, you can choose I Want To Locate The Program Manually and then skip to step 5 of this practice exercise.) If you cannot find an appropriate program in the list, you can browse to the WordPad application by using the \Program Files\Windows NT\Accessories path on the system volume.

4. In the list of programs, select the one for which you want to assign compatibility settings. Click Next to continue.

5. In the compatibility mode step, choose to emulate Microsoft Windows XP (Service Pack 2). Click Next.

6. Under Select Display Settings For The Program, select the Disable Visual Themes and Disable Desktop Composition check boxes. Click Next to continue.

7. Under Does The Program Require Administrative Privileges, select the Run This Program As An Administrator check box. Although this might not be required for the program you selected, enable the option for the purposes of this practice exercise. Click Next to continue.

8. Verify the compatibility settings that you have chosen, and then click Next to continue.

9. The Program Compatibility Wizard automatically launches the program, using the settings you have specified. Assuming that the program runs correctly, close it to continue.

10. To keep the original settings for the application, select the No, I Am Finished Trying Compatibility Settings option. If the compatibility settings did work properly (and were required), you would usually choose the Yes, Set This Program To Always Use These Compatibility Settings option. Click Next.

11. On the Program Compatibility Data page, you have the option to send information about this program to Microsoft. Because this is a practice exercise, select No, and then click Next.

12. Click Finish to complete the Program Compatibility Wizard. Settings for your application should be unchanged from their original values.

Practice 2: Updating Device Drivers

In this practice exercise, you use features in Device Manager to search for updated drivers for a particular device. The steps use the display adapter driver as an example, but other types of hardware can be substituted if necessary.

1. Open Device Manager by opening Control Panel and clicking Hardware And Sound. In the Device Manager section, click View Hardware And Devices. Note that all of the hardware attached to the computer is displayed here. A yellow exclamation mark indicates that the device is not functioning properly, and a red X indicates that the hardware is disabled.

2. Expand the Display Adapters section. Right-click the name of the display adapter and select Update Driver Software. (If you have multiple display adapters in the computer, select one of them for this exercise.)

3. On the How Do You Want To Search For Driver Software page, choose the Search Automatically For Updated Driver Software option. The program attempts to connect to the Internet and search local driver databases.

4. Assuming that an appropriate display adapter driver is already installed, you are shown a recommendation to keep the driver. Click Close to keep the existing driver. If an updated driver is available, you are prompted to install it for the device.

5. When finished, close Device Manager.

Lesson Summary

- A common approach can be used to troubleshoot hardware devices whether they're installed before or after Windows Vista.
- Windows Vista provides several ways to resolve program compatibility issues, including a wizard and the ability to adjust compatibility settings manually.
- You can reinstall Windows Vista, using the clean installation method.

Lesson Review

You can use the following questions to test your knowledge of the information in Lesson 3. The questions are also available on the companion CD if you prefer to review them in electronic form.

NOTE   Answers

Answers to these questions and explanations of why each answer choice is correct or incorrect are located in the "Answers" section at the end of the book.

---

1. Which compatibility option should you enable if the user interface of an individual application is no longer rendered properly after installing Windows Vista?

    A. Disable Visual Themes

    B. Run Program In 640x480 Screen Resolution

    C. Disable Desktop Composition

    D. Privilege Level

Chapter Review

To further practice and reinforce the skills you learned in this chapter, you can perform the following tasks:

- Review the chapter summary.
- Review the list of key terms introduced in this chapter.
- Complete the case scenarios. These scenarios set up real-world situations involving the topics of this chapter and ask you to create a solution.
- Complete the suggested practices.
- Take a practice test.

Chapter Summary

- Two main installation types are supported by Windows Vista: clean installation and in-place upgrade.
- Perform a clean installation by booting the computer to the Windows Vista product CD/DVD.
- Use the Windows Vista Upgrade Advisor to evaluate a computer's hardware compatibility prior to installation of Windows Vista.
- Upgrade media cannot be used to perform a clean installation.

Key Terms

Do you know what these key terms mean? You can check your answers by looking up the terms in the glossary at the end of the book.

- basic input/output system (BIOS)
- clean installation
- in-place upgrade
- Windows Vista Upgrade Advisor

Case Scenarios

In the following case scenarios, you apply what you've learned about installing Windows Vista. You can find answers to these questions in the "Answers" section at the end of this book.

Case Scenario 1: Evaluating Windows Vista Installation Options

You are working as a Consumer Support Technician. A customer brings in his computer along with a new copy of Windows Vista Home Basic. The computer is currently running Windows XP Media Center Edition. He states that he has several programs installed that will work with Windows Vista, but he is unable to find some of his original installation media.

1. Which installation type is supported in this scenario?
2. How will the customer's data and settings be retained?
3. What steps should be taken before installing Windows Vista?

Case Scenario 2: Disk Partitioning

You are working as a Consumer Support Technician. A customer brings in her computer along with a new copy of Windows Vista Home Premium. The computer is currently running Windows 2000. The customer states that she would like to retain her existing hard disk partitioning, which includes a C and D drive, and not to delete data on D.

1. Which installation type is supported in this scenario?
2. How will the customer's data and settings be retained?
3. What steps should be taken before installing Windows Vista?

Suggested Practices

To help you successfully master the exam objectives presented in this chapter, complete the following tasks.

Planning for and Troubleshooting the Installation of Windows Vista

▶ **Practice 1: Evaluate Upgrade Paths**

In this practice exercise, you evaluate the upgrade options for several different computers. This helps you determine the options that are available for users of various operating system versions and editions.

Select three computer configurations (real or hypothetical) in which each has a different edition of Windows 2000 or Windows XP, such as Windows XP Professional.

For each configuration, list the installation types supported for the following editions of Windows Vista:
- ❑ Windows Vista Home Basic
- ❑ Windows Vista Home Premium
- ❑ Windows Vista Business
- ❑ Windows Vista Ultimate

▶ **Practice 2: Application Compatibility**

In this practice exercise, you work with the application compatibility settings in Windows Vista. This helps you identify the available options for troubleshooting programs that do not run properly on Windows Vista.

On a computer running Windows Vista, select an application that you've installed and evaluate what impacts compatibility settings have. For example, change the display-related settings for a specific application and disable some of the new features of Windows Vista. Then, run the program and see the effects that it has on the user interface of the program. Also, apply different values for the settings found in Table 2-2.

Take a Practice Test

The practice tests on this book's companion CD offer many options. For example, you can test yourself on just one exam objective, or you can test yourself on all of the 70-623 certification exam content. You can set up the test so that it closely simulates the experience of taking a certification exam, or you can set it up in study mode so that you can look at the correct answers and explanations after you answer each question.

MORE INFO   **Practice tests**

For details about all the practice test options available, see the "How to Use the Practice Tests" section in this book's introduction.

Chapter 3

Configuring and Customizing the Windows Vista Desktop

For most users, the most noticeable aspect of an operating system is its user interface—the portion of the platform with which the user directly interacts. In the case of Microsoft Windows, one of the major strengths of the platform is usability through a graphical user interface (GUI) with which many users are already familiar. From accessing programs to opening and managing documents, there Windows Vista provides consistent ways to complete tasks.

Important goals for the Windows desktop and other user interface components are to provide information in a logical, consistent, and easy-to-understand way, and to provide intuitive ways to work with applications, documents, and operating system settings. Although there is a tremendous amount of complexity in the underlying operating system code and features, the purpose of the user interface is to present this as simply as possible.

With Windows Vista, Microsoft has included many new enhancements over previous versions of the Windows GUI. Although the general methods of accomplishing tasks remain similar to previous versions of Windows (such as Windows 2000 and Windows XP), the new additions and changes include functional and aesthetic usability improvements. Overall, the enhancements to the user interface can provide numerous advantages for users. As a customer support provider, you can help users make the most of their Windows Vista experience by guiding them through the various options that are available. Because users have different needs and backgrounds, some simple configuration changes can help optimize their operating system environment.

In this chapter, you'll look at perhaps the most conspicuous change in Windows Vista, the improved user interface. You'll cover details related to configuring Windows Aero and managing desktop settings. Some options might be purely aesthetic in nature, but various settings can improve productivity and provide for a better end-user experience. You'll also look at another new and useful feature, the Windows Sidebar. By providing helpful information directly on the Windows Vista desktop, this feature allows users to stay up to date without opening many different applications or Web pages.

Exam objectives in this chapter:
- Configure Windows Aero.
- Configure Windows Sidebar.

Lessons in this chapter:

Before You Begin

To work through the lessons and practice items in this chapter, you should have an installation of Windows Vista Home Premium, Windows Vista Business, or Windows Vista Ultimate installed and ready for use.

For the exercises in Lesson 1, you should be running Windows Vista on hardware that supports the Windows Aero user interface feature.

A basic understanding of working with the Windows platform will be helpful.

Lesson 1: Configuring Windows Aero and Desktop Settings

From the moment users log on to their computers, they rely on the ability to accomplish tasks such as launching applications and working with documents quickly and easily. Perhaps the easiest way to identify whether a computer is running Windows Vista is to take a look at the desktop and GUI features. From the look of the taskbar to the layout of the Start menu, these components are easily identifiable as part of the Windows Vista operating system (OS).

The Windows Vista user interface includes many improvements over previous versions of the Windows platform. Although it provides enhancements to usability and functionality, there's an aesthetic aspect that can't be ignored. To accommodate a variety of different preferences, the look and feel of many different settings can be customized. In this lesson, you'll cover details related to configuring these options, using Control Panel and other settings.

After this lesson, you will be able to:

- Describe the features of Windows Aero, including transparency effects.
- Enable and disable Windows Aero user interface features.
- Troubleshoot issues related to enabling Windows Aero.
- Customize the various desktop settings of Windows Vista, based on users' preferences.
- Configure other desktop settings, including themes, backgrounds, and color schemes.

Estimated lesson time: 30 minutes

Working with Windows Display Settings

Windows Vista has been designed with a look and feel that is easy to configure and customize, using simple GUI-based tools. Most of these options are available directly from within Control Panel, although there are other ways to access the same settings more quickly. In this section, you'll walk through various display-related settings and the effects that they will have on the look and feel of the desktop.

Accessing Display Settings

The first step in configuring display settings is to find out how to access these various options. There are two main ways in which you can access display-related settings in Windows Vista, as follows:

- **Using Control Panel**   You can access most of the Windows Vista configuration settings through Control Panel. Users access Control Panel by clicking Start → Control Panel. In the Control Panel Home window, clicking Appearance And Personalization enables you to access links to additional options (see Figure 3-1). Common tasks, such as changing the desktop background and modifying desktop themes, are accessible from here. If you prefer to use the Control Panel Classic view, you can access these options by clicking the Classic View link. The Classic view is similar to that in previous versions of Windows. You can also use the integrated search feature within Control Panel to find appropriate settings.

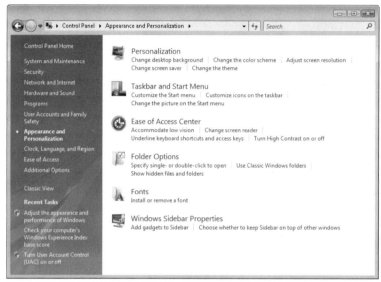

Figure 3-1   Accessing the Appearance And Personalization options in Control Panel

■ **From the desktop**   By right-clicking the desktop and choosing Personalize, users can quickly jump to the Personalization window (see Figure 3-2). This is the same window that you access through Control Panel, but you can access it using fewer mouse clicks.

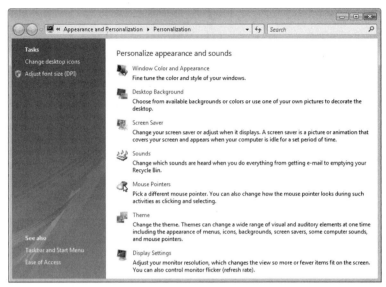

Figure 3-2   Viewing options for personalizing appearance and sounds

Regardless of the method used to access the settings, all of the options are the same. When supporting customers and other users, you can always instruct them to close any open windows and return to the Personalization window as a starting point. In the remainder of this lesson, you'll walk through the available settings in more detail.

Managing Windows Display Settings

The most noticeable features of a computer's display include several settings that are configured for the video adapter. By default, Windows Vista tries to choose the most appropriate settings for the computer based on the capabilities of the installed graphics adapter and display devices.

You can configure the primary properties by using the Display Settings dialog box (see Figure 3-3). The main configuration options include the following:

Figure 3-3   Accessing the Display Settings properties

- **Resolution**   *Resolution* refers to the number of pixels that are displayed on the screen. Common resolutions include 1024 x 768 and 1280 x 1024. It is also becoming increasingly common for desktop and notebook displays to include widescreen configurations, such as 1680 x 1050. In general, higher resolutions provide the ability to view more information on the screen at one time (although the text and application windows might appear smaller).

- **Colors**   The number of bits used to represent colors can affect the quality of the overall display. This setting is generally most noticeable in photos and other images. In general, users should select the maximum number of colors supported by their video adapter. To use Windows Aero features, you must select the Highest (32-bit) option.

- **Screen refresh rate**   The refresh rate indicates the number of times the screen is redrawn per second (the rate is measured in Hertz [Hz]). For cathode ray tube (CRT) monitors, higher refresh rates result in a more stable image with less visible flickering. Some users might find that they experience headaches or fatigue when running at a refresh rate that is too low. In general, users should select the highest refresh rate that their monitor and video adapter can support. The maximum refresh rate will vary based on the capabilities of the video card, the capabilities of the monitor, and the desktop resolution setting. To access these options, click Advanced Settings, and then click the Monitor tab (see Figure 3-4).

Figure 3-4   Viewing and setting the screen refresh rate

For LCD-based displays, manufacturers usually recommend an optimal refresh rate. Windows Vista typically detects this refresh rate automatically, but you can also find the information in the display's menu system or documentation.

■ **Multiple monitors**   Many users have discovered the usability and productivity benefits of having multiple monitors attached to the same computer. To support multiple monitors, the computer must have a video card with multiple outputs, or it might have multiple independent video cards (each connected to one monitor). Assuming that the computer has this capability, users can specify the physical arrangement of the monitors in the Display Settings dialog box (see Figure 3-5). Options include the ability to specify which is the main monitor (the display on which the Start menu and other programs will appear) and to extend the desktop onto other monitors. If you're not sure about how the current monitors are numbered, you can click Identify Monitors to display the numbers on each screen briefly.

Figure 3-5   Configuring Display Settings options for multiple monitors

On CRT-based displays, users often choose their resolution settings based on personal preferences. Some types of computer displays (such as LCD flat-panel monitors) use a fixed number of pixels to generate an image. These displays work best at their recommended optimal resolution. When run at either a higher or a lower resolution, text might become difficult to read, and images will appear grainy. In most cases, Windows Vista is able to detect the supported resolutions of the video adapter and the optimal resolution of the connected display devices automatically.

Working with Windows Aero

The Windows Aero user interface is a new feature in certain editions of Windows Vista. It has been designed to take advantage of hardware acceleration features that are present in most modern video cards. Windows Aero features provide benefits related to usability, as well as an updated look and feel. Windows Aero is included in the premium editions of the Windows Vista platform, including Windows Vista Home Premium, Windows Vista Business, and Windows Vista Ultimate. (See Chapter 1, "Preparing to Install Windows Vista," for more details.)

Windows Aero Features

Windows Aero is a collection of several different features that can make interacting with the desktop and programs quicker and more intuitive. These features include:

- **Transparent glass borders**   In earlier versions of Windows, application title bars and other user interface components were completely opaque. That is, a window that was active would completely obscure any windows that were located beneath it. Windows Aero provides users with the ability to see underlying windows through what appears to be glass (see Figure 3-6). This feature can help users more easily keep track of multiple open windows.

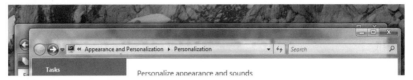

Figure 3-6   Transparency effects that allow users to see through particular windows

■ **Shadow effects for open windows**   Application windows now have a more 3-D look through the use of shadows in window borders. This creates the effect of having the windows themselves floating slightly above the desktop and other windows.

■ **Enhanced window management buttons**   A feature common to almost all standard Windows applications are the minimize, restore, and close buttons that are located in the top-right corner of open windows. In past versions of Windows, the buttons were fairly small, and users would sometimes click the wrong one. Windows Aero adds a glowing effect whenever one of these window items is highlighted (see Figure 3-7). This can help users more easily identify which icon they wish to click based on color.

Figure 3-7   Viewing enhanced window management button effects

■ **Window animations**   When users have multiple windows open on the desktop at the same time, it can sometimes be confusing to figure out what happens when applications are maximized and minimized. Windows Aero enables animations that help users visualize when application windows are launched and when they're minimized to the taskbar.

■ **Other look and feel enhancements**   With Windows Aero, common window elements such as buttons and user controls appear to glow softly when you hover the mouse over them. This helps users identify which areas of the GUI are interactive.

NOTE   **Visualizing Windows Aero**

Some of these user interface features can be difficult to visualize when you read about them in text. If you've used a system that supports Windows Aero, you're probably already familiar with the visual effects (although they might have been somewhat subtle). If you haven't, I highly recommend you access a computer that supports Windows Aero and try out all of these features firsthand. Sometimes a picture really is worth a thousand words.

Although these features might seem relatively minor when it comes to productivity, they can be very helpful when combined. If you find yourself demonstrating Windows Vista, you'll likely find that potential customers or other end users will be impressed by these effects.

Enabling Windows Aero

During the installation process of an edition of Windows Vista that supports Windows Aero, the operating system will perform a quick system test to determine whether the installed hardware configuration is capable of supporting Windows Aero user interface enhancements. Assuming that a suitable video adapter is installed and that the appropriate drivers are available, Windows Vista enables Windows Aero by default. (For complete details on system requirements for enabling Windows Aero, see Chapter 1.)

Customizing Windows Aero Options

In some cases, users might want to enable or disable various Windows Aero user interface features manually due to aesthetic preferences, issues with application compatibility, or performance reasons. You can quickly and easily change these settings while the operating system is running.

When Windows Aero is enabled, you use the Window Color And Appearance dialog box to specify details related to the appearance of the Windows Aero glass effects. Figure 3-8 shows an example of the options that are available. They include the following:

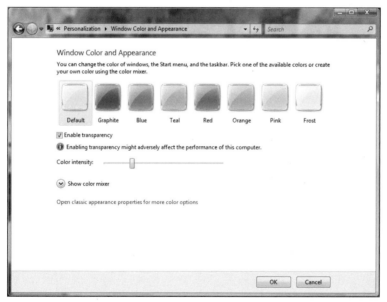

Figure 3-8   Adjusting Window Color And Appearance settings

- **Color**   You can choose from one of the default colors included within Windows Vista. Selecting one of these options automatically makes changes to the other settings, such as color intensity. This is the quickest and easiest way to choose a color, and it can help you get back to something more familiar if you've accidentally changed any of the other settings.

- **Enable Transparency** This check box specifies whether portions of the user interface will enable you to see the contents of windows that are located beneath it. You can disable all transparency effects by clearing this check box.
- **Color Intensity** This slider allows you to specify the intensity of the selected color. The ideal setting will largely be a matter of personal preference and can range from shades that are very light to ones that are exceedingly bright.
- **Color Mixer** In addition to choosing from the standard built-in colors included with Windows Vista, you can also choose your own colors, based on preferences. The three main parameters are hue, saturation, and brightness. The easiest way to see the effects of these parameters is to open a few windows and then use trial and error to find the settings you want. The changes will be applied live, as you make them.

Overall, the various Windows transparency features can have a significant effect on the aesthetics of using Windows Vista.

Troubleshooting Windows Aero

Because there are specific hardware requirements for enabling the Windows Aero user interface, a common customer support issue will be related to troubleshooting systems on which Windows Aero is not enabled. A good first step to finding the source of the problem is to verify that Windows Aero is supported on the installed edition of Windows Vista and to make sure that the system meets the minimum system requirements (both topics are covered in more detail in Chapter 1).

Verifying Display Hardware

When attempting to enable Windows Aero, it's often helpful to get details related to the properties of the video card. You can do this in the Display Settings dialog box by clicking Advanced. The Adapter tab (shown in Figure 3-9) and Monitor tab provide details related to the type and amount of video memory that is present. Other details, including the manufacturer and model of the graphics chipset, are also provided.

Figure 3-9   Viewing the properties of the display adapter

Verifying Display Configuration Settings

There are several display-related settings that must be properly configured for Windows Aero to be enabled and to work properly. These include the following:

- **Window Color And Appearance**   If the transparency effects of Windows Aero are not being properly displayed, a good first step is to verify the Window Color And Appearance settings. The Enable Transparency check box should be selected. If this check box is disabled, other issues are preventing you from enabling transparency effects.

- **Desktop Theme settings**   The selected Desktop Theme should be set to Windows Vista. When users make changes to some settings, the item might appear in the list as Modified Theme (or another name if the settings have previously been saved). If you suspect that some settings are preventing Windows Aero from running, a good troubleshooting step is to select the Windows Vista theme, which resets the options to their defaults.

- **Color scheme**   The color scheme selected in the Appearance Settings dialog box should be Windows Aero. (You access this dialog box from the Personalization window by first clicking Window Color And Appearance and then clicking Open Classic Appearance Properties For More Color Options.)

- **Display settings**   The computer's display must be configured to use the Highest (32-bit) color depth setting. You can verify this setting by using the Display Settings dialog box.

- **Refresh rate**   The refresh rate of the display must be set to greater than 10Hz. For most LCD and CRT displays, the rate should be set significantly higher. If Windows Vista is unable to determine the optimal settings, you can usually find this information in the monitor's product documentation.

Assuming that all of the settings are configured properly, there are still scenarios that might prevent Windows Aero from working. These include the following:

- **Hardware-related changes**   Changes to device drivers or driver settings might prevent Windows Aero features from running properly. Although it is more common to upgrade computers than it is to downgrade them, Windows Vista can automatically detect if an incompatible video adapter has been installed or if the total amount of physical memory has been lowered. In these cases, Windows Aero will automatically be disabled.

- **Running legacy applications**   To maintain compatibility with some applications that do not support new display features, Windows Vista might temporarily disable Windows Aero when these applications are launched. When this happens, a notice appears in the system tray. The desktop and all windows will then revert to a basic mode that does not include the glass features of Windows Aero. Over time, this situation should become less common as vendors and application developers update applications to provide full support for the enhanced Windows Vista user interface.

- **Memory limitations**   The primary purpose of an operating system is to run applications. Ideally, a computer will have enough physical memory to run several applications and Windows Aero at the same time. If Windows Vista detects that the amount of physical memory is getting low, it might automatically decide to disable advanced Windows Aero features. This enables Windows Vista to provide maximum resources to applications and should improve overall performance. If you suspect that a lack of available memory is preventing Windows Aero from working properly, you should try closing all open programs and stopping any unnecessary services. (For more details, see Chapter 5, "Optimizing Windows Vista Performance.")

This might seem like a long list of configuration options to check, but you can often troubleshoot in a matter of a few minutes the most common issues that prevent Windows Aero from running.

Configuring Other Windows Display Options

In addition to the primary display-related settings you've covered thus far, Windows Vista includes several other options that enable users to change the appearance of their desktop. In this section, you'll look at these settings and their effects.

Configuring Theme Settings

So far, you've looked at many different settings that can affect the overall look of Windows Vista. In some cases, you might want to tweak one or two settings manually, but what if you want to save a collection of settings so that you can use them again? That's where Theme Settings come in. As shown in Figure 3-10, the Theme Settings dialog box enables you to select or save a theme.

Figure 3-10   Adjusting theme settings

The themes that are built in and included by default are Windows Vista (which reverts to the initial display that you see after you complete the installation process) and Windows Classic (which looks like earlier versions of the Windows platform). You can also click Browse to find additional theme files. These files have a default file extension of .theme and can be found on the Internet. Finally, after you have a collection of settings that you'd like to use later (or that you might want to share with others), you can click Save As to save your own .theme file. Using the Theme Settings dialog box is a good way to store and apply collections of visual settings.

Choosing a Desktop Background

A quick and easy way for a user to personalize his or her desktop settings is by changing the desktop background. Windows Vista ships with numerous wallpapers that have been professionally composed and optimized for viewing on computer displays. In addition, users can choose to use their own images as wallpapers. To access these options, in the Personalization Control Panel window, click Desktop Background. The available options are shown in Figure 3-11.

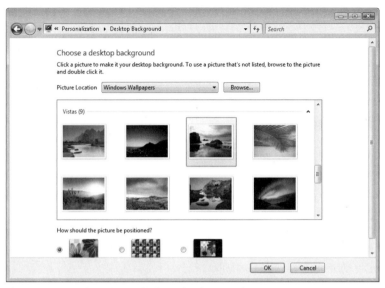

Figure 3-11   Choosing a desktop background

The Picture Location drop-down list defaults to Windows Wallpapers, which is the initial location of built-in backgrounds. Users can also select from other commonly used file locations, such as the user account's pictures folder, or they can choose to use a solid color. To specify the location of a background file manually, click Browse. Some pictures are intended to fill all or part of the screen, whereas others are designed to be tiled. The picture position options at the bottom of the dialog box enable you to specify the most appropriate option: stretched to fit the whole screen, tiled, or centered.

Selecting a Color Scheme

Windows Vista includes several different color schemes that can alter the appearance of the user interface. If Windows Aero is enabled, the best method for changing color settings is through the Window Color And Appearance dialog box (described earlier in this chapter). If you're not using Windows Aero, however, you can access the classic display settings in Window Color And Appearance by clicking Open Classic Appearance Properties For More Color Options. Figure 3-12 shows the available options.

Figure 3-12   Modifying Windows Appearance settings

The available color schemes include the following:

- **Windows Aero**   Assuming that the installed edition of Windows Vista supports the Windows Aero feature, this option enables features such as transparency within the user interface.

- **Windows Vista Basic**   This color scheme provides the basic look and feel of Windows Vista without the 3-D features of Windows Aero.

- **Windows Standard**   For users who prefer the look of versions of Windows released prior to Windows Vista, this color scheme provides window titles that use a fade effect.

- **Windows Classic**   The Classic color scheme is based on early versions of the Windows user interface.

- **High Contrast**   For some users who are visually impaired, increased contrast can help make windows and text more readable. Several different options are available, each of which provides a different set of high-contrast colors.

In addition to the basic color scheme options, users can also specify whether effects such as font smoothing, shadows under menus, and showing window contents while dragging are enabled. You access these settings by clicking Effects in the Appearance Settings dialog box. When running on older hardware, disabling some of these options might make the user interface more responsive.

Finally, for the most in-depth customization, in the Appearance Settings dialog box, users can click Advanced to specify the exact colors they want to use for each component of the user interface. As shown in Figure 3-13, you can specify details such as fonts for title bars and icon spacing. Users who have particular preferences for fonts and colors should be able to get the effect that they need using the many different user interface options.

Figure 3-13 Configuring Advanced Appearance settings

Working with Desktop Usability Enhancements

So far, you have focused on user interface enhancements and options that control the display of the desktop itself. Windows Vista also includes several features that can help make operating system users more productive. This is especially true for users who often have many different programs open at once.

Using Flip 3D

One of the most visually impressive features of the Windows Vista user interface is the Windows Flip 3D window navigation option. After Windows Aero is enabled, users can access Flip 3D by pressing the Windows key along with the Tab key. When users press these keys, a live view of each open window is presented at an angle so that they can see the contents of all windows at the same time. Windows that have actively changing contents (such as a video playing in Windows Media Player) are viewable in a "live" format.

Using Flip 3D should be intuitive to most users. Repeatedly pressing the Tab key while holding down the Windows key cycles through the programs in forward order. Holding down the Shift key in addition to the Windows key and then pressing the Tab key enables you to cycle through the programs in reverse order. Additionally, users can click any of the windows with the left mouse button to make that window active.

Enhancements to Alt+Tab

Many Windows users routinely use the Alt+Tab keystroke combination to switch between applications. In addition to the Flip 3D method of navigating among open applications, Windows Vista now presents a live preview of all open windows when you press the Alt+Tab keystroke combination. This makes it significantly easier for the user to determine which application or window he or she wants to select. For example, if multiple presentations are open in Microsoft PowerPoint, the live preview can show the contents of each open document.

Another useful enhancement is the ability to use the mouse to click one of the items in the Alt+Tab list of programs. This is particularly helpful when several programs are running concurrently, and you want to avoid pressing Tab multiple times to cycle through them all.

Using Live Taskbar Previews

For users who commonly run multiple programs, it can be helpful to get information about a running program quickly without actually switching the focus to it. For example, you might want to check on the progress of a file download or other long-running task quickly without moving away from your e-mail program, or you might have several different documents of a similar type open, and you want to switch to a particular one.

Live taskbar previews are a new feature in Windows Vista that enables the user simply to hover the mouse pointer over the title of an application in the Windows taskbar to see an immediate preview of the contents of the window. Because this is a "live" preview, the user can see any changes or progress as it's occurring.

Improving Efficiency with Keyboard Shortcuts

Anil Desai

One way in which you can significantly improve the efficiency of working with Windows operating systems is through the use of keyboard shortcuts. Novice users often rely heavily on the mouse to perform actions such as starting programs and managing files. Although this method certainly works, it is not always the most efficient way to perform tasks.

The Windows platform provides useful ways to accomplish common tasks through keyboard shortcuts. Rather than navigating menus or performing multiple mouse clicks to find a setting or option, you can often do it more quickly with one or more keystrokes. For example, in typing, it's much easier to use keyboard shortcuts for cutting, copying, and pasting text (Ctrl+X, Ctrl+C, and Ctrl+V, respectively). There's definitely a learning curve, but all of this can greatly improve efficiency. Windows Key–based shortcuts, such as Windows-D (to display the desktop), and Windows-M (to minimize all open applications) can also be used.

You can find a complete list of keyboard shortcuts for use with Windows Vista by searching for "keyboard shortcuts" in Windows Help and Support. There's even a feature to create your own key combinations to open applications that you use frequently. Finally, keep in mind that many modern keyboards offer buttons for performing tasks such as scrolling, zooming, and controlling media player functions.

If you're up to the ultimate test of your keyboard capabilities, try unplugging your mouse for a few hours. At first, it's likely that you'll be stumbling around to figure out certain commands (make sure you know how to get to the Help and Support Center). After a few such exercises, you'll probably find that you're reaching for your mouse far less frequently!

Quick Check

1. What are two ways to access the Personalization window?
2. How can you disable Windows Aero transparency effects?

Quick Check Answers

1. You can access this window by using Control Panel or by right-clicking on the desktop and choosing Personalize.
2. In the Window Color And Appearance dialog box, clear the Enable Transparency check box.

Practice: Configuring Windows Aero and Desktop Settings

These practice exercises will walk you through the many different Windows Aero desktop configuration settings. You should perform these exercises on a computer that meets the hardware requirements for Windows Aero and is running an edition of Windows Vista that supports Windows Aero (see Chapter 1 for more details). Because many desktop settings are based on personal preferences, it's important to try several different options wherever possible.

▶ **Practice 1: Enable and Disable Windows Aero Transparency Effects**

In this exercise, you will walk through the steps that are required to enable and disable the Windows Aero transparency effects. This exercise assumes that Windows Aero is initially enabled.

NOTE UAC approval

Depending on your security settings, some steps might prompt you for User Account Control (UAC) approval. Whenever necessary, you should approve the operation. For more information about UAC, see Chapter 6, "Configuring Windows Vista Security."

---

1. Start Windows Vista and log on to the computer.
2. Click Start and open Control Panel.
3. If it is not already selected, click the Control Panel Home link to view all of the available options.
4. Click Appearance And Personalization.
5. Click Personalization to open the Personalization window.
6. Click Window Color And Appearance.
7. To disable Windows Aero, clear the Enable Transparency check box, and then click OK.
8. You will notice that the title bars for any open windows are now opaque, and you can't see any underlying programs or the desktop.
9. To enable window transparency, open the Window Color And Appearance dialog box, select the Enable Transparency check box, and then click OK.
10. Verify that transparency effects are working by opening several applications and viewing the contents of underlying programs.
11. When finished, close any open dialog boxes, and then close Control Panel.

▶ **Practice 2: Customize Windows Desktop Settings**

In this exercise, you will work with several different desktop settings that can be used to change the look and feel of the Windows Vista desktop. This exercise assumes that Windows Aero features are enabled.

1. Start Windows Vista and log on to the computer.
2. Right-click the desktop and choose Personalize to open the Personalization window. Note the various options that are available.
3. To change the desktop background, click Desktop Background. In the drop-down list, select Windows Wallpapers (if it is not already selected), and choose one of the available wallpapers that is included with Windows Vista. Alternatively, you can click Browse to locate another graphics file that you might have available on the computer.
4. Click the various options in the How Should The Picture Be Positioned section. Note the effects of tiling vs. centering the wallpaper. When finished, click OK to save the changes.
5. In the Personalize Appearance And Sounds window, click Display Settings.
6. Note the current desktop resolution and number of colors. Attempt to change the settings to use either a higher or lower resolution, and then click Apply to view the effects. Note the effects that these settings have on the size of text and windows that are shown. In some cases, you might see a blank or unreadable screen if you select a resolution that is not supported by your hardware. If this occurs, simply wait 15 seconds, and Windows Vista automatically reverts the display to the previous settings.

7. Click Advanced Settings to view the properties of the installed video adapter. Make note of the total amount of graphics memory as well as the amounts of dedicated versus shared system memory.

8. When finished, click Cancel to close the adapter properties, and then click OK to close the Display Settings dialog box. Close Control Panel and any other open windows.

Lesson Summary

- Windows Aero provides numerous visual and functional enhancements to the Windows Vista desktop.

- Display adapter settings such as resolution, refresh rate, number of colors, and multiple monitors can be configured using the Display Settings dialog box.

- Users can enable, disable, and configure Windows Aero settings by using the Window Color And Appearance dialog box.

- When troubleshooting Windows Aero, users can verify the specifications of the display adapter by accessing the Display Settings dialog box.

- There are several display settings that might prevent Windows Aero from working properly, including hardware specifications, color and appearance settings, and running applications that do not support Windows Aero enhancements.

- Users can customize desktop themes, desktop backgrounds, and color schemes by using the display properties in Control Panel.

- Windows Flip 3D, live taskbar previews, and Alt+Tab enhancements can help users manage multiple open windows and programs more efficiently.

Lesson Review

You can use the following questions to test your knowledge of the information in Lesson 1, "Configuring Windows Aero and Desktop Settings." The questions are also available on the companion CD if you prefer to review them in electronic form.

NOTE Answers

Answers to these questions and explanations of why each answer choice is correct or incorrect are located in the "Answers" section at the end of the book.

1. You are helping a new Windows Vista user customize his desktop settings. The user would prefer to change the desktop appearance to look more like previous versions of Windows while he is learning to use Windows Vista. Which of the following will allow him to accomplish this goal?

    A. Lower the resolution setting for the graphics adapter.

    B. Increase the refresh rate for the graphics adapter.

        C. Change the color scheme to Windows Aero in the Appearance settings.

        D. Change the color scheme to Windows Standard or Windows Classic in the Appearance settings.

2. A customer has asked you for help with changing the color of the Windows Aero "glass" that is used in window title bars. You have verified that Windows Aero and transparency effects are enabled. Which of the following options will enable you to change the color?

        A. Window Color And Appearance

        B. Desktop Background

        C. Theme

        D. Display Settings

Lesson 2: Working with the Sidebar

In the early days of desktop computers, users would often perform only one or a few simple tasks on their computers at a time. Often, this involved opening a word processor, spreadsheet, or other application to perform a single task. Modern users tend to require access to many different applications and types of information simultaneously. For example, within a typical day, users might check their e-mail, monitor stock quotes, view up-to-date weather forecasts, and visit several news sites.

Although all of these tasks can be accomplished using traditional applications such as Web browsers, it can be difficult and time-consuming to navigate to all of the required information. Additionally, the task of juggling multiple open applications and browser windows can become a challenge in itself. Often, the amount of effort required to download, install, and configure new applications prevents users from easily accessing the information they need. It would be much simpler to access commonly used information directly from the desktop by using small utilities that are easy to install and customize. That's where the Windows Vista Sidebar feature comes in. In this lesson, you'll look at the purpose and function of Windows Sidebar, along with details on how to configure it.

After this lesson, you will be able to:
- Describe the purpose and features of Windows Sidebar.
- Provide examples of gadgets for Windows Sidebar that are included with Windows Vista.
- Enable and disable Windows Sidebar.
- Add, remove, and reposition gadgets for Windows Sidebar.
- Set up and manage RSS feeds by using Windows Sidebar.
- Download and install new gadgets for Windows Sidebar.

Estimated lesson time: 45 minutes

Understanding Windows Sidebar

Microsoft designed Windows Sidebar as an optional desktop component that allows for running small but useful applications called gadgets. Windows Vista ships with a variety of useful gadgets. Third-party developers can also create their own gadgets and make them available for download. For example, a Web-based stockbroker could provide customized quotes based on a user's portfolio.

Before you get into the technical details of working with Sidebar, it's important to understand the types of benefits this feature is intended to provide. As mentioned earlier, it is possible to download and install separate applications that provide all of the same functionality. The primary goal with gadgets for Windows Sidebar is to provide users with a quick and easy way to access the types of data and functionality they require without having to go through the trouble of downloading and installing full Windows-based applications. It provides for a secure and easy-to-configure environment that's always available on the desktop. Figure 3-14 shows a sample of Windows Sidebar in action, including several running gadgets. In this screen, some of the gadgets are placed directly on the Windows Sidebar, and two others are located directly on the Windows desktop.

Figure 3-14   Windows Sidebar, along with several running gadgets

As you'll see in this lesson, a new gadget can be downloaded, installed, and customized within a matter of minutes. Unlike traditional programs, gadgets for Windows Sidebar are designed to run continuously on the user's computer and can perform tasks such as periodically updating a weather forecast or providing stock market updates. Furthermore, users can show, hide, and move gadgets quickly and easily. They no longer need to worry about constantly rearranging application windows just to see the information they want. Now that you have an overview of the goals for Windows Sidebar, let's look at how to configure it.

Configuring Sidebar Properties

Enabling and configuring Windows Sidebar is a simple, straightforward process. If Windows Sidebar is already running, you can right-click any blank area of it and select Properties. You can also right-click the Sidebar system tray icon, if it is present, and select Properties.

If Windows Sidebar is not already running on your system, you can find the Sidebar configuration application by searching for "sidebar," using the Start menu. Regardless of the method you choose, you will see a dialog box similar to the one shown in Figure 3-15.

Figure 3-15   Configuring properties for the Windows Sidebar

The first option is to determine whether Windows Sidebar should start automatically whenever Windows Vista is started. If this check box is selected, the gadgets for Windows Sidebar will launch automatically after a user logs on to the system. This is the most convenient option for users who rely on gadgets for Windows Sidebar to be available at all times. If the computer is low on resources such as physical memory, manually launching Windows Sidebar might help reduce startup times.

The Arrangement options enable you to specify where and how Windows Sidebar appears on the desktop. The Sidebar Is Always On Top Of Other Windows check box specifies that running gadgets will always appear on top of other windows. Although this is useful for making sure that information is always visible, it can sometimes be inconvenient because user interface components such as scrollbars might be hidden. Other options include the ability to specify on which side of the screen Windows Sidebar will appear.

Finally, if you have multiple monitors connected to the computer, you can choose on which monitor you want Windows Sidebar to appear. There are also buttons for viewing a list of running gadgets and for restoring the default gadgets for Windows Sidebar (both options are covered later in this lesson).

Managing Gadgets

Although gadgets for Windows Sidebar have primarily been designed to be small, lightweight applications, they can sometimes consume significant computer resources such as processor time and memory. This is especially true when simultaneously running many different gadgets. A poorly designed gadget might cause the system to slow down overall. For these reasons, it's important to keep track of which gadgets are installed and running on the system. In this section, you'll look at ways in which you can manage and configure Windows Sidebar.

NOTE   **Using gadgets through the Web**

Although the focus in this chapter (and on Microsoft Exam 70-623) is on using gadgets within Windows Sidebar, you can also use gadgets on the Windows Live Web site. This can be particularly helpful when you want access to some handy utilities, but you're not using your own computer running Windows Vista. For more information, see the Windows Live Gallery at *http:// gallery.live.com/*.

Windows Vista Default Gadgets

Windows Sidebar, by itself, does not perform any useful functions for users. Instead, it's the actual gadgets for Windows Sidebar that can be used to provide information and manage user interaction. The initial release of Windows Vista ships with numerous gadgets for Windows Sidebar (see Figure 3-16), including the following:

Figure 3-16   Viewing a default list of gadgets for Windows Sidebar included with Windows Vista

- **Calendar**   A simple graphical calendar that enables you to view either the current month or the current day. The interface allows you to click sections to view details about a day or time.
- **Clock**   This displays the current date and time using an animated analog clock. The configuration settings include eight different visual styles. You can also change the time zone of the clock to any area of the world, and you can even add multiple clocks to Windows Sidebar at the same time.
- **Contacts**   A list of individuals and their associated contact information can quickly be viewed or edited using this gadget. The actual data for the contacts is stored in the Windows Contacts application.
- **CPU Meter**   Technical users often like to monitor resource usage on their computers. This gadget displays two frequently updated gauges that reflect the current CPU use and amount of memory that is in use. This information can be helpful when running multiple programs to ensure that enough system resources are still available.
- **Currency**   This gadget is used to convert between different world currencies. Because these values fluctuate daily, up-to-date information is downloaded from the Internet as needed.
- **Feed Headlines**   Many users like to stay current on the latest news and information from their favorite Web sites. This gadget can be configured to download and display updated headlines automatically. You'll learn more details about this gadget later in this lesson.
- **Notes**   Often, when working on their computers, users will want a quick and easy way to jot down some brief notes. Like their physical counterparts, these electronic desktop notes allow you to write and store small pieces of information quickly. Note pages can be added and removed as needed.
- **Picture Puzzle**   Gadgets for Windows Sidebar aren't limited to productivity. The Picture Puzzle is a simple tile-based game that can be played from directly within Windows Sidebar. Numerous pictures are available, and a timer keeps track of how long it takes you to solve the puzzle.
- **Slide Show**   This gadget automatically displays all of the pictures in a specific folder. It can be configured to show them in continuous or random order. Options allow for choosing the duration of each display, the folder of the images, and manual controls for advancing through the pictures.
- **Stocks**   A common task for Internet users is to keep up to date with the performance of their investments and the market in general. The Stocks gadget can provide this information. By default, it shows details for common U.S. indexes. Users can also add their own favorite investments to receive updates on prices.
- **Weather**   This gadget presents information on the current temperature and conditions in a specific area and can show additional forecast details. Configuration options include the geographic location for which to display weather and the temperature units (Fahrenheit or Celsius).

Overall, the default gadgets for Windows Sidebar provide a good overview of some of the types of functions that can be performed within Windows Sidebar.

Attaching, Detaching, and Arranging Gadgets

You can freely move gadgets for Windows Sidebar around the screen. Although the exact details of behavior vary based on the type of the gadget, there are two main locations in which you can place them. The first is within the vertical strip of the Windows Sidebar itself. This portion of the screen allows multiple gadgets to appear in a vertical line. When a gadget is included in the Sidebar area, it is referred to as *attached*. Many gadgets are designed to take up less desktop space when they are attached to the Windows Sidebar.

You can also detach items from Windows Sidebar by dragging gadgets onto the desktop area. Gadgets that are placed directly on the desktop often show a larger user interface with more information. For example, when it is docked, the Weather gadget shows only the current temperature and weather. When it is moved to the desktop, it shows information for the current day as well as the forecast for the next two days (see Figure 3-17). Similarly, the Stocks and Feed Headlines gadgets have different docked and undocked displays.

Figure 3-17   Comparing the docked and undocked views of the Weather gadget

If you've cleared the check box to have the Sidebar always appear on top of other windows, you can always right-click the Sidebar and choose Bring Gadgets To Front to make them visible.

Another useful option allows you to specify the opacity of each gadget. Similar to the Windows Aero glass effect, this option provides a semitransparent effect for the display. Users can change the opacity setting by right-clicking a gadget and choosing the appropriate percentage value. There's a trade-off related to opacity: lowering the opacity will make underlying windows easier to see, but it can also make the gadgets themselves more difficult to read.

Adding Gadgets

The process of adding gadgets to Windows Sidebar or to the desktop is simple: Just right-click the Sidebar and select Add Gadgets. A list of all of the gadgets that are currently installed and available on the local computer will be shown. To add a gadget, you can click its icon and drag it to the desired location.

Alternatively, you can right-click it and choose Add from the menu. This adds the selected gadget to the first available position on the Sidebar. You can also click See Details to view additional information about installed gadgets, including the version, a description of its purpose, and details about the author or publisher (see Figure 3-18).

Figure 3-18   Viewing details when adding a gadget for Windows Sidebar

A useful feature is that you can add multiple instances of the same gadget to the desktop or Windows Sidebar at the same time. This is particularly useful for those gadgets that have configuration settings. For example, if you're interested in keeping track of the current temperature in two different cities, you can add two instances of the Weather gadget, each configured with a different geographic location.

Removing Gadgets

The process of removing gadgets can easily be accomplished in two ways. First, you can click the X that appears when you hover over a particular gadget. This removes it from the display, whether it is attached or detached.

Because the user interface portion of gadgets can vary significantly, sometimes it's easier just to view a list of the running gadgets for removal purposes. You can do this by accessing the properties of Windows Sidebar and clicking View List Of Running Gadgets. As shown in Figure 3-19, a text-based list of running items will be displayed. You can easily remove an item by selecting its name and clicking Remove.

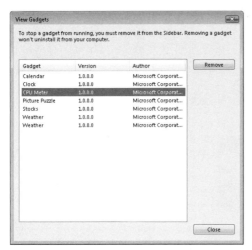

Figure 3-19   Viewing a list of running gadgets

It is important to note that when you remove a gadget, it remains available on the system. If you want to add it again, you can just use the Windows Sidebar Add Gadgets option. Alternatively, if you're reasonably sure that you will never want to use a gadget again, you can choose to uninstall it from your system by right-clicking the appropriate item in the Add Gadget dialog box and choosing Uninstall.

If you have accidentally deleted one of the default gadgets that was initially installed with Windows, you can restore it by accessing the Windows Sidebar properties and clicking Restore Gadgets Installed With Windows. After this is done, you'll again be able to add the default gadgets to Windows Sidebar, using the process described in the previous section. If all of the default gadgets are still present on the system, the option to restore the default gadgets is unavailable.

Configuring Gadget Settings

Most gadgets provide for at least a few configuration options. For example, the Clock gadget that is included with Windows Vista provides several different visual styles. It also provides the ability to name the clock and to specify the time zone. Figure 3-20 shows these options. Similarly, the Stocks gadget enables users to specify which stocks or indexes they would like to view. There are some gadgets, such as the CPU Meter, that do not provide any configuration options.

Figure 3-20   Viewing options for the Clock gadget

The process of configuring a gadget is simple and can be done in one of two ways. You can right-click any running gadget and choose Options from the shortcut menu. Another option is to click the Configure icon that appears when you hover the mouse over a portion of the gadget. Both methods will display the properties and options for that gadget. To make any setting changes take effect, click OK.

Downloading and Installing New Gadgets

Although the built-in gadgets for Windows Sidebar that are included with Windows Vista are useful, the real power of Windows Sidebar is that it allows third-party developers to create their own utilities and applications. The easiest method for finding new gadgets is to click Get More Gadgets Online in the Add Gadgets dialog box. This link launches a Web browser and connects you to the Windows Vista Gadgets Web site. You can also visit the site manually by going to *http://gallery.microsoft.com*.

On the site, you can view the entire list of gadgets for Windows Sidebar, which is always growing as developers add their newest creations. When you choose to download a gadget, you will be prompted for confirmation. After the gadget is downloaded, Windows Vista automatically adds it to Windows Sidebar. The new item now appears in the list of available gadgets when you choose to add a new one to the desktop. It's helpful to note that this display has multiple "pages" that you can navigate by using the arrows at the top-left corner of the screen. As with the default gadgets, you can configure settings, attach, detach, and remove the gadgets.

NOTE **Evaluating gadgets**

Although the potential for clever and useful gadgets for Windows Sidebar is practically unlimited, users should exercise some caution when choosing what to download. Poorly implemented gadgets might not work as expected or might use a significant amount of computer resources.

One good indicator about the quality of a gadget is other users' ratings. You can see how other people feel about the gadget and read their comments. Of course, it's a good idea to return the favor: if there's a gadget that you like or dislike, post an opinion so others can benefit from your experience.

Configuring RSS Feeds

In the not-too-distant past, tasks such as viewing maps, finding contact information, and keeping up with the news were handled without computers. The popularity of the Internet changed that, and many people now depend on online resources far more than their physical counterparts. Perhaps one of the most useful aspects of the Internet is the ability to find just about any information at any time. In fact, the major problem has become related to having too many different sources of information.

One way to collect information from throughout the Internet is to visit Web sites manually. Although this often provides a good experience, it can be difficult to isolate just the information you need. Often, the presence of numerous ads and inconsistencies in site navigation can result in a less-than-ideal experience.

Understanding RSS

The RSS standard has been created to provide developers of Web-based content with a method for making this information easily available to the user, other sites, and applications. The data itself is made available in Extensible Markup Language (XML) format and can be accessed using any application or service that supports RSS.

The benefit to users is the ability to obtain news and other updates from a large variety of different sites and services and view them all in one place. The RSS data itself is often referred to as a *feed* because it provides data that can be consumed elsewhere. Feeds are generally updated based on the frequency of Web content updates. Visitors to a Web site or service can usually access RSS-based data by clicking an RSS link or icon. Numerous applications (both GUI-based and Web-based) for reading feed-based information are available on the Internet.

NOTE **What does RSS stand for?**

The RSS acronym is somewhat enigmatic in that it doesn't represent a single specific term. It has sometimes been expanded to mean Really Simple Syndication or Rich Site Summary. Regardless of the terminology, it refers to an XML-based standard that enables content producers to make their information available in a consistent format.

Adding the Feed Headlines Gadget

Windows Vista ships with a gadget for Windows Sidebar that is designed to view RSS feeds within Windows Sidebar. The gadget is called Feed Headlines, and it works like many of the other gadgets. Figure 3-21 shows a sample view of the Feed Headlines gadget.

Figure 3-21 Viewing RSS information using the Feed Headlines gadget

The user interface continually shows the latest headlines obtained from RSS feeds. Users can click a link to see details related to that specific headline. In most cases, the content that is included with an RSS feed is limited to a brief summary of the total information. Readers who want the complete content of an article or item will need to visit the provider's Web site.

Configuring Feed Headlines Options

Users can modify the properties of the Feed Headlines Gadget to display some or all of the information that they're interested in. Figure 3-22 shows the available configuration options.

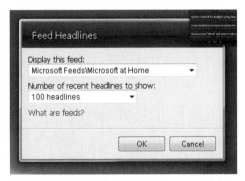

Figure 3-22 Configuring properties of the Feed Headlines gadget

The top drop-down list includes a list of all of the RSS feeds that are available on the computer. You can add feeds by using compatible applications such as Microsoft Internet Explorer 7 (which is discussed in Chapter 8, "Configuring Parental Controls and Browser Security"), Microsoft Outlook, or one of several third-party products. This model enables users to subscribe to and view RSS feeds by using several different methods. Because you can add several different instances of the Feed Headlines gadget to Windows Sidebar, a wide variety of information can be made readily available on the Windows desktop.

Overall, the use of the Feed Headlines gadget can help users better manage information from many different sources in a consistent manner.

Quick Check

1. What are some advantages of using Windows Sidebar instead of installing full Windows applications?
2. What is the difference between gadgets for Windows Sidebar that are attached and those that are detached from Windows Sidebar?

Quick Check Answers

1. Gadgets for Windows Sidebar are quick and easy to install and can be configured to always be available on the Windows desktop. The process for adding new gadgets is simple, and gadgets can be arranged based on users' preferences.
2. Attached gadgets appear in a vertical strip that is part of Windows Sidebar itself. They generally show a smaller user interface. Detached gadgets can be placed anywhere on the desktop and often have a larger display.

Practice: Configuring Windows Sidebar

In this practice, you configure Windows Sidebar to show a variety of different gadgets. In addition to the steps in these exercises, you should try to download and install new gadgets, if possible.

▶ **Practice 1: Add and Configure Gadgets for Windows Sidebar**

In this practice exercise, you work with adding gadgets to the Windows Sidebar display and to the system desktop. This exercise assumes that Windows Sidebar is currently enabled. (For information about enabling Windows Sidebar, see the text in Lesson 2, "Working with the Sidebar.")

1. Start Windows Vista and log on to the computer.
2. Right-click Windows Sidebar and select Add Gadgets. This displays a list of all of the available gadgets installed on the computer.
3. Right-click the Weather gadget and select Add. Note that the gadget is attached to Windows Sidebar by default.
4. Add a second instance of the Weather gadget to Windows Sidebar by right-clicking it and selecting Add. Note that two instances of the gadget appear attached to the Sidebar.
5. Close the Add Gadgets dialog box.

6. Right-click the uppermost Weather gadget in Windows Sidebar and choose Options. Search for any city in the Options dialog box and click OK to select.

7. Next, perform the same configuration step for the second Weather gadget but select a different city. Note that each Weather gadget can show information about a different city.

8. Drag the uppermost Weather gadget to an area of the desktop and note the difference in display. Many gadgets display more information when they are in a detached location.

9. Remove both Weather gadgets from the display by right-clicking each one and clicking Close Gadget. This returns the Windows Sidebar configuration to its initial display.

Lesson Summary

- Windows Sidebar enables users to add small applications called gadgets to the user interface.
- Users can easily add gadgets to or remove gadgets from Windows Sidebar.
- Gadgets can be added to Windows Sidebar in an attached or detached configuration.
- Most gadgets for Windows Sidebar provide configuration settings that enable users to customize their behavior based on personal preferences.
- Users can download and install new gadgets from third-party developers.
- RSS feeds provide a consistent method by which users can collect and view information from a variety of different sources.
- The Feed Headlines gadget shows recent headlines from particular RSS feeds that have been configured on the computer.

Lesson Review

You can use the following questions to test your knowledge of the information in Lesson 2. The questions are also available on the companion CD if you prefer to review them in electronic form.

NOTE Answers

Answers to these questions and explanations of why each answer choice is correct or incorrect are located in the "Answers" section at the end of the book.

---

1. A user has added several gadgets to her Windows Sidebar and would like them to be visible even when other application windows are open. Which Windows Sidebar option or command will enable her to achieve this goal?

    A. Bring Gadgets To Front

    B. View List Of Running Gadgets

    C. Sidebar Is Always On Top Of Other Windows

      D. Restore Gadgets Installed With Windows

      E. Opacity

2. A user would like to remove the Clock gadget from Windows Sidebar but would like to have the ability to add it back quickly again in the future. Which of the following operations meets these requirements?

      A. Uninstalling the gadget

      B. Closing the gadget

      C. Changing the Opacity to 0%

      D. Placing the gadget directly below another gadget

      E. Detaching the gadget from Windows Sidebar

3. A customer has subscribed to numerous RSS feeds by using Internet Explorer and would like to view headlines directly on the desktop. Specifically, he has eight different feeds configured on the system and would like headlines from three of them to appear within separate gadgets. How can he achieve this configuration?

      A. Add a single Feed Headlines gadget to Windows Sidebar and select the All Feeds option.

      B. Add a single Feed Headlines gadget to Windows Sidebar and select only the three feeds that he would like to monitor.

      C. Add three separate Feed Headlines gadgets to Windows Sidebar and configure each to display one of the three feeds that he would like to monitor.

      D. Add three separate Feed Headlines gadgets to Windows Sidebar and select the All Feeds option.

Chapter Review

To further practice and reinforce the skills you learned in this chapter, you can perform the following tasks:

- Review the chapter summary.
- Review the list of key terms introduced in this chapter.
- Complete the case scenarios. These scenarios set up real-world situations involving the topics of this chapter and ask you to create a solution.
- Complete the suggested practices.
- Take a practice test.

Chapter Summary

- Windows Aero provides an enhanced user experience through features such as window transparency and Flip 3D.
- Users can customize desktop settings based on their preferences. Options include desktop themes; backgrounds; and displaying adapter settings such as resolution, number of colors, and refresh rate.
- Windows Sidebar allows users to add and arrange small applications called gadgets for Windows Sidebar. Several useful gadgets are included with Windows Vista.
- The Feed Headlines gadget enables users to view information from RSS feeds that are configured on the computer.

Key Terms

Do you know what these key terms mean? You can check your answers by looking up the terms in the glossary at the end of the book.

- Desktop theme
- Feed Headlines
- Flip 3D
- gadgets
- Live taskbar previews
- RSS
- Windows Sidebar

Case Scenarios

In the following case scenarios, you will apply what you've learned about configuring and customizing the Windows Vista desktop. You can find answers to these questions in the "Answers" section at the end of this book.

Case Scenario 1: Customizing the Windows Vista Desktop

You are supporting a customer who has recently installed Windows Vista Home Premium and would like to change several display-related settings based on personal preferences. Specifically, he would like to increase the amount of information that is displayed on his CRT monitor and would like to make some visual changes to colors used on the desktop.

1. How can the user configure the display to show more information on the screen at once?
2. The user likes the transparency effects of Windows Aero but would prefer to define his own custom color for the glass. How can he configure this?
3. The user has made numerous display-related settings and would like to save them all so they can be easily restored if needed. How can he do this?

Case Scenario 2: Configuring Windows Sidebar

You are assisting a customer who has recently upgraded to Windows Vista. She believes that Windows Sidebar will be very helpful and would like to configure it to display numerous gadgets. Currently, Windows Sidebar does not appear on the desktop, and there is no Windows Sidebar icon in the system tray.

1. How should she enable Windows Sidebar?
2. The customer has added two Weather gadgets to Windows Sidebar and would like each to show information about a different city. How can she configure this?
3. How can the user view headlines from all of the RSS feeds that have been added to the system?

Suggested Practices

To help you successfully master the exam objectives presented in this chapter, complete the following tasks.

Customizing Windows Vista Based on User Preferences

- **Practice 1: Explore Windows Desktop Options** Make changes to several different settings on a computer running Windows Vista. Specifically, you should view the effects of disabling transparency, changing the method of smoothing screen fonts, modifying the color of glass effects, and saving desktop themes. Note that if you would like to restore the original configuration of Windows Vista, you can do this using the Themes icon in Control Panel.

- **Practice 2: Manage Windows Sidebar Preferences** If it is not already running on a computer running Windows Vista, enable Windows Sidebar. Change various configuration options such as opacity and the option to keep gadgets running visibly on top of other windows and view the effects. Add several instances of the Clock, Weather, and Feed Headlines gadgets to Windows Sidebar and configure each to use a different set of properties. When finished, practice removing gadgets from Windows Sidebar.

Take a Practice Test

The practice tests on this book's companion CD offer many options. For example, you can test yourself on just one exam objective, or you can test yourself on all of the 70-623 certification exam content. You can set up the test so that it closely simulates the experience of taking a certification exam, or you can set it up in study mode so that you can look at the correct answers and explanations after you answer each question.

MORE INFO Practice tests

For details about all the practice test options available, see the "How to Use the Practice Tests" section in this book's introduction.

Chapter 4
Configuring Windows Vista Features

In the early days of computers, users considered themselves lucky just to be able to track and organize information on a single machine. Over time, however, the benefits of sharing data have become readily apparent. There's no greater example than the public Internet, a network through which users from throughout the world can create and access information.

One of the primary benefits of using modern operating systems such as Windows Vista is the ability to share information with others. In fact, one of the primary motivations for many customers to purchase a new computer is to access the Internet. Common tasks include sending and receiving e-mail, managing calendar information, and collaborating with others. Windows Vista includes several applications that provide methods of sharing information, using the Internet or a local area network (LAN). The main customer goals include communications and entertainment.

In this chapter, you'll learn about many different applications and features of Windows Vista. Lesson 1, "Working with Windows Communication Features," focuses on programs that are designed to help users communicate and share information. Lesson 2, "Using Windows Media Features," focuses on media-related functionality.

Exam objectives in this chapter:
- Post-installation: Customize and configure settings.
  - ❏ Evaluate user requirements and recommend, set up, and configure appropriate applications.
- Configure, troubleshoot, and repair networking.
  - ❏ Configure Media Center.

Lessons in this chapter:

Before You Begin

This chapter covers a broad range of media and communications features in Windows Vista. To follow the text and complete all of the exercises in this chapter, you need a computer that is running Windows Vista Home Premium or Windows Vista Ultimate. In Lesson 1, you need to have an e-mail account to set up and test sending and receiving messages. Additionally, you need a second computer to test the Windows Meeting Space feature.

In Lesson 2, you learn about configuring a TV tuner card for use with Windows Media Center. This requires a compatible hardware TV tuner device. To configure media sharing with other devices, you need to have access to a Microsoft Xbox 360 console that is located on the same network. Even if you do not have access to all of these types of devices, you can still follow the text.

Lesson 1: Working with Windows Communication Features

As a Consumer Support Technician, you're likely to be asked about how to configure Internet-connected applications. Although the steps are generally easy to perform, they require some background knowledge about the underlying features and concepts. In this lesson, you'll learn how you can use Windows Mail for e-mail and newsgroups, how you can manage tasks and appointments with Windows Calendar, and how you can create meetings with Windows Meeting Space.

After this lesson, you will be able to:

- Enable or disable optional components of Windows Vista using the Windows Features dialog box.
- Create and configure new e-mail and newsgroup accounts in Windows Mail.
- Use the Junk E-mail filter and message rules to manage information in Windows Mail.
- Connect to news servers and access newsgroups, using Windows Mail.
- Use Windows Calendar to keep track of tasks and appointments and to share scheduled information with other users.
- Set up and join meetings for sharing applications and handouts, using Windows Meeting Space.

Estimated lesson time: 75 minutes

Managing Windows Features

All editions of Windows Vista include a large number of different operating system features and services. By default, the most commonly used programs are enabled and available for use after installation. For example, tools such as Windows Mail and various networking options are automatically available. In some cases, however, you might need to turn specific features on or off. For example, you might disable a feature because you are sure that you do not need it, and you don't want to make it available.

In other cases, you might need to enable less commonly used features of the operating system. These features are sometimes provided for compatibility reasons, such as compatibility with earlier versions of Microsoft Internet Information Services (IIS), or they might be seldom-used options that are required by only some users (for example, the Telnet Server and Telnet Client features).

To make changes to which features are turned on or off, open Control Panel and click Programs. Clicking Turn Windows Features On Or Off launches the Windows Features dialog box (see Figure 4-1). It is important to note that Windows Features are components of the operating system; they are not programs that you can manage by clicking Uninstall A Program in Control Panel.

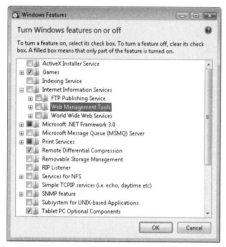

Figure 4-1 The Windows Features dialog box

The complete list of available Windows Features is a very long one. To help organize them, they are grouped together into folders, which can each be expanded to display the available subfeatures. There are three states for the check boxes in each section:

- **Checked** Indicates that the feature is enabled and that all associated lower-level items (if any) are also checked.
- **Cleared** Indicates that the feature is not enabled, and all lower-level items (if any) are also cleared.
- **Filled** Indicates that the feature is partially enabled. That is, at least one lower-level item is selected within the hierarchy.

Users should be advised not to enable or disable features unless they are fairly certain about their purpose. In some cases, modifications can cause system-related problems such as applications and operating system options not working as expected. For example, some applications on the computer are likely to require Microsoft .NET Framework 3.0. Disabling it prevents those applications from running.

To apply the changes, click OK in the Windows Features dialog box. Windows Vista automatically determines which files it should add and remove and which operating system changes it must make. The entire process can take several minutes and depends on how many different types of changes Windows Vista must perform. In some cases, it might be necessary to restart the computer.

Configuring Windows Mail for E-Mail

One of the most important capabilities for most Internet users is the ability to send and receive e-mail. Therefore, it should come as no surprise that Windows Vista includes a new e-mail program called Windows Mail. Windows Mail is a replacement for Microsoft Outlook Express, which was included in earlier versions of the Windows platform. It includes a wide variety of new and enhanced features, including the following:

- Support for accessing multiple e-mail accounts, using a variety of different options
- Integrated search functionality for quickly finding information stored in even very large mailboxes
- Built-in support for browsing newsgroups
- Junk e-mail and phishing filters for added security

Windows Mail is designed to provide a core set of messaging functionality in a program that is easy for users to configure. You can launch Windows Mail by searching for it in the Start menu or by accessing the All Programs group. Windows Mail is configured as the default e-mail program for new installations and is easily accessible using Start menu shortcuts. Figure 4-2 shows the main user interface.

Figure 4-2   The Windows Mail main user interface

The default view includes three main sections. The left side of the interface displays a list of folders, including the e-mail Inbox, Outbox, and other commonly used groupings. The right side of the interface includes two main sections. The top section is used to show a list of the messages that are present in the selected folder or group. The bottom section shows the contents of the message itself. This layout allows users to view all of the most important information easily without having to open each message in a separate window (although that is still an option).

Although it does not provide all of the functionality of programs such as Office Outlook, Windows Mail is an excellent product for home and small-business users who just need to perform basic tasks. In this section, you'll learn how you can configure and use Windows Mail.

MORE INFO   **Web-based e-mail vs. Windows Mail**

Customers are likely to ask you about the advantages of using a client-based mail program (such as Windows Mail) compared with using a Web-based messaging service. Many Internet users have chosen to obtain free or paid e-mail accounts that they can access through Web browsers. Examples include Windows Live Hotmail, Google's Gmail, and Yahoo! Mail. The primary benefit of these services is that they are quick and easy to set up. Generally, the only requirement is a standard Web browser. Usually, all information is stored online. The primary drawback of Web-based e-mail is usability and portability. Advanced users will appreciate the many different ways in which they can access e-mail, using Windows Mail. They'll also have the ability to read downloaded messages and compose responses even when they're not connected to the Internet. Both options have benefits, and users might choose to use both client-based and Web-based e-mail.

Preparing to Create E-Mail Accounts

Generally, the first step you must perform when using Windows Mail is to configure e-mail accounts. The process is fairly simple, although certain pieces of information are required. Usually, this information is available from the customer's Internet service provider (ISP) or from various online services. In general, have the following details before beginning the process of configuring new e-mail accounts:

- The user's name (for example, "Denise Smith").
- The user's logon information, which generally includes a logon that is the same as the e-mail address and a password.
- The user's e-mail address (for example, Denise Smith@TestISP.com).
- The user's e-mail server types and addresses.
- Any additional security configuration details that might be required. For example, server port numbers might be modified from their default settings.

As a Consumer Support Technician, you might need to assist users who aren't aware of the technical terms and details of configuring e-mail. Next, you'll learn how to use this information to create an e-mail account.

Creating E-Mail Accounts

As mentioned earlier, Windows Mail provides support for multiple e-mail and newsgroup accounts. When a user first launches Windows Mail, the New Account Setup Wizard automatically displays. To begin the process of creating and organizing e-mail accounts manually, click Tools, and then select Accounts. Figure 4-3 shows an example of the Internet Accounts dialog box. By default, the settings for e-mail accounts are blank because no e-mail accounts have been configured.

Figure 4-3   The Internet Accounts dialog box in Windows Mail

To begin the process of setting up a new e-mail account, click Add. The first step of the process enables you to select the type of account that you want to create. In addition to e-mail accounts, Windows Mail also supports newsgroup and directory service accounts. The process walks you through the steps required to create and configure a new e-mail account.

MORE INFO   **Other account types**

You learn about working with newsgroups later in this lesson. The Directory Services feature is primarily designed for larger organizations that have a Windows Active Directory directory service infrastructure. It is, therefore, outside of the scope of Exam 70-623 and is not covered further.

The first step of the process asks for a display name that Windows Mail should display in the *From* field in e-mail messages. Users are often confused by this step because they expect to enter their e-mail address. Although this works, the e-mail standard is for users to provide their first and last name (and, optionally, a middle initial). Generally, they should not use their last name first. Figure 4-4 shows an example.

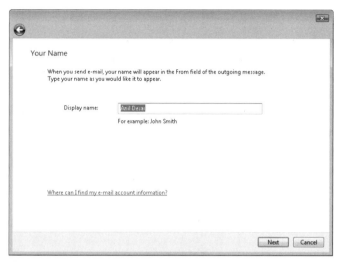

Figure 4-4   Providing the display name for a new e-mail account

The next step prompts for the full Internet e-mail address of the user account. This is the address that is used when recipients choose to reply to messages. This and all subsequent information should be available from the customer's e-mail provider.

To send and receive messages, the e-mail account must include details about server addresses. Windows Mail supports two server types for incoming mail:

- **Post Office Protocol version 3 (POP3)**   This is the most common method for accessing e-mail. This protocol allows for receiving messages and for performing other basic functions such as deleting messages from the server.

- **Internet Message Access Protocol (IMAP)**   IMAP is a newer messaging protocol than POP3. It provides basic functionality for sending and receiving e-mail, but it also allows users to perform other operations. For example, they can directly access and organize messages on the e-mail server without downloading them.

Both protocols use the Transmission Control Protocol/Internet Protocol (TCP/IP) standard and require the proper configuration of the Windows Vista networking options (for more information about configuring networking, see Chapter 9, "Configuring Windows Vista Networking"). Figure 4-5 shows the server setup options, along with some sample values. POP3 and IMAP server addresses are generally valid Internet Domain Name System (DNS) names, although small-business owners might have their own local mail servers.

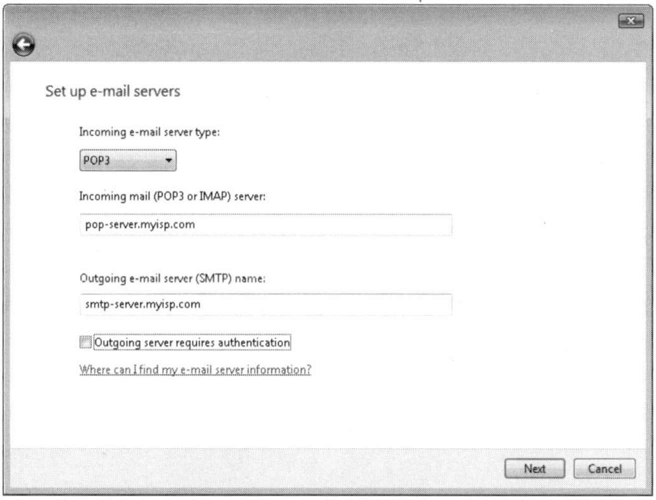

Figure 4-5   Specifying e-mail server settings

MORE INFO   **Support for HTTP-based messaging**

Windows Mail does not support direct access to Web-based e-mail using the HTTP protocol. Depending on the features provided by their Web-based e-mail provider, users might have the option of sending and receiving messages using the POP3 or IMAP protocols. If those protocols are supported, users can configure the settings just as they would for any other type of supported server.

POP3 and IMAP are the primary protocols for receiving e-mail. In addition to providing the incoming server address, users must provide the address of the outgoing e-mail server. Outgoing e-mail messages are sent using Simple Mail Transfer Protocol (SMTP). SMTP is the standard by which messages are sent throughout the world. It is also the primary method by which e-mail servers send messages between each other. In some cases, the server address might be the same for the POP3 and SMTP server. Many e-mail server providers allow users to send SMTP messages without requiring authentication. If a customer's ISP requires SMTP authentication, you must select the Outgoing Server Requires Authentication check box and then configure Windows Mail with the appropriate user name and password for the SMTP server.

The Internet Mail Logon step requires the user to provide the required credentials to log on to the mail server. Often (but not always), the e-mail user name is the same as the user's e-mail address. The password is usually provided by the e-mail provider or was created when the account was originally set up. For security purposes, users can choose to be prompted for the password each time a send and receive operation is performed. For convenience, the password can be remembered automatically, so it is not required each time.

After the necessary details have been provided, users can complete the setup process and click Finish. It is a good idea to check for messages automatically at this time. Windows Mail attempts to perform a send and receive operation and provides the resulting details.

Troubleshooting E-Mail Account Issues

Most users are able to get up and running with e-mail quickly, as long as they have the required account setup details. When problems do occur, an error message displays in the Send And Receive dialog box. Figure 4-6 provides an example. In this case, the cause of the error is that Windows Mail could not contact the POP3 server. The most likely cause of this is incorrect POP3 server address details.

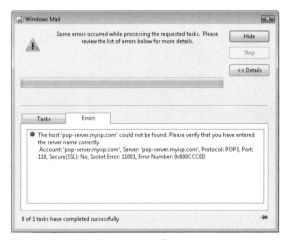

Figure 4-6   Viewing an e-mail error message

After you create an e-mail account, you can view, modify, and change additional options by selecting it and clicking Properties in the Internet Accounts Properties dialog box. Figure 4-7 shows an example of the General tab settings. The steps that were performed to create a new account included only the most commonly required configuration settings.

In some cases, Windows Vista might require additional details. For example, on the General tab, users can choose to provide a reply address that is different from their e-mail address, a helpful feature for people who have more than one e-mail account. Another helpful feature is the ability to provide a name for the connection (the default is to use the POP3 or IMAP4 server address information). The Include This Account When Receiving Mail Or Synchronizing check box determines whether the account is included in standard send and receive operations. Users can temporarily disable the use of an account without losing their settings by clearing this check box.

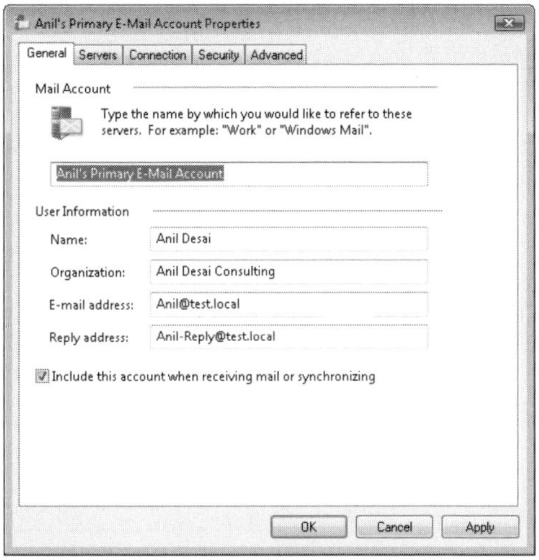

Figure 4-7   Viewing general settings for an e-mail account

When troubleshooting issues with sending and receiving e-mail, one of the most common sources of errors is the server settings. Figure 4-8 shows the options that are available on the Servers tab. On this tab, you can verify that the server addresses are correct and optionally provide additional authentication details for a user's SMTP server.

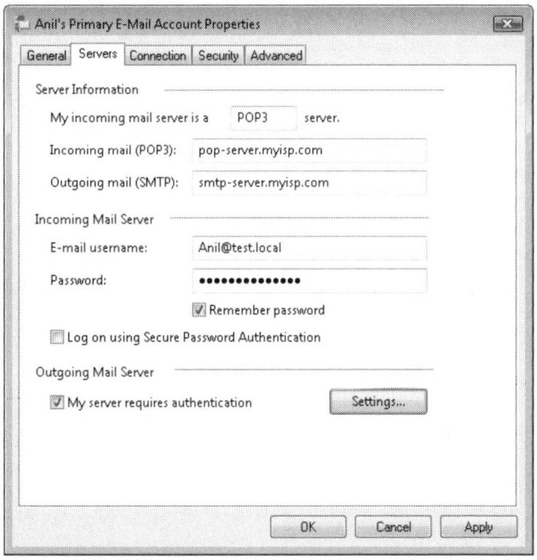

Figure 4-8   Viewing server settings for an e-mail account

The Connection tab provides settings that are useful for customers without a persistent Internet connection. The Security tab includes options for configuring security certificates. For most home and small-business users, this is not necessary.

Configuring Advanced Settings

The Advanced tab contains numerous options that are helpful when troubleshooting connection and other related issues. Figure 4-9 shows the available options. The POP3, IMAP, and SMTP protocol specifications include standard TCP/IP port numbers for communications. Windows Mail automatically chooses these default values. Some e-mail services might change the default server port numbers for security reasons or based on network considerations. Based on the type of e-mail server chosen for the account, users can manually change their settings. Additionally, they can specify whether they want to enable Secure Sockets Layer (SSL) to encrypt communications. This setting requires that the server support SSL.

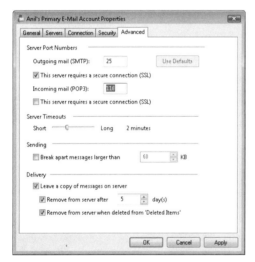

Figure 4-9   Configuring advanced settings for an e-mail account

The Server Timeouts setting is set to a default of one minute. This tells Windows Mail to stop waiting automatically after this amount of time when sending or receiving messages. In some cases, slow or unreliable Internet connections might cause connections to take longer than this amount of time. In those cases, you can increase the timeout to up to five minutes. You can use the Sending section to break large messages into chunks if required by the outgoing e-mail server. This option is not required for most e-mail servers.

Finally, there is a set of useful options related to delivery. These settings determine how e-mail messages are managed on the server. When using POP3, the default operation is for messages to be deleted automatically from the mail server after they are downloaded. This helps keep the size of the mailbox on the server small. What if the user wants to download the same messages to multiple computers? Or what if the user wants to be able to access messages through a Web-based interface and by using Windows Mail? In these cases, you can choose to leave a copy of the messages on the server. You can then choose to have Windows Mail delete the messages after a specified number of days, permanently delete them from the server when the user removes them from the Deleted Items folder in Windows Mail, or both. Both options instruct Windows Mail to delete messages during a send and receive operation.

Importing and Exporting Accounts

In addition to manually creating and configuring e-mail accounts, users can choose to import and export their settings. The Internet Accounts dialog box provides buttons for this functionality. The settings files are known as Internet Account Files, and they use the default extension of .iaf. These files can be copied to other computers running Windows Vista to simplify the setup and configuration process for Windows Mail.

The Internet Accounts dialog box also provides other useful functions. When you configure multiple e-mail accounts, it is possible to use the Set Order button to change the order in which Windows Mail uses e-mail accounts for send and receive operations. Additionally, you can configure one of the e-mail accounts using the Set Default button. This makes that account the default selection when sending and receiving messages. Finally, it is possible to remove e-mail accounts. When you delete an account, it is no longer included in send and receive operations. However, all messages that have already been downloaded for the account are saved on the local computer until you manually delete them.

Working with Windows Mail

After you have properly configured Windows Mail, most users find the user interface to be intuitive. In this section, you learn about the major features of the user interface.

Understanding Default Mail Folders

The main folders that are shown on the left side of the Windows Mail interface include the following:

- **Inbox** This is the location into which all new mail messages are placed.
- **Outbox** Messages that are waiting to be sent are located in this folder. Unless there is a configuration issue, Windows Mail sends these messages during the next send and receive operation.
- **Sent Items** This folder contains a copy of all of the messages that a user sends using Windows Mail.
- **Deleted Items** This folder acts much like the Recycle Bin in Windows Vista. By default, Windows Mail stores deleted messages here, so you can restore them if necessary. You can permanently delete the items by right-clicking the folder and selecting Empty 'Deleted Items' Folder.
- **Drafts** This folder stores all messages that a user creates and saves. Windows Mail does not automatically send these messages.

■ **Junk E-mail** This folder contains suspected junk e-mail messages. Users should periodically review the contents of this folder to look for any incorrectly categorized messages.

In addition to the default mail folders, users can create their own personal folders for organizing and categorizing messages. Dragging and dropping is the easiest method for moving messages into such folders.

Configuring Junk E-Mail Settings

A common annoyance related to sending and receiving e-mail messages is that of junk e-mails. As a Consumer Support Technician, you're very likely to be asked for advice about reducing the wasted time and space junk e-mail can cause. Most of these messages are sent as unsolicited commercial communications, but they can also be a serious security concern. It is very difficult to keep e-mail addresses truly private. Fortunately, Windows Mail provides an automatic junk e-mail filtering feature. You can access its settings by clicking Tools and selecting Junk E-mail Options (see Figure 4-10).

Figure 4-10 Configuring Junk E-mail Options settings

The primary concern with automatic junk e-mail filtering is the potential of filtering out legitimate messages. Preventing these "false positives" has to be balanced with the ability to filter out as many unwanted messages as possible. The available options with their descriptions are as follows:

■ **No Automatic Filtering** Mail from blocked senders is still moved to the Junk E-mail folder.

■ **Low** This moves the most obvious junk e-mail to the Junk E-mail folder.

- **High**   Most junk e-mail is caught, but some regular mail could be caught as well. Check your Junk E-mail folder often.
- **Safe List Only**   Only mail from people or domains on the Safe Senders List is delivered to the Inbox.

The default setting, Low, is designed to err on the side of caution (that is, it is least likely to mark legitimate messages incorrectly as junk e-mail). By default, Windows Mail stores suspected junk e-mail messages in the Junk E-mail folder, so users can review them manually. There is also an option to delete these messages permanently if users are confident with their settings.

In addition to using the automatic filtering options, users can choose to create their own Safe Senders and Blocked Senders e-mail lists, as shown in Figure 4-11. Although it can be difficult to maintain these lists manually, the Safe Senders tab offers two helpful options. The first is to trust any e-mail addresses automatically that are in the Windows Contacts list (enabled by default). The second option is to include people automatically to whom the user sends e-mail messages.

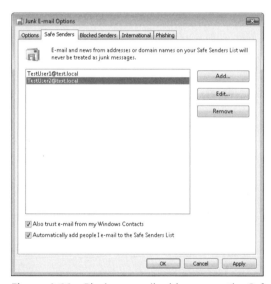

Figure 4-11   Placing e-mail addresses on the Safe Senders List

Many junk e-mail messages are sent from countries other than the user's home country, sometimes written in foreign languages. These are obvious indications that the message is not legitimate. The International tab (shown in Figure 4-12) provides users with the ability to filter out messages automatically that are sent from certain top-level Internet domains. Figure 4-13 shows some of the options. Most top-level domain names are based on the country of origin, and users who don't often interact with people outside their country can use these options to reduce the number of junk messages they receive.

Figure 4-12   Configuring International Junk E-mail options

Figure 4-13   Configuring the list of blocked top-level domains

Another option on the International tab is to block messages based on their regional encoding. Encoding options are used to specify the language in which the message is written. Figure 4-14 provides an example of the available options.

The final tab in the Junk E-mail Options dialog box is Phishing. Phishing is a method by which seemingly legitimate e-mails attempt to trick users into accessing Web sites and providing sensitive information. For example, a message might appear to have come from a bank or credit card provider and require the user to access the site to log on. Windows Mail can attempt to detect these messages automatically and optionally move them to the Junk E-mail folder. For more information about avoiding phishing, see Chapter 8, "Configuring Parental Controls and Browser Security."

Figure 4-14   Blocking e-mails based on regional encoding settings

Junk e-mail can be annoying and potentially dangerous. By enabling the advanced filtering options of Windows Mail, however, users can save time and keep their computers secure.

Configuring Message Rules

Managing large volumes of e-mail messages can be a time-consuming and error-prone process. For example, users who receive many messages every day are likely to overlook important messages or spend too much time trying to manage lower priority communications. One solution to this is to set up automatic rules for how Windows Mail should manage these mail messages. Windows Mail includes a Mail Rules feature that you can configure by clicking Message Rules on the Tools menu and then clicking Mail. Figure 4-15 shows an example of a new mail rule.

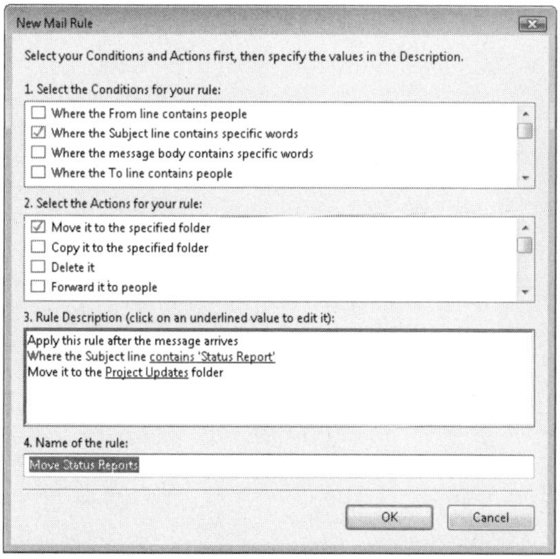

Figure 4-15   Creating a new mail rule

There are many different options that allow for automatically identifying messages based on details such as the sender, the subject, contents of the message, and the To address. Windows Mail can then move or copy these messages to a specific folder, or it can delete or forward them. You can create multiple rules and specify the order in which Windows Mail processes those rules. Overall, message rules can greatly reduce the common problem of "information overload."

Customizing the Window Layout

Windows Mail is likely to become one of the most frequently used applications for many Internet-enabled users of Windows Vista. In addition to all of the features you have learned about already, customers can change many different details about the configuration of the user interface. Panels and panes can be hidden, shown, or rearranged based on preferences. Figure 4-16 provides an example of the options that are available when clicking Layout on the View menu.

Figure 4-16   Configuring window layout settings in Windows Mail

As a Consumer Support Technician, you might be required to assist new Windows Mail users with issues in which information might appear to have disappeared. A good first troubleshooting step is to verify the window layout and other view options to make sure that they have not been incorrectly modified.

Quick Check

1. What are the three main messaging protocols that are supported by Windows Mail?
2. What are two ways in which users can reduce the number of messages received directly to their Windows Mail Inbox folder?

Quick Check Answers

1. Windows Mail supports Post Office Protocol version 3 (POP3), Internet Message Access Protocol (IMAP), and Simple Mail Transfer Protocol (SMTP).
2. Users can automatically filter out unwanted e-mail by using the Junk E-mail options. They can also use message rules to configure Windows Mail to perform actions automatically based on message details.

Real World

Anil Desai

A Chinese proverb states:

When I hear, I forget

When I see, I remember

When I do, I learn

As a Consumer Support Technician, one of your main goals is to learn about the many different features of Windows Vista, not only to prepare for Exam 70-623, but also to provide expert advice and configuration help. The best way to do this is to have first-hand knowledge of working with various programs. This chapter covers many different communications-related and media-related applications. Each program has its own set of features and configuration options. Whenever possible, I recommend you use these programs to learn about their many different nuances and capabilities.

Sometimes, you'll find features almost unavoidable. For example, you'll find many situations that require you to create and configure network connections (a topic that is covered in Chapter 9). I use Windows Media Center with my Xbox 360 all the time. Therefore, I've become very familiar with its capabilities and options.

In other cases, however, you might not have a need for a particular program. For example, because I normally use Outlook for e-mail and calendaring tasks, I didn't have a need to use these features in Windows Mail and Windows Calendar. In those cases, it's helpful to try to find ways in which your customers might want to use the programs. For example, imagine that a customer would like to download e-mail from several different accounts but use only one reply-to address. Alternatively, create situations in which parents might want to keep track of their children's appointments by using Windows Calendar. Then, try to implement these configurations on a test computer. Overall, it's often easiest and most effective to learn by doing.

Using Windows Mail to Access Newsgroups

In addition to providing support for creating, sending, and receiving e-mail, the Windows Mail application also includes functionality for accessing newsgroups. Newsgroups use the Network News Transport Protocol (NNTP) to provide access to a news server. When connected to a news server, users can view messages posted by others and post their own topics or reply to existing messages. This is an excellent way for users to interact with each other. In this lesson, you'll learn how to configure Windows Mail to use newsgroups.

Configuring Newsgroup Accounts

Windows Mail is automatically configured to access a default news server. You can create new news server configurations by accessing the Accounts option on the Tools menu. Click Add to start the process and select Newsgroup Account for the new account type.

The first step of the process asks you to provide a display name. This name is shown to everyone who can view messages that you have posted in a newsgroup. If you are connecting to a private news server, you generally should use your real name. In public forums, however, you might choose to create a new name that is not personally identifiable to help ensure security and privacy. The same suggestions apply to the second step, providing your e-mail address. A common source of junk e-mail and other annoyances is organizations that automatically collect e-mail addresses online, especially from newsgroup servers. To avoid this, you might choose not to include your primary e-mail address.

The third step requires you to enter the network address of the NNTP server (see Figure 4-17). The address of the news server is generally provided by the service provider's Web site. In addition, some news servers might require authentication. You can select the My News Server Requires Me To Log On check box to be prompted for logon credentials in the next step.

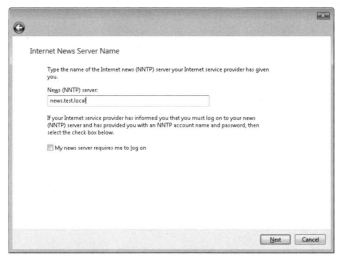

Figure 4-17   Configuring the news server name

When connecting to a news server that supports it, you can choose to use your Windows Live ID to use advanced features. Figure 4-18 shows the available options.

Figure 4-18   Providing a Windows Live ID when connecting to a compatible server

After you have completed the configuration, the new account appears in the Internet Accounts dialog box. As with e-mail accounts, you can choose to configure various additional settings by selecting a news account and clicking Properties. Figure 4-19 shows the settings that are available on the Advanced tab.

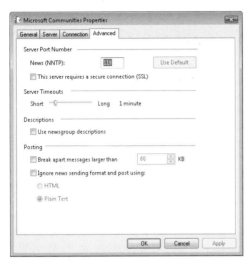

Figure 4-19   Configuring advanced settings for a news server

The default for the Server Port Number value is 119 because this is the standard port used by the NNTP protocol. If the server supports it, you can also enable an encrypted SSL connection to the server.

Subscribing to Newsgroups

As mentioned earlier, by default, Windows Mail is automatically configured to provide access to the Microsoft Communities news server. This service is designed for users of the Windows platform to ask questions and provide responses related to various operating system features and applications. Newsgroups are generally named using a multipart set of topics. After you have configured a news server account, you can right-click it and select Newsgroups to view a list of available groups (see Figure 4-20). To display a particular newsgroup automatically when you access a news server, select the newsgroup, and then click Subscribe. Newsgroups that have been added are considered subscriptions because you are able to view updated articles after they're posted.

For example, a newsgroup is designed for topics related to Windows Mail itself, named microsoft.public.windows.vista.mail. For more information, see the Microsoft Communities home page at *http://www.microsoft.com/communities/default.mspx*.

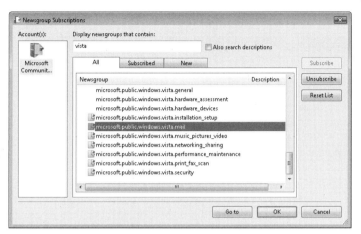

Figure 4-20   Subscribing to newsgroups

Exam Tip   Accessing news servers such as Microsoft Communities can be an excellent way to prepare for Exam 70-623. In some cases, you might be puzzled about a technical issue, and you might want to get assistance from others. In other cases, you might want to see common questions that others are asking and offer your own advice. When using any newsgroup, there are several important rules of etiquette. Apart from being courteous and respectful, be sure to search for similar postings before posing a question to avoid duplication. Be sure that you are posting your question to the appropriate newsgroup. When used correctly, newsgroups can be one of the most important resources you have (in addition, of course, to this book!).

Reading and Posting Messages

When you activate a particular message group by clicking its name in the left panel of Windows Mail, you automatically have the ability to read messages that have been posted. By default, the newest messages are shown at the top of the list. Responses to messages are grouped, and you can use the plus sign (+) next to a topic to view associated replies (see Figure 4-21).

Windows Mail also enables you to post new messages to a newsgroup. In general, you should search for similar messages before creating your own topic. Also, be sure to describe your problem and issue completely. All too often, people are frustrated with a problem and have difficulty focusing on providing the necessary details. This reduces the usefulness of many of the communications.

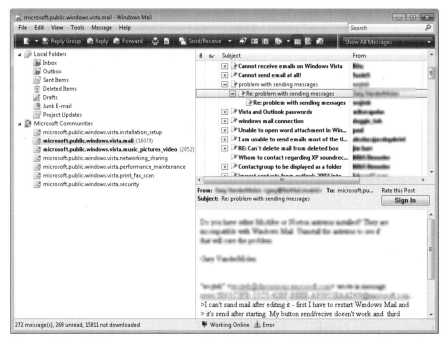

Figure 4-21   Reading newsgroup postings in Windows Mail (details have been obscured to protect users' privacy)

If you simply want to test the posting functionality, be sure to do it in a designated test newsgroup and not in an actual active group. For example, on the Microsoft Communities server, there is a group called microsoft.public.test. Overall, keep in mind that thousands of users will be able to see your post. Therefore, be sure that your messages are polite, complete, and accurate.

Using Windows Calendar

Computers are useful for tracking all kinds of personal information, and keeping track of appointments and events is no exception. Windows Vista includes Windows Calendar, which uses a simple, intuitive user interface for recording information about upcoming meetings, tasks, and related details. Windows Calendar also provides a feature that makes it easy to share calendar appointments with other people. Figure 4-22 shows an example of a daily view in the application. In this section, you'll learn how to work with Windows Calendar.

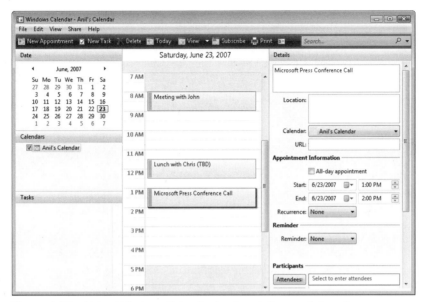

Figure 4-22 Using Windows Calendar to view daily appointments

Managing Calendars and Groups

In its simplest configuration, you can use a single Windows Calendar file for all of your appointments. This is useful if, for example, you just want to keep track of a single type of event. More commonly, users want to keep different types of events separate for organizational purposes. For example, a small-business user might have separate calendars for personal and social events, another for business appointments and meetings, and a third for keeping track of details such as tax filings.

The process of creating a new calendar is simple: just click the New Calendar item on the File menu. A new calendar appears in the Calendars section. Windows Calendar gives each calendar a separate color to help keep events visually separate.

Another useful feature for organizing calendars is the ability to create groups. This enables you to manage similar types of calendars together for administrative purposes (you'll see examples later in this lesson). To create a new group for calendars, click New Group on the File menu. After you have created a new group, you can drag and drop the calendars into and out of them.

Creating Tasks and Appointments

Appointments are events that occur at a specific date and time. To create a new appointment, place the cursor on the date or time of the event in the calendar view. Then, click the New Appointment button in the toolbar, or choose New Appointment on the File menu. You can type the text of the appointment either directly in the calendar (if the current view is large enough) or in the details pane. This section enables you to specify additional information, including the following:

- A description of the appointment.
- Location.
- On which calendar the item should appear.
- A URL for reference to a Web site or other online location.
- Details about the start and end time for the appointment. (Optionally, you can choose for it to be an all-day appointment and configure the appointment to recur.)
- An amount of time before the event that a reminder should be displayed.
- A list of participants that you would like to invite to the meeting. You can enter e-mail addresses manually, or you can click Attendees to choose them from the list stored in Windows Contacts.

Windows Calendar also enables you to create and track tasks. The primary difference between a task and an appointment is that tasks generally have a start date and due date (rather than specific beginning and end times), and they are not necessarily placed at a certain time of the day. Tasks also don't have attendees. To create a new task, click New Task on the toolbar or select New Task on the File menu. The list of tasks appears in the bottom left section of the user interface. Users can place a check mark next to a task to signify that it is complete. Figure 4-23 shows an example of Windows Calendar in which there are multiple appointments and task items.

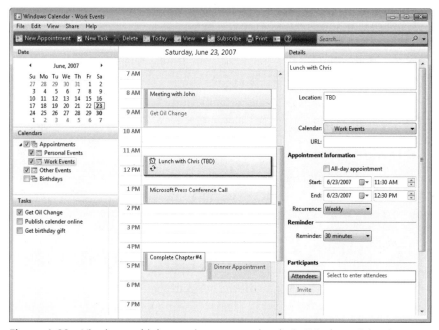

Figure 4-23   Viewing multiple appointments and tasks in Windows Calendar

Viewing Calendar Information

You can view calendar events by using several different view options. The first option is to choose the time span shown in the calendar portion of the user interface. The options are as follows:

- Day
- Work Week
- Week
- Month

To change the view, click the drop-down arrow next to the View button on the toolbar or select the appropriate item from the View menu. Note that there are convenient keyboard shortcuts that can make it easier to switch between views. If you choose to show information for many days on the display, then summary text is shown for each event. You can always click Today to return to the current date.

In addition to controlling the date range that is shown, you can manage which events and tasks are shown in the calendar view by selecting the check box for the associated calendar or calendar group. This enables you to view information from multiple calendars in a single view or to view just one type of information. For example, when at work, you might be most interested in details about meetings. At other times, you might want to view all of the types of upcoming events.

Sending Calendar Information

Although calendars are certainly helpful when used on an individual basis, they can be even more useful when shared with other people. A common example in a home-based environment is for parents to be able to keep track of their children's after-school activities. You can share calendar information in several different ways. The simplest method is to send appointments through e-mail. The iCalendar format enables users to send appointment-related data in a standard format. These files usually have an .ics extension and can easily be attached to an e-mail message (see Figure 4-24).

Note that the message is being sent using Windows Mail. If you are using a different e-mail program, Windows Calendar uses your default program. The message has an attachment that includes the .ics file for a group of appointments. To send a new appointment or group of appointments, select the specific item, and then click Send Via E-mail on the Share menu. A new e-mail message is generated. The recipient can open the attachment to have the event added to his or her calendar. Because the iCalendar format is a standard, programs other than Windows Calendar can use it.

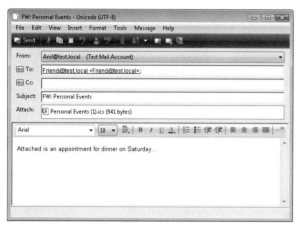

Figure 4-24   Sending appointment information through e-mail

Publishing a Calendar

Although sending individual appointments through e-mail can be useful, it can quickly become difficult to manage when there are many different users who need to stay up to date with their friends, family members, and coworkers. An easier way to do this is to use the Windows Calendar publishing feature. Publishing calendar information also relies on the iCalendar format, but the data can be stored in a central location that is accessible to many people. The options include local file folders and shared network folders. (For more information about configuring shared folders, see Chapter 10, "Managing Network Sharing".) In addition, you can publish calendar data to a compatible Web server on the Internet.

To enable publishing, on the Share menu, select Publish. Figure 4-25 shows the options that are available. The first option is the Calendar Name text box. It is usually helpful to include the name of the individual and the types of events that are included. The Location To Publish Calendar text box specifies where the calendar data is published. This can be a local folder path, a network folder path, or the URL of a compatible Web host. The link opens a Web site that provides more details for available services. A very useful option is the Automatically Publish Changes Made To This Calendar check box. When selected, this setting ensures that the published information is updated whenever you add or change appointments. Finally, you can determine whether you want to publish notes, reminders, or tasks.

The publishing process also enables you to generate an e-mail message to inform others of the location of your shared calendar. When other users connect to and download the .ics file, they can add the events and other details to their own calendars (see Figure 4-26).

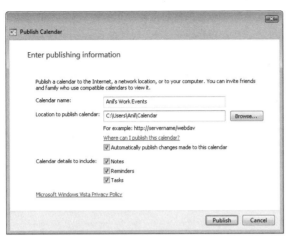

Figure 4-25   Publishing calendar-related information

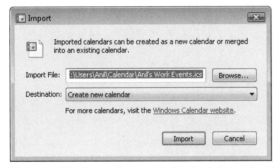

Figure 4-26   Importing new calendar information by using an .ics file

You can choose to stop publishing calendar information from the Share menu by choosing Stop Publishing.

Subscribing to Calendars

Although manually connecting to and downloading iCalendar files is an option, it does take time and effort for people to obtain that data. To make this process easier, Windows Calendar includes a Subscribe command on the Share menu. The only configuration option is to specify the path to the shared calendar files. This might be in a local folder, but it is more commonly stored on a shared network folder or on a compatible Internet server.

Windows Calendar provides a great deal of functionality for tracking tasks and appointments in a simple and easy-to-learn user interface.

Using Windows Meeting Space

An important design goal for Windows Vista is to give users the ability to share information easily. All too often, users have to share files through removable media (such as USB flash memory drives) or by using e-mail to transmit files. Although these methods work, it's often much simpler for people to connect directly to a shared workspace. For example, if several users are located in a meeting room, they might already have available network connections. All that is required is some type of application for making the files available. Of course, an important requirement is for the data to remain secure by allowing only authorized users to connect to it.

Microsoft designed Windows Meeting Space to meet the security and usability requirements to share information. In this lesson, you'll learn how to set up and configure this feature.

Setting Up a Meeting Space

The first step in working with Windows Meeting Space is to set up this feature. To start the process, launch Windows Meeting Space from the Start menu by searching for it or clicking the appropriate icon on the All Programs menu. Figure 4-27 shows the first screen of the setup process.

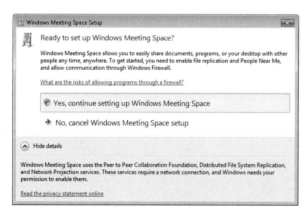

Figure 4-27   Starting the Windows Meeting Space setup process

The details section of the dialog box provides a list of the required services and configuration details as follows:

- A current network connection
- Peer to Peer Collaboration Foundation
- Distributed File System Replication
- Network Project services

Typically, the relevant components are enabled automatically. After you click the button to start the setup process, you'll see the People Near Me dialog box (see Figure 4-28). This configuration is necessary to identify other users uniquely in the environment. The display name is what users see when you are participating in a meeting. You can also choose to specify from which types of people you can receive invitations. The options are as follows:

- **Anyone** This setting allows any user to send an invitation (although you must still accept it to connect).
- **Trusted Contacts** These people appear in your Windows Contacts list or have a security certificate on the local computer.
- **No One** This setting effectively disables the ability to receive invitations.

Figure 4-28 Configuring People Near Me settings

After you define the People Near Me settings, Windows Meeting Space retains them for the next time you use Windows Meeting Space or other collaboration features.

Starting a New Meeting

One member of the group that would like to create a meeting should use the Start A New Meeting link to create a meeting space. Figure 4-29 shows the available options.

Figure 4-29 Creating a new meeting space

The main setting is the name of the meeting. This is what other users see when they launch Windows Meeting Space. Additionally, you must enter a password to be used by the attendees. Because anyone on the network could potentially connect, it is recommended that you use a strong password. Clicking the Options link enables you to configure additional functions. You use the Visibility Options section to specify whether the meeting is automatically seen by others on the network. In typical small-business and home environments, this makes it much easier for people to connect. If a wireless network adapter is present in the computer, the Network Options section enables you to create an ad hoc wireless network. (See Chapter 9 for more information about setting up wireless networks.)

MORE INFO Creating a strong password

The strength of a password is based on several different characteristics. For example, the length of the password, inclusion of different types of characters such as numbers and symbols, and avoiding obvious personal information can help keep information secure. For more tips and guidelines, see "Strong Passwords: How to Create and Use Them" at *http://www.microsoft.com/protect/yourself/password/create.mspx*.

After you create the meeting, you see a screen that is similar to the one in Figure 4-30.

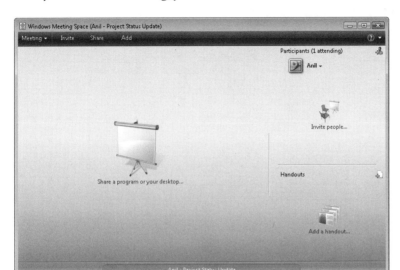

Figure 4-30 A new meeting that is ready for users to join

Inviting Meeting Attendees

After you create a new meeting space, you can choose to invite attendees to the meeting by clicking the Invite People link or by clicking the Invite button on the toolbar. You can send an invitation through e-mail or by creating an invitation file. Both methods generate a Windows Meeting Space invitation file with a .wcinv extension.

Joining a Meeting

After you have started Windows Meeting Space, the program automatically searches for meetings that are located on the network. If a meeting space is found, you can see the details as shown in Figure 4-31. To join the meeting, simply click it and provide the password.

You can also join a meeting by using the Open An Invitation File command. This is useful if you have received a .wcinv file through e-mail or if one is located on the network. After the meeting has been joined, all of the attendees see a similar view.

Figure 4-31   Viewing a list of available meetings

Sharing Information in Windows Meeting Space

When multiple users are present in a meeting space, they can share information in a variety of ways. The first option is to set personal status information done by selecting the user's own identity in the Participants section and choosing a status. The available options are as follows:

- Available
- Busy
- Be Right Back
- Away

The main information sharing options include sharing handouts and sharing either a program or the desktop. To share a handout, click the Add A Handout link. The notice informs you about how handouts work. The handout file itself is copied to each of the participants' computers. Only one participant can modify the contents of the file at a time because the changes are copied for each of them. The original shared file, however, remains unmodified.

The second option is to share the desktop or a program. This feature enables others to view information on one participant's computer. To start sharing, click the Share A Program Or Your Desktop link. The resulting dialog box enables you to specify whether you want to share the entire desktop or only a specific application window.

After sharing starts, all of the participants are able to see the user's application or desktop window within Windows Meeting Space. Figure 4-32 shows an example. If an application is shared, a status message of Currently Sharing appears in the program's title bar.

Figure 4-32   Viewing a shared application in Windows Meeting Space

At any given time, only one user can have control of the program. Participants can click Request Control at the top of the interface to request the ability to interact with the program or the desktop. The user who has control can choose to view the window as others see it for verification purposes. There is also an option to view the shared content in full screen mode.

Ending a Meeting

When the meeting is finished, participants can choose the Leave Meeting item on the Meeting menu. If handouts were created and modified, each participant is given the option of saving them. After all participants leave the meeting, the meeting is ended.

Windows Meeting Space provides a very useful method of sharing documents and program windows between users who are located on the same network.

Quick Check

1. What are two ways in which potential attendees can join a Windows Meeting Space meeting?
2. What are the main sharing options in Windows Meeting Space?

> **Quick Check Answers**
> 1. Potential participants can open Windows Meeting Space and select the meeting if it is advertised on the network. If it is not, they can choose to join the meeting by providing the invitation file.
> 2. Participants can share files by using the handouts feature, or they can share a program or the entire desktop by using the sharing features.

Practice: Using Windows Communications Features

In these practice exercises, you use the built-in applications of Windows Vista to share information and access newsgroups. Specifically, you'll use Windows Mail to access public newsgroups and Windows Meeting Space to create and join a new meeting.

▶ **Practice 1: Accessing Newsgroups in Windows Mail**

In this practice exercise, you use the newsgroup features of Windows Mail to connect to the Microsoft Communities server and browse the contents of newsgroups. For practice purposes, the steps create a new connection to this news server (even though it is likely that one already exists by default on your local computer).

1. Open Windows Mail from the Start menu.
2. On the Tools menu, select Accounts to open the Internet Accounts dialog box.
3. To create a new account, click Add.
4. For the first step, select the Newsgroup Account option, and then click Next.
5. In the Display Name text box, type either your own name or an alias. This practice exercise does not involve posting any messages, so privacy should not be an issue. Click Next.
6. For the e-mail address, type **Test@test.local**. Click Next to continue.
7. For the NNTP server address, type **msnews.microsoft.com**. Click Next.
8. If prompted, in the Internet Community News Windows Live ID Sign-In section, choose the Never Use Community Features That Require Windows Live ID option. Click Next.
9. To complete the process of creating the account, click Finish.
10. You should see an account called msnews.microsoft.com in the Internet Accounts dialog box. Optionally, click Properties to view the available options. When finished, click Close.
11. You receive a message that gives you the opportunity to subscribe to newsgroups. Click the Show Available Newsgroups, But Don't Turn On Communities option. Windows Mail starts to download the complete list of available newsgroups.

12. On the All tab, search for "Vista" to display a list of Windows Vista newsgroups.

13. Select the microsoft.public.windows.vista.mail newsgroup, and then click Subscribe. Optionally, subscribe to additional newsgroups that have topics you might want to view. When finished, click OK.

14. In the left pane of Windows Mail, select the microsoft.public.windows.vista.mail newsgroup. Note that a list of message headers appears.

15. Click various messages and expand groupings to view the contents.

16. When finished, close Windows Mail. You can delete the news account you created in this practice by clicking the Tools menu and selecting Accounts. In the list of accounts, select the msnews.microsoft.com account and click Remove.

▶ **Practice 2: Using Windows Meeting Space**

In this practice exercise, you create a new Windows Meeting Space and then join the meeting from another computer on the network running Windows Vista. The steps in this exercise assume that you have not yet configured Windows Meeting Space on either computer.

1. Start Windows Meeting Space from the Start menu.

2. If you have not yet configured it, the People Near Me dialog box opens. Choose the Anyone option for invitations and enter an appropriate user name. Click OK to continue.

3. In the Windows Meeting Space window, click Start A New Meeting.

4. Type a descriptive name for the meeting, and then create a strong password. Click the right arrow to create the meeting. The new meeting starts automatically.

5. On a second computer, repeat steps 1, 2, and 3 of this practice. In step 3, enter a different name in the People Near Me dialog box so you can simulate different users connecting to the meeting.

6. In the Windows Meeting Space window, click Join A Meeting Near Me.

7. Select the name of the meeting that you created in step 5, provide the password, and then click the right arrow to connect.

8. From either computer, click Add A Handout and specify a local file that you want to share. Note the details about revisions in the confirmation box.

9. Click Share A Program On Your Desktop, and then choose to share the entire desktop.

10. Verify that both computers can see the handouts and that one of the computers can see the shared desktop of the other computer.

11. When finished, click Leave Meeting on both computers and close Windows Meeting Space.

Lesson Summary

- You can enable and disable Windows Vista features by using the Windows Features dialog box in Control Panel.
- Windows Mail supports the POP3, IMAP, and SMTP protocols for sending and receiving e-mail.
- You can import and export account settings to simplify setup of Windows Mail on multiple computers.
- You can automatically detect and move unwanted e-mail messages, using the Junk E-mail filter options.
- Users can create message rules to perform actions automatically on e-mail messages.
- Windows Mail provides the ability to connect to NNTP news servers and to read and post messages.
- Windows Calendar enables users to create multiple calendars that contain tasks and appointments.
- Users can share calendar information, using iCalendar files or by publishing and subscribing to other people's calendar data.
- Windows Meeting Space enables users to share their desktop or a program and to share files over the network.

Lesson Review

You can use the following questions to test your knowledge of the information in Lesson 1, "Working with Windows Communication Features." The questions are also available on the companion CD if you prefer to review them in electronic form.

NOTE Answers

Answers to these questions and explanations of why each answer choice is correct or incorrect are located in the "Answers" section at the end of the book.

---

1. You are a Consumer Support Technician assisting a customer with setting up Windows Mail. The customer has reported that the majority of e-mail she receives from her multiple e-mail accounts are junk messages. She would like to filter out as much of this junk e-mail as possible and allow messages only from certain people to be displayed in the Inbox. Which two actions should she take to meet these requirements? (Select two. Each correct answer presents part of the solution.)

   A. Configure the Junk E-mail filter to No Automatic Filtering.

   B. Configure the Junk E-mail filter to High.

   C. Configure the Junk E-mail filter to Safe List Only.

    D. Add the acceptable senders to the Safe Senders List.

    E. Add unacceptable senders to the Blocked Senders List.

    F. Use the Blocked Top-Level Domain List to remove messages from known junk e-mail domains.

2. You are assisting a father who would like to configure Windows Calendar for himself and for his three children. He has created four separate Windows Vista user accounts: one for himself, and one for each of the children. He would like the ability to view information about his children's appointments on his own Windows Calendar. How can he most easily meet these requirements? (Choose two. Each correct answer presents part of the solution.)

    A. Have all three children subscribe to the father's calendar.

    B. Have all of the children publish their calendars to a shared folder location.

    C. Have the father publish his calendar to a shared folder location.

    D. Have the father subscribe to each of the children's shared calendars.

3. A customer is planning to use Windows Meeting Space over a public wireless network. She would like to prevent other users from detecting the meeting. She still wants three of her coworkers to be able to access the meeting. How can she most easily do this? (Choose two. Each correct answer presents part of the solution.)

    A. Choose to start a new meeting but use a blank meeting name.

    B. Use a strong password when creating the meeting.

    C. Configure the People Near Me settings to allow invitations from trusted contacts.

    D. Choose to send the meeting invitation through e-mail.

    E. Select the Do Not Allow People Near Me To See This Meeting option when creating the meeting.

Lesson 2: Using Windows Media Features

Several years ago, the idea of using personal computers as the primary method of working with photos and video seemed somewhat far-fetched. Hardware was significantly slower, and new devices such as digital cameras were just becoming popular. Vendors of specific hardware products provided programs for managing media. The situation today is significantly different. Now, many home and small-business users find themselves relying on computers to send, receive, and store media. The primary challenge has changed from making this possible to keeping track of large volumes of data. Dealing with thousands of photos, music files, recorded video programs, and related data can be difficult.

It probably comes as no surprise that Windows Vista Home Premium and Windows Vista Ultimate include several new and updated features for managing media. Apart from enhancements to Windows Explorer and other key components of the operating system, there are specific applications for working with media. Windows Photo Gallery is designed for viewing and editing digital photos. It also includes options for common operations such as sending photos through e-mail, burning photos to CD or DVD media, and e-mailing pictures. Windows Movie Maker provides the ability to assemble video and compile it to a file or burn it to removable media. It includes features such as animated transitions and has an easy-to-learn user interface. Windows Media Center goes a big step toward making computers an integral component of customers' entertainment environments. It allows for watching and recording live television and for accessing a wide variety of content online. Windows Media Player has been enhanced in Windows Vista to provide a much more intuitive user interface for playing and organizing video and audio content.

As a Consumer Support Technician, you will frequently field customers' requests for your expertise and recommendations about working with media applications. The Windows Vista media features have been designed to be quick and easy to learn, but there are several additional techniques that can be very helpful. In this lesson, you'll learn ways in which you can use Windows Media Player, Windows Movie Maker, Windows Media Center, and Windows Photo Gallery.

MORE INFO   Configuring media devices

The focus of this lesson is using the primary media applications that are included with Windows Vista. For more information on configuring devices such as MP3 players and digital video cameras, see Chapter 11, "Managing and Troubleshooting Devices."

> **After this lesson, you will be able to:**
> - Configure and use Windows Media Player to play, organize, burn, and synchronize audio and video content.
> - Use Windows Photo Gallery to view and organize picture and video files.
> - Use Windows Movie Maker to import media, credit movies, and publish them.
> - Configure Windows Media Center to access media files on the local computer and on extender devices.
> - Manage and troubleshoot file associations that are related to Windows programs.
>
> **Estimated lesson time: 60 minutes**

Using Windows Media Player

Windows Media Player is the primary application for playing audio and video files on Windows Vista. In addition to being a player, it actually provides functionality for organizing your music library, synchronizing with portable devices, and burning content to CD or DVD media. All of these features make Windows Media Player an important hub for accessing media content. In this section, you'll learn how to configure and use the many different features that are included in Windows Media Player.

MORE INFO   Sharing media with other devices

For more information about sharing photos, videos, and music with other devices (such as an Xbox 360 console), see the details on enabling media sharing in Chapter 10.

Setting Up Windows Media Player

You can launch Windows Media Player from the Start menu by searching for it or by selecting its icon in the All Programs menu. When you launch Windows Media Player for the first time, it starts a brief setup process to configure the initial settings for Windows Media Player. The options are Express Settings and Custom Settings. The Express Settings option uses the default settings, including choosing file associations, selecting an online music store, and opting to sending anonymous usage data to Microsoft. For many users, this is the most appropriate option.

The Custom Settings option enables you to configure various initial settings. It is most useful when users are running other media applications on the same computer or if they want to modify the default settings. The first step in this process is related to Privacy Options settings (see Figure 4-33). To provide an improved user experience, Windows Media Player has the ability to access information from the Internet. The first three settings pertain to allowing the program to download information, including media related to music, details about music files, and usage rights for music that is protected by Digital Rights Management (DRM). DRM is a system designed to prevent the illegal duplication of music and video files. DRM systems work by requiring a media player application to connect automatically to the Internet to determine whether the user has the appropriate rights to play the file. All three of these options require outbound access to the Internet, which some users might consider a privacy issue.

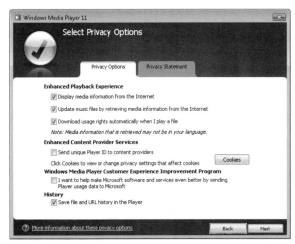

Figure 4-33   Configuring Privacy Options settings in Windows Media Player

The Send Unique Player ID To Content Providers check box is cleared by default. When enabled, this setting allows Windows Media Player to send a unique identifier automatically to content providers so that they can customize their experience. Customers can also choose to send anonymous usage information to the Microsoft Customer Experience Improvement Program. There is an option related to whether file and URL history are stored within Windows Media Player. The next step involves determining whether a new Windows Media Player shortcut should be created on the desktop and whether it should appear in the Quick Launch toolbar.

The Custom Settings option also enables users to specify whether they want to make Windows Media Player the default music and video player. If this option is selected, all of the file types that are supported by Windows Media Player are associated with the program. This means that when any of those file types are played, Windows Media Player is automatically launched. The second option allows users to select manually which file associations are set up. (You'll learn more about file associations later in this lesson.)

The final option enables users to specify an online music store. The default is the URGE music service, which has partnered with Microsoft. If you select this option, the appropriate software is downloaded and installed. Users can also choose not to set up the store and finish the installation.

After the process is complete, Windows Media Player is launched. Figure 4-34 shows the default Library view of the player. Windows Vista includes several sample music files that the library automatically indexes.

Figure 4-34   Viewing music information in the Windows Media Player Library view

Working with Windows Media Player

Microsoft designed Windows Media Player with an intuitive user interface that most customers find quick and easy to learn. Rather than relying on standard menus, the primary portion of the user interface is divided into numerous sections that pertain to specific commonly used tasks, as follows:

- **Now Playing**   This section always shows any audio or video files that are currently playing as well as any media files that you have queued for playback (see Figure 4-35). When playing audio files, Windows Media Player can display visualizations. A visualization is a display feature that shows graphics that are designed to match the music that is playing. Options for managing visualizations are available by right-clicking in the main portion of the display.

Figure 4-35   Playing music in Windows Media Player

- **Library**   Many customers have large collections of music files on their computers. The Library view provides a convenient way of viewing all of these files. The Library section on the left side of the display enables users to access content based on artist, album, song name, genre, year, and rating. To play a music file or set of music files, users can right-click the item in the center display and choose the appropriate option.

- **Rip**   The term *rip* refers to copying content from a music or other audio CD. Ripping involves copying and compressing the data and storing it in the computer's file system. The Rip Music tab automatically displays information about the disc that has been inserted in the CD/DVD-ROM device. If the automatic downloading of information from the Internet is allowed, Windows Media Player attempts to download all of the details about the CD (including song titles, the album title, and related data).

- **Burn**   Burning media involves copying files that are currently located on the computer's hard disk to writable CD media. Generally, this requires Windows Media Player to convert the files automatically to an uncompressed format that standard CD and DVD players can read. For this option to be available, the computer must be configured with a CD or DVD writing device. To add items for burning to media, users can select and drag the appropriate items to the Burn List section, located on the right side of the screen.

- **Sync**   Many users have portable media devices such as MP3 players to which they want to copy music. Often, they want to add, remove, or replace songs that are stored on the device. Windows Media Player is able to detect a wide variety of different types of devices automatically. When a new device is plugged in, users are given the option of specifying whether the device should be made available to Windows Vista. If it is, users can drag and drop items from the library for synchronization with the removable media device. The Start Sync button begins the process of copying the information.

MORE INFO   **Recommending portable music devices**

The portable music player industry provides a large range of options to consumers. Because many players have different hardware and software requirements, customers are often confused about which options work best. When evaluating products for customers who plan to use Windows Media Player, look for the Plays for Sure logo. This designation specifies that the product has been designed to be compatible with the synchronization features in Windows Media Player 11. For more information about compatible products, see *http://www.microsoft.com/windows/windowsmedia/playsforsure/default.aspx*.

- **Online Music Store**   For users who have selected a default online music store, an icon appears in the top-right corner of the Windows Media Player user interface for choosing to access the site. You can also access most music sites directly by using a Web browser, but browsing through Windows Media Player often provides a simplified experience for hearing samples of files and downloading purchased songs.

Each of these task sections also includes additional commands that you can access by clicking the small downward arrow that is located under the icon. For example, in the Now Playing section, menus are available for choosing visualization settings.

Configuring Windows Media Player Options

In addition to the standard tasks that are available in the default Windows Media Player view, the program includes many different configuration options. To access these settings, in the drop-down menu for any of the available tasks, select More Options. All of these commands open the Options dialog box, but they automatically display the most relevant collection of settings. Figure 4-36 shows an example of accessing basic player settings.

The many different settings that are available are generally self-explanatory. For example, on the Rip Music tab, there are options for determining where ripped music should be stored. The details also enable you to choose the format for compression along with related details about the audio quality (see Figure 4-37).

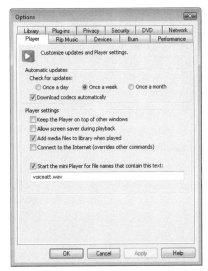

Figure 4-36 Player tab settings in the Options dialog box

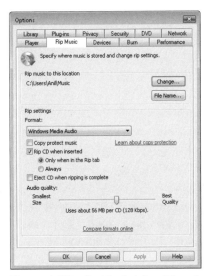

Figure 4-37 Rip Music tab settings in Windows Media Player

Exam Tip One of the best ways to learn about the many different options of Windows Media Player is to browse through the different tabs in the Options dialog box. If you are unsure of the exact purpose of a feature, click Help to view associated descriptions. It's certainly not necessary to memorize each option when preparing for Exam 70-623. Rather, focus on the types of available configuration settings and how customers can use them.

Installing Codecs

Compression is one of the primary technology features that enables for computers to store large quantities of audio information. For example, a standard uncompressed audio CD can be as large as approximately 700 MB. When compressed, the total size of the disc is usually less than 100 MB. This enables users to store more information on their computers.

There are two major compression methods. The first is lossless compression, which ensures that the quality of the resulting compressed file retains 100 percent of the quality of the original file. The compression is obtained by using mathematically lossless algorithms. The effects are similar to compressing files such as Microsoft Word or Microsoft PowerPoint documents. The other method, lossy compression, actually results in the quality of the compressed audio or video being lower than the quality of the source material. The benefit, however, is that the content usually achieves a much higher level of compression. Often, users are unable to detect the differences and find the slight loss in quality to be an acceptable trade-off for reduced storage space requirements.

The actual software that performs the compression and decompression is known as a codec (or compressor/decompressor). Windows Media Player supports several different types of compression, by default. For example, it can automatically play Windows Media Audio (.wma), Windows Media Video (.wmv), and MP3 audio files. Users who download media from the Internet might find that they need to obtain additional codecs to play a file in Windows Media Player. In some cases, Windows Media Player is able to download the required codec automatically (this option is enabled on the Player tab of the Options dialog box). In other cases, users might need to download the required codec manually. For more information about downloading plug-ins for Windows Media Player, see the WMPlugins Web site at *http://www.wmplugins.com/*. Some codecs are available free, but others must be purchased.

As a Consumer Support Technician, a common issue that you will run into is users who report that they cannot play a standard DVD in their computer. Assuming that they have a compatible DVD-ROM device, the most likely cause of the issue is that they do not have an appropriate DVD decoder installed. In some cases, hardware or software that the customer has already purchased might include the appropriate codec. In other cases, the user needs to purchase, download, and install one from one of various online vendors.

Using Windows Photo Gallery

Customers who often use their digital cameras and Internet connections to download photos can collect hundreds or thousands of pictures on their computers. Because many devices use nonintuitive default file names, the process of organizing these files can become very difficult. Windows Photo Gallery has been designed to provide a quick and easy way to view and organize graphics files. In this section, you'll learn how this application works.

MORE INFO   **Windows Photo Gallery and hardware requirements**

Most of the features and functions in Windows Photo Gallery run properly as long as the computer meets the minimum Windows Vista system requirements. (For more details on these requirements, see Chapter 1, "Preparing to Install Windows Vista.") Some features, such as certain slide show options, might require additional video hardware capabilities. When this occurs, the application informs the user of the specific requirements that have not been met.

Working with Windows Photo Gallery

There are two main ways in which you typically access Windows Photo Gallery. The first is by launching the program directly. You can do this by searching for it in the Start menu or by selecting it from the All Programs group. When you open it in this way, Windows Photo Gallery automatically shows a list of known photo and video files on the computer. Figure 4-38 shows the default view of the application.

Figure 4-38   The default view of Windows Photo Gallery

The other way to launch Windows Photo Gallery is by double-clicking a file of an associated file type (you'll learn more about setting file type associations later in this lesson). For example, if a bitmap (.bmp) file is opened, Windows Photo Gallery opens automatically and displays the file.

Adding Folders to Monitor

By default, Windows Photo Gallery automatically accesses photos and video files that are stored in the computer's default locations. This includes the contents of the current user's Pictures and Videos folders (located within the C:\Users*Username* folder). Additionally, the contents of the Public Pictures and Public Videos folders are included. Windows Vista includes several default photos and videos as samples.

To add additional folders to be monitored, from the File menu, select Add Folder To Photo Gallery. This enables you to browse to a local or network folder and view those files directly. It is also possible to add files manually by dragging and dropping them from Windows Explorer into the Windows Photo Gallery view.

Viewing and Managing Media

The default Windows Photo Gallery view displays all of the known photo and video files that are available. To enable you to work with large numbers of files, the left side of the interface can organize the display based on many different criteria. Examples include the date the picture was taken, specific folder locations, and tags.

Tags are pieces of information that are attached to files to help identify their content. Any image can contain one or more tags. There are two main methods of adding tags. The first is to double-click an image to open it in the photo viewer. The right side of the user interface includes a list of all of the tags that are assigned to that image (see Figure 4-39).

Figure 4-39 Viewing tags related to a picture file

Manually typing tags can become a tedious process when dealing with large numbers of files. Fortunately, there's an easier way. To add a tag to many different files at the same time, select the files on the right side of the main Windows Photo Gallery interface, and then drag and drop them onto a tag item on the left side of the interface. The tag is automatically added to those files.

Photo and video capture devices such as digital cameras and digital video recorders automatically add information to file properties. You can access these properties by right-clicking the file, selecting Properties, and then clicking the Details tab. Figure 4-40 shows an example. Although it is not as easy to do, you can also modify picture properties directly in this dialog box.

Figure 4-40   Viewing details about a photo

Importing Files

After taking photos with a digital camera or recording video, users often want to download the contents directly to their computers. Windows Photo Gallery includes an Import From Camera Or Scanner command on the File menu to allow for automatically downloading the files. The Import Pictures And Videos dialog box attempts to locate any media files that are on the device and then allows the user to select one or more items to import. This is a quick and easy way to add media to the computer without having to worry about file system locations. To configure the details of where imported media files are stored, from the File menu, select Options, and then click the Import tab. Figure 4-41 shows the available options.

Figure 4-41   Configuring Import tab settings for Windows Photo Gallery

Fixing Photos

When viewing an individual photo, users often want to correct common mistakes or make changes to what was captured. The Fix button on the toolbar of the photo viewer is designed to make this process quick and easy. The available options are shown in Figure 4-42 as follows:

- Auto Adjust
- Adjust Exposure
- Adjust Color
- Crop Picture
- Fix Red Eye

These commands address the most common operations performed on photos. In some cases, users might be happy with the Auto Adjust option, which attempts to determine mathematically the best color and exposure settings. Alternatively, they can manually adjust these options using slider bars or other tools. By default, Windows Photo Gallery automatically saves a copy of the original image when you choose one of the fix options. You can configure the application to automatically delete backups from the File menu by selecting Options and clicking the General tab. Automatically deleting the backup files frees additional disk space on the computer.

Figure 4-42   Fixing photos in Windows Photo Gallery

E-Mailing Photos

Users often want to share photos with their friends and family through e-mail. A potential problem, however, is that the original photos that are captured by a digital camera are often very large. This makes the process of sending files slow and, in some cases, can result in attachments that exceed the limit of an e-mail service provider. The E-mail button provides an easy way of resizing the file and automatically creating an e-mail message with an attachment. Figure 4-43 shows an example of the picture size options. Smaller file sizes result in less detail, but the file size is also smaller.

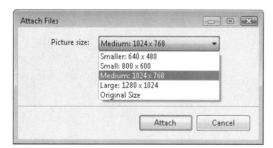

Figure 4-43   Selecting picture size details for e-mailing a photo

Using Windows Movie Maker

Windows Movie Maker is a digital video editing application that enables users to create their own movies. It also allows users to compile these productions to files or burn them to media such as a DVD. In the past, dealing with video files was challenging. The files are often very large and must be cut into smaller pieces. Typical tasks include assembling media content into segments and creating transitions between them. Windows Movie Maker provides a simple but powerful way of dealing with these files (see Figure 4-44). In this section, you'll learn how to work with Windows Movie Maker.

Figure 4-44   The default display of Windows Movie Maker

Understanding Hardware Requirements

Working with video files often requires additional system specifications beyond the minimum hardware required to run Windows Vista. To use Windows Movie Maker, the computer must have a graphics adapter that is capable of providing hardware acceleration. In addition, users who want to capture their own video need a digital video recorder device that is compatible with Windows Vista. The most common types of recorded devices use either USB or IEEE 1394 (FireWire) connections.

Windows Movie Maker is designed to work directly with digital video. If users want to access analog video (such as movies recorded on VHS videotapes), they need to use an analog capture device. These devices are available from third-party manufacturers and can convert analog signals into digital ones.

Understanding the User Interface

The Windows Movie Maker user interface is divided into several different sections. The top menu bar includes the standard Windows options, such as the ability to load and save files. The toolbar includes context-sensitive shortcuts that change based on the specific item you select. The left side focuses on the major types of tasks that you perform when creating movies: importing media, editing the media, and finally publishing the movie.

The center portion of the interface shows options for media, effects, or transitions that you can drag to the storyboard or timeline. The storyboard or timeline is located at the bottom of the window and provides the location where the final sequence for the movie is created. The storyboard view is a simpler way of working with clips. It allows for dragging imported media and effects directly without worry about the total time of each segment. The timeline view is more advanced and allows for controlling the duration of clips as well as for changing the audio portion and controlling title overlays.

Finally, the right side of the user interface provides a video player that you can use to preview clips or the finished movie. It includes a Split command for using the current time to create a new media clip. Although Windows Movie Maker might seem confusing to users at first, most customers find that it provides an intuitive way of working with video content.

Importing Media

The first step in working with video in Windows Movie Maker is importing the data to be used in the final movie. The content can come from a variety of different sources. The Import section in the Tasks list of the Windows Movie Maker interface provides the following options:

- From Digital Video Camera
- Videos
- Pictures
- Audio Or Music

After you import the media files, they are available for dragging to the timeline and storyboard.

Editing Movies

The main components of a movie include imported media, effects, transitions, and titles and credits. To add any of these options to the movie, select the associated editing item, and then drag and drop it onto the timeline or storyboard. Figure 4-45 shows an example of the available effects that you can add to a component of the movie.

Figure 4-45   Choosing from among available Windows Movie Maker effects

To preview a portion of the video, select it in either the timeline or storyboard, and then play it in the media player. Figure 4-46 shows an example of a movie clip that contains multiple images and videos.

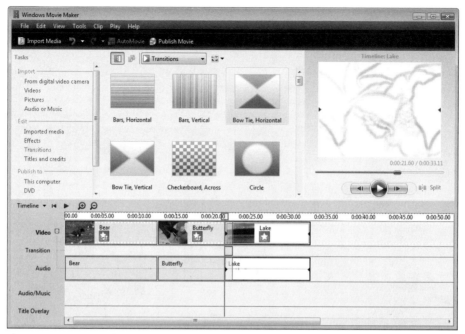

Figure 4-46   Assembling a movie using the Timeline view

Publishing Movies

The final step in creating a movie is publishing it. The publishing process compiles all of the files, effects, transitions, and other details that are in the storyboard and timeline down to the required type of file. Publishing destinations include the following:

- **This computer**   Creates a local file that includes the entire contents of the movie. Options are available for selecting the quality and format of the resulting file (see Figure 4-47). The Movie Settings section shows the details along with the estimated file size (if applicable).

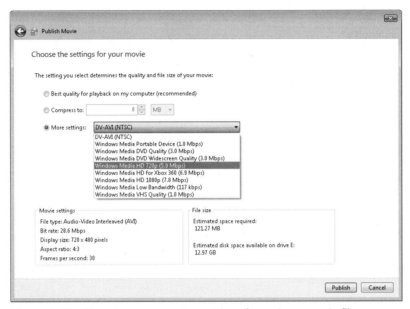

Figure 4-47 Choosing compression settings for saving a movie file

- **DVD** Burns the video to DVD media, using the Windows Vista burning application. The resulting video might not be playable in all DVD players but will be accessible on computers running Windows Vista.
- **Recordable CD** Compresses the resulting movie to fit on a recordable CD, if possible.
- **E-mail** Significantly compresses the video to make it the smallest possible size for sending through e-mail.
- **Digital Video Camera** Outputs the finished movie to a digital video camera that supports it. Many digital video cameras can record content directly from a computer.

Windows Movie Maker places all of the common steps that are required to create a video file together into an easy-to-learn user interface.

Using Windows Media Center

Over time, computers have increasingly become a part of the consumer's entertainment experience. The process of downloading and sharing photos, music, and video files has become common for many users. However, most of these operations have remained limited to display only on a computer. For many home users, the ability to access media content in their living room and on their televisions would be a welcome addition. Microsoft designed Windows Media Center to bring multimedia experiences to all areas of the home. It includes the ability to record and watch live TV using a TV tuner card and to access many different types of online content. It also supports the use of "extender" devices such as the Xbox 360 for bringing multimedia into rooms that do not have PCs. In this section, you'll learn the details of working with Windows Media Center.

MORE INFO   Obtaining Windows Media Center

Windows Media Center is included with Windows Vista Home Premium and Windows Vista Ultimate. For more information about features included in each edition of Windows Vista, see Chapter 1. Prior to Windows Vista, the Media Center feature was available only in an operating system version known as Windows XP Media Center Edition. Most customers who used this version acquired it with the purchase of a new computer.

Understanding the Windows Media Center System Requirements

Some features of Windows Media Center require hardware and software features that exceed the minimum system requirements of Windows Vista. First, users who want to record analog or digital television content must purchase and install a compatible TV tuner device. These devices can receive and decode analog or digital television signals. They often accept input from an antenna (for over-the-air broadcasts) or from a digital or analog physical connection (such as coaxial cable). The devices can be internal Peripheral Component Interconnect (PCI) cards or external USB devices. Whenever possible, you should look for devices that specifically state that they are designed for use by Windows Media Center.

To record two programs at once, users can choose to install more than one TV tuner in the computer. Customers should also ensure that they have adequate disk space to store the content they want to record. Some types of media can use large volumes of disk space. For example, recording a 30-minute television show in high-definition (HD) quality can require approximately 4.0 GB of space.

It is still possible to use Windows Media Center without installing a TV tuner card. In this case, users are not able to record TV, but they can still use the program to access photos, video, and music files that are stored on the computer.

Performing the Initial Setup

You can launch Windows Media Center by searching for it in the Start menu or by finding the application icon in the All Programs group. When a user starts Windows Media Center for the first time, the user must perform some initial configuration steps. The Windows Media Center user interface is optimized to run within a window on a computer and for use while attached to a television set. A keyboard can be used to perform all functions, and a mouse is also supported. The standard graphical display of Windows Media Center uses large fonts to improve readability on standard-definition televisions.

Figure 4-48 shows the initial setup page when running Windows Media Center for the first time. The Express Setup option uses the most common settings and is the quickest and easiest way for users to get up and running. Users are able to make settings changes later if the defaults are not what they want to use.

Figure 4-48 Performing the initial configuration of Windows Media Center

The Custom Setup option walks users through the entire process, step by step. The entire process is spread across numerous steps (to limit the amount of information shown on each screen). The Enhanced Playback step allows users to specify whether Windows Media Center should be allowed to connect to the Internet to download additional content and information, including music information (such as album cover art) as well as links to additional content such as online TV programs.

The Optional Setup section enables users to configure Windows Media Center based on their speaker options. This is particularly useful if the computer is connected directly to a home theater receiver or to specific speaker types. The other optional setting is to specify which folders are monitored for music, pictures, and video content. Figure 4-49 shows the options.

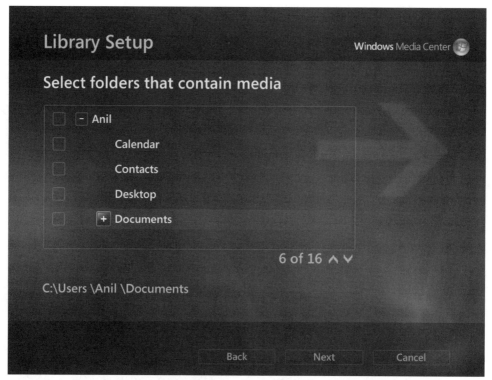

Figure 4-49   Adding folders to watch in Windows Media Center

Configuring a TV Tuner

After you install a TV tuner device in the computer, users need to perform an initial configuration process. The first step enables users to select whether the configuration process should be performed manually or automatically.

If you choose the manual option, the following steps must be completed:

1. Choosing whether to use the Program Guide.
2. Agreeing to the terms of service for the Program Guide (if enabled).
3. Entering the ZIP code (which is used for determining which program guide options are available).
4. Downloading the TV Program Guide over the Internet.
5. Testing the signal strength of the antenna (see Figure 4-50). This is helpful for determining which TV stations are available and the strength of each signal. Users can also attempt to reorient or relocate their antenna to get better reception.

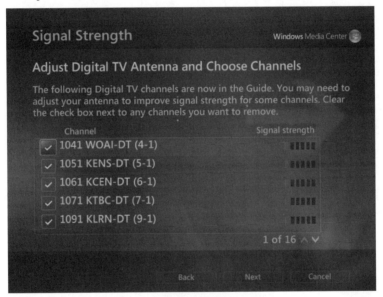

Figure 4-50   Testing the signal strength of a digital TV tuner

After the TV tuner setup process is complete, users are able to record TV programs and access the Program Guide to view TV listings automatically.

Working with Windows Media Center

The main Windows Media Center user interface is shown in Figure 4-51. You can access the various options by moving up or down (using the keyboard, a mouse wheel, or another controller). You can select the options for a particular type of media by moving left or right.

The user interface is designed to organize all of the many available functions intuitively. Figure 4-52 shows an example of the Music Library view, which includes album art and additional details.

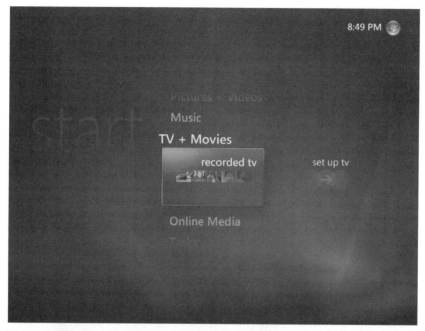

Figure 4-51   The main Windows Media Center screen

Figure 4-52   Using the Windows Media Center Music Library

Many different options and settings are available in the Settings section. Figure 4-53 shows the different categories that you can access after the initial setup process completes.

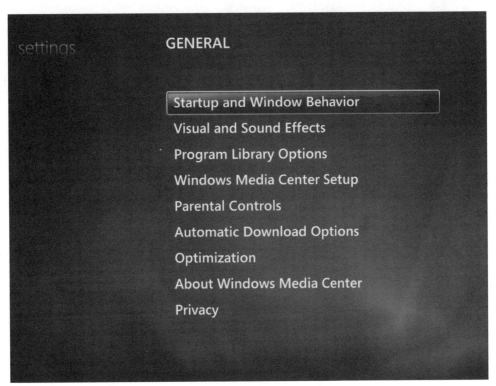

Figure 4-53   Accessing general setup and configuration options

Adding a Windows Media Center Extender

One of the most useful features for Windows Media Center home users is the ability to add compatible extender devices. An extender device is able to connect to Windows Media Center using a network and to display content on a television or other device. One example of an extender is the Microsoft Xbox 360 console. Other compatible devices are available from third-party hardware vendors.

The primary benefit is that the computer running Windows Media Center does not have to be located in the same room as the TV device. For security reasons, the process of setting up an extender requires obtaining an eight-digit setup key from the extender device and providing it within Windows Media Center. Figure 4-54 provides an example of this setup step.

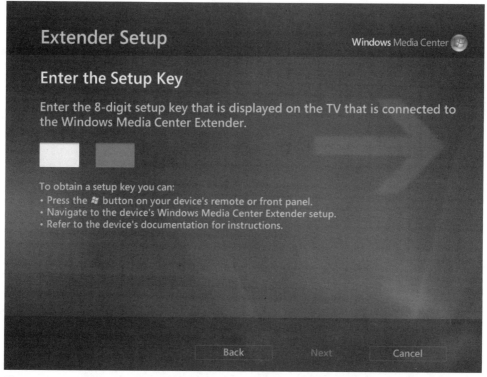

Figure 4-54   Configuring an extender device in Windows Media Center

Managing and Troubleshooting File Associations

Due to the popularity of working with media files on home computers, there are dozens of vendors that provide programs for viewing, managing, and creating audio and video content. File associations are used to determine the default application that is launched when a program is executed. For example, when a user clicks a Microsoft Word document (which is identified by a .doc or .docx file extension), Windows Vista launches Microsoft Word, and the document is loaded and displayed.

Users can change the default application that is associated with various file types by managing file associations. One method of choosing the appropriate application for a file is to right-click the file and select Open With. The resulting menu shows the registered programs that are able to open or work with that file. For example, when you right-click an MP3 file, you can choose which media player application should open the file.

When you install new applications, users might find that their file associations have been modified. For example, a new music player application that is installed along with a portable MP3 player might become the default program for playing back MP3 files. In previous versions of Windows, the process of selecting default applications was tedious and involved searching through long lists of file types. Windows Vista includes a new method of changing file associations. To access these settings, open Control Panel, click Programs, and then click Default Programs. Figure 4-55 shows the available options. In this section, you'll learn two ways of associating file types with programs.

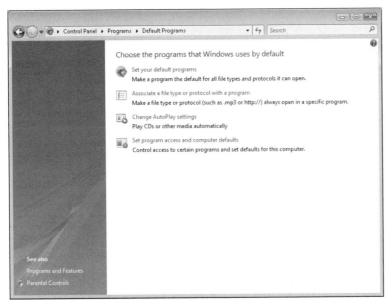

Figure 4-55   Viewing default program options in Control Panel

Setting Default Programs

A typical operation for fixing file associations is to reset all of the supported file type associations for a specific program. For example, if several different types of media files are no longer automatically opening in Windows Media Player, you can quickly resolve the problem with just a few mouse clicks. To access this feature, click Set Your Default Programs in the Default Programs Control Panel window (see Figure 4-56).

Windows Vista automatically lists all of the current programs that are registered with the system and that are manageable using the Set Default Programs dialog box. To change file associations, select one of the programs on the left side of the user interface. The right side shows some basic information about the program. It also shows how many of the default file types that are supported by the application are currently assigned to it.

There are two main commands. The first, Set This Program As Default, automatically determines which types of files are supported by the application and then associates those files with the program. For example, when you select Windows Photo Gallery, all of the different image file formats (such as .jpg, .bmp, and .png) are automatically associated with Windows Photo Gallery.

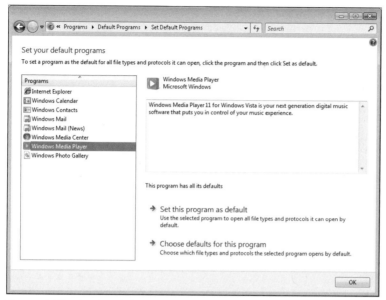

Figure 4-56 Setting default program settings

The second option, Choose Defaults For This Program, enables users to specify which of the program's default associations should be set. Figure 4-57 shows an example for the Windows Media Player application. Note that, in addition to setting file associations, protocols can also be configured. These settings usually apply to accessing a certain type of media (such as an audio file), using a URL in a Web browser such as Microsoft Internet Explorer.

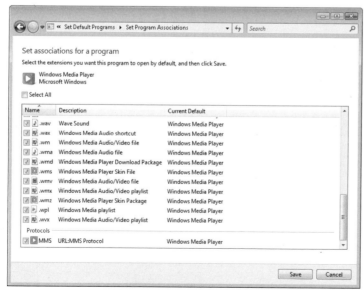

Figure 4-57 Setting associations for a specific program

You can add or remove associations from the program by using the associated check boxes. The method of changing program defaults can be the quickest way of getting the desired file association configuration.

Associating File Types with Specific Programs

In addition to setting default programs based on installed programs' capabilities, it is also possible to set file associations manually for each specific file type. Although the process is generally more time-consuming, it does allow for fine-grained configuration. To access these settings, click the Associate A File Type Or Protocol With This Program link in the Default Programs dialog box. As shown in Figure 4-58, the system displays a list of all of the known file types that are registered on the local computer.

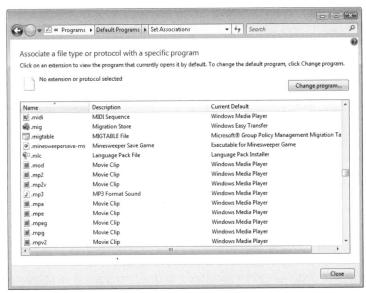

Figure 4-58 Manually associating a file type with a specific program

The complete list includes hundreds of items. The list can be sorted based on the name, description, or the current default program. To change the association, select a file, and then click Change Program. A list of known compatible programs is provided.

You can choose one of the listed programs, or you can click Browse to locate the program file that should be associated with the extension.

Using Set Program Access and Computer Defaults

Windows Vista provides default shortcuts and settings that pertain to commonly used types of programs. For example, in the Start menu, users might see items labeled Internet and E-mail.

These links are designed to load the system's default applications for these functions. When multiple programs that support the same functionality are installed, however, users might want to change the default setting. A common example is when multiple Web browsers are available, and users want to change the default browser that is opened by the Internet link.

You can modify the associated program defaults by clicking the Set Program Access And Computer Defaults link in the Default Programs Control Panel window. Figure 4-59 shows an example of the settings.

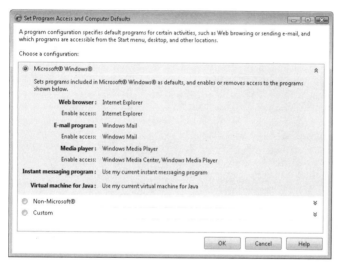

Figure 4-59   Setting program access and computer defaults options

The user interface includes three main options. The first option, Microsoft Windows, specifies that all of the default program associations are set back to their initial configuration when you installed Windows Vista. The text specifies which associations are removed and which are added (if applicable). The second option, Non-Microsoft, automatically attempts to use a non-Microsoft program when other default options are available. For example, if the Mozilla Firefox browser is installed, it becomes the default Web browser for the system.

The final option, Custom, enables you to select default applications individually (see Figure 4-60). This section of the dialog box includes a list of all of the registered applications for each type of program. You use the options to determine which file associations should be changed.

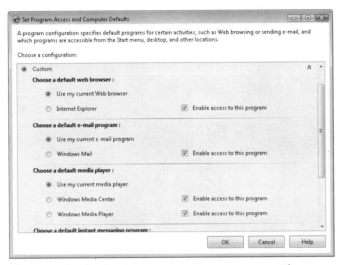

Figure 4-60   Configuring custom program access settings

The file associations features enable users to remain in control of which applications are used by default for working with media and other file types.

Changing AutoPlay Settings

Windows Vista includes a convenience feature called AutoPlay that automatically reacts to the insertion of new media or devices on the computer. For example, when an audio CD is placed in a drive, users are given the option of what they want to do. Users can specify what they wish to do (and optionally to retain the setting for that media type in the future). For most types of media, there are many different available options.

The Default Programs Control Panel window includes a Change AutoPlay Settings link for changing the default behaviors for various file types. Figure 4-61 shows an example.

In addition to choosing one of the available options, you can also choose Take No Action (which doesn't perform any automatic action) or Ask Me Every Time (which presents a prompt for what the user wants to do). Finally, there is a Reset All Defaults button that you can use to clear the settings for every type of media.

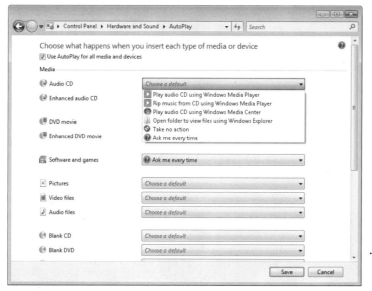

Figure 4-61   Changing AutoPlay settings in Control Panel

Quick Check

1. What is the most likely cause of a DVD movie failing to play in Windows Media Player?
2. What are two ways to add pictures for viewing in Windows Photo Gallery?
3. What types of media can you import into a Windows Movie Maker project?

Quick Check Answers

1. The most likely cause is a missing codec for decoding DVD media. This codec can be obtained from third-party vendors online.
2. You can choose to add folders to watch from the File menu, or you can drag and drop files into the Windows Photo Gallery interface.
3. Windows Movie Maker enables you to import video files, video data from a digital video camera, pictures, and audio.

Practice: Working with Windows Media Features

In these practice exercises, you apply the information you've learned about working with the media-related applications of Windows Vista. Wherever possible, the steps rely on using the sample music, photos, and video files that are included with Windows Vista.

▶ Practice 1: Working with Windows Media Player

In this practice exercise, you walk through some ways in which you can use Windows Media Player to organize and play back audio files. The steps assume that you have performed the initial configuration steps for Windows Media Player and that you have not moved or deleted the sample music files that are included with Windows Vista. To hear the music files, you need to have configured a sound card and speakers on the computer.

1. Open Windows Media Player from the Start menu or by finding it in the All Programs group.

2. If it is not already selected, click the Library tab at the top of the user interface.

3. To sort the list of music in different ways, start by clicking the Artist link on the left side of the user interface. Notice that the albums appear sorted by the artist's name. You can also click the column headings to sort by other defaults such as number of tracks, the length of the tracks, and your ratings.

4. Double-click any of the album titles to view the songs that are part of the album.

5. Right-click the name of a song and select Add To Now Playing. The song should start playing through your speakers.

6. Next, click the Genre link to view a list of music sorted by the type and style of the artist.

7. Create ratings for some of the sample songs by clicking the appropriate number of stars for each song.

8. Click the Rating link to view a list of songs based on their ratings. You can always change ratings for particular music by using the star icons located next to a track name.

9. When finished, close Windows Media Player.

▶ Practice 2: Using Windows Movie Maker

In this practice exercise, you create a new movie, using Windows Movie Maker. The steps assume that you have not deleted any of the sample audio or video files that were included with Windows Vista.

1. Open Windows Movie Maker from the Start menu or by clicking its icon from the All Programs group.

2. In the Import section of the user interface, click the Videos link.

3. Choose to add the three sample videos that are included with Windows Vista: Bear, Butterfly, and Lake. If the default path does not show these files, they are located within the Public user folder (for example, C:\Users\Public\Public Videos\Sample Videos). Note that thumbnail images of the videos appear in the Clips section of the user interface.

4. In the bottom portion of the user interface, verify that the title shows the Storyboard view. (If it doesn't, you can change it by using the drop-down menu that shows Timeline.)

5. Drag the Bear video to the first spot on the storyboard. Drag the Butterfly movie to the second spot and the Lake video to the third spot.

6. To add transition effects between the videos, select Transitions from the top drop-down list. Drag two different transitions to the location between the video clips.

7. To add effects to the video clips, select Effects from the top drop-down list. Drag three separate effects onto each of the video clips.

8. To preview the movie, select the Bear clip in the Storyboard, and then click the Play button on the right side of the user interface. Notice that the transitions and effects have been added to the video.

9. To publish the video, click the This Computer link in the Publish To section.

10. Choose a name and file system location for the destination movie, and then click Next.

11. Select the default option, Best Quality For Playback On My Computer, and then click Publish.

12. It might take several minutes for the movie to be saved. You can double-click the movie file in Windows Explorer to open it in Windows Media Player or the associated video player application.

13. When finished, close Windows Movie Maker. You can choose to save the project if you would like to edit it further.

Lesson Summary

- With Windows Media Player, you can play, rip, burn, and synchronize audio and video content.
- Users can install additional codecs to add playback functionality to Windows Media Player.
- With Windows Photo Gallery, you can organize and tag photos and video files.
- Windows Movie Maker enables users to create and publish movies that are assembled from digital video data, picture files, and audio files.
- Windows Media Center includes support for recording television on computers that include a digital or analog TV tuner.
- Users can use a Windows Media Center extender device (such as an Xbox 360 console) to access content in other rooms of the house.
- The Default Programs section in Control Panel enables you to edit which programs are associated with which file types.

Lesson Review

You can use the following questions to test your knowledge of the information in Lesson 2, "Using Windows Media Features." The questions are also available on the companion CD if you prefer to review them in electronic form.

NOTE   Answers

Answers to these questions and explanations of why each answer choice is correct or incorrect are located in the "Answers" section at the end of the book.

---

1. You are a Consumer Support Technician assisting a new user of Windows Vista with troubleshooting a problem with viewing images. In the past, she was able to open several different types of images by double-clicking them. Now, when she attempts to open .jpg files in Windows Explorer, the images are not automatically displayed. She would like .jpg files and all other image types to appear in the Windows Photo Gallery viewer. How can she most easily resolve this problem?

   A. Open Windows Photo Gallery and drag the .jpg files onto the image viewer.

   B. Open Windows Photo Gallery and add all of the folders that contain .jpg files to the gallery.

   C. In Control Panel, choose Set Your Default Programs and configure Windows Photo Gallery to be associated as the default for all of its supported file types.

   D. In Control Panel, choose Set Program Access And Computer Defaults and configure Windows Photo Gallery to be the default graphics viewer.

2. You are assisting a customer who has recently purchased Windows Vista Home Premium. He would like to have his Xbox 360 console, located in his living room, access audio and video files, using Windows Media Center. The computer does not currently have a TV tuner card installed. The computer running Windows Vista and the Xbox 360 are configured on the same network. Which of the following steps should the customer perform first to enable the console to connect to his computer?

   A. Generate a setup key on the Xbox 360 console.

   B. Generate a setup key on the computer running Windows Vista.

   C. Add a TV tuner card to the computer running Windows Vista.

   D. Set Windows Media Center as the default player for video files on the computer running Windows Vista.

Chapter Review

To further practice and reinforce the skills you learned in this chapter, you can perform the following tasks:

- Review the chapter summary.
- Review the list of key terms introduced in this chapter.
- Complete the case scenarios. These scenarios set up real-world situations involving the topics of this chapter and ask you to create a solution.
- Complete the suggested practices.
- Take a practice test.

Chapter Summary

- Windows Mail can be used to send and receive e-mail messages and connect to newsgroup servers.
- Windows Calendar enables tasks and appointments management and sharing appointments with other users.
- Windows Meeting Space enables users to collaborate by sharing desktop applications and by sharing files called handouts.
- Windows Media Player provides features for playing audio and video files and for organizing, ripping, burning, and synchronizing audio with other devices.
- Windows Photo Gallery can display and organize large collections of graphics files.
- Windows Media Center enables users to access photos, music, and video content through an extender device and to record television programs by using a TV tuner card.
- File associations can be configured using the Default Programs item in Control Panel.

Key Terms

Do you know what these key terms mean? You can check your answers by looking up the terms in the glossary at the end of the book.

- codec
- file associations
- Internet Message Access Protocol (IMAP)
- Network News Transfer Protocol (NNTP)

- Post Office Protocol (POP3)
- Simple Mail Transfer Protocol (SMTP)
- TV tuner
- Windows Media Center Extender

Case Scenarios

In the following case scenarios, you apply what you've learned about configuring the media and communications features of Windows Vista. You can find answers to these questions in the "Answers" section at the end of this book.

Case Scenario 1: Configuring Windows Mail

You are a Consumer Support Technician assisting a customer with configuring Windows Mail in Windows Vista. The customer has been using a Web-based e-mail service for several years but would like to switch to using Windows Mail. You have verified that her e-mail provider allows for downloading and sending messages, using standard Internet protocols. The customer is particularly concerned about receiving junk e-mail and other unwanted messages. She would also like to be able to categorize messages automatically based on details in the subject line of each message.

1. What information should the customer have before setting up Windows Mail to access her account?
2. What are some of the Junk E-mail filter settings that can help reduce the number of unwanted messages?
3. How can the user automatically categorize messages?

Case Scenario 2: Working with Windows Media Center

You are assisting a new Windows Vista Home Premium user with configuring Windows Media Center in his home. He would like the ability to record two different television shows at the same time. If possible, he would like also to convert his old analog VHS tapes to digital format for preservation. The customer's children want to be able to access music and recorded TV from their Xbox 360 console, which is located in the living room.

1. In addition to the basic requirements for Windows Vista, what additional hardware is required to meet these goals?
2. What is the process for enabling the Xbox 360 to access Windows Media Center over the network?
3. How can the customer copy analog content into Windows Media Center?

Suggested Practices

To help you successfully master the exam objectives presented in this chapter, complete the following tasks.

Using Windows Mail and Windows Calendar

■ **Practice 1: Working with Windows Mail**   Configure Windows Mail to access your own primary e-mail account or a test account that is available from an e-mail service provider. Be sure to collect all of the information you need prior to starting the process. Before checking for new mail, choose to leave all messages on the server by using the advanced options. Create message rules to move messages automatically to specific folders when they are received. Also, configure Windows Mail to connect to the Microsoft Communities news server. Post a test message to a test newsgroup and verify that the message has been posted.

■ **Practice 2: Working with Windows Calendar**   Open Windows Calendar and create several appointments and tasks. Create multiple calendars and calendar groups to allow for categorizing different events. Publish your calendar to a local folder or a shared network location. On another computer running Windows Vista, subscribe to the published Windows Calendar. Make a change on the initial computer and verify that the appointments automatically appear on the second computer.

Using Windows Media Center

■ **Practice 1: Working with Windows Media Center**   Launch Windows Media Center and walk through the initial setup process. Look at the different types of content you can access, including photos, videos, and music. Also, work with the various online content options, including streaming video. If you have access to a TV tuner card, configure it for use in Windows Media Center. Download and access the Program Guide to record specific shows. If you have access to an Xbox 360 console, configure it to work as a Windows Media Center extender device.

Take a Practice Test

The practice tests on this book's companion CD offer many options. For example, you can test yourself on just one exam objective, or you can test yourself on all of the 70-623 certification exam content. You can set up the test so that it closely simulates the experience of taking a certification exam, or you can set it up in study mode so that you can look at the correct answers and explanations after you answer each question.

MORE INFO   Practice tests

For details about all the practice test options available, see the "How to Use the Practice Tests" section in this book's introduction.

Chapter 5
Optimizing Windows Vista Performance

Over time, standard computer hardware has improved dramatically in terms of performance, and new applications and operating system features have been designed to take advantage of those capabilities. By taking full advantage of faster systems, users can enjoy better productivity and a more pleasant experience. The Windows Vista operating system is no exception. To offer the best user experience, it includes many components and features that can be useful for all types of users. Not surprisingly, some of these features require additional resources. For example, Chapter 3, "Configuring and Customizing the Windows Vista Desktop," discussed detailed requirements for the new Microsoft Windows Aero user interface. Other features such as Windows Media Center can require significant CPU, memory, and hard disk resources to complete tasks such as recording and playing high-definition television feeds.

The goal for many computer users is to get the best performance out of their computer hardware. Although some audiences (such as dedicated gamers) might be more actively involved in performance tuning, all users can benefit from applications running more quickly. A common complaint that you'll hear as a Consumer Support Technician is that a system just doesn't "feel" like it's running as fast as it should. There are numerous technical causes for these problems. In some cases, hardware or driver configuration issues might be the cause. It's also possible that malware or other unwanted programs and services are consuming large amounts of system resources. Regardless of the underlying causes, your primary job will be to identify and resolve them.

Microsoft has made performance a key consideration for Windows Vista, and there are many methods for both monitoring and optimizing performance. In this chapter, you'll look at ways in which users and technical professionals can monitor Windows Vista to measure resource use and identify bottlenecks. Then, you examine how you can apply this information to optimizing performance. The result is ensuring that the users you support have the best possible experience with the Windows Vista operating system.

Exam objectives in this chapter:
- Evaluate user's system and recommend appropriate settings to optimize performance.
- Configure Windows Defender.

Lessons in this chapter:

Before You Begin

A basic understanding of computer hardware resources such as CPU, memory, hard disk, and network subsystems will be helpful when working through the content of this chapter. Access to one or more computers running Windows Vista for testing purposes would also be very useful. Finally, the Windows ReadyBoost performance feature requires the use of a removable memory device (such as a SmartCard or USB flash memory stick) that meets the required performance characteristics.

Lesson 1: Using the Windows Vista Performance Tools

As a Consumer Support Technician, some of the most common issues you'll troubleshoot are related to performance. Some computer users might be able to state only that their system "feels slower" than it did when they first purchased or upgraded it. Users who are more technical will be able to describe specific tasks or operations that seem to take longer than they should. The first step to solving the problem is measuring current performance and pinpointing potential problems.

When trying to optimize performance, it is often tempting to make several different changes to see whether the system feels faster. Although this method might work in some cases, it often leads to less-than-ideal configurations. A better solution is to use measured statistics and other evidence to determine what might need to change. In this lesson, you'll cover details related to how Consumer Support Technicians can take a methodical and systematic approach to monitoring the performance of their computers.

After this lesson, you will be able to:

- Describe the Windows Vista tools you can use for troubleshooting common performance-related problems.
- Launch and use Task Manager to get details related to the performance of running applications, processes, and services.
- Use the Windows Sidebar CPU Meter gadget to get an overview of performance.
- Use the Resource Monitor to examine details related to CPU, disk, network, and memory performance.
- Use the Reliability Monitor to determine potential causes of performance issues.
- Generate Performance Reports by using the Reliability and Performance Monitor.
- Describe the Windows Experience Index and how you can use it to evaluate the performance of a computer running Windows Vista.

Estimated lesson time: 45 minutes

Using Performance Monitoring Tools

The process of improving overall system performance usually begins with monitoring the current system. Often, this involves measuring performance statistics related to system components such as the CPU, memory, hard disk, and network adapters. The goal is to identify any system resource bottlenecks that might reduce overall performance. After you identify potential problems, you can move toward resolving those issues (a topic covered in Lesson 2, "Improving System Performance").

In this section, you'll look at an overview of several different performance monitoring tools that are available in Windows Vista. Details include how you use them to monitor performance and ways in which this information might be helpful for resolving common issues.

Real World

Anil Desai

The process of performance monitoring involves many different aspects that you must keep in mind. First, there's an element of mystery solving. After you've identified a problem, you need to collect performance-related clues that help you pinpoint the source of the issue. Second, you need a solid understanding of the ways in which operating systems and applications interact with the underlying computer hardware. So how do you learn these skills?

Troubleshooting actual performance issues is probably the best way to learn and apply performance monitoring skills. Perhaps you're wondering what's happening when a particularly slow application is launched. Is the hard disk a bottleneck? Is there a lack of physical memory? Is the problem network related (perhaps a slow Internet connection)? The steps you take (and tools you use) to determine the source of the problem can greatly improve your support skills. Perhaps the best advice is always to collect and use evidence when making changes. It's often too easy to just "twiddle a few knobs" and hope that will magically fix the issue.

Performance monitoring skills go far beyond just supporting an operating system such as Windows Vista. If you decide to move into an IT professional role (such as working as a system administrator for a corporation), these abilities will help you tremendously in keeping systems running at their best. Overall, the key is to practice troubleshooting these issues whenever possible.

Understanding Task Manager

Modern operating systems can run dozens of different processes and applications, all at the same time. Some of these processes are obvious; for example, when you use Microsoft Word to write a new document, it's easy to see that it's running. Other applications and services might not have a user interface. When working with the Windows Vista operating system, you'll often want to get a quick view of all of the processes that are running on the system. The Task Manager is a quick way to obtain these details.

There are several ways to launch the Task Manager utility, including the following:

- **Start menu** Searching on the string "taskmgr" quickly provides a link to open the application.
- **Taskbar** When you right-click the Windows Vista taskbar, you'll see an option to launch Task Manager directly. This helps ensure that Task Manager is located only a couple of clicks away, regardless of the number of applications that are running on the system.

- **Keyboard shortcut**   You can quickly open Task Manager by using the Ctrl+Shift+Esc keyboard combination. Although it might not be the easiest method to remember, this shortcut enables you to launch Task Manager even when many other windows are open.

The Task Manager user interface automatically updates with the latest details and statistics related to system performance. For example, whenever you start a new application or service, it appears on the corresponding tab of the interface.

The first three tabs of the Task Manager interface provide details related to programs that are currently running on the computer. Specifically, there are three main views that show this information. Each describes details about a particular type of program that is running on the system.

Monitoring Applications

Most users are aware that they can run numerous programs at the same time within Windows Vista. For example, it's common for users to have Word, Microsoft Outlook, Microsoft Internet Explorer, and other applications running simultaneously. You can see most running programs in the Windows Taskbar and the system tray.

The Task Manager Applications tab shows the current programs that are running on the local computer (see Figure 5-1). Generally, this list corresponds to the open applications that you see on the desktop and in the taskbar.

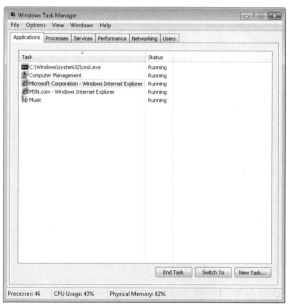

Figure 5-1   Viewing a list of running applications

From a performance monitoring standpoint, this is a good place to check first when encountering performance issues. In some cases, an application might not be responding to the operating system, or unwanted programs might be running. You can easily close these applications by right-clicking the appropriate item and selecting End Task. After you end the task, the system resources it was using (such as CPU time and memory) are returned to the operating system.

NOTE   Exercise caution when stopping programs

When managing applications, processes, and services, it might be tempting simply to shut down a variety of processes that do not seem to be needed. Keep in mind that there are potentially dozens of tasks and services that are required for Windows Vista to run properly. Stopping certain programs from running might cause system instability or prevent important functions from occurring. Also, data loss could occur if a program is not properly terminated. If you want to free up memory by closing Word, for example, it's best to use the application's Exit option.

In general, if you're in doubt about the purpose or function of a particular task, you should leave it alone. Tools such as Windows Defender and antivirus products are often able to determine automatically any unwanted or malicious programs.

Monitoring Processes

The Processes tab in Task Manager lists all of the tasks currently running on the system. In general, every application that is running has at least one associated task. However, the Processes tab contains details related to processes that might not have a user interface or that are running as part of the operating system itself. Figure 5-2 shows an example.

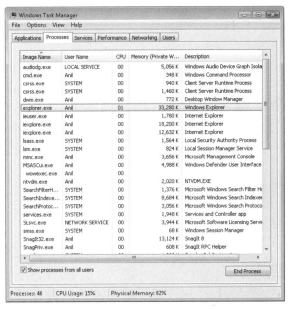

Figure 5-2   Monitoring processes in Task Manager

It can sometimes be difficult to determine what a particular process is used for. Task Manager provides many different pieces of useful information, including the following:

- **Image Name**   This is the name of the actual executable file that is running on the system. In some cases, you can use this name to determine the purpose of the program that is running.
- **User Name**   This is the name of the user context under which the program is running. If the Show Processes From All Users check box is selected, processes from all users are shown. Otherwise, only processes that were launched by the current user are included. Some programs have the name of a user account, whereas others are launched under special system accounts.
- **Image Path Name**   This information provides the fully qualified path for the executable. If the executable name does not provide enough information, sometimes viewing in which folder it is stored can be helpful. This column is not shown by default but can be added using the Select Columns command in the View menu.
- **Description**   This text displays an easy-to-read description of the process that is running, if one is available.
- **CPU**   This listing shows the current percentage of CPU time the process is using.
- **Memory**   This category shows the total amount of memory the process is using.

You can add additional columns to the view by clicking View and choosing Select Columns. These details can be very helpful when troubleshooting performance issues. For example, in some cases, processes might be using large amounts of memory when they are actually not needed. Simply closing the related application (or ending the process) resolves the problem. It is also possible that unwanted processes are running on the system.

One other useful option is changing the priority of a particular process. By default, most processes run under the Normal priority. This tells Windows Vista to provide the same amount of CPU and other resources to each process. It's possible for one or more processes to start consuming a large amount of system resources. In this case, you can right-click the process and choose the Set Priority option to lower its priority. The process continues to run, but other applications on the system get a higher preference for system resources.

Monitoring Services

Windows services are programs that are designed to run independently of a user. Unlike applications such as Internet Explorer, they do not require users to start them manually. Usually, services do not have a user interface, and the operating system manages them automatically. An example is the Windows Defender service, which is designed to start and run whenever the operating system is running. You can configure, start, and stop services by using the Services item in Control Panel. You can launch this tool from the Start menu or by opening Control Panel, clicking the System And Maintenance link, clicking the Administrative Tools link, and then double-clicking Services.

The Services tab in Task Manager shows details related to services that are configured on the computer. The Name and Description columns provide details related to the purpose and function of the service. As with applications and processes, you can right-click a service and choose to stop it. This is useful when you suspect that a particular service is using significant system resources.

Monitoring Performance

So far, you have looked at ways in which you can obtain details about applications, processes, and services that are running on a system. Often, you'll want to get details about overall system resource usage first. The Task Manager Performance tab can provide a quick overview of CPU and memory resources and how they're being used (see Figure 5-3).

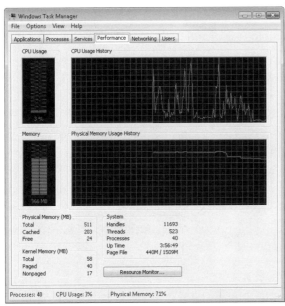

Figure 5-3 Monitoring performance in Task Manager

The CPU Usage and CPU Usage History graphs show the percentage of time that the system's CPU(s) are in use. When the levels are consistently high (for example, above 80 percent), it might indicate that a particular program is slowing down the system. It is also possible that the system might need a hardware upgrade to improve performance.

Similarly, the Memory and Physical Memory Usage History graphs show details about how much random access memory (RAM) the system is using. In most situations, the amount of physical memory that is being used should be less than the total amount of memory being used. Launching numerous applications or running memory-intensive operations can cause these numbers to increase significantly.

The bottom of the display shows additional details related to the number of processes that are running, how long the system has been running, and statistics related to how physical memory is currently allocated. All of these details can provide a quick overview of system resource use and help identify a potential hardware constraint that might be causing slow performance.

Gadgets for Windows Sidebar

The Windows Sidebar provides a great way to keep useful performance-related information available on the desktop. Windows Vista includes the CPU Meter gadget, which is available as part of the operating system (see Figure 5-4). This gadget displays two gauges that show the current amount of CPU use and the percentage of system memory that is currently in use.

Figure 5-4   Using the CPU Meter gadget to monitor CPU and memory use

The CPU Meter provides a convenient way to determine how current system resources are being used. If CPU or memory use is frequently high, this might indicate that there is a performance issue or that the computer could benefit from a hardware upgrade. For more details about using and configuring Windows Sidebar, see Chapter 3.

Resource Monitor

Earlier, this lesson mentioned the importance of monitoring CPU, disk, network, and memory resources on the computer. Although tools such as Task Manager can provide some of these details, the Resource Monitor is designed to provide a quick overview of the details in a single user interface. You can launch the Resource Monitor from the Start menu or from Task Manager by clicking the Performance tab and then clicking Resource Monitor. You can also access the Resource Monitor by searching for the Reliability and Performance Monitor from the Start menu. Figure 5-5 provides an overview of the default view of the Resource Monitor in the Reliability and Performance Monitor application.

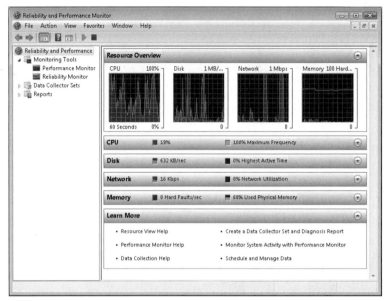

Figure 5-5   Monitoring resource usage with Resource Monitor

The graphs at the top of the display provide a quick overview of resource usage over time. Spikes or sustained high values can indicate a potential performance bottleneck. Because statistics vary based on the capabilities of the underlying hardware, Windows Vista might automatically rescale each graph to reflect current values.

Isolating Performance Issues

The first step in troubleshooting system performance operations often focuses on determining which system resource is being overconsumed. You can use the Resource Monitor's graphs to identify this information quickly. The next step often involves determining which process or processes are using those resources.

To show these details, you can click any of the four sections to expand that portion of the display. Alternatively, you can click one of the graphical displays to expand or collapse the relevant section. The resulting list shows statistics related to processes currently running and how much of that type of resource they're using (see Figure 5-6). You can sort column values easily by clicking them.

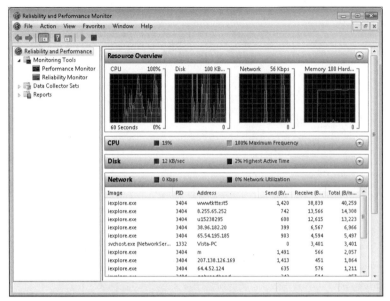

Figure 5-6   Viewing which resources are consuming the most network-related resources

For example, suppose that a user has reported that it is taking far longer than expected to download Web pages. If the problem started after the installation of certain programs, they might be a possible cause of the issue. To get more details, you can launch the Resource Monitor and expand the Network section. By sorting the list by the Total (B/Min) column, you can identify which processes are using the most network bandwidth. (You sort a column by clicking its column heading. Click once to sort the column in descending order; click the column heading a second time to sort in ascending order.)

Reliability Monitor

Changes to a system are often the root cause of performance-related issues. Users might notice a significant decrease in performance after installing a new application, or the installation of new video drivers might lead to slower than expected performance in graphically intensive applications. You can use the Windows Vista Reliability Monitor to obtain a quick overview of important events that might be affecting the system's overall reliability (see Figure 5-7).

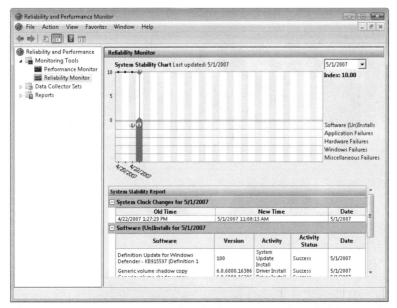

Figure 5-7 Viewing reliability-related information in the Reliability Monitor

When attempting to isolate the source of performance-related complaints, it's useful to consider reliability-related information. The Reliability Monitor keeps track of events such as the following:

- Installation of software
- Removal of software
- Application failures
- Hardware failures
- Windows failures
- Miscellaneous failures

Details related to each type of event are shown in the System Stability Report at the bottom of the details pane. If the onset of a performance problem can be correlated with one of these events, the Reliability Monitor can often help determine the root cause of the issue.

Using Performance Monitor

Windows Vista includes a powerful tool called Performance Monitor. As its name implies, Performance Monitor provides a method for collecting and viewing statistics about particular areas of system performance. There are literally hundreds of performance counters that are available for monitoring in a default Windows Vista installation. In addition, new applications and services often install their own performance counters.

Performance Monitor provides numerous views of statistics and details. Figure 5-8 provides an example. You can view the data over intervals of time. The default display collects new statistics every second and displays 100 points of information (for a total duration of 1 minute and 40 seconds).

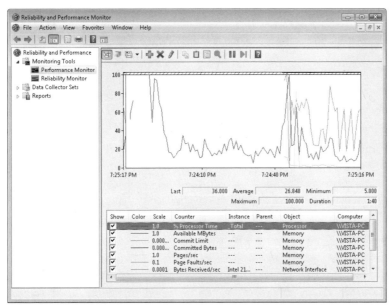

Figure 5-8   Viewing performance statistics with Performance Monitor

Performance Monitor is most useful for troubleshooting specific types of problems. For example, if you suspect that a computer could benefit from a memory upgrade, you can view numerous statistics related to memory performance (see Figure 5-9). Although the list of potential statistics to monitor might seem overwhelming, this data can be useful for performing very detailed performance troubleshooting.

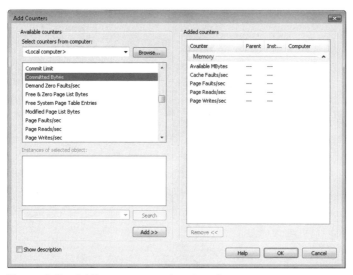

Figure 5-9   Adding memory-related performance counters

NOTE   The full power of Performance Monitor

Performance Monitor is a tremendously useful tool for analyzing and troubleshooting computers. The sheer number of objects and counters can be overwhelming, however. Rest assured, you do not need to memorize all of the options that are available for Exam 70-623. Instead, you should focus on the types of data that you can collect and the overall process of using Performance Monitor.

Using Data Collector Sets

Windows Vista automatically tracks a great deal of information related to overall system performance and operations. The data itself, however, can be difficult to collect without using several different tools and inspecting various log files and settings. The Data Collector Sets feature in the Reliability And Performance Monitor console is designed to help make the process easier.

Each Data Collector Set contains a list of types of information that Windows Vista should record when you start a particular set. This might include performance statistics, application information, Registry values, and operating system settings details. There are four built-in system Data Collector Sets that are included with Windows Vista. They are as follows:

- **LAN Diagnostics**   Used for collecting performance and configuration data related to network services on the local computer. It is useful for troubleshooting network connectivity or performance problems.
- **System Diagnostics**   Returns a report that shows details about the hardware configuration of the computer, the applications and processes that are running, and how current system resources are being used.

- **System Performance** Generates a report that shows performance statistics related to CPU, memory, disk, and network statistics.
- **Wireless Diagnostics** Collects details related to the network configuration and hardware related to wireless network connections.

In addition to using the built-in Data Collector Sets, software developers and system administrators can create their own sets for troubleshooting purposes.

Running a Data Collector Set

You must start Data Collector Sets to collect information and generate reports. You can begin this process from within the Reliability And Performance Monitor console by right-clicking a Data Collector Set and selecting Start. The icon for the item changes to show that it is currently running. After the process is complete, a report is made available. You access the report by expanding Reports in the console tree, then expanding either User Defined or System, expanding the relevant category for the report, and then selecting the appropriate report.

Viewing Reports

The Reports section in the Reliability And Performance Monitor console allows you to view the results that are generated when you run a Data Collector Set. Figure 5-10 shows an example. You can also choose to view the latest report for a particular Data Collector Set by right-clicking its name and selecting Latest Report.

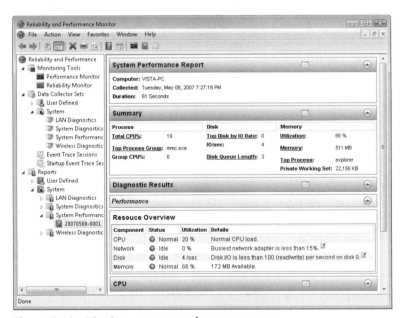

Figure 5-10 Viewing a system performance report

The report itself is highly informative and allows for drilling down into additional details. For example, the Resource Overview section of the System Performance Report provides a high-level summary of the performance of CPU, network, disk, and memory resources. A green light indicates that performance is within acceptable ranges, whereas a yellow or red light indicates that there is a potential resource constraint. You can view in-depth statistics by expanding one or more sections in the report. Figure 5-11 shows an example of the types of details that are provided.

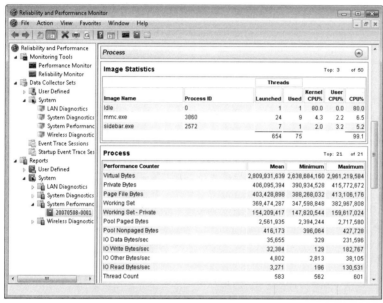

Figure 5-11   Viewing additional details related to memory performance

You can generate multiple reports at different times, and it is often useful to compare the results from earlier reports to detect any changes that might account for performance problems. Overall, you can generate, collect, and analyze a great deal of information simply by running the appropriate Data Collector Set.

Viewing System Information

Often, when working with a computer, you'll want to gather technical specifications related to its hardware and software configuration. You can obtain the details by using several different tools and options, but you would likely need to access many different sections in Control Panel. You'd also have to look for details in the file system, Start menu, and the Registry. All of this can be a time-consuming process. Fortunately, there's a better way.

The System Information utility is designed to collect and present data from the entire Windows Vista system. You can launch it from the Start menu. Figure 5-12 shows an example of the System Summary view. Important details include the operating system name and version, the system manufacturer and model (if available), and details related to the CPU, memory, and other hardware options.

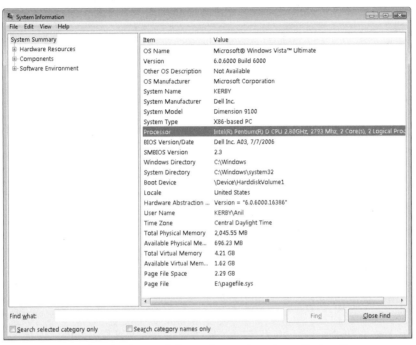

Figure 5-12   Using the System Information tool to view a System Summary

In addition to the System Summary, you can easily drill down into the other major sections. These include the following:

- **Hardware Resources**   This section shows a list of the actual resources that are used by various devices and components in the computer. This information is particularly helpful when troubleshooting hardware-related issues (a topic covered in Chapter 11, "Managing and Troubleshooting Devices").

- **Components**   This section provides details related to the various devices that are connected to the computer. For example, if you're troubleshooting a performance issue related to the network, you can drill down to collect details about the network adapter that is in the system.

- **Software Environment**   This section provides numerous views that can identify the current configuration of the system. A particularly useful section related to performance optimization is the Startup Programs view. As shown in Figure 5-13, this provides a list of all of the programs that are scheduled to run when the computer is started, along with the full command and location of the startup configuration details.

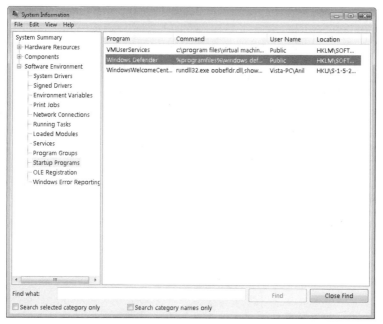

Figure 5-13   Viewing a list of startup programs by using the System Information tool

Working with System Information

Although it is limited to viewing (and not modifying) configuration information, the System Information tool also provides some additional functionality. On the View menu, the Remote Computer option allows this utility to connect to a computer over the network. This is a very useful feature if you're managing multiple computers on a home network or in a test environment.

You can save the data collected by the System Information tool so you can open it later on either the same or another computer running Windows Vista. The default file extension is .nfo. Another useful feature is the ability to export system information to a text file. This enables you to store configuration details for later viewing.

Finally, the sheer volume of information that's available through the System Information tool can be daunting. The Find button at the bottom of the window provides a convenient way to locate particular pieces of information without having to navigate to the appropriate section manually.

Understanding the Windows Experience Index

Evaluating the overall performance characteristics of a computer can be a challenging task. Often, you must consider many different subsystems such as CPU, memory, hard disk, and network components. Performance-related details are very important in a variety of different scenarios. For example, when evaluating software packages, potential users must be able to determine whether the software will run properly on their systems. Traditionally, long lists of technical specifications are provided, and customers are expected to determine whether their systems meet or exceed the requirements.

Most consumers lack the technical knowledge to be able to collect and analyze performance specifications for computer hardware. As a Consumer Support Technician, it's important for you to be able to translate these requirements in a way that is meaningful to users and customers. You also need to be able to run a standard set of tests that can indicate the performance characteristics of a particular computer running Windows Vista.

Evaluating System Performance

To make the process of evaluating system performance easier for both software vendors and consumers, Microsoft has developed a new set of measurements that you can use to approximate the performance of the components within a typical computer. This calculation is known as the Windows Experience Index. The overall base score returned for the entire computer is based on the lowest score of any of the components.

The specific components that are measured include the following:

- **Processor**   Calculations per second
- **Memory (RAM)**   Memory operations per second
- **Graphics**   Desktop performance for Windows Aero
- **Gaming graphics**   3D business and gaming graphics performance
- **Primary hard disk**   Disk data transfer rate

Windows Vista includes a built-in set of tests that you can run for each of these components. Performance-related tests such as these are often called benchmarks. Each of these components receives a particular score when you run the measurement process. The numbers themselves have no units and are designed for relative comparisons. For example, a computer that has a processor component rating of 4.0 is significantly faster than one that has a rating of 2.0.

Viewing the Windows Experience Index Score

By default, Windows Vista performs a Windows Experience Index measurement at the end of the operating system's installation process. You can then view these details by clicking System And Maintenance and then Performance Information And Tools in Control Panel. Figure 5-14 provides an example of a sample Windows Experience Index rating collected from within Windows Vista.

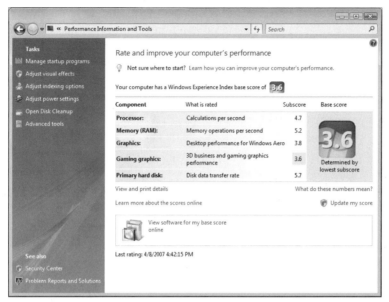

Figure 5-14   Viewing the Windows Experience Index rating for a computer

Of course, it's possible for the system's performance characteristics to change. Changes to the hardware configuration or the installation of new drivers require you to rerun the Windows Experience Index tests.

Using Windows Experience Index Scores

Windows Experience Index scores can be helpful to users in determining the overall performance of their computers. You can also use these scores to assess potential upgrades. For example, if a system's lowest score is for the graphics component, upgrading to a newer or faster video card might provide the most benefit. The scores are also helpful for evaluating software requirements. Rather than stating technical requirements, a minimal score (such as 3.5) can be provided to users.

Software packages that have specific requirements might include recommendations for one or more components. For example, games and entertainment software might require a gaming graphics score of at least 4.5 (see Figure 5-15). Overall, the Windows Experience Index can make the job of evaluating system performance easier for consumers, vendors, and support professionals.

Figure 5-15 Comparing information about a game with the computer's Windows Experience Index rating

---

Quick Check

1. Which Windows Vista performance tool displays graphs related to CPU, memory, disk, and network performance?
2. Which Windows Vista performance feature can you run to generate reports related to system configuration and performance?

Quick Check Answers

1. The Resource Monitor provides graphs that monitor the usage of these system resources.
2. You use Data Collector Sets, which are available from within the Reliability And Performance Monitor console, to collect these details and generate reports.

Practice: Working with the Windows Vista Performance Tools

In these exercises, you perform several tasks on the local computer while monitoring the performance of the system. The goal is to become familiar with the types of information that you can collect with the numerous performance tools available in Windows Vista. In addition to the steps in the practice exercises, you can perform various tasks (such as downloading a large file from the Internet or launching multiple programs) and monitor CPU, memory, disk, and network performance.

▶ **Practice 1: Monitor System Resource Usage**

In this practice exercise, you use the Reliability And Performance Monitor console to track resource usage during various tasks.

1. Open the Reliability And Performance Monitor console from the Start menu.

2. To view details about the reliability of the local computer, under the Monitoring Tools folder, click Reliability Monitor. Make a note of any recent failures, such as application failures, hardware failures, Windows failures, and miscellaneous failures. View the details for any failures that are present.

3. Click any of the items in the Software (Un)Installs row to get details about which applications were added or removed from the system.

4. To start monitoring performance, in the console tree, click the top-level Reliability And Performance item. You will see graphs and details related to CPU, disk, network, and memory performance. This is the same display that you see if you launch the Resource Monitor directly from within Task Manager. Keep this window open while performing the following steps.

5. To generate disk activity, run the Disk Defragmenter program from the Start menu and click Defragment Now when it becomes available.

6. Switch back to Reliability And Performance Monitor and view details related to CPU and disk activity.

7. To get more details about which processes are using the most disk resources, click the Disk graph. Sort the expanded section by the Read B/Min column and note which processes have the highest amount of disk read use.

8. Close the Disk Defragmenter. You might choose to cancel the disk defragmentation process to save time.

   In this step, you update the Windows Experience Index on the computer and monitor the usage of system resources.

9. Open Control Panel and search for Experience. In the results of the search, click the Check Your Computer's Windows Experience Index Base Score link.

10. Verify that Reliability And Performance Monitor is still running, and then click Update My Score to start the process.

11. While the test is running, switch back to Reliability And Performance Monitor and view the details related to the usage of system resources. Note that, depending on the stage of the testing, the display might flicker or update slowly.

12. When the Windows Experience Index process is complete, close all open programs and windows.

▶ **Practice 2: Use Data Collector Sets**

In this exercise, you generate a System Performance report by running a Data Collector Set and viewing the results. This exercise assumes that you have not made any changes to the default settings of the built-in Data Collector Sets.

1. Open the Reliability And Performance Monitor console using the Start menu.

2. Expand the Data Collector Sets folder, expand the System folder, and click the System Performance item. Note that the right pane shows details related to the types of information that will be collected and where the information will be stored.

3. To start the data collection process, right-click the System Performance item and choose Start. This begins the data collection process.

4. While the data collection process is running, right-click the System Performance item and choose Latest Report. This opens the appropriate report in the Reports section of the Reliability And Performance Monitor console. If the report hasn't yet completed, you will see a message stating that it is being generated. The process should take approximately 60 seconds, and the report will appear automatically.

5. Examine the details of the report by scrolling through the various sections. To get more information, you can expand various sections of the report.

6. Answer the following questions based on the information from the System Performance report:

   a. What was the time range for the data collection used by the report?

   b. What was the total CPU use percentage?

   c. What is the amount of memory use?

   d. Which files were causing the most disk I/Os during the test?

   e. Which three processes were using the most memory during the test?

7. When finished, close the Reliability And Performance Monitor console.

Lesson Summary

■ Windows Task Manager provides a quick and easy way to view details about running applications, processes, and services.

■ The Task Manager Performance tab provides a graph and statistics related to CPU and memory usage.

■ The CPU Meter Windows Sidebar gadget provides a way to display processor and memory usage information on the desktop.

■ The Resource Monitor displays graphs of CPU, memory, disk, and network resource use, and it allows for viewing which processes are accessing those resources.

■ Reliability and Performance Monitor enables you to run and view information collected by Data Collector Sets.

- You can use the System Information tool to collect, view, and save details related to the hardware and software configuration of a computer.
- The Windows Experience Index provides ratings of the performance of a computer running Windows Vista.

Lesson Review

You can use the following questions to test your knowledge of the information in Lesson 1, "Using the Windows Vista Performance Tools." The questions are also available on the companion CD if you prefer to review them in electronic form.

NOTE Answers

Answers to these questions and explanations of why each answer choice is correct or incorrect are located in the "Answers" section at the end of the book.

---

1. You are helping a customer troubleshoot a problem related to Windows Vista system performance. The customer reports that, after she installed a new application, Task Manager shows that her CPU use is constantly at 100 percent. The desktop and taskbar currently show no open programs. Which Task Manager tab will most likely help identify which program is using the majority of CPU time?

   A. Applications

   B. Processes

   C. Services

   D. Performance

2. A user reports problems related to slow network performance during certain times of the day. Because the problems started soon after he installed a network-based application, you suspect that the new program might be using significant network resources. Which tool can you use to identify most quickly which processes are currently using the most network resources?

   A. Windows Experience Index

   B. Task Manager

   C. Performance Monitor

   D. Resource Monitor

Lesson 2: Improving System Performance

In many ways, it is human nature to want to optimize the way a system or device behaves. Most of us would like our cars to accelerate faster, especially if it requires only a few minor modifications. The same is true for working with operating systems. Although some users are willing to dedicate time and effort to squeeze every last bit of performance out of their systems, most are not aware of the many ways in which they can configure their systems to run more efficiently.

An important goal for the Windows Vista operating system is to provide the best possible performance for users. When people can use programs more quickly, they tend to be more productive. Numerous enhancements have been included in the core operating system to improve memory, disk, CPU, and network performance.

As a Consumer Support Technician, you're likely to hear complaints about performance issues. For example, a customer might mention that her system is running more slowly after she installed a new application. There are many different aspects related to troubleshooting these issues, and determining which applications and processes should be running is based on the particular needs of the user. Sometimes, it might make sense to remove an application or process that is not used. Spyware, viruses, malware, and other unwanted programs are common examples.

In this lesson, you'll look at ways you can optimize the configuration of Windows Vista to improve overall performance based on user needs.

After this lesson, you will be able to:
- Use MSConfig to troubleshoot startup-related problems.
- Use Windows Defender to configure startup programs.
- Improve performance by using the Disk Defragmentation tool.
- Start and stop services based on users' needs.
- Enable and configure Windows ReadyBoost to improve system performance.

Estimated lesson time: 45 minutes

Developing a Performance Optimization Approach

Perhaps one of the most important aspects of troubleshooting is having a clear and well-defined process. Technical professionals often jump into making changes quickly without a full understanding of the problem. This can lead to less-than-optimal configurations or other related problems.

A performance optimization approach should include several steps, including these important steps in the process:

- **Establish a baseline**   Because the goal of making performance-related changes is to improve overall performance, it's important to know how the system is working currently. Sometimes a baseline must be collected over a long period of time (for example, an entire week or month). In the case of a consumer operating system such as Windows Vista, it's likely that the user has one or more applications that are not running as fast as he or she would like. Taking some brief measurements, such as the time to open a particularly resource-intensive application, can be helpful in determining whether changes have helped the problem.

- **Identify bottlenecks**   Defined simply, a bottleneck is the slowest step in a given process. Given a particular process or workload, it's possible for the CPU, memory, hard disk, or network subsystem to be the overall rate-limiting component. Through the use of performance monitoring, you can determine which aspects of the system are most overworked. These are the areas on which to focus to realize the most improvement.

- **Implement a change**   This step involves actually trying to improve performance. You'll look at many different examples in this lesson, but one idea to keep in mind is that you should minimize the number and types of changes that you make at the same time. For example, if you have three different ideas about how to improve disk-related performance, it's best to make one change first and then measure its effects. Making multiple changes at the same time can cause a variety of problems. Imagine, for example, that you made three different changes. One increased performance by 15 percent, another decreased performance by 10 percent, and the third had no effect. In this case, you have an overall positive effect (a 5 percent increase in performance), and you might conclude that the changes were a positive step. Note, however, that one of the changes actually decreased performance. It would have been easier to detect this by making only one change at a time.

- **Measure performance**   After you've made a change to the system, it's time to determine its effects. Ideally, you will have some kind of test that you can run to see whether you've improved performance. In the previous lesson, you looked at how the Windows Experience Index can provide a basic benchmark of overall performance. Other measures might include the amount of time it takes to start an application or to perform a particularly resource-intensive task. If the change was beneficial, it should probably be retained (unless, of course, it causes some unintended negative effects). Otherwise, it should be rolled back, and another approach should be attempted.

- **Repeat the process (if needed)**   The process of performance optimization can often continue indefinitely. For example, you can continue to isolate and reduce bottlenecks to squeeze more capacity out of a system. The problem, however, is that at some point, the amount of effort it takes to perform optimizations will outweigh the potential benefits. For example, if it takes several hours of time to find a way to increase performance by 2 percent, many users will not find this to be a worthwhile investment. Although it doesn't sound like optimization, often the rule for the process is to stop when performance is good enough.

It is important to keep the steps of the performance optimization process in mind when looking at ways to troubleshoot Windows Vista performance issues.

Using Performance Information and Tools

One of the potential challenges related to changing operating system settings is finding all of the available options. The Performance Information And Tools link in Control Panel provides a starting point for viewing the many available options and utilities. Figure 5-16 shows the tasks that can be launched quickly by using the links on the left side of the window.

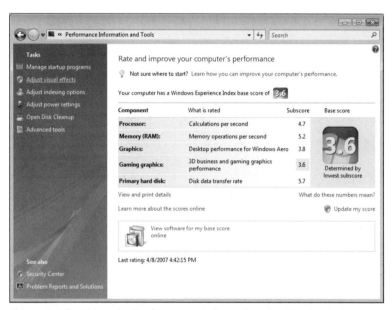

Figure 5-16   Using the Performance Information And Tools window

In addition to these tasks, clicking Advanced Tools in the left pane of the Performance Information And Tools window shows numerous other features that you can launch directly from within Control Panel (see Figure 5-17).

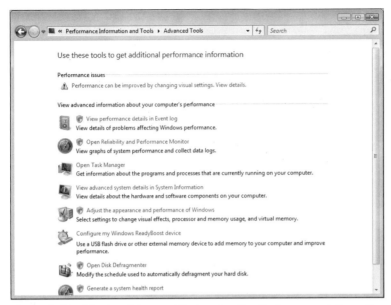

Figure 5-17   Viewing Advanced Tools using the Performance Information And Tools window

You can also launch all of these tasks in other ways. For example, you can access Windows Defender through the Start menu. Indexing, visual effects, and power settings can also be accessed directly from within Control Panel. Overall, however, the Performance Information And Tools window provides a good starting point for the optimization process. You'll learn more about these tasks in this lesson.

Managing Startup Programs

Like most modern operating systems, Windows Vista provides programs with the ability to launch automatically during the startup process. This provides users with ready access to the applications and services that they plan to use. Perhaps the most noticeable examples include the Windows Sidebar, Windows Defender, and other applications that might automatically run whenever a user logs on to the system.

Although automatically running applications on startup or during the logon process can be convenient, it can also lead to performance problems. In some cases, unwanted applications such as malware might be configured to run without requiring any user interaction. Often, users are completely unaware that the program is running. Many of these applications and processes can consume significant system resources, thereby reducing performance.

When attempting to diagnose performance-related problems in Windows Vista, it's often helpful to determine which applications or programs are configured to run automatically. The actual configuration details might be stored in one of several different places, including the

Startup folder and several sections in the Windows Registry. Tracking down these different locations can be difficult. In Lesson 1, you saw how the System Information tool can be used to view details about startup programs. In this section, you'll look at two ways in which the startup settings can be managed.

Configuring Startup Items with MSConfig

Windows Vista includes a System Configuration application known as MSConfig. It can be launched from System Configuration or Msconfig in the Start menu. This utility includes several different tabs that you can use to determine how Windows Vista operates. Specifically, with relation to performance optimization, the Startup tab is very useful. As shown in Figure 5-18, this tab provides a list of all of the programs that are configured to run automatically during the Windows Vista startup process.

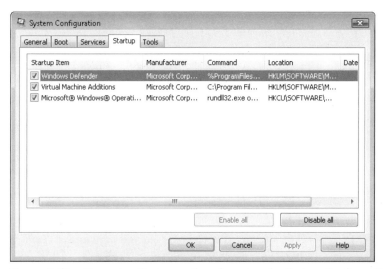

Figure 5-18   Managing Startup options by using the System Configuration (MSConfig) utility

The columns include the following details:

- **Startup Item**   The name of the startup item.
- **Manufacturer**   The manufacturer of the software. This is most commonly the name of a software or hardware company (such as Microsoft Corp.) that created the application.
- **Command**   The full text of the actual command that is being run. Several startup items might include configuration switches as part of the command line.
- **Location**   The file system or Registry location in which the startup information is stored for each item.
- **Date Disabled**   Displays the date on which an item was disabled. By default, this column is blank.

You can disable a startup item by clearing the check box next to the name of that item. This option is a convenient way to troubleshoot potential performance problems caused by these items because clearing an item's check box does not remove the command and other information permanently. If you disable an item, Windows Vista does not run it during the next reboot or logon operation. Additionally, there is a Disable All button that you can use to clear the check boxes automatically for all of the startup items in the list. This option can be useful in cases in which numerous startup programs are making the system slow and unresponsive. A typical performance troubleshooting process involves enabling or disabling an item, rebooting the computer, and re-evaluating system performance.

There is also another way to disable all startup items from running. The General tab (shown in Figure 5-19) includes several options for enabling or disabling device drivers and services. The Selective Startup option includes a Load Startup Items check box. If you clear this check box, no startup items run, regardless of their configuration on the Startup tab.

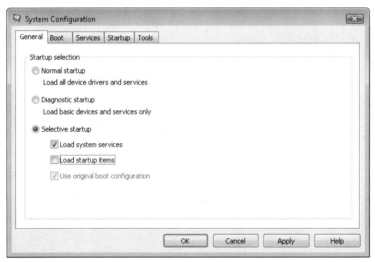

Figure 5-19   Choosing startup selections in the System Configuration utility

More details related to using features in MSConfig for troubleshooting purposes are covered in Chapter 12, "Troubleshooting Windows Vista."

Managing Startup Programs with Windows Defender

Windows Defender is an antispyware utility that is included with the Windows Vista operating system. Although its focus is on detecting and removing potentially malicious software, Windows Defender provides an option for managing startup programs. You can open Windows Defender from the Start menu or by clicking the Windows Defender system tray icon (if it is present). You can launch this option by clicking Tools in the Windows Defender Home view and then clicking the Software Explorer link. You can also directly access this view by clicking Manage Startup Programs in the Performance Information And Tools Control Panel window.

By clicking the Startup Programs category in the Windows Defender Software Explorer, you can view a list of all of the programs that are configured to run during the Windows Vista startup process. By default, the list of items is grouped by the publisher of the software and sorted by the name of each application or process. You can change the grouping to view information based on startup type by right-clicking any item and choosing Startup type (see Figure 5-20). The groups include the User Profile Startup Folder, the Current User Registry Key, and the Local Machine Registry Key.

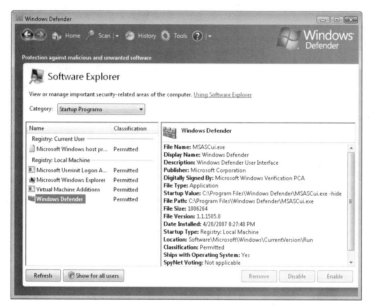

Figure 5-20 Viewing a list of startup programs (sorted by Startup Type) in Windows Defender Software Explorer

You can obtain more details about a particular item by selecting it in the list. The right pane then shows a long list of details about the application or process. Some of the details include the file name of the program, the location of the file, the size of the file, the date it was installed, and the location of the startup information. Another useful detail specifies whether the program shipped with the operating system. In general, programs that shipped as part of Windows Vista should be considered safe and are often required for the operating system to work properly.

The Classification section is based on a centralized database known as SpyNet. The Windows Defender Software Explorer can automatically query this database over the Internet to determine which applications are known and which are not. Spyware, malware, and other malicious programs will automatically be prevented from running on the system. Of course, it is also possible for some third-party applications and services to be listed as Not Yet Classified.

When managing startup items, there are three primary configuration operations that you can perform:

- **Disable** This command prevents a specific item from running at system startup or during the logon process. The definition of the item (including the command and its file system or Registry location) will remain in the system. Disabling is most useful for situations in which it is possible that the startup item will be needed again.
- **Enable** Startup items that have been marked as disabled can be configured to run at startup by re-enabling them.
- **Remove** This command permanently removes an item from the list of startup programs. This usually involves the deletion of a shortcut or the removal of the associated Registry key. The Remove command is most appropriate for removing software items that are known to be unwanted.

Windows Defender also includes a category for viewing which processes are currently running on the system and for optionally terminating them. If a particular program is known to be causing problems, you can use the End Process command to stop that program immediately and return system resources. Chapter 12 provides more details related to using Windows Defender for removing unwanted programs and processes.

Real World

Anil Desai

Users rely on you as a Consumer Support Technician to help them make positive decisions about the configuration of their systems. In some cases, the tasks that you will perform on their behalf are clear. For example, if a known malware program is using significant system resources, you should probably terminate it and remove it from the startup item configuration.

Other cases might not be as simple. For example, what if you see a program in the Windows Defender Software Explorer that is listed as Not Yet Classified? Perhaps you don't recognize the program, or you have a hunch that it is not needed. Should you remove it? A good first step is to ask the customer whether he or she recognizes the name of the program. If not, and you think it is possibly the source of a performance problem, you should choose to disable it. Because you can easily re-enable it in the future, this is often a better option than removing it entirely.

Additionally, it's important to keep customers informed of the changes you've made. In some cases, they might not encounter any issues for several days, until they try to access a particular application or function. Overall, your primary goals should be to resolve the issue but also to do no harm.

Viewing Performance Information in the Event Log

The Windows Vista operating system keeps track of numerous different events that occur while the system is running. The types of messages include notifications from applications, system-related details, and security events. With relation to performance monitoring and optimization, particular portions of the event logs can be useful.

Operations such as the time it takes to boot the computer are measured and recorded. In some cases, events can clearly identify that the system is working more slowly than is expected. These details can help verify reports from users about slow system performance. They can also be used to measure the effects of making changes.

Event Viewer is the standard application used to monitor events that are recorded on the system. By default, Windows Vista includes dozens of groupings for events. You can launch Event Viewer directly from the Start menu, but the default display shows all of the available event logs on the system. This often makes it challenging to filter the display to show just the information you need.

One easy way to filter the information to view performance-related details is to use the Performance Information And Tools Control Panel window. To do this, in Control Panel, click System And Maintenance and select Performance Information And Tools. Click Advanced Tools, and then click View Performance Details In Event Log. This automatically launches the Event Viewer console and opens the Diagnostics-Performance section. Figure 5-21 shows an example of the types of events that you can view. (If necessary, you can close the Actions pane to allow more room for you to review these events. To close the Actions pane, click the Show/Hide Action Pane button on the toolbar.)

The actual events that are stored are organized into three levels: Information, Warning, and Error. By selecting an item in the list, you can view the details of the issue. Often, the explanatory text gives you insight into the issue and possible ways to resolve it. For example, the process of opening many different windows while the Windows Aero user interface is enabled might reduce overall system responsiveness. Windows Vista automatically monitors for this issue and logs an event whenever it occurs. If the event is occurring frequently, you might decide to either upgrade the computer's display adapter or disable the Windows Aero desktop feature (a topic that was covered in Chapter 3). Overall, the Event Viewer can be an indispensible tool for viewing information about how Windows Vista is performing.

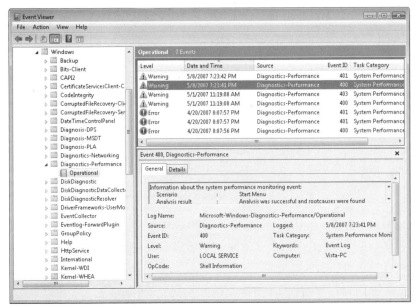

Figure 5-21   Viewing performance-related event information

Configuring Windows Features

The Windows operating system platform includes many potentially useful applications and services. For security and performance reasons, many of these options are not enabled by default on computers running Windows Vista. This approach helps ensure that system resources are not being used for programs that the user might not need. Some examples include network applications such as the Telnet client and server and Tablet PC Optional Components. Each of the available options is known as a Windows Feature.

You can easily turn Windows Features on or off based on users' needs. If a user or application requires a particular feature, you should probably enable it. Alternatively, if you find that a feature is using a significant amount of system resources even if it is not being used, you can choose to disable it. These functions are available by using the Uninstall A Program link in the Programs section of Control Panel. The Turn Windows Features On Or Off link launches the Windows Features dialog box (see Figure 5-22).

Figure 5-22   Viewing options in the Windows Features dialog box

You can turn some of the features in the list on or off simply by using the check boxes that are located next to them. In addition, you can view some services and components that provide additional subfeatures by expanding the respective sections. When you click OK, Windows Vista goes through the process of enabling and disabling the relevant features. In some cases, you might be required to reboot the system before the configuration will complete.

Configuring Windows ReadyBoost

One of the easiest methods of improving overall system performance is to add more physical memory (RAM) to the computer. Physical memory is consumed by applications, processes, and services. When many different applications are run on the computer at the same time, however, Windows Vista must try to make the most efficient use of the available memory. Often, the operating system will need to store memory information on the hard disk. This operation is known as *paging*, and it can slow system performance significantly.

The obvious solution to this problem is to add more physical memory to the computer. There are, however, some potential barriers to this solution. First, purchasing memory can be costly (although prices have decreased dramatically over time). Second, the physical computer itself might not have enough room for expansion. Some systems are physically limited by the number of available memory slots and might have limitations on the storage capacity of installed memory. Finally, there's the issue of installation: many end users are not comfortable with opening their computers and installing additional memory.

Understanding Windows ReadyBoost

Windows Vista includes a feature called Windows ReadyBoost that allows users to use external memory devices to improve performance. Compatible devices include USB memory drives (often called flash drives or thumb drives), and multimedia cards such as those that are used for portable devices like digital cameras.

ReadyBoost uses a method known as write-through caching to improve performance. This works by automatically storing data to the memory device as well as to the hard disk. Writing to a memory device can be slower than writing to a hard disk. The write-through cache approach ensures that the system does not have to wait for the data to be written to the memory device. It also protects against any potential data loss that might occur if the item is unplugged from the system. For smaller operations, reading from a memory device can be faster than reading from a hard disk. Depending on the patterns of disk activity, Windows Vista can then read the data directly from the memory device rather than going to the physical hard disk. This operation is often significantly faster than accessing the same data from the hard disk.

NOTE   The role of Windows ReadyBoost

When helping users determine how to upgrade their systems, you're likely to come across questions about which types of upgrades are best. Should the user purchase and install more physical memory, or will Windows ReadyBoost meet their requirements? The ideal solution is to install more physical RAM in the computer. Memory chips that are installed on the motherboard of a computer run far faster than their flash-based counterparts. Windows ReadyBoost is a good second choice if the user is unable or unwilling to upgrade. A good rule of thumb is to use physical memory whenever possible.

Windows ReadyBoost Requirements

There are several technical and performance requirements that must be met for a device to be compatible with Windows ReadyBoost. The device should be connected directly to a USB 2.0 or media reader port on the computer for maximum performance. When recommending devices to users, it's best to look for information that specifies that the device is compatible with Windows ReadyBoost. Additionally, Windows ReadyBoost is limited to using up to a maximum of 4.0 GB of space for the Windows ReadyBoost cache, even if the size of the memory device is larger.

Enabling Windows ReadyBoost

The process of enabling the Windows ReadyBoost feature is simple. The first step is to connect an external memory device to the computer. For example, you might connect a USB flash drive to a USB 2.0 port on the physical computer. By default, Windows Vista automatically tests the performance of the device. If it meets the requirements, Windows Vista then prompts you as to whether you would like to use the device with the Windows ReadyBoost feature. If the device did not meet the performance requirements, you can choose to retest it or to stop retesting it in the future. The same options are also available by viewing the ReadyBoost tab in the properties of a memory device. Figure 5-23 shows the available options.

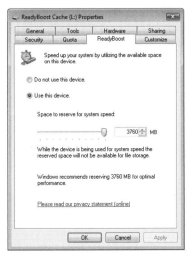

Figure 5-23 Enabling Windows ReadyBoost for an external memory device

To enable Windows ReadyBoost, the Use This Device option should be selected on the Ready-Boost tab of the Properties dialog box for the device. Windows Vista also attempts to detect automatically whether a memory device meets the requirements for ReadyBoost when it is plugged in. If it does, you can choose the Speed Up My System option to access these settings directly. The slider enables users to choose how much memory they would like to use on the device. All of the space that is used by Windows ReadyBoost will be unavailable for storing other files. Therefore, users should decide whether they want to use all of the available space, or if they want to use only some of it. After you apply the settings, Windows Vista automatically starts using the external memory device to improve performance. As mentioned earlier, users can remove the memory device at any time without risking the loss of data.

Managing Services

In addition to standard programs that are configured to run on a Windows Vista–based computer, services provide important functionality for keeping the system running properly. Examples include the Workstation service (which enables accessing files and resources over the network), the Windows Time service (for automatically synchronizing the system clock), and the Offline Files service (for automatically synchronizing files between computers).

The default list of services included with Windows Vista is a long one, although most of the services are not enabled by default. Many of these perform important system functions. In addition, the installation of new software might result in the installation of new services.

Viewing Service Configuration Information

Services are programs that are designed to run in the background without requiring user input. They usually run on the system whether or not a user is logged on. This often makes it difficult to "see" which services are running. Even though they usually don't have a user interface, services do consume system resources while they are running. In Lesson 1 of this chapter, you looked at ways in which to use the Services tab in Task Manager to view details about which services are currently running.

The primary method of configuring, starting, and stopping services is the use of the Services console. You open this console by first opening Control Panel and then clicking System And Maintenance. Click Administrative Tools, and then double-click Services. Figure 5-24 shows the default display of the Services interface.

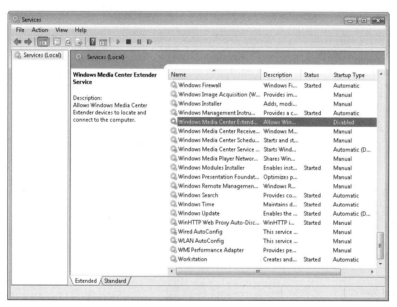

Figure 5-24   Managing services by using the Services console

The important configuration-related details include the following:

- **Name**   The friendly name of the service. Generally, this will provide an overview of the feature or functionality that the service provides.
- **Description**   A description of the purpose and function of the service in greater detail. Often, the text will also mention which types of functionality might be affected if the service is stopped or disabled.
- **Status**   Information that specifies the status of the service. The most common values are blank (indicating that the service is not running), or Started (indicating the service is running).

- **Startup Type**　Startup options that are generally configured in one of three states. Automatic specifies that the service should start whenever the computer is started. Manual specifies that the service will not start automatically, but it can be started manually (by either a user or another program). Finally, Disabled specifies that the service cannot be started by a user or other program. This option is useful when troubleshooting potential performance-related issues.

- **Log On As**　A field that shows details about which account will be used. Because services do not depend on a user to launch them manually, they must run under the security settings of a particular user account. Most services that are included with the Windows Vista operating system will run using a built-in account such as Local System or Local Service. You can also provide credentials related to a particular user account.

Although the standard Services console display is simple, it does provide the capability to sort the information. A common task is to click the Status column heading to show all of the services that are currently running at the top of the list. You can also click the Startup Type column heading to sort by whether a service is set to Automatic or Manual. If a service has an Automatic startup type, but it is not running, that might indicate a potential configuration issue.

Starting and Stopping Services

The Services console allows you to start and stop services easily. The easiest method is to select the service you want to manage and then click the relevant buttons in the console toolbar. The buttons are as follows:

- **Start Service**　Starts the service if it is currently stopped.
- **Pause Service**　Tells the service to run in a paused state.
- **Stop Service**　Stops the service if it is currently running.
- **Restart Service**　Stops the service and then immediately restarts it.

The actual effects of each operation are dependent on the service itself. Some services might execute cleanup-related tasks (such as deleting temporary files) before ending. Although not all services can be paused, some can be placed in this state temporarily to prevent them from responding to requests or events.

Overall, by monitoring and managing services, you can identify possible performance issues. You can also make sure that only required programs are using system resources.

Optimizing Disk Performance

Just about every application (and the Windows Vista operating system itself) relies on the computer's hard disk system. Hard disk storage is used for storing files and for performing temporary operations. The operating system also uses disk space to supplement the amount of available memory. As a Consumer Support Technician, you've likely heard the complaint that users' systems tend to slow down over time. One potential reason is that information is not organized as efficiently on the hard disk. In this section, you'll look at ways in which you can optimize disk performance.

Disk Cleanup

Over time, it's likely that applications will leave unnecessary files on the computer's hard disk. Examples include temporary Internet files, application installation components, and error report files. Finding and safely deleting these items can be tricky because they're often scattered in many regions of the file system. Apart from the obvious loss of usable disk space, unwanted files can lead to decreased performance due to fragmentation.

The Disk Cleanup tool provides a quick way to identify temporary files that the system no longer needs. You can access it through the Start menu or by clicking Disk Cleanup in the Properties dialog box for a particular hard disk. The latter option is helpful if you want to restrict the cleanup operation to a single logical hard disk partition.

When you launch the program directly, it performs an automatic scan of the hard disk. The resulting display shows an overview of the types of files that it finds, along with estimates related to the potential amount of disk space that can be recovered (see Figure 5-25).

Figure 5-25   Using the Disk Cleanup utility to remove unnecessary files

The list of types of files that might no longer be needed includes the following:

- Downloaded Program Files
- Temporary Internet Files
- Debug Dump Files
- Microsoft Office Temporary Files
- Office Setup Files

- Recycle Bin
- Setup Log Files
- System Error Memory Dump Files
- System Error Minidump Files
- Temporary Files
- Thumbnails
- Windows Error Report Information

It's important to note that some of these types of files can be useful in improving the user experience. For example, thumbnail files help Windows Explorer show previews of files such as photos and videos more quickly. The contents of the Recycle Bin are useful for recovering files that have been deleted accidentally.

The process of performing a disk cleanup simply requires you to select the check boxes for the relevant types of files and then click OK. The files are automatically removed from the system. In addition, the More Options tab in the Disk Cleanup dialog box provides a way to access utilities quickly for managing Programs And Features and for configuring System Restore And Shadow Copies features.

Disk Defragmentation

Most modern computers include very large hard disks that allow for the storage of many gigabytes of data. This places a heavy burden on the file system because Windows is often responsible for moving, copying, and deleting many files. The ideal arrangement for files is for them to be stored contiguously. This means that the entire contents of the file are physically stored together on the hard disk.

Due to usage patterns, however, this might not always be possible. For example, on a hard disk that is nearly full, it might be necessary to spread the contents of a 2.0 GB video file across different sections of the disk. Each of these sections is referred to as a fragment of the file. Disk fragmentation can lead to a decrease in overall performance because, whenever the file must be read, the physical hard disk must perform more work to load data that is scattered in different locations.

Fortunately, there is an easy way to counteract this problem: the Windows Vista Disk Defragmenter. You can launch this utility from the Start menu or by clicking Defragment Now on the Tools tab of the Properties dialog box for a particular hard disk. When the program launches, it shows the options that are available, as shown in Figure 5-26.

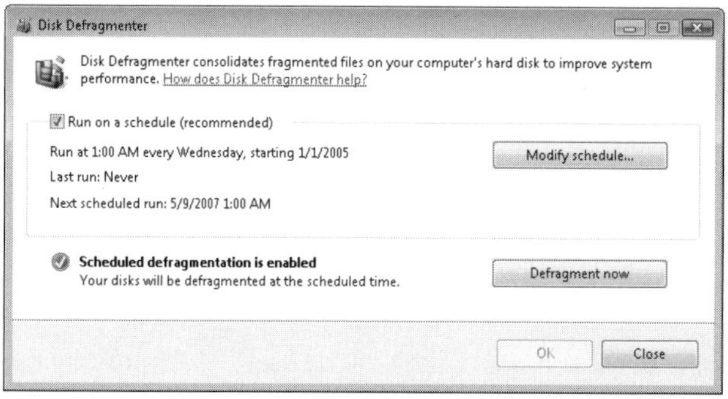

Figure 5-26 Configuring the Disk Defragmenter

The Disk Defragmenter program offers two options. The first is to start a disk defragmentation pass manually by clicking Defragment Now. This starts the defragmentation process immediately. The other option is to configure the process to run automatically based on a schedule (see Figure 5-27). It is a good idea to schedule defragmentation operations regularly to maintain overall disk performance over time. The defragmentation process places a significant load on the disk system, and users are likely to notice the impact if it is run while they are actively using their systems. Therefore, it's a good idea to run the process during periods of no user activity on the computer.

Figure 5-27 Configuring a Disk Defragmenter schedule

Other Performance Optimization Options

So far, you have examined many different ways in which you can optimize the performance of Windows Vista. In addition to these methods, there are a few services and features that can be configured to improve system responsiveness. Although there might be a trade-off in relation to functionality, computers that are low on system resources can often benefit from these features.

Adjusting Visual Effects

Chapter 3 discussed ways in which the Windows Aero user interface can improve aesthetics and productivity and how these features require significant system resources. Fortunately, you can configure systems to choose the best balance of options to optimize responsiveness. The Performance Information And Tools window in Control Panel includes a link entitled Adjust Visual Effects. This link opens the Performance Options dialog box that allows for changing settings related to visual effects used by the Windows desktop (see Figure 5-28).

Figure 5-28   Viewing details related to visual effects

The Visual Effects tab provides several options that control which user interface features are enabled. The default setting is to let Windows automatically determine which options should be enabled. When this option is selected, Windows Vista determines whether there is a potential performance problem and makes changes accordingly. The next two options are to adjust for best appearance or for best performance. The best-performance option disables all of the visual effects, whereas the best-appearance option enables them all. Finally, you can choose the Custom option to select which specific features to enable.

Users might complain to you that it takes too long to launch programs or that the system does not seem responsive enough (especially when numerous applications are running at the same time). For these users, disabling some of the Visual Effects tab settings can improve the usability of the system.

Managing Indexing Options

One of the most useful productivity features of Windows Vista is the ability to perform a search from the Start menu or directly from within applications such as Windows Explorer.

The Windows Search indexing process can place a significant load on systems, however. It is responsible for analyzing many different file types and for storing the results to make searches faster.

You can launch the Indexing Options configuration utility directly from the Start menu or by clicking Adjust Indexing Options in the Performance Information And Tools Control Panel window. As shown in Figure 5-29, the tool provides an overview of which file system locations and applications will be indexed.

Figure 5-29   Managing indexing options

If some locations are not frequently searched, users can click Modify to remove those paths. Clicking Advanced presents additional options, including the location of the index files. Users can also specify whether certain file types should not be indexed. Overall, by configuring Indexing options based on users' needs, you can help reduce hard disk and CPU use.

Quick Check

1. Which two programs can you use to disable a program that is configured to run at system startup?
2. Which Control Panel item provides links to many different performance management tools and options?

Quick Check Answers

1. You can use both The System Configuration (MSConfig) and Windows Defender Software Explorer tools to configure startup items.
2. The Performance Information and Tools Control Panel item provides these links.

Practice: Improving System Performance

These practice exercises walk you through some steps to improve overall system performance. To complete Practice 2, you need an external memory device that is compatible with Windows ReadyBoost. The most common options include USB flash drives and memory cards.

▶ **Practice 1: Configure Startup Items**

In this practice exercise, you obtain a list of startup options by using the MSConfig utility as well as Windows Defender. Because software configurations will vary, you can optionally choose to disable a startup item and reboot the computer to ensure that it does not load during the startup process.

1. Launch the System Configuration (MSConfig) utility from the Start menu.
2. On the General tab, note the various startup options that are available.

   The default setting is Normal Startup, but you can also choose to perform a Diagnostic Startup or a Selective Startup. Leave the Normal Startup option selected.
3. Click the Startup tab.

   The tab shows a listing of all of the programs that are configured to load during the startup process. Note that the information includes the name of the program, the manufacturer (if available), the command, and the location in which the startup commands are stored.
4. Clear the check box for one of the startup items, and then click Apply.

   Note that the Date Disabled column shows the current date and time. This program will not run automatically during the next system restart.
5. To re-enable the startup item, select its check box and click Apply. This returns the configuration to its original settings.
6. Click Cancel to close the System Configuration utility.
7. Open the Windows Defender program by using the Start menu.
8. From the Windows Defender home page, click Tools, and then select Software Explorer. The default view shows a list of all of the current startup programs.
9. Right-click any startup item on the list and choose to sort the list by Startup Type.

   Note that some programs are configured to run during system startup, whereas others automatically run whenever a user logs on to the system.
10. Click any startup item to view additional details about the program.

    Note the various details that are provided, including the command and path to the program. Note that you can also disable or permanently remove a startup item from the list.
11. When finished, close Windows Defender.

▶ **Practice 2: Configure Windows ReadyBoost**

In this exercise, you walk through the steps required to configure a removable media device to support Windows ReadyBoost.

1. Install a compatible removable media device (such as a media card or a USB flash device) into the computer.

2. Windows Vista might automatically run a performance test on the device and prompt you to enable Windows ReadyBoost. For the purpose of this exercise, choose not to enable Windows ReadyBoost if prompted.

3. From the Start menu, open the Computer item and locate the new removable memory device. Right-click the device and select Properties.

4. Click the ReadyBoost tab. By default, the Do Not Use This Device option is selected.

5. To enable Windows ReadyBoost, select the Use This Device option. The slider bar can be used to determine how much space should be allocated for Windows ReadyBoost. Note that any space you allocated to Windows ReadyBoost will be unusable for other storage on the device.

6. Select the recommended amount of memory and click OK to enable Windows Ready-Boost. This initializes the ReadyBoost file on the memory device.

7. Windows ReadyBoost runs automatically in the background and works to optimize memory and disk-related performance. If your memory device has a light or other indicator of activity, you will see it blinking actively. Otherwise, you can always return to the Windows ReadyBoost Properties dialog box to view the settings for this feature.

Lesson Summary

- The Performance Information And Tools Control Panel item provides a quick way to access numerous tools and utilities that can be used to optimize performance.

- Use MSConfig to enable or disable startup items.

- Windows Defender Software Explorer provides details about startup items and allows users to enable or disable them.

- The Windows Vista event log contains diagnostic information related to performance.

- Users can enable and disable Windows features by using the Add/Remove Programs Control Panel item.

- Windows ReadyBoost enables users to improve performance by using external memory devices.

- Disk performance can be improved through the use of the Disk Cleanup and Disk Defragmenter utilities.

- Performance can be improved by enabling or disabling visual effects and by modifying indexing options.

Lesson Review

You can use the following questions to test your knowledge of the information in Lesson 2, "Improving System Performance." The questions are also available on the companion CD if you prefer to review them in electronic form.

NOTE Answers

Answers to these questions and explanations of why each answer choice is correct or incorrect are located in the "Answers" section at the end of the book.

---

1. You are helping a user troubleshoot a performance problem that occurred soon after he installed a new application he downloaded from the Internet. He reports that the system takes much longer to start since the program was installed. Which tool(s) can you use to prevent the item from starting automatically? (Choose all that apply.)

    A. Windows ReadyBoost

    B. Windows Defender

    C. Disk Cleanup

    D. System Configuration (MSConfig)

    E. Disk Defragmenter

2. You are helping a customer who frequently copies and moves large video files on her computer. She reports that the system seems to be slowing down over time, and it now takes far longer to copy a large file than it did in the past. She has not installed any new software or made any configuration changes. Which of the following will most likely improve performance?

    A. Disabling all startup items

    B. Disabling some or all of the visual effects options

    C. Defragmenting the hard disks

    D. Stopping unnecessary services

Chapter Review

To further practice and reinforce the skills you learned in this chapter, you can perform the following tasks:

- Review the chapter summary.
- Review the list of key terms introduced in this chapter.
- Complete the case scenarios. These scenarios set up real-world situations involving the topics of this chapter and ask you to create a solution.
- Complete the suggested practices.
- Take a practice test.

Chapter Summary

- Windows Vista includes numerous tools for monitoring performance, including Task Manager, Resource Monitor, Performance Monitor, Data Collector Sets, System Information, and the Windows Experience Index.
- Windows Vista performance can be improved by managing startup items, configuring services, enabling Windows ReadyBoost, and maintaining hard disks.

Key Terms

Do you know what these key terms mean? You can check your answers by looking up the terms in the glossary at the end of the book.

- Data Collector Sets
- Event Viewer
- Performance Monitor
- Reliability Monitor
- Resource Monitor
- Services
- System Configuration (MSConfig) tool
- System Information (MSInfo) tool
- Task Manager
- Windows Defender Software Explorer
- Windows Experience Index
- Windows ReadyBoost

Case Scenarios

In the following case scenarios, you apply what you've learned about monitoring and optimizing Windows Vista performance. You can find answers to these questions in the "Answers" section at the end of this book.

Case Scenario 1: Monitoring Performance

You are a Consumer Support Technician who is helping a user troubleshoot a computer running Windows Vista. The user recently installed four separate programs that he downloaded from the Internet. He is now experiencing server system performance issues. First, he has noticed that the system takes far longer to start up than it did before he installed the programs. Also, performance of network-related tasks such as browsing Web sites is much slower than it was before the programs were installed.

1. How can you determine quickly which programs are using the most network resources?
2. How can you speed up the startup time for the computer?
3. How can you generate an overall report of the performance of the system?

Case Scenario 2: Optimizing Performance

You are a Consumer Support Technician who is helping a customer improve performance of a computer running Windows Vista. The customer commonly uses her system to run multiple applications at the same time. Performance always slows down noticeably when she has numerous applications running at the same time. Specifically, operations such as switching between open applications can take several seconds. The customer also reports that she is running low on disk space and would prefer not to have to purchase another hard disk drive. The current computer is configured with the maximum amount of physical memory that the system allows, and it is not possible to upgrade it.

1. How can you add more memory to the system to improve performance?
2. How can you improve the responsiveness of the desktop interface?
3. How can you make more hard disk space available for use by programs?

Suggested Practices

To help you successfully master the exam objectives presented in this chapter, complete the following tasks.

Monitoring and Improving System Performance

- **Practice 1: Monitoring applications and processes**   Open the Windows Task Manager and Resource Monitor tools and step through the various tabs to get information about programs that are running on the system. Answer the following questions: Which process is using the most memory? Which services are started on the system? Which application or process is generating the most disk activity?

- **Practice 2: Disable a startup item**   Use the System Configuration (MSConfig) utility and Windows Defender Software Explorer to view a list of enabled startup items. Disable at least one startup item, and then restart the computer to verify that it no longer runs automatically. Re-enable the startup item, and then reboot the computer to return it to its original state.

- **Practice 3: Enable Windows ReadyBoost**   Install a memory card or USB flash device into a computer running Windows Vista and enable Windows ReadyBoost. If possible, use various performance monitoring tools to measure the effects of adding external memory to the system.

Take a Practice Test

The practice tests on this book's companion CD offer many options. For example, you can test yourself on just one exam objective, or you can test yourself on all of the 70-623 certification exam content. You can set up the test so that it closely simulates the experience of taking a certification exam, or you can set it up in study mode so that you can look at the correct answers and explanations after you answer each question.

MORE INFO   Practice tests

For details about all the practice test options available, see the "How to Use the Practice Tests" section in this book's introduction.

Chapter 6
Configuring Windows Vista Security

As a Consumer Support Technician, there's a good chance that you're aware of potential security issues that occur on customers' computers. It's not uncommon to hear complaints related to system slowdowns after visiting an unfamiliar Web site or installing a new application. Cleaning computers that have been infected by viruses or spyware can be a difficult and time-consuming process. The ideal solution is to prevent them from being infected in the first place. That leads to increasing security. Often, it's necessary to reduce the permissions that are granted to users on their own computers.

Security and usability are often at odds: increasing one often decreases the other. This makes the true goal of configuring and managing security settings a balancing act. Imagine, for example, if you were required to enter five different pieces of personal information to log on to a computer. In many ways, this system might be more secure than one that just required a single password. However, it would make the act of using your computer cumbersome and frustrating. You might even resort to writing down the necessary information on a piece of paper that you store near the computer (thereby negating the real benefits of the security itself). The net result would be that the drawbacks of implementing security overshadowed its potential benefits. On the other hand, you cannot simply grant all users full permissions to make changes to all areas of their systems. This often leads to the installation of malicious software or accidental file deletions and operating system changes.

Users rely on your expertise as a Consumer Support Technician to help them ensure that their systems remain secure. They expect to be reasonably protected from malware such as viruses, unwanted third-party applications, and security issues. Customers also expect you to help keep their systems usable and performing well over time.

One of the fundamental design goals Microsoft mandated for Windows Vista was to make the product as secure as possible while retaining compatibility with the vast library of existing programs that have been written for the Windows platform. Numerous features have been designed to meet this goal. In this chapter, you'll learn ways in which you can create, configure, and manage standard and administrator user accounts. Then, you'll learn about the User Account Control (UAC) feature of Windows Vista, including many different options that can be configured to meet users' needs. These are critical aspects of working with a secure operating system, whether in a home or small business environment.

Exam objectives in this chapter:
- Customize and configure user accounts.
- Configure User Account Control.

Lessons in this chapter:

Before You Begin

A basic understanding of computer security issues and concepts such as user accounts and permissions will be helpful as you learn the concepts in this chapter. You should have already installed Windows Vista and created at least one user account. Some of the practice exercises require you to be running Windows Vista Home Premium, Windows Vista Ultimate, or Windows Vista Business. Other editions of Windows Vista (such as Windows Vista Enterprise) will also work, but some of the default security settings might be different from those described in the text.

Lesson 1: Managing User Accounts

Modern operating systems such as Windows Vista have been designed to meet the needs of many different users. Accordingly, the operating system provides a method for creating multiple user accounts on a single installation of Windows Vista. You can configure and customize each user account based on the needs of the individual who will be using it. For example, desktop settings, screen savers, shortcuts, and user-specific data files are all stored separately for each account. In general, give each user of a system his or her own account.

From the standpoint of a consumer—a typical home or small-business user—it's common for a computer to include multiple user accounts. For example, a family of four might have separate accounts for each parent and each child. A small business might have various employees that occasionally use a single shared computer to perform specific tasks.

Regardless of the purpose of a particular user account, there are security-related considerations that should be addressed. In this lesson, you'll learn about the different types of accounts that are available in Windows Vista and how to create and manage them.

After this lesson, you will be able to:
- Describe the differences between standard and administrative user accounts.
- Provide examples of tasks that can be performed by administrative user accounts but not by standard user accounts.
- Create new standard and administrative user accounts.
- View and modify details about a user account.

Estimated lesson time: 45 minutes

Understanding User Account Types

When a user logs on to a computer running Windows Vista, he or she must provide valid credentials that prove his or her identity. Most commonly, a user performs a logon by using a combination of a user name and a password. Each user account has its own collection of settings and permissions. These include the following:

- **User profile** A user profile contains all of the operating system preferences that are defined separately for each user account. Examples include desktop wallpaper options, the Windows Sidebar configuration, and application shortcuts. By default, user profiles are located in the C:\Users folder.
- **Application settings** Each user profile has its own collection of application settings. These settings usually pertain to personal preferences for an application (such as default paths, toolbar layouts, and related details). They are stored either in the user-specific portion of the registry or in configuration files that are stored within the profile.

- **User data folder**   Each user has his or her user data storage location on the computer. This enables multiple users of the same computer to keep their files separate from each other.

- **Other user-specific folders**   To improve consistency and usability for operating system users, each user profile includes several shortcuts to special folders. Examples include Music, Pictures, Saved Games, Documents, Downloads, and Videos. Each user will have his or her separate shortcuts and storage locations for these default folders.

- **Security privileges and policy settings**   Each user account has a set of security-related actions that it can perform. For example, users might have restrictions related to logon hours or installing applications.

- **File system permissions**   These are details related to which actions the user can take on which files. For example, a user will be allowed to create and delete documents in his or her own user data folder but will not be able to access another user's data folder.

The two main types of user accounts in Windows Vista are Standard User and Administrator. In this lesson, you'll learn about the purposes of each account type, along with differences in the permissions they are granted. In Lesson 2, "Understanding User Account Control (UAC)," you'll look at details related to how the UAC feature can be used to enable the temporary elevation of privileges.

Standard User Accounts

The default type of user account in Windows Vista is a standard user account. This account is designed to provide basic permissions for completing common daily tasks. It allows users to launch applications, create new documents, and modify basic system configuration settings. In general, these operations affect only the user who is logged on to Windows Vista. They do not include systemwide changes such as the installation of new software.

Administrator User Accounts

Accounts that have Administrator permissions have the capability of performing any operation or task on the system. This includes all of the permissions that are granted to a standard user account plus the ability to make major operating system changes, install new software, and create and modify other user accounts. Administrator accounts also have the ability to set permissions for other users on the system.

There are potential security considerations for users who use an administrative account for daily computer use. The primary issue is that unwanted software can make changes to the operating system or to data without the user's permission. This is because all programs run, by default, using the security permissions of the user who launched them. A related issue is that such users have the ability to perform actions that could lead to operating system instability or corruption. For example, a novice user who is running as an Administrator might accidentally delete critical operating system files or programs, thinking that they are not needed. These are all reasons why Microsoft designed the UAC feature as a major component of Windows Vista.

Therefore, it is recommended that most users log on to their computers using a standard user account. One potential problem with this approach is that applications often expect to have full permissions on the system. You'll learn about ways in which this situation can be addressed in Lesson 2.

Windows Vista creates a default account called Administrator during the installation process. This account has full permissions on the system and is generally not designed for regular use. For this reason, the default Administrator account is disabled on new installations. For in-place upgrade installations of Windows Vista, the setup process disables the built-in Administrator account only if there are other active Administrator accounts on the system. If there aren't any, the account remains enabled.

The Guest Account

A third type of account that is created with default Windows Vista installations is the Guest account. This account is designed for users who require temporary access to a computer and don't need to store their user-specific profile settings permanently. For example, if a friend is visiting your home and just needs to launch a Web browser to check her e-mail, you can allow her to use the Guest account. Users who log on as a guest have a very limited set of permissions. For example, they cannot access other users' files or perform systemwide tasks such as installing software or hardware.

For security reasons, the built-in Guest account is disabled by default. This prevents users from having an option to log on to the system as Guest.

Comparing User Permissions

When working with standard and Administrator user accounts, it's important to understand which actions each type of user is allowed to perform. Specifically, it's important to understand a list of permissions that are granted to standard user accounts. In this section, you'll learn examples of operations that can be performed by each type of account.

Permissions of Standard User Accounts

The following actions can be performed by a standard user account:

- Perform basic system management tasks. The built-in Windows Vista applications and tools indicate operations that require elevated permissions with a shield icon next to the control.
- Change personal user settings such as passwords, desktop wallpaper, system sounds, and screen savers.

- Access removable media such as memory storage devices and CD/DVD media.
- Create a local area network (LAN) connection.
- Connect to a wireless network.
- Personalize display settings, including desktop resolution and number of colors.
- Use Remote Desktop to connect to remote computers.
- Perform basic configuration settings in Control Panel. For example, a user can change power management settings.
- Enable or disable accessibility options such as the screen magnifier.
- Connect and configure some external devices, such as universal serial bus (USB) storage or Bluetooth devices.

It is important to note that these are the default settings for a standard user account. Administrators can manually change the permissions and privileges of users to meet their requirements. Also, in some cases, a background service or process might perform important tasks that the user cannot perform directly. One example is the disk defragmentation service, which is configured to run under a specific user account.

Permissions of Administrator Accounts

Administrator accounts, as mentioned earlier, have full permissions on a computer system. This includes the ability to change or delete files owned by any user on the system and to make changes to the operating system. Examples of operations that can be performed by an Administrator account but not by a standard user account include the following:

- Installing new software on the computer
- Adding new hardware and installing device drivers on the computer
- Making changes to configuration of the Automatic Updates feature
- Accessing files that are in secure locations, such as the Windows folder and the Program Files folder
- Configuring Windows Firewall (including enabling, disabling, and adding exceptions)
- Performing a complete system backup and restore operation
- Creating new user accounts, removing user accounts, and configuring the user account type
- Managing the behavior of the UAC feature

Again, this is just a sample of the types of operations that a standard user account cannot perform.

Exam Tip   Exam 70-623 tests your ability to identify which types of operations require privilege escalation. One great way to learn these is to "poke around" the Windows Vista user interface. Open Control Panel items and Administrative Tools to see the actions you can perform as a standard user and which ones require additional permissions. This will help give you a good idea of the limits of standard user accounts without having to memorize long lists of potential actions.

Managing User Accounts

So far, you have looked at details related to the different types of accounts that are available on a computer running Windows Vista. In this lesson, you'll see how you can use that information to perform actual user account–related tasks. Many of these operations will require you to log on to the computer by using an account that has Administrator permissions.

Adding User Accounts

The Windows Vista Control Panel provides utilities that enable you to create and manage user accounts quickly and easily. To access the relevant settings, you need to have Administrator permissions on the computer. You can open the Manage Accounts window by clicking the Add Or Remove User Accounts link in the User Accounts And Family Safety section of the default Control Panel. Figure 6-1 shows an example of the available options and settings.

Figure 6-1   Using the Manage Accounts window in Control Panel

The default view shows a list of all of the users who are currently configured on the computer and an overview of their settings. The Create A New Account link starts the process of creating a new user (see Figure 6-2). The details that are required include the name of the new account. Usually, this corresponds to the individual who will be using that logon. The other option is related to whether the account should be created as a standard user (the default option), or as an Administrator.

Figure 6-2   Creating a new user account

After you click Create Account, the new account is available for logon. Generally, you will want to configure various properties of the account before you make it available for use by individuals.

Configuring User Accounts

There are several different operations that are commonly performed when managing user accounts. You can access these by clicking the name or icon of an account in the Manage Accounts window. Figure 6-3 shows the options that are available.

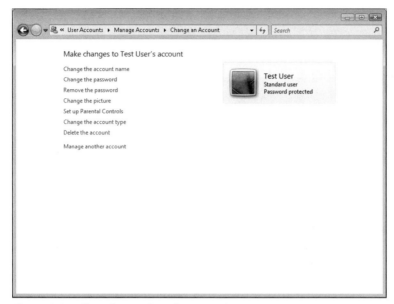

Figure 6-3 Changing settings for an account

The options include the following:

- Change The Account Name
- Change The Password (or Create A Password if the account does not currently have one)
- Remove The Password (if one is currently configured)
- Change The Picture
- Set Up Parental Controls
- Change The Account Type
- Delete The Account

The built-in Guest account has a limited set of options and commands. As mentioned earlier, this account is disabled by default. When you click the Guest account, you have the option of turning it on. If you click the Guest account item when it is turned on, you see the Turn Off The Guest Account link. The only other option that is available for a Guest account is the ability to change the picture that is used.

Changing Passwords

A common operation for users is to change their password. By default, standard users can change only their own passwords. It is a good practice for users to change any initial password that has been provided to them by an administrative user. Administrators have the ability to set, remove, or modify the password for any account. Figure 6-4 shows the Change Password dialog box.

Figure 6-4   Changing an account's password

Passwords are case-sensitive; that is, capital and lowercase letters must be entered exactly as they have been defined. When changing a password, it might be necessary to enter the old password first. This is done to ensure that a user does not simply walk up to a computer to which someone is already logged on and make a change without knowing the original password. To make it easier to remember passwords, you can configure a password hint to be shown to all users who attempt to use the account through the logon screen. For this reason, this hint should be something that will help only the intended user access the system.

Performing Advanced User Account Configuration

The Manage Accounts window has been designed to provide access to the most common account-related operations on a computer running Windows Vista. In some cases, however, you might need to perform advanced operations. You can do this by using Local Users And Groups within the Computer Management console (see Figure 6-5). To access this console, in the Start menu, right-click Computer and choose Manage. Alternatively, if the Administrative Tools program group is available in the Start menu, select Computer Management.

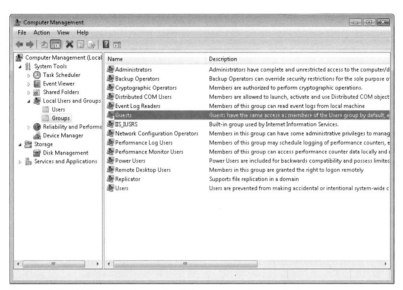

Figure 6-5 Using the Computer Management console to manage user accounts

The two main folders are Users and Groups. The Users folder contains a list of all of the user accounts created on the system. Depending on the software and services you have installed on the computer, it's possible that you'll notice some accounts that might not have been present in the Manage Accounts Control Panel item. Often, these accounts are designed to provide support for special software or services that require particular sets of permissions on the computer. You can view and modify detailed settings for a user by right-clicking the account and selecting Properties. User accounts have several different options, such as those shown in Figure 6-6.

Figure 6-6 Viewing the General properties tab for a Windows user account

The Groups folder within Local Users And Groups displays a list of all of the security groups that are defined on the computer. You use groups to manage permissions for collections of users. A general practice is to place users in groups and then to assign permissions to the groups themselves. Because you can easily change the membership of a group, this simplifies the process of managing permissions.

MORE INFO   Centrally managing advanced user settings

Most home and small-business users do not have reasons to configure advanced user settings and permissions manually. In general, you should encourage customers to use the features in Control Panel for managing security settings.

In corporate network environments, many of these options are more important. Most larger organizations have dedicated IT staff that are able to manage such settings centrally, using Windows Active Directory directory service.

In addition to the Administrators and Users groups, there are several other groups that pertain to collections of permissions that might be required for certain types of operations. For example, members of the Remote Desktop Users group are able to access this computer using the Remote Desktop feature, and members of the Backup Operators group can bypass standard file system security for performing a backup operation. Most groups include descriptive text that provides information about their purpose and function.

To view the members of a group, right-click the group name in the list and select Properties. The General tab shows a list of the user accounts that are currently members of the group (see Figure 6-7). The Add button also provides you with the ability to include new members in the group.

Figure 6-7   Viewing properties of a Windows Vista group

> ## Quick Check
>
> 1. What is the recommended type of account to use for daily computer use?
> 2. Which type of account should you create or enable for a user who requires temporary access to the computer?
>
> ### Quick Check Answers
>
> 1. Use a standard user account for performing common operations on the computer.
> 2. The Guest account has been designed to allow users temporary access to a computer. It provides a minimal set of permissions for performing common tasks.

Practice: Creating and Managing User Accounts

In this practice exercise, you will work with the user account management tools provided with the Windows Vista operating system.

▶ **Practice: Create and Configure New Accounts**

This exercise familiarizes you with the process of creating a new user account. To complete this exercise, you need to log on to the computer as an administrator initially.

1. Open Control Panel and click User Accounts And Family Safety. This opens the main window for security and safety-related settings.
2. Under User Accounts, click Add Or Remove User Accounts.
   You now see a list of all of the users who are currently configured on the computer.
3. Click Create A New Account to start the process of adding a new account.
4. Type **Test User** as a user name, and then choose the default Standard User option for the account type. This creates an account that has permissions to accomplish many common tasks, but it will not be able to change system settings.
5. Click Create Account.
   You now see the new user account in the Manage Accounts window.
6. To view and modify the settings of the Test User account, click it.
7. Click Change The Picture and select a different picture for the user account. Click Change Picture to complete the configuration. The picture you select appears on the Windows Vista logon screen.
8. By default, the new user account has not been assigned a password. To increase security, click Create A Password.
9. Type **test!123** in the New Password and Confirm New Password text boxes.
   Note that you can optionally provide a password hint to help the user remember his or her logon information. Remember that this hint is visible to all users of the system

(whether or not they have logged on), so be sure that it is something that is understood only by the user who will be using the account.

10. Click Create Password.

11. Close the Manage Accounts window and close Control Panel.

12. To test the new account, start by logging off the computer.

13. Next, test the new account by using it to log on to the system. You should see the Test User account as an option. Click this account, and then provide the password that you assigned in step 9 to log on to the system. During the first logon, Windows Vista creates a new user profile and sets up the default system settings for new accounts.

14. Try performing several different types of tasks using the new account. Make a note of which types of operations are allowed and which ones require you to type in administrator credentials.

15. When finished, log off the computer. Optionally, you can delete the Test User user account by logging on as an administrator and using the Manage Accounts window.

Lesson Summary

- For security reasons, it is recommended that users run with a minimal set of permissions whenever possible.

- Standard user accounts have limited permissions on the system but are able to perform most common day-to-day tasks.

- Administrator user accounts have full permissions on the computer, but users can run with minimal permissions for most tasks.

- You can enable the Guest account for use by individuals who might need to access the system occasionally.

- The Manage Accounts window in Control Panel enables administrators to create new accounts and modify account settings.

- You can use Local Users And Groups in the Computer Management console to perform advanced security configuration, including group membership.

Lesson Review

You can use the following questions to test your knowledge of the information in Lesson 1, "Managing User Accounts." The questions are also available on the companion CD if you prefer to review them in electronic form.

NOTE Answers

Answers to these questions and explanations of why each answer choice is correct or incorrect are located in the "Answers" section at the end of the book.

---

1. You are a Consumer Support Technician explaining the limitations of a standard user account to a customer. Which of the following operations require the user to provide approval for privilege escalation when running in Admin Approval Mode? (Choose all that apply.)

   A. Changing the user's own password

   B. Installing new device drivers

   C. Installing a new accounting software package

   D. Changing the desktop wallpaper

2. You are a Consumer Support Technician assisting a user with configuring security on his Windows Vista–based laptop. The customer mentions that he often has friends and co-workers that want to use his computer temporarily to perform tasks such as checking stock quotes on a Web site. The customer wants to ensure that users cannot make permanent changes to his system configuration. Which of the following types of accounts are most appropriate for these individuals to use?

   A. Administrator

   B. Guest

   C. Standard User

   D. Power User

Lesson 2: Understanding User Account Control (UAC)

As mentioned earlier, one of the primary design goals for Windows Vista was to make it an extremely secure desktop operating system. This process has involved significant engineering effort in all areas of the Windows platform. Many of these improvements have been performed so that users might not readily notice them. Others, however, do require user interaction.

As a Consumer Support Technician, it's likely that you've heard about the User Account Control (UAC) feature of Windows Vista. The primary purpose of UAC is to ensure that users and applications are granted the lowest level of permission they require to complete their tasks. The benefits include ensuring that people and programs cannot make potentially disastrous changes to their systems. In this lesson, you'll learn about the purpose and function of UAC and how you can configure it based on customers' requirements.

After this lesson, you will be able to:

- Describe common security issues and considerations related to desktop operating systems.
- Describe the purpose and function of a UAC file and registry virtualization and Admin Approval Mode.
- Perform permissions elevations, including answering of prompts for consent and prompts for credentials.
- Enable and disable UAC by using Control Panel.
- Configure the behavior of UAC by using Local Security Policy settings.

Estimated lesson time: 60 minutes

Understanding Common Security Risks and Threats

In the area of computer security, it is often wise to know the methods of the "enemy." That is, it's important to understand ways in which malicious programs or people might be able to perform unwanted actions on your computer. Some of these actions might include the following:

- **Using system resources**   Malicious programs might use CPU, memory, disk, and network resources to perform their tasks. In one example, users' computers are used to launch an attack on another site or computer without their knowledge. In those cases, users might notice that their computer appears to be working more slowly than before.

- **Tampering with critical system files or data**   In some cases, the data might simply be destroyed. In other cases, it might be transmitted to other computers. Regardless, these changes can cause data loss and instability of the operating system.

- **Attempting to obtain personal information such as credit card numbers, user names, and passwords** Often, this data is then transmitted to a remote computer, where it might be used for actions such as identity theft.

- **Tracking system usage** Software that is commonly referred to as spyware often runs in the background on a computer, unknown to users. It collects information such as Web sites that are visited and then reports this information back to the distributor of the software. Apart from violating security, this can lead to system slowdowns and instability.

- **Displaying unwanted advertisements** It is a common practice for applications to include additional software that is installed with little or no warning to the user. The additional code can perform operations such as automatically loading content from Web sites.

Some of these programs might be designed with a specific purpose in mind (for example, collecting potentially useful personal financial data). In other cases, the programs might have no purpose other than to annoy the user. Regardless of the authors' goals, it's obvious that malware should be prevented from running on desktop computers.

Understanding the Security Goals of Windows Vista

A fundamental principle of managing security is giving users and applications a minimal set of security permissions. This ensures that they can perform the most common operations that they need to accomplish tasks, but it greatly limits the potential damage that a malicious program can cause. For example, users rarely (if ever) need to modify operating system files directly. By preventing them from performing this action, the operating system can avoid the mistaken or malicious deletion of critical components. By default, applications that a user launches inherit all of the permissions of that user. If a user can open a Microsoft Word document, type a letter, and then e-mail it, a program could easily perform the same actions automatically. Therefore, it's important to place restrictions.

Microsoft had two primary goals when designing security for the Windows Vista operating system. The first was to ensure that users and applications were granted a minimal set of permissions for completing common operations. The other goal, however, was to ensure compatibility with earlier applications. In previous versions of Windows, it was very common for programs to assume that they had full access to the computers on which they were running. They could easily perform tasks such as reading and writing files from the file system and making modifications to the system registry. Because developers relied on these capabilities, it was often necessary for users to log on to their systems with accounts that had full administrative permissions. If the permissions were not available, the application might fail to run or might return errors to the user. Based on the two goals of security and compatibility, let's look at some new architectural features in Windows Vista.

> ### Real World
>
> *Anil Desai*
>
> There's no doubt about it: things would be far simpler for everyone involved if security were not a concern. In the early days of desktop computing, users and programs expected to have full control of their computers. Accordingly, application developers designed their programs under the assumption that they would also have these permissions and rights. Users would be able to perform any action they required on their systems. Unfortunately, having these abilities also increases potential security risks.

It is very important to understand that maintaining complete end-to-end security requires a team effort. It has been said that a chain is only as strong as its weakest link. It's not enough for a few users to follow the rules: all must do so. Application developers, home and business users, and Consumer Support Technicians must all exercise discipline to minimize security issues.

For example, from a network standpoint, having the world's most sophisticated and powerful firewall software won't prevent users from using their initials as their password. A malicious user might easily circumvent all of this protection simply by guessing the password. Similarly, you can easily disable the many security features in Windows Vista with just a few mouse clicks.

So how can you, as a Consumer Support Technician, do your part? Perhaps the most important aspect of ensuring security for the customers you support is to make sure that they understand the importance of features such as UAC. Users often don't see the benefits of limiting what they can easily do on their systems. This can lead them to circumvent or disable the features altogether. When, on the other hand, they see the potential benefits of security, they are much more likely to use best practices. Overall, it's your job to help lead the security team effort.

Understanding the UAC Process

In previous versions of Windows, it was most common for users to log on to their computers by using an account that had Administrator permissions. This meant that the user (and any program that he or she launched) would be able to perform any operation on the computer. This includes reading and writing to critical operating system files and accessing data stored anywhere on the system. In Windows Vista, it is recommended that users log on to the computer, using a limited set of permissions. In Lesson 1, you learned about the details of working with standard and administrative user accounts.

Microsoft designed the UAC feature of Windows Vista to allow users to log on to their computers using a standard user account. They can perform the majority of their tasks using a limited set of permissions. During the logon process, Windows Explorer (which provides the user interface for Windows Vista) automatically inherits the standard level of permissions. Additionally, any programs that are executed using Windows Explorer (for example, by double-clicking an application shortcut) also run with the standard set of user permissions. Many applications, including those that are included with the Windows Vista operating system itself, are designed to work properly in this way.

Other applications, especially those that were not specifically designed with the Windows Vista security settings in mind, often require additional permissions to run successfully. These types of programs are referred to as *legacy applications*. Additionally, actions such as installing new software, and making configuration changes to programs such as Windows Firewall, require more permissions than what is available to a standard user account. Windows Vista can automatically detect when an application is attempting to use more than standard user privileges.

Understanding Standard User Mode

When a user logs on to Windows Vista by using a standard user account, Windows Explorer and all other processes that are launched run with a minimal set of permissions. In this mode, UAC requires the user to provide credentials to the system whenever an application or operation requires elevated permissions. When an application or process requests access to more permissions, the user is prompted for approval. This process is known as application elevation because it allows Windows Vista to give a program a full set of permissions. Figure 6-8 shows a sample screen. After the credentials are provided and accepted, the program runs with elevated permissions. The user, however, still continues to have only a limited set of permissions.

Figure 6-8   Providing administrator credentials for application elevation

In a typical consumer environment, the user might already have knowledge of the user name and password of an Administrator account on the computer. By providing those details, he or she is implying that he or she wishes to allow the program to run in an elevated way. Other users of the computer who do not have these credentials will be unable to perform administrator-level actions.

Another way in which the standard user mode can be used is often called the "over the shoulder" method. In this case, a parent or supervisor might want most users to run under the standard user mode. Whenever there is a need to elevate privileges, this person can provide the necessary credentials. For example, a mother might want her child to log on to the computer as a standard user. Whenever the child needs to perform tasks such as changing system settings or installing new software, the mother must provide the necessary credentials.

Understanding Admin Approval Mode

In some cases, users might want to log on to the computer by using an Administrator account but still have the security benefits of running with minimal permissions. UAC provides this ability by using the Admin Approval Mode. The user account technically has full permissions on the system, but UAC limits which actions the user can perform. This effectively makes the account behave like a standard user account for most operations. Actions that require additional permissions can be performed, but the user must first approve them.

When an application requests elevated privileges, the default prompt Windows Vista shows to the user is one that asks the user to provide consent (see Figure 6-9). This method ensures that the user is aware when an application is attempting to run with elevated privileges. It can also help prevent situations in which malware applications attempt to modify the system. However, by default, it does not require the user to provide credentials for an Administrator account, because the current account already has this ability. Later in this lesson, you'll see how you can change UAC settings to require credentials in Admin Approval Mode.

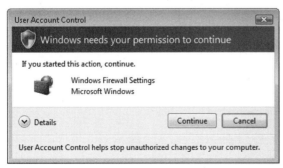

Figure 6-9   Providing consent for an application to run with elevated privileges

Additional Security Features

In addition to the UAC elevation prompts in Windows Vista, there are several other security-related enhancements that have been designed to increase safety and provide compatibility for earlier applications. In this section, you'll learn about how they work.

File System and Registry Virtualization

Two important areas of security-related concerns are the Windows file system and the registry. The file system contains files ranging from operating system components to user data. In the past, applications were designed with the assumption that they would be able to access these files and settings freely. These earlier applications often fail to run properly when they cannot make those changes.

To prevent direct access to secure file system locations (such as the operating system and Program Files folders), Windows Vista uses a technique called virtualization. This method works by monitoring for when applications request direct access to the file system or registry. When this occurs, the operating system automatically redirects the requests to the appropriate location. For example, if a previous program is attempting to write a configuration file to the Program Files folder, Windows Vista automatically intercepts that request and writes the file to a subfolder of the User profile. This is a much safer operation, and it still enables the application to run without modifications.

NOTE Temporary compatibility measures

Microsoft designed file system and registry virtualization technology primarily for compatibility with the vast library of earlier applications that were written for previous versions of Windows. Over time, many applications will be designed and updated to use safer models for file and registry access. Therefore, virtualization is being used as a temporary measure to bridge the gap until that happens. It is not intended to be used as a long-term compatibility solution.

Understanding the Secure Desktop

One method by which malicious applications might attempt to collect sensitive information from the user is by emulating a standard application or window. This is particularly true of the UAC elevation prompt. Users might be prompted for credentials by an unauthorized application that appears to be a standard Windows dialog box. The program collects user names and passwords and then might use this information to compromise security.

To prevent this problem, Windows Vista displays elevation prompts, using a secure desktop. The secure desktop automatically dims the desktop background and prevents all applications from launching any new prompts or windows until the user makes a decision related to the UAC elevation prompt. In this way, the user can be assured that the UAC prompt is coming from the Windows Vista operating system itself.

Identifying Tasks That Require Privilege Elevation

Although you can perform the majority of common tasks in Windows Vista as a standard user, there are various functions that require elevated privileges. Built-in operating system tools and applications use a shield icon next to the appropriate button or link to indicate that privilege elevation is required (see Figure 6-10). This helps users understand when they are performing potentially unsafe actions.

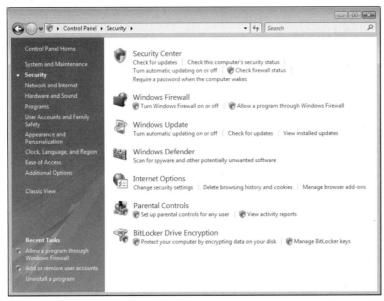

Figure 6-10   Tasks that require administrator permissions are shown with a shield icon

Responding to Elevation Prompts

A common source of security-related and configuration-related issues occurs when users install unknown applications. In some cases, this might be done deliberately, but in other cases, users might be tricked into running a setup program without knowing it. UAC automatically attempts to verify whether an application is a known program or potentially unsafe. Figure 6-11 shows an example of the approval dialog box that is presented to users.

In addition to providing the name of the program and its publisher (if available), the details include the full path to the application. This can help users determine whether they really want to install the program. Options include allowing or disallowing the program to run.

Figure 6-11 A prompt for an unknown application

Running Programs with Elevated Privileges

In some cases, users always want to run a particular program using Administrator permissions. For example, a customer might know that her former accounting software requires elevated permissions, and she does not want a prompt to appear automatically every time she launches the application. Run This Program As An Administrator offers the option to run a program always as an administrator. You can configure this setting on the Compatibility tab of a program or shortcut (see Figure 6-12).

Figure 6-12 Using Compatibility tab settings to run a program as an administrator

In some cases, the Run This Program As An Administrator check box might be disabled. For example, the application might be a built-in program that is included with Windows Vista and might not require elevated credentials. In those cases, the check box is disabled.

Another way to launch a program with elevated permissions is to right-click a program or shortcut and select Run As Administrator. This setting launches the application with Administrator permissions. Unless UAC is disabled, the user is prompted to provide consent or credentials.

Understanding Installer Detection

Perhaps one of the most common tasks that requires elevated privileges is the process of installing new software. Setup programs and installers often need to write directly to secure file system locations (such as the Program Files folder) and make changes to the registry.

Windows Vista uses methods to identify installation programs automatically and automatically prompts for approval of elevation when the application is run. This helps prevent common error messages and issues that users encounter when attempting to install programs, using standard user permissions.

NOTE   **Choosing new applications**

Whenever possible, recommend that customers select software that includes the Certified for Windows Vista logo. This helps ensure that the product has been designed for compatibility with UAC and other security features. More information about various Windows software logos is available in Chapter 1, "Preparing to Install Windows Vista."

Enabling and Disabling UAC

To ensure security of new Windows Vista installations, the UAC feature is enabled by default. When users log on to the computer, they start launching processes under the context of a standard user.

There are several different ways to control the behavior of the UAC feature. In some cases, customers might ask you for information about how to disable the feature altogether. You can access the Use User Account Control (UAC) To Help Protect Your Computer check box from within Control Panel . This check box is available by clicking User Accounts And Family Safety and then clicking User Accounts. You can also access this check box by searching for UAC in Control Panel. As shown in Figure 6-13, the dialog box provides a single check box that determines whether UAC is enabled.

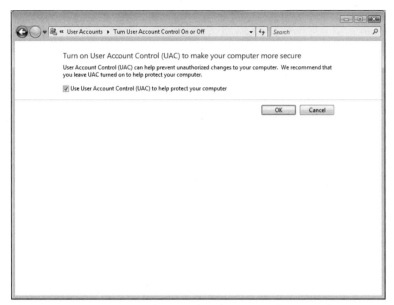

Figure 6-13 Viewing details related to the status of the UAC feature

NOTE Questioning the decision to disable UAC

When a customer asks how he or she can completely disable UAC, it's a good idea to get some more information about why he or she is making this request. Is the customer frustrated with the frequency of elevation and consent prompts? Is he or she having difficulty running certain applications? Often, users don't understand the value of the UAC feature and therefore see it as only an annoyance. As a Consumer Support Technician, explain the purpose and function of UAC, including how it can help prevent security issues and increase system reliability. It's quite likely that customers might decide that disabling the feature completely is too much of a risk and that changing various settings might be a much better overall solution. Remember, your goal should be to strike a balance between security and usability.

After selecting to enable or disable UAC, you are prompted to reboot your computer, which is necessary to make the changes effective. When you disable UAC, users receive a notification of this whenever they log on to the computer or access security-related settings in Control Panel. This is done to remind users that they are at risk of potential security issues. You'll look at ways in which you can fine-tune the behavior of UAC later in this lesson.

Managing UAC Settings with Local Security Policy

In addition to the default behavior of UAC, there are several different options that you can use to control the specific way in which this feature works. You define these settings by using policy settings on the computer. To access them, open the Local Security Policy console from the

Start menu. The utility is available in the Administrative Tools program group (if the Start menu options are set to display it) or by searching for Local Security Policy. The default interface shows several different groups of settings, each of which has dozens of available options.

To access the properties of the UAC functionality, expand Local Policies, and then select the Security Options folder. The right side of the console shows all of the available policy options along with their current settings. UAC-related policies are prefixed by the text User Account Control (see Figure 6-14).

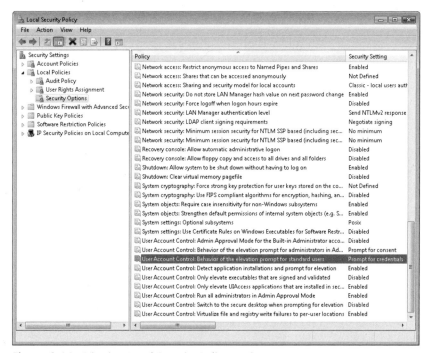

Figure 6-14 Viewing Local Security Policy settings

Each of the settings pertains to some aspect of system behavior or permissions. For example, you can use the Accounts: Guest Account Status option to specify whether the built-in Guest account is enabled. To make changes to a policy setting, double-click the item in the list. For most options, the first tab that is shown, Local Security Setting, provides the options for the setting (see Figure 6-15).

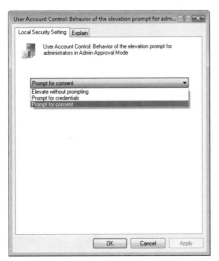

Figure 6-15   Viewing options for a policy setting

It's often difficult to understand the exact purpose of every available option. Fortunately, the Local Security Policy console also includes details about specific options on the Explain tab. The text that is displayed here (see Figure 6-16) provides background information about the policy, along with details about the effects of these settings. Most explanations also include details about the default setting for the option. This can be very helpful in troubleshooting configuration issues. In some cases, links to more information are provided. Overall, this can help you determine the purpose and function of each setting.

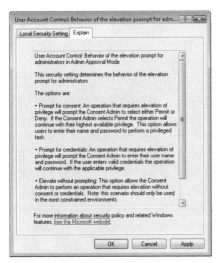

Figure 6-16   Viewing explanatory text for a policy setting

NOTE **Resisting the urge to tweak**

With all of the options available in the Local Security Policy console, it might be tempting to try to change configuration settings just to see what happens. Although this can be a good method for learning, it's important to make these changes on noncritical systems (such as a test computer). Keep in mind that it is possible to "break" certain functionality with improper settings.

In relation to controlling the behavior of UAC, there are nine different settings that you can configure manually. These are as follows:

- **User Account Control: Run All Administrators In Admin Approval Mode**   This setting can be considered a "master switch" that determines whether UAC is enabled on the local computer. The default setting is Enabled. The status of this setting corresponds to the Turn User Account Control (UAC) On Or Off setting in Control Panel. When the status is set to Disabled, Admin Approval Mode, file system and registry virtualization, and all related settings are effectively disabled. It is important to keep in mind that the other settings might appear to be properly configured, but they do not have any effect when this setting is disabled.

Exam Tip   Instead of memorizing the names of each of the UAC-related Group Policy settings, concentrate on the meanings and effects of each. On the exam, you'll be expected to understand how the settings are used, but you won't be tested on the exact wording of each setting.

- **User Account Control: Admin Approval Mode For The Built-In Administrator Account** This setting specifies the UAC options for the built-in Administrator account. By default, this setting is set to Disabled, which means that users who log on with the Administrator account have full permissions on the system. In general, it is recommended that the default Administrator account not be used. If you do have a need to enable the Administrator account, you can add security by enabling this policy setting.
- **User Account Control: Behavior Of The Elevation Prompt For Administrators In Admin Approval Mode** This setting specifies the type of elevation prompt that will be presented to administrative users when a program or process requests additional privileges. The settings include:
  - ❑ Prompt For Consent (the default).
  - ❑ Elevate Without Prompting.
  - ❑ Prompt For Credentials.

The default setting provides a balance between security and usability. To improve security, you can require that administrators provide a user name and password to elevate permissions. Alternatively, you can choose to eliminate the prompt altogether.

■ **User Account Control: Behavior Of The Elevation Prompt For Standard Users**   This setting determines how elevation prompts will be shown to standard users. The default setting, Prompt For Credentials, requires the user to provide logon information for an Administrator user every time an application or process requests elevated permissions. In some cases, you might want to prevent elevation from occurring at all. That's the purpose of the Automatically Deny Elevation Requests option.

■ **User Account Control: Detect Application Installations And Prompt For Elevation**   When users attempt to install an application, Windows Vista automatically attempts to elevate privileges. This is a useful feature, because most setup and installation programs require access to the file system and other protected areas of the computer. The default setting for consumer-focused editions of Windows Vista is for this option to be enabled. This means that users automatically see an elevation prompt whenever they launch an installer. The Disabled option is primarily used in company network environments in which IT staff can control the installation of software, using centralized methods.

■ **User Account Control: Only Elevate Executables That Are Signed And Validated**   One important potential security risk related to working with applications and software is in trusting the publisher of the application. Malware could easily create a new executable or shortcut that appears to be a familiar application (such as Microsoft Word), but that actually launches malicious code that could damage the system. One way to validate a program is to use a method based on Public Key Infrastructure (PKI) technology. This method allows trusted third parties to validate whether the publisher of the software is who it claims to be.

This option is set to Disabled, by default, because PKI technology has dependencies on other services such as a Certificate Server. Home and small-business users are unlikely to have the necessary infrastructure to do this.

■ **User Account Control: Only Elevate UIAccess Applications That Are Installed In Secure Locations**   Some applications might need to run with elevated privileges on Windows Vista. Developers of these applications can create a setting that instructs the operating system to prompt for elevated privileges automatically whenever the program is launched. One potential problem is for malware (such as programs downloaded from the Internet) to request full permissions and then make undesired changes to the system. This setting specifies that only applications that are located within known secure file system locations (such as the Program Files folder and subfolders of the Windows folder) are able to request elevation. This helps ensure that only properly installed programs are able to run with elevated permissions. The setting can be disabled, although this will reduce overall security.

■ **User Account Control: Switch To The Secure Desktop When Prompting For Elevation**   One method that malware authors have at their disposal is the possibility of tricking a user into providing sensitive information to a program. For example, a program could be designed to look very similar to the standard UAC elevation prompt. A user might provide a user name and password for privilege escalation, but the application itself is recording or sending this information elsewhere. To help prevent this type of intrusion, the default setting in Windows Vista is to use a secure desktop when an elevation prompt is presented. When this occurs, the entire desktop background is dimmed, and only the prompt is shown. Other applications will be unable to overwrite the prompt or create new windows that take the focus. When you disable this option, the UAC prompt appears like any other window. However, it is then possible for other applications to create a false UAC prompt.

■ **User Account Control: Virtualize File And Registry Write Failures To Per-User Locations** This setting is designed to provide compatibility with legacy applications that request direct access to the file system or to the registry. When a program attempts to perform one of these actions, Windows Vista automatically redirects the request to a safe, virtual location. The benefit is that the program can still run successfully, but all write operations occur safely. When you disable this setting, earlier applications are prevented from directly writing to file system and registry locations. In most cases, this means that the applications fail to run correctly.

NOTE   Educating customers

When supporting customers who are attempting to understand the purpose of various security settings, you might be tempted just to make various changes on their behalf. It's important, however, that you keep the customer informed of the effects of your modifications. After all, if a security issue or malware infection were to occur on customers' systems due to a change you made, you want to ensure that the user agreed with it. Generally, the more educated customers are with relation to security, the more likely they are to exercise good judgment.

Quick Check

1. What is the default elevation prompt that a user receives when running under Admin Approval Mode?
2. How can you modify UAC to disable the use of the secure desktop?

Quick Check Answers

1. The user is prompted for consent and is not required to provide logon credentials.
2. You can change this setting by using the Local Security Policy console. Specifically, you can set the User Account Control: Switch To The Secure Desktop When Prompting For Elevation option to Disabled.

Practice: Working with UAC

These practice exercises walk you through steps that can be used to configure and customize the behavior of UAC in Windows Vista. The exercises assume that you have created at least one Administrator account and one standard user account (for more information about creating accounts, see Lesson 1).

▶ **Practice 1: Configure UAC Behavior**

In this exercise, you configure UAC to prevent standard user accounts from performing system-level tasks, even if they have information about administrator credentials on the computer. It is important that you have at least one Administrator account configured on the computer before beginning. This exercise also assumes that all UAC options are set to their default values.

1. Log on to the computer using an Administrator account.
2. From the Start menu, open the Local Security Policy console.
3. Expand the Local Policies folder and select Security Options.
4. Double-click User Account Control: Behavior Of The Elevation Prompt For Standard Users.
5. On the Local Security Setting tab, change the setting to Automatically Deny Elevation Requests.

   This setting specifies that users who log on with a standard user account are not prompted to provide elevation credentials. Therefore, they are unable to run programs with administrator permissions.
6. Log off the computer and log on as a standard user.
7. From the Start menu, open Control Panel and click an item that has a shield next to it.

   Examples include Add Or Remove User Accounts or Allow A Program Through Windows Firewall. Note that you do not receive a UAC elevation prompt. The resulting dialog box states: "This program is blocked by group policy. For more information, contact your system administrator."
8. To change the UAC back to its initial settings, log off the computer and log on again as an administrator. Use the Local Security Policy console to change the User Account Control: Behavior Of The Elevation Prompt For Standard Users setting to Prompt For Credentials.

▶ **Practice 2: Run Programs with Administrator Credentials**

This practice demonstrates two different methods of running a standard program as an administrator. This exercise assumes that you are logged on to the computer as a member who has administrator permissions with Admin Approval Mode enabled. To complete this exercise, you need to install a program that requires administrator permission on the computer. Place a shortcut to the program on your desktop to follow these steps.

1. Log on to Windows Vista using an Administrator user account.
2. Double-click the program shortcut to open the program.

   You should receive a UAC elevation prompt that asks for approval to run under elevated permissions.
3. Choose Cancel to prevent the program from running.
4. To avoid the elevation prompt, right-click the program shortcut and choose Run As Administrator.

   Note that the program launches and that you do not receive a prompt for UAC elevation.
5. Close the program.
6. To configure the program always to run using administrator credentials, right-click the program shortcut and choose Properties.
7. Click the Compatibility tab, and then select the Run This Program As An Administrator check box. Click OK to save the settings.
8. Double-click the program shortcut and note that you are not prompted for UAC approval.
9. To change the shortcut settings back to the defaults, right-click the shortcut and select Properties. On the Compatibility tab, clear the Run This Program As An Administrator check box. Click OK to save the changes.

Lesson Summary

- Common computer security risks include viruses, adware, and other software that are collectively known as malware.
- For security reasons, users should log on to their computers by using a minimal set of permissions.
- Important design goals for Windows Vista include improving security settings while maintaining compatibility with earlier applications.
- The UAC process allows users to run with minimal permissions and provides prompts when programs require additional permissions.
- In the UAC Standard User Mode, users will be prompted to provide credentials whenever an application requires additional permissions.
- Admin Approval Mode allows a user to log on as an administrator but to run under a minimal set of permissions for most operations.
- File system and registry virtualization prevents direct access to secure operating system locations while still providing for backward compatibility with former applications.
- UAC settings and options can be modified using the Local Security Policy tool.

Lesson Review

You can use the following questions to test your knowledge of the information in Lesson 2. The questions are also available on the companion CD if you prefer to review them in electronic form.

NOTE Answers

Answers to these questions and explanations of why each answer choice is correct or incorrect are located in the "Answers" section at the end of the book.

---

1. Which of the following Local Security policy options can you set to disable all UAC functionality and options effectively?

    A. User Account Control: Virtualization File And Registry Write Failures

    B. User Account Control: Admin Approval Mode For The Built-In Administrator Account

    C. User Account Control: Only Elevate Executables That Are Signed And Validated

    D. User Account Control: Run All Administrators In Admin Approval Mode

2. You are a Consumer Support Technician assisting a customer with configuring UAC features in Windows Vista. The customer would like to run using a minimal set of permissions but would like to be able to perform privilege escalation without providing credentials. Which of the following settings should you recommend?

    A. An Administrator user account with Admin Approval Mode enabled

    B. An Administrator user account with Admin Approval Mode disabled

    C. A standard user account with the behavior of the elevation prompt set to Prompt For Credentials

    D. A standard user account with the behavior of the elevation prompt set to Automatically Deny Elevation Requests

Chapter Review

To further practice and reinforce the skills you learned in this chapter, you can perform the following tasks:

- Review the chapter summary.
- Review the list of key terms introduced in this chapter.
- Complete the case scenarios. These scenarios set up real-world situations involving the topics of this chapter and ask you to create a solution.
- Complete the suggested practices.
- Take a practice test.

Chapter Summary

- Windows Vista includes standard and Administrator user account types.
- User Account Control (UAC) is designed to help users run with a minimal set of permissions on their computers while still being able to support earlier applications.
- The process of privilege escalation allows standard users to perform tasks and run programs that require Administrator permissions.

Key Terms

Do you know what these key terms mean? You can check your answers by looking up the terms in the glossary at the end of the book.

- Admin Approval Mode
- consent
- credentials
- elevation prompt
- Local Security Policy
- privilege escalation
- User Account Control (UAC)

Case Scenarios

In the following case scenarios, you apply what you've learned about user accounts and UAC in Windows Vista. You can find answers to these questions in the "Answers" section at the end of this book.

Case Scenario 1: Creating User Accounts Based on Customers' Requirements

You are a Consumer Support Technician assisting a customer in setting up a new Windows Vista–based computer for use by her family. You have asked several questions to determine how you should set up the computer. The customer would like to create four separate user accounts: one for herself, one for her husband, and one for each of her two children. The parents require the ability to install new software and hardware on the computer occasionally. They would like to make this process as simple as possible. The parents also need to run several applications that they know require administrator permissions. The children should not be able to perform advanced system functions unless a parent is present. Overall, the customer wants to minimize risks related to the installation of malicious software or the accidental deletion of important system files.

1. What type of user account should you configure for the parents?
2. What type of user account should you configure for the children?
3. How can the parents specify which applications should be run automatically as an administrator?

Case Scenario 2: Configuring UAC Settings Based on Customers' Requirements

You are a Consumer Support Technician assisting a customer in setting up security in Windows Vista. The customer did not perform the initial configuration of his computer, and he would like to change the behavior of UAC. Specifically, he would like to configure his computer so that he does not need to provide credentials every time he is prompted for privilege elevation. He also wants to ensure that all programs remain visible whenever an approval prompt is displayed. Overall, he wants to achieve these goals without significantly reducing the security of the system.

1. What type of user account should you configure for the customer?
2. Which tool should you access to make changes to the behavior of UAC?
3. Which UAC option should you change to keep desktop applications visible when an elevation prompt is displayed?

Suggested Practices

To help you successfully master the exam objectives presented in this chapter, complete the following tasks. It is recommended that you make security-related changes on a test computer and that you keep a record of the changes you are making so that they can be reversed if necessary.

Practice 1: Working with User Account Types

Create two new user accounts within Windows Vista. The first should be configured as a standard user account, and the second should be an Administrator account. Log on under the standard user account and note which types of actions require you to provide administrator credentials. Then, log on as the administrator and make note of the difference in behavior of the UAC prompts. When finished, delete both user accounts.

Practice 2: Configuring UAC Settings

Use the Local Security Policy console to modify UAC-related settings. Make a note of the initial settings before you make any changes. Verify the results of the settings. For example, you might choose to disable Admin Approval Mode temporarily. Verify that you no longer receive UAC elevation prompts when logging on as an Administrator. Another option is to choose to disable the secure desktop when prompting for elevation. When finished, reset all options to their initial values.

Take a Practice Test

The practice tests on this book's companion CD offer many options. For example, you can test yourself on just one exam objective, or you can test yourself on all the 70-623 certification exam content. You can set up the test so that it closely simulates the experience of taking a certification exam, or you can set it up in study mode so that you can look at the correct answers and explanations after you answer each question.

MORE INFO   Practice tests

For details about all the practice test options available, see the "How to Use the Practice Tests" section in this book's introduction.

Chapter 7

Using Windows Security Center

The tasks involved in ensuring that computer systems remain secure can be challenging, even for knowledgeable users. To keep an operating system protected from issues such as the installation of malware or network-based attacks often requires examining numerous operating system settings. It also requires the use of several different features and applications. In some cases, if even one of these settings or programs is incorrectly configured, the overall security of the system can be significantly decreased.

Windows Vista includes numerous security features that you can use together to protect users' computers. It also includes simplified methods for monitoring and configuring these security methods. The problem is that examining and modifying all of these many settings can be tricky. Security tools and features such as Windows Firewall, Windows Defender, Automatic Updates, and third-party products require some level of expertise to configure.

As a Consumer Support Technician, customers rely on your knowledge to help keep their computers secure. Although you could verify numerous security settings manually, the process would be time-consuming and error-prone. In this chapter, you'll learn how you can use the Windows Security Center to get a quick view of overall system security through a single, simple application. Generally, this information will help you quickly and easily identify potential configuration problems throughout the system. It will also provide an easy way for users to ensure that their systems remain optimally configured over time.

Exam objectives in this chapter:
- Configure Windows Vista Security.
    - ❏ Configure Windows Security Center.
    - ❏ Configure Windows Updates.
    - ❏ Configure Windows Defender.

Lessons in this chapter:

Before You Begin

To complete the practice exercises in this chapter, you'll need to have access to at least one computer that is running a consumer edition of Windows Vista (Windows Vista Home Basic, Windows Vista Home Premium, Windows Vista Ultimate, or Windows Vista Business). Unless otherwise noted, the contents of the text and practice items assume that you are running Windows Vista using its default settings and that no additional security software (such as an antivirus scanner) is installed.

Lesson 1: Using Windows Security Center

The steps required to secure a modern operating system fully, such as Windows Vista, can be complicated. Potential sources of security issues include network-based attacks and the installation of unwanted or malicious software. Because most home users have access to the Internet, it's important that their systems remain protected against common types of attacks. The same is true for small-business users; they often require their own computers to be able to talk to each other while limiting the types of operations that can occur over the Internet.

Important types of security software include antispyware, antimalware, and antivirus scanners. Network security features include components such as Windows Firewall and the configuration of public and private networks. Finally, as you learned in Chapter 6, "Configuring Windows Vista Security," it's important for users to run under a set of minimal permissions. That's where the User Account Control (UAC) feature comes in.

The Windows Security Center is designed to provide you with an overview of the status of security based on all of these different settings, regardless of which tools are needed to manage them. In this lesson, you'll learn how to use Windows Security Center to monitor the security configuration of Windows Vista.

After this lesson, you will be able to:

- Describe the purpose and function of Windows Security Center.
- Launch Windows Security Center and obtain an overview of current security-related settings.
- List the different areas of security that are monitored by Windows Security Center, along with potential sources of warnings.
- Resolve security-related configuration issues that are reported by Windows Security Center.
- Modify the ways in which Windows Security Center notifies users about potential security configuration issues.

Estimated lesson time: 45 minutes

Overview of Windows Security Center

Windows Security Center is an application that is included with all of the consumer-based editions of Windows Vista. Windows Vista includes numerous security-related features and settings. To get an overview of the available options, you can open Control Panel and click Security. Figure 7-1 shows the default display.

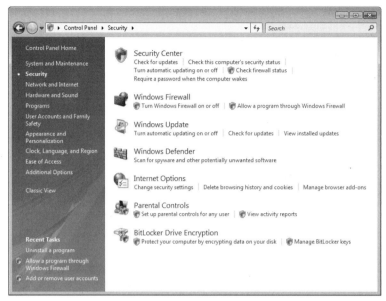

Figure 7-1   Viewing security-related configuration options in Control Panel

The first available link provides access to Security Center. Figure 7-2 shows the basic user interface of the Windows Security Center application.

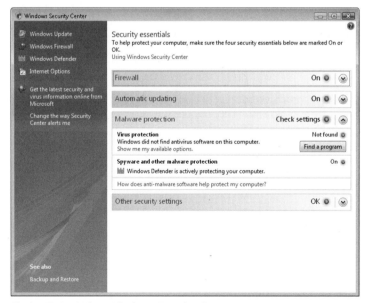

Figure 7-2   Using Windows Security Center

Microsoft designed Windows Security Center to provide you with an overview of the various different security configuration features and to provide a quick method of detecting any potential problems. The default display provides information related to the following four different types of security features:

- Firewall
- Automatic updating
- Malware protection
- Other security settings

The color of each section provides you with an overview of the status of each of these areas. Green indicates the current settings are optimal from a security standpoint and that this feature or setting is correctly configured based on recommendations. Yellow indicates that there is a potential issue with the configuration of current security settings or that the security level could not be determined. Finally, red indicates that one or more configuration settings might not be configured according to security recommendations.

Understanding Security Details

Initially, all of the Windows Security Center sections are displayed in a collapsed view. This allows you to get an overview about the overall status of security easily. However, you can also expand each section by clicking the title of the item or the arrow on the right side of the bar. When expanded, each section provides additional details related to the item's status. This is especially useful for items that are colored yellow or red, indicating that there is a potential configuration setting or feature that could be improperly configured.

NOTE   Security in previous versions of Windows

Microsoft first introduced the Security Center feature to the Microsoft Windows platform in Windows XP Service Pack 2. If you're supporting users who are running this version of Windows, you will find several of the features and settings to be similar to those of Windows Vista. It is still important to keep in mind that Windows Vista includes numerous features and additions that make it more secure than earlier versions of the Windows platform.

Changing Windows Security Alerts Settings

In cases in which the configuration of security-related applications and settings is not set based on recommendations, Windows Vista can automatically alert users about the issue by displaying an icon or notification in the system tray. The icon, called Windows Security Alerts, provides a shield icon with explanatory text about the issue. You can configure the exact behavior of Windows Security Alerts by clicking Change The Way Security Center Alerts Me in Windows Security Center. Figure 7-3 shows the available options.

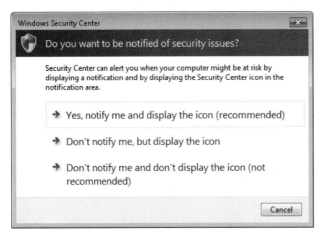

Figure 7-3   Viewing notification options for Windows Security Center

The options include the following:

- Yes, Notify Me And Display The Icon (Recommended)
- Don't Notify Me, But Display The Icon
- Don't Notify Me And Don't Display The Icon (Not Recommended)

The default and recommended option is to display the notification and the icon. This setting is useful because it helps ensure that users are notified whenever there is a problem related to configuration settings. If users want more information about the problem, they can click the notification. They can also launch Windows Security Center by right-clicking the shield icon in the system tray and then choosing Security Center from the shortcut menu. These features ensure that users are aware of their security status even when they do not manually open Windows Security Center.

Now that you have a basic idea of the purpose of Windows Security Center, you'll look at each of the major areas in more detail.

Configuring Windows Firewall

From a usability standpoint, it's often helpful to enable computers to communicate with each other without any restrictions. If you can trust all of the computers and users in the environment, this will allow for the easy flow of information. In many environments, however, security risks require limited network connectivity. The goal is to enable authorized communications and keep unwanted network traffic out.

A firewall is designed to provide a logical layer of protection between computers in a networked environment. For example, home users might want their home computers to communicate with each other but want to prevent users on the Internet from accessing their computers directly. Microsoft designed Windows Firewall to restrict inbound and outbound traffic based on a series of configurable rules. The goal is to ensure that only certain types of applications and services are able to connect to the computers.

Understanding Inbound Filtering

Filtering inbound traffic can be very useful in preventing many kinds of common network-based attacks. Especially when computers are directly connected to the Internet, it's common for other computers and malicious users to scan for computers that are not properly protected and try to access them.

For example, if an application such as a Web server can be directly accessed from another computer, it's possible for malicious users to exploit known vulnerabilities in the product to gain access to the system. A firewall can prevent inbound access to the Web server at the network layer, thereby avoiding these potential problems. It does this by blocking all traffic that is inbound to the computer. In some cases, applications or services might need to access the computer for legitimate purposes. In these cases, you can create exceptions for known applications.

Understanding Outbound Filtering

Outbound filtering limits network access for applications and services that are running on the local computer. For security reasons, not all outbound Internet access should be allowed. A common method of compromising security is to have unwanted applications connect to the Internet or to other computers. In some cases, these applications might be used to download unwanted advertisements and directly display them on the screen. More serious problems include collecting data and password information from the local computer and transmitting it to another computer on the Internet.

In some cases, outbound access is required. For example, applications such as Web browsers and antivirus scanners might need to connect to the Internet regularly to obtain data. Features of Windows Vista (such as online help, Windows Update, and Windows Defender) can benefit greatly from having access to the Internet. The standard approach to meeting these requirements is to provide a list of exceptions in the outbound firewall configuration. These settings define which applications and services are able to communicate across the firewall.

Managing Firewall Settings

There are two main management methods for the configuration of Windows Firewall. You can find both by opening Firewall from the Start menu or by accessing Security in Control Panel and then clicking Windows Firewall. The default Windows Firewall window shows a simplified display of overall firewall settings. It provides details related to the current status of Windows Firewall (see Figure 7-4).

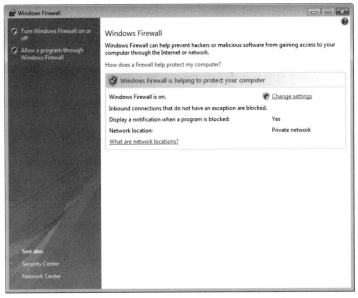

Figure 7-4   Viewing an overview of the status of Windows Firewall

Users can click Change Settings to make modifications to the current configuration of Windows Firewall. The General tab of the Windows Firewall dialog box (shown in Figure 7-5) provides a master setting that determines whether the firewall is enabled.

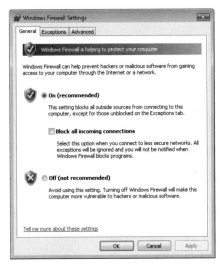

Figure 7-5   Viewing the General tab settings for Windows Firewall

It is strongly recommended that you configure the firewall to On. When you choose this option, the Block All Incoming Connections check box is available. Selecting this check box prevents other computers from accessing any resources on the local computer, regardless of the configuration settings in other tools and applications. Therefore, this option is most useful when running in insecure environments such as a public network.

Users who want to be able to set up a home network to share media and other files will likely want to leave the check box cleared. The last option is to disable Windows Firewall completely. In most cases, use this setting only for temporary troubleshooting because disabling the firewall can leave the system open to numerous types of network attacks.

The Exceptions tab includes a list of all of the different types of applications that are allowed to communicate through Windows Firewall (see Figure 7-6). Because many network-enabled and Internet-enabled applications require this access, users can specify which applications are allowed to connect. By default, the Windows Firewall list includes a default set of allowed outbound connection options. These settings allow commonly used applications to communicate with other networks.

When you install new applications or enable new operating system features, Windows Vista might prompt you to approve automatic changes to the firewall configuration. Regardless of your choice, you'll be able see which programs are able to access remote networks, such as the Internet, by using the Exceptions tab. By limiting the list to only known applications, you can prevent malware and other programs from automatically connecting to the Internet or to other computers.

Figure 7-6   Viewing Exceptions tab settings for Windows Firewall

Finally, the Advanced tab enables users to configure which network connections use the Windows Firewall. In most cases, it's best to leave the firewall settings on for all connections. In some cases, however, it might be necessary to disable Windows Firewall. For example, some users might connect to their work networks from home. If their work network already has adequate security software and settings, it might be preferable to turn off the firewall for that particular connection.

The primary goal of the basic Windows Firewall tool is to provide a quick and easy way for users to modify the most common settings. The Windows Vista firewall also has many additional features and functions that you can use to manage better which types of connections are permitted. You can access these additional settings by launching the Windows Firewall With Advanced Security console. (You can launch this console from the Start menu or through Administrative Tools). Figure 7-7 shows the default types of settings that are available. It is beyond the scope of this book (and the 70-623 exam) to look at creating and managing firewall rules, but it is helpful to know that these features are available if necessary.

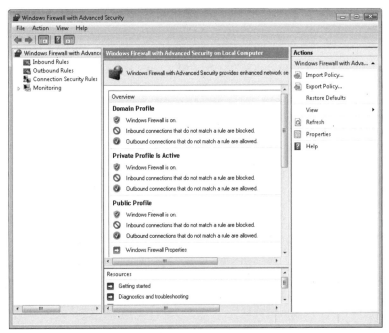

Figure 7-7 Using the Windows Firewall With Advanced Security console

Exam Tip When preparing for Exam 70-623, you should be familiar with the process of viewing and creating firewall exceptions. There's no need to memorize the list of common applications and network ports that are available. Just keep in mind what you might do to troubleshoot an application that appears to be configured properly but is unable to connect to other computers or to the Internet.

Configuring Automatic Updating

A critical aspect of maintaining security is to keep operating systems up to date. Over time, security or reliability problems might be found, and updates are necessary to avoid any potential problems. For example, a security vulnerability might be found in a component of Windows Vista. Malicious users who are aware of this can target systems that haven't been updated, and such users might be able to make modifications to the system or access sensitive data.

To reduce these risks, Windows Vista includes an automatic update feature that can be used to download new updates to the operating system. Windows Update works by periodically contacting servers at Microsoft over the Internet to obtain a list of available updates. It then compares the current state of the computer (including which updates have already been installed and which features are enabled) and determines whether updates are required. If they are required, Windows Update can optionally download and install them.

Windows Security Center provides an overview of the current settings for related to automating updates. Figure 7-8 provides an example.

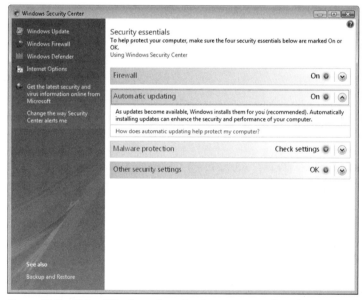

Figure 7-8 Using Windows Security Center to monitor the status of automatic updates

The recommended configuration setting for automatic updates is for new updates to be installed automatically. When this setting is chosen, the Automatic Updating item appears green in Windows Security Center.

Changing Windows Update Settings

In addition to the recommended configuration of automatically downloading and installing updates, users have several other options. You can change the settings for Windows Update by first clicking Security in Control Panel, clicking Windows Update, and then clicking Change Settings (see Figure 7-9).

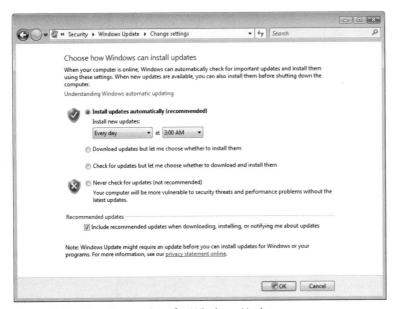

Figure 7-9   Changing settings for Windows Update

The options include the following:

- **Install Updates Automatically (Recommended)**   This option specifies that Windows Vista automatically attempts to download and install all updates based on the defined schedule. Options include choosing a particular day and time to run every week or choosing Every Day. As mentioned earlier, when you select this option, the Windows Security Center Automatic Updating section appears green.

- **Download Updates But Let Me Choose Whether To Install Them**   This option specifies that Windows Vista should automatically download updates but that it does not install these updates until a user chooses to do so. The benefit of this method is that it minimizes the potential performance impact to the system while updates are being installed. The problem, however, is that the user might forget to install the updates, thereby leaving the system without the updates for significant periods. For this reason, Windows Security Center shows the Automatic Updating item as yellow when this option is selected.

- **Check For Updates But Let Me Choose Whether To Download And Install Them**   This option instructs Windows Vista to contact the Windows Update servers periodically for information about new updates, but it does not automatically download or install them.

When this option is selected, Windows Security Center shows a yellow warning for Automatic Updating.

- **Never Check For Updates (Not Recommended)**   This setting effectively disables Windows Update and prevents Windows Vista from checking for, downloading, and installing any new updates that might be available. This option is particularly risky because users of the computer will be unaware of potential security problems. For this reason, Windows Security Center displays the Automatic Updating item in red when this option is selected.

When supporting customers' computers running Windows Vista, the recommended option of automatically downloading and installing updates is often the most appropriate. In some cases, users might want more control over which updates are installed and when. One possible reason for this is to limit the performance impacts of installing the updates and then requiring a system reboot. It is important to make users understand, however, that keeping their systems updated by installing updates as soon as possible is a critical component of overall system security.

Using Windows Security Center to Modify Update Settings

Whenever Windows Security Center shows a yellow or red warning for the Automatic Updating item, the details of the item includes a Change Settings button that enables users and Consumer Support Technicians to change their settings quickly and easily without having to open another dialog box manually. Figure 7-10 shows the options that are available.

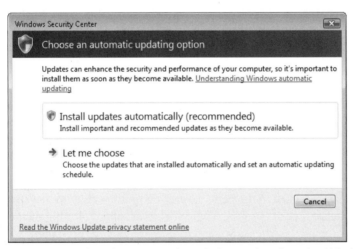

Figure 7-10 Changing automatic updating settings by using Windows Security Center

The first option automatically configures the Windows Update settings to the recommended value to download and install updates automatically based on a schedule. Clicking the second option opens the Windows Update Change Settings dialog box, which enables the user to make other selections. When changes are made and applied, the Windows Security Center display is automatically refreshed to show the current security status of the computer.

Real World

Anil Desai

In the early days of desktop computers, the most common configuration (especially in a home environment) was to have computers run in a stand-alone configuration. Often, the only way to get data between systems was by using removable media such as floppy disks (a process that is humorously referred to as "sneakernet"). Over time, the benefits of connecting computers together using a network became indispensible. Today, it's not uncommon for homes and small businesses to have multiple computers, and they need to be able to communicate with each other. The rise in popularity of the Internet brought another leap in connectivity. Now, just about every computer in the world has the potential to connect with any other.

The downside of networking is that computers are now vulnerable to a wide array of potentially malicious software infections and attacks. As a Consumer Support Technician, your customers rely on you to provide them with protection against these potential problems. Although you have many technical features and applications to help you take care of the job, it's important also to educate users about potential security issues.

Computer users who are new to the Internet often trust everything they read. Offers to install software that will magically improve system performance and or reveal get-rich-quick schemes are very common on the Internet. It can be helpful to instill a healthy dose of skepticism in newer users. They should always consider the source of the information they're receiving, and they should practice "defensive computing" wherever possible.

A common method of obtaining sensitive information is through the use of phishing or social engineering. These methods trick users into providing details such as name, address, national ID numbers, credit card information, and passwords. They can also be surprisingly effective, especially with trusting users. Often, a basic understanding of common schemes is enough to prevent such schemes from being effective.

Another security issue is related to the perception of computing risks. When supporting end users, I have often talked to customers who are almost afraid of using their computers because of these risks. They tend to hear about data loss, identity theft, and other issues in the popular media. Often, the reports are overly sensationalized in popular media. There are certainly risks with performing any type of action such as connecting to the Internet, but it can be helpful to reassure customers that, with a little diligence, systems and information can remain well protected. Overall, there are numerous potential security risks, but most can be addressed with a little knowledge and care.

Configuring Malware Protection

Some of the most common threats to standard desktop operating systems are collectively known as malware. These types of software can perform a wide array of unwanted operations on a computer. One example is a type of software that is installed on a computer with little or no notification to the end user. The program might automatically download and display advertisements from the Internet or collect and transmit information to another computer.

Viruses are programs that are generally designed to do damage. They might be installed through a security vulnerability or by tricking users into downloading and installing them. When run, they can cause serious system-related problems, including data corruption. Regardless of the details, these programs should clearly be avoided.

Antimalware products are available from Microsoft and a number of different vendors. These programs have been designed to protect systems against the installation and operation of malware by providing several layers of protection. For example, they might examine all downloaded programs and verify that users want to install them when they are launched. Another method is to scan the computer's file system periodically, looking for signatures of known malware programs. These features often integrate with other products such as firewall configurations.

Microsoft designed Windows Security Center to show basic details related to the configuration of malware protection. There are two items that you can find in the details of this section:

- Virus Protection
- Spyware And Other Malware Protection

The default configuration of Windows Vista includes Windows Defender, which is designed to provide numerous security-related functions, including scanning for malware. It also relies on the Windows Update feature to download and install new malware definition updates regularly. You'll learn about configuring Windows Defender in more detail later in this lesson.

As with the other sections in Windows Security Center, there are three main indications for the malware protection item:

- **Green** Indicates that malware protection is installed, is up to date, and is configured properly.
- **Yellow** Specifies that an antimalware configure setting is different from the recommended value, or that the antimalware software is outdated. The indicator also appears yellow if Windows Vista is unable to find compatible antimalware programs on the system.
- **Red** This indicator specifies that an antivirus or antimalware program is not currently installed or is turned off. This leaves the computer potentially vulnerable to security-related problems.

Changing Antivirus Options

Windows Vista does not include an antivirus application. Therefore, unless a third-party hardware or software vendor has included a specific product that is able to detect and remove viruses, the default setting appears as Not Found. Third-party antivirus developers can add certain features that automatically assist users in ensuring that the features are properly configured.

For example, if an antivirus product is installed but its virus definitions are out of date, Windows Security Center can provide a direct link that launches the application and shows options for resolving the problem. Although the user can accomplish this task manually, it requires the user to find the relevant program and change the settings.

NOTE   Evaluating antivirus products

Numerous Windows-based antivirus products are available on the market. When evaluating features, users generally have the best experience with products that are certified for Windows Vista. (See Chapter 1, "Preparing to Install Windows Vista," for more information on Windows Vista software certification logos.) These products are most likely to integrate properly with Windows Security Center. In addition to virus detection and removal capabilities, it's helpful to keep in mind the performance effects of particular antivirus solutions. Some of these products can use significant amounts of memory, CPU, and disk resources, which can cause systems to slow down noticeably.

For Windows Security Center to be able to monitor the installation and configuration of an antivirus product, it must be designed with Windows Vista in mind. In some cases, you might have installed an antivirus product that is not automatically detected by Windows Security Center. In this case, you can click Show Me My Available Options in the details of the Malware Protection section. Figure 7-11 shows the two available options.

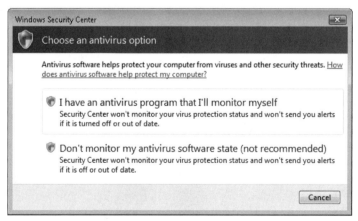

Figure 7-11   Changing antivirus options in Windows Security Center

The first option tells Windows Security Center that you have installed or will install an antivirus program and that you do not want to see any further prompts related to this configuration setting. The other option is not to monitor the status of antivirus software at all. Clicking this setting still makes the malware protection configuration appear in yellow, but you will not receive further alerts or details related to antivirus programs.

Configuring Windows Defender

In addition to monitoring antivirus programs, the malware protection section in Windows Security Center can detect the presence of antispyware or antimalware products. By default, Windows Defender is configured to provide this functionality. If users continue to use the default settings, they see that Windows Defender is listed in the details under Malware Protection.

In some cases, users might want to change the configuration settings of Windows Defender. Available options include details related to how frequently and when automatic spyware scans are performed. To change these settings, open Windows Defender from the Start menu. Click Tools, and then click Options to open the Options dialog box (see Figure 7-12).

Figure 7-12   Viewing configuration options in Windows Defender

The Options dialog box includes numerous settings that you can use to define how and when Windows Defender runs. The major sections and options include the following:

■ **Automatic Scanning**   The settings in this section determine whether Windows Defender automatically scans the system based on a schedule. If automatic scanning is enabled, users can specify the days and·times at which the scans will be performed. Additionally, there is an option to check for updated definition files automatically before performing the scan. Finally, if users want to remove or disable any spyware automatically that has been detected, they can choose to apply the default actions automatically.

■ **Default Actions**   When Windows Defender detects malware, it automatically categorizes the item into an alert level. The possible levels are High, Medium, and Low. By default, the action that Windows Defender takes is based on settings defined in the definition files. You can override these default actions by selecting either Remove or Ignore as the default action for each alert level. The settings affect options that are displayed when Windows Defender finds malware as well as the automatic actions it takes during a scheduled scan.

■ **Real-Time Protection Actions**   One of the most powerful features of Windows Defender is its ability to monitor for system modifications automatically that might be unautho- rized. This feature, known as real-time protection, is enabled by default. Figure 7-13 shows the many different options that are available. In some cases, users might want to disable one or more of the security agents while still allowing real-time protection to be enabled. Other options include customizing how and when Windows Defender notifies the user when potential security issues occur.

Figure 7-13   Viewing Real-Time Protection Options in Windows Defender

■ **Advanced Options**   This section enables you to specify which types of files Windows Defender scans and to provide a list of exceptions. Exceptions might be useful if you have large files that contain only data or known information, and you want to reduce the usage of system resources during the scan process. Options are also available for creating a restore point before any detected malware is removed from the system.

- **Administrator Options** These options are "master switches" for the functionality of Windows Defender. They allow you to specify whether Windows Defender is enabled and which users will be able to change its configuration.

For most users, the default settings of Windows Defender provide the ideal balance of security and usability. In some cases, particular applications or services might require settings to be temporarily modified. Alternatively, users might want to change options such as the default scan frequency to reduce potential performance impacts.

Instead of using Windows Defender, users also have the option of installing their own third-party antimalware products. If the program has been designed for compatibility with the Windows Security Center, its status and details should appear in this section. It is important to note that customers should generally use only one type of antimalware product at a time. Having more than one enabled can cause various compatibility issues.

Finally, if you have chosen not to install a particular antimalware solution (or if you are running a product that is not detected by Windows Security Center, you can click Show Me My Available Options under Malware Protection in Windows Security Center. As shown in Figure 7-14, there are two main options that are available:

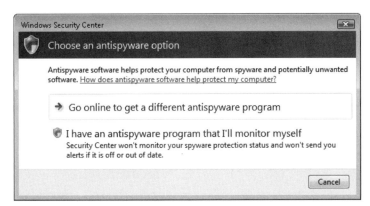

Figure 7-14 Viewing available options when an antispyware product is not installed

- **Go Online To Get A Different Antispyware Program** This option launches a Web browser and navigates to Microsoft's third-party antispyware product page.
- **I Have An Antispyware Program That I'll Monitor Myself** Selecting this option effectively disables the Windows Security Center automatic spyware check. The user does not receive notifications if malware definitions are out of date or if there are other configuration issues.

Configuring Other Security Settings

The final section of the Windows Security Center console is titled Other Security Settings. The two main features that you manage here include Internet Security Settings and User Account Control (UAC). Internet Security Settings is based primarily on the configuration of Microsoft Internet Explorer, such as Internet zones, the phishing filter, and other options. For more information about configuring Internet Explorer and browser security, see Chapter 8, "Configuring Parental Controls and Browser Security." UAC is a critical option for ensuring that users run under a set of minimal permissions. For more details about enabling and disabling UAC, see Chapter 6.

It is important to note that the overall status of the Other Security Settings section is based on the least secure option in the details. For example, if UAC is turned off, but Internet security settings are properly configured, the Other Security Settings item still appears red. You need to check into the details to determine which items are raising the warning.

Overall, Windows Security Center is a useful application for centrally monitoring and managing security settings. By including important details related to Windows Firewall, automatic updating, malware protection, and other security settings, it brings together important system information from numerous different security tools.

Quick Check

1. How can you get a quick overview of all of the security-related settings on a computer running Windows Vista?
2. How can you remove the Windows Security Center icon from the system tray?

Quick Check Answers

1. Launch Windows Security Center and use the color and status information for each of the monitored areas.
2. Open Windows Security Center, click Change The Way Security Center Alerts Me, and then select the Don't Notify Me And Don't Display The Icon option.

Practice: Monitoring Security with Windows Security Center

In these practice exercises, you use Windows Security Center to monitor the overall configuration of a computer running Windows Vista. The steps in these exercises assume that you are running Windows Vista with its default security settings and that you have not installed any third-party security management software. Although you might be able to complete the steps even if other software is installed, you might notice that the specific text and information that is displayed might vary.

▶ **Practice 1: Modify Firewall Settings**

In this exercise, you make changes to the settings of Windows Firewall and view the effects displayed in Windows Security Center. Keep in mind that disabling the firewall can temporarily put your computer at risk. If you are currently connected to a public network or are running in an insecure environment, you might want to disable your network connection temporarily.

1. Launch Windows Security Center by opening Control Panel, clicking Security, and then clicking Security Center.
2. Note that the Firewall setting is currently shown in green, indicating that this setting is configured as recommended.
3. Click the Windows Firewall link in the left pane of the Windows Security Center dialog box.
4. Verify that the default display shows that the firewall is currently enabled.
5. To modify the firewall settings, click Change Settings.
6. On the General tab of the Windows Firewall Settings dialog box, choose Off to disable the firewall functionality. Click OK to save the setting.
7. Notice that the Windows Firewall window now shows that your computer is not protected. Close the Windows Firewall window.
8. If it is not currently visible, switch to the Windows Security Center window. Note that the display has automatically changed to indicate that there is a problem with the Firewall item.
9. If necessary, expand the Firewall section to see the details about the configuration. Note that the text states that Windows Firewall is turned off. To re-enable the Windows Firewall, click Turn On Now.
10. Verify that the display now shows that Windows Firewall is enabled.
11. When finished, close Windows Security Center.

▶ **Practice 2: Change Notification Options**

In this exercise, you change the way in which Windows Security Center notifies you of potential security configuration issues. Specifically, you disable notifications and then re-enable them. The steps of this exercise assume that the initial configuration is for the Windows Security Center icon and notifications to be enabled.

1. Notice that the system tray currently displays the Windows Security Alerts shield icon. The color of the icon indicates whether the current configuration is as expected (green), whether there are potential security issues (yellow), or whether some settings are either improperly configured or disabled (red).
2. Launch Windows Security Center by right-clicking the Windows Security Alerts icon in the system tray and selecting Open Security Center.

3. Click Change The Way Security Center Alerts Me to view a list of available notification options.

4. To remove the system tray icon and any notifications, click Don't Notify Me And Don't Display The Icon. Note that the Windows Security Alerts icon no longer appears in the system tray.

5. To re-enable the Windows Security Alerts icon, click Change The Way Security Center Alerts Me, and then click Yes, Notify Me And Display The Icon. Note that the system tray icon reappears, and any security alerts are disabled in a notification balloon.

6. When finished, close Windows Security Center.

Lesson Summary

- Microsoft designed Windows Security Center to provide a quick overview of the status of the Windows Vista security settings.

- Users can customize the way in which Windows security alerts are displayed.

- The Firewall section of the Windows Security Center shows whether Windows Firewall is enabled and properly configured.

- You can use the Windows Firewall section in Windows Security Center to enable or disable the firewall and to configure exceptions for outbound connections.

- The Automatic Updating section of Windows Security Center shows whether the Windows Update feature is set to the recommended configuration.

- The Malware Protection section of Windows Security Center determines whether antivirus and antimalware software is installed, enabled, configured properly, and up to date.

- The Other Security Settings section of Windows Security Center monitors the status of the UAC feature and Internet security settings.

Lesson Review

You can use the following questions to test your knowledge of the information in Lesson 1, "Using Windows Security Center." The questions are also available on the companion CD if you prefer to review them in electronic form.

NOTE Answers

Answers to these questions and explanations of why each answer choice is correct or incorrect are located in the "Answers" section at the end of the book.

1. You are a Consumer Support Technician who is assisting a customer with configuring her computer, which is running Windows Vista, for security. You open Windows Security Center and notice that the Malware Protection section is not displayed in green. Which of the following is a possible reason for this? (Choose all that apply.)

   A. No antivirus software is currently installed on the computer.

   B. User Account Control (UAC) is turned off.

   C. Windows Defender is currently disabled.

   D. Windows Firewall is currently disabled.

   E. Windows Update is not configured to download and install updates automatically.

2. You are assisting a customer with troubleshooting a security-related problem on a computer running Windows Vista. Specifically, the customer has noticed that he has been receiving many different pop-up ads and offers to install unwanted software. You have verified that Windows Defender is properly configured and that many pieces of malware have been automatically removed from the system. You suspect that the problem is related to the configuration of Internet Explorer. Which of the sections in Windows Security Center should you examine to determine if the recommended settings are being used?

   A. Firewall

   B. Automatic Updating

   C. Malware Protection

   D. Other Security Settings

Chapter Review

To further practice and reinforce the skills you learned in this chapter, you can perform the following tasks:

- Review the chapter summary.
- Review the list of key terms introduced in this chapter.
- Complete the case scenarios. These scenarios set up real-world situations involving the topics of this chapter and ask you to create a solution.
- Complete the suggested practices.
- Take a practice test.

Chapter Summary

- Windows Security Center provides a quick way to view the overall status of the numerous security options for Windows Vista.
- Windows Security Center monitors details related to the configuration of the firewall, automatic updating, malware protection, and other security settings such as User Account Control (UAC) and Internet Explorer security settings.

Key Terms

Do you know what these key terms mean? You can check your answers by looking up the terms in the glossary at the end of the book.

- inbound filter
- outbound filter
- Windows Defender
- Windows Firewall
- Windows Firewall with Advanced Security
- Windows security alerts
- Windows Security Center
- Windows Update

Case Scenarios

In the following case scenario, apply what you've learned about using Windows Security Center. You can find answers to these questions in the "Answers" section at the end of this book.

Case Scenario: Troubleshooting Security Issues with Windows Security Center

You are a Consumer Support Technician assisting a customer with troubleshooting various security problems. The customer has mentioned that his children made changes to various system settings while he accidentally let them log on as administrators. Recently, the system has had several spyware installations, and the computer appears to be running more slowly than usual. You open Windows Security Center and notice that there are several warnings.

1. What are some likely causes of warnings displayed in the Malware Protection section?
2. What is the most likely cause of warnings displayed in the Firewall section, and how should you resolve them?
3. What are some likely causes of warnings displayed in the Automatic Updating section?

Suggested Practices

To help you successfully master the exam objectives presented in this chapter, complete the following tasks.

Working with Windows Security Center

Practice 1 helps familiarize you with the information provided in Windows Security Center. Practice 2 involves changing which security settings are monitored.

■ **Practice 1: Monitoring Security Using Windows Security Center** Launch Windows Security Center and make a note of the current security configuration of the computer. Make changes to Windows Vista security settings to view the effects they will have on the information shown in Windows Security Center. For example, change the configuration of Windows Updates to display a yellow warning in the Security Center. Then, change the settings to display a red warning. Do the same for other sections, including Firewall, Malware Protection, and Other Security Settings.

■ **Practice 2: Monitoring Virus Protection Status** Open Windows Security Center and expand the Malware Protection section to view details related to the monitoring of virus protection. If no antivirus program is installed, specify that Windows Security Center should no longer monitor for one. Download and install a third-party antivirus product that is compatible with Windows Vista. (Note that free trial versions are available from several vendors.) View the changes in Windows Security Center.

Take a Practice Test

The practice tests on this book's companion CD offer many options. For example, you can test yourself on just one exam objective, or you can test yourself on all of the 70-623 certification exam content. You can set up the test so that it closely simulates the experience of taking a certification exam, or you can set it up in study mode so that you can look at the correct answers and explanations after you answer each question.

MORE INFO Practice tests

For details about all the practice test options available, see the "How to Use the Practice Tests" section in this book's introduction.

Chapter 8
Configuring Parental Controls and Browser Security

Windows Vista provides a wide array of features that enable users to perform tasks that range from connecting to Web sites to playing games. All of these features can be helpful (and entertaining), but there's always the potential for misuse. For example, left uncontrolled, children might be able to access content that their parents do not believe is appropriate for them. There is always the chance of accessing malicious Web sites and installing unwanted software from the Internet. All of these potential negatives add some inherent risk to using some of the most useful features of computers.

Windows Vista includes many different methods for addressing these potential problems. As you've learned in several chapters of this book, security is an important component of Windows Vista. Microsoft has included many different security and privacy features in the Microsoft Internet Explorer 7 Web browser. These features can help reduce the chances of accessing malicious content on the Web and installing unwanted software. Windows Vista also includes a Parental Controls feature that enables parents to place restrictions on which content their children can access. They can also set up rules such as limits on the time that children can spend using the computer.

As a Consumer Support Technician, you're likely to encounter customers who are concerned about the security of their computers. They'll want your advice on how to ensure security and privacy for themselves and their children. In this chapter, you'll learn about how you can configure the security features of Internet Explorer. You will also learn about the capabilities of the Parental Controls feature.

Exam objectives in this chapter:
- Configure Windows Vista Security.
    - Configure Parental controls.
    - Configure Internet Explorer 7+.

Lessons in this chapter:

Before You Begin

To complete the lessons in this chapter, you need a computer running any edition of Windows Vista. To complete the practice exercises, you need to configure at least one account that is running as an Administrator on the computer. (For more information about configuring user account security, see Chapter 6, "Configuring Windows Vista Security.")

Lesson 1: Configuring Parental Controls

Through Internet access, computers have a tremendous amount of potential. Users can access a wide variety of Web sites, ranging from informational to entertainment resources. Windows Vista also provides a great platform for playing games. Although these capabilities provide users with significant benefits, they can also come at a cost. For example, it is often difficult to restrict which content is accessible. For situations in which parents want to be able to manage the types of content that their children can access, it can be very difficult to create and enforce rules.

In this lesson, you'll learn how you can use the Parental Controls features in Windows Vista to limit the types of access that are available to children. Although this is the primary use for this feature, there are other applications. For example, perhaps you might want to restrict some shared computers to only specific Web sites or restrict the times during which users can access them. Regardless of the purpose, Parental Controls are a good way to help limit the types of content users can access.

After this lesson, you will be able to:
- Define how to set up user accounts to enable Parental Controls.
- Define Web Restrictions settings to filter inappropriate content.
- Configure time limits for computer use.
- Manage content-related restrictions for gaming software.
- Restrict which applications children can run on the computer.
- Configure and review activity reports to monitor children's activities.

Estimated lesson time: 50 minutes

Understanding Parental Controls

The Windows Vista Parental Controls feature is designed to provide several different types of restrictions on how children access programs and Web sites. It can also control when they can use the computer. The specific types of restrictions include the following:

- **Web Restrictions**   Managing which Web sites children can access
- **Time Limits**   Specifying when children are allowed to log on to the computer and how long they can use it
- **Games**   Controlling access to games and other entertainment software based on third-party content ratings
- **Allowing Or Blocking Programs**   Preventing children from running specific applications on the computer

You'll learn how you can enable and configure each of these options later in this lesson. To enforce these settings, the Parental Controls feature is integrated with several other operating system features. For example, filtering Web sites requires interactions with Internet Explorer (which you'll learn about in Lesson 2, "Securing Internet Explorer 7"). Similarly, games-related restrictions are based on ratings provided as a part of certified Games for Windows entertainment titles. This integration enables Parental Controls settings to manage which types of content children can access.

Configuring User Accounts

Parental Controls restrictions are based on the creation and management of user accounts. Users who have Administrator accounts are able to create new user accounts and enable controls on them. Standard user accounts may have restrictions placed on them. The primary method of managing user accounts is by accessing Control Panel and selecting User Accounts And Family Safety. The Add Or Remove User Accounts link launches the Manage Accounts window (see Figure 8-1). For more information about creating and managing user accounts, see Chapter 6.

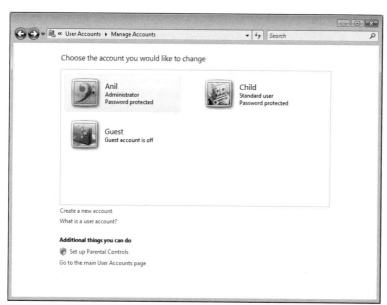

Figure 8-1   Accessing the Manage Accounts window

NOTE   **A note about user names**

Although it might seem a little strange, the screen shots in this lesson use a standard user account simply named Child. This helps identify the account for which Parental Controls are enabled. Customers usually use their children's first names for the user account names.

Typically, parents create and use an Administrator account for themselves. They then create a separate user account for each of the children for whom they want to restrict access. Although it is possible to allow multiple children to share the same user account, it is generally preferable to create individual accounts for each user. You can also access the Parental Controls feature by clicking the Set Up Parental Controls link at the bottom of the Manage Accounts page.

Enabling Parental Controls

By default, Parental Controls are not enabled in Windows Vista. You can start the process of creating and managing these settings by accessing Control Panel. The User Accounts And Family Safety section includes a Set Up Parental Controls For Any User link. Figure 8-2 shows the default view of the Parental Controls window.

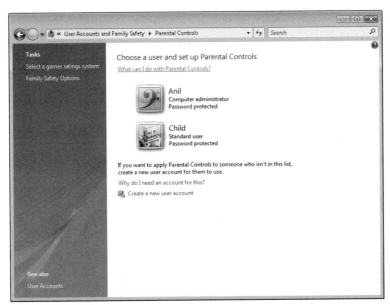

Figure 8-2   Accessing the Parental Controls configuration window

The main Parental Controls window provides access to several different functions. As mentioned in the previous section, the first step in configuring a computer to enable Parental Controls is to create at least one standard user account for a child. (If you have not done so already, you can create the child's account by clicking the Create A New User Account link in the Parental Controls window.) To enable restrictions, start by clicking the name of the account that the child uses to log on to the computer. This provides a list of all of the major types of controls that you can manage (see Figure 8-3).

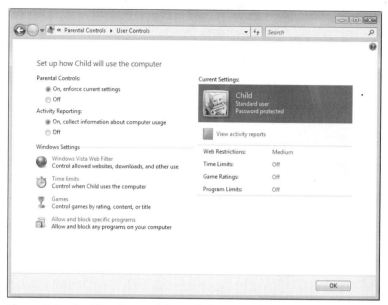

Figure 8-3   Enabling Parental Controls for a standard user account

The first two options determine whether Parental Controls are enabled for this user account. When you select On, Enforce Current Settings, all of the other restrictions are enforced when the user logs on to the computer. This option is also useful for testing purposes because it does not automatically change any of the other settings on the system. For example, if you suspect that Parental Controls are preventing access to a particular program, you can temporarily select the Off option to see whether that resolves the problem. Because all of the other settings remain at their original values, you can then easily reenable Parental Controls without reconfiguring all of the options. When you click OK to save the settings, the Parental Controls window shows the message "Parental Controls On" for the child's user account.

Real World

Anil Desai

Windows Vista includes numerous features that enhance security and oversight significantly over which types of content children can access. These improvements can help filter out unwanted materials. They are not, however, perfect. Determining which types of content are appropriate is often a matter of significant subjectivity. Some types of filtering (such as Web site access) are based on voluntary ratings. The majority of online businesses use valid settings, but some might ignore or circumvent the guidelines.

So how can parents help ensure that their children are accessing acceptable content only? One of the most important security measures is not directly related to technology. Parents should educate their children about the potential security risks and other problems associated with accessing unapproved content. The children should also feel confident in reporting those issues to their parents. Additionally, parents should review the content regularly that their children access. In some cases, natural curiosity might lead children to access unexpected content. Children can also be extremely clever in their attempts to circumvent security-related configuration options.

Overall, the task of maintaining parental control and oversight must be a team effort to be successful. By informing and educating children about potential risks, you can decrease their ability to access undesirable content.

Defining Web Restrictions

Web restrictions settings enable parents to define which types of content are accessible to children who are using the computer. To access these settings, first enable Parental Controls for the child's user account. Then, click the Windows Vista Web Filter link in the User Controls dialog box for the child's account to access the available options. Figure 8-4 shows the default settings for Web restrictions.

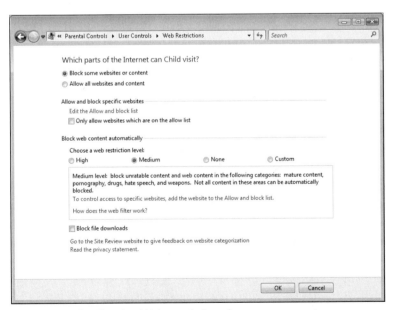

Figure 8-4 Configuring Web restrictions for a user account

The first option, Block Some Websites Or Content, is the master setting that determines whether Web filtering is active. When it is active, parents can specify a wide array of options to manage which content is accessible.

Allowing and Blocking Web Sites

In some cases, parents might want to determine actively which Web sites are available to their children. These settings can be managed by clicking the Edit The Allow And Block List link in the Web Restrictions dialog box (see Figure 8-5).

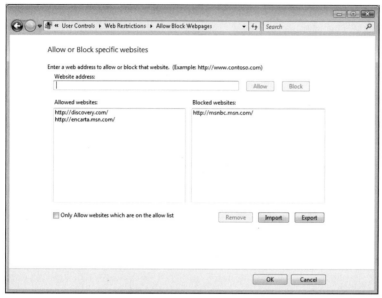

Figure 8-5   Defining the list of allowed and blocked Web sites

The Allow Or Block Webpages dialog box contains two columns: one for a list of allowed Web sites, and another for a list of blocked Web sites. The Website Address text box enables users to specify a complete Uniform Resource Locator (URL) to a particular site. One easy way to obtain the URL if it is not known is for a parent to open Internet Explorer, navigate to the site, and then copy and paste the URL. The Allow and Block buttons determine how the Web site is managed.

There are two main approaches to managing which sites are accessible. The first is to define a list of allowed Web sites and to prevent children from accessing any other sites. The other approach is to block access specifically to a list of Web sites. In general, blocking access to specific Web sites might be easier to configure (especially when considering the other options that you'll learn about in this lesson). Defining a list of allowed Web sites can be tedious and time-consuming, but it can offer the best protection against access to unwanted content.

The Only Allow Websites Which Are On The Allow List check box specifies which approach is used. When the check box is selected, the list of blocked Web sites is effectively unused because all sites are blocked unless they appear on the Allowed Websites list. Parents can remove an entry from either list by selecting it and clicking Remove.

Managing lists of Web sites can be a time-consuming process. When parents need to configure these settings on multiple computers, it is often difficult to type in each site address manually on every computer. The Import and Export buttons enable parents to save the current collection of settings to a file that they can import to other computers or allow other accounts to use on the same computer.

Blocking Sites Based on Content

When configuring Web restrictions, it is practically impossible to define specific Web site exceptions for every site on the Internet. The primary goal for parents is to ensure that inappropriate content is not available to children. Because site contents often change, it is important to be able to filter the content dynamically. Many Web site operators are just as concerned as parents about the suitability of their content. Because they often do not want children to visit their sites, they can choose to rate their own content voluntarily. This information is sent to the Web browser automatically with each page request. Although the system does not prevent potentially malicious Web site operators from misstating these details purposely, it does provide a reasonable level of protection.

To ease the task of filtering Web content, the Web Restrictions dialog box contains a section titled Block Web Content Automatically (see Figure 8-6). This feature works by analyzing the content of a particular Web page or Web site automatically and then testing it based on a variety of built-in algorithms. There are four main settings for the Web restriction level, as follows:

- **High**   This setting blocks all sites except those that specifically include information that they are approved for children. Therefore, this is the most secure option, but it is also the most restrictive.
- **Medium**   This setting automatically blocks content that does not contain rating details and analyzes the page for a variety of unsuitable content.
- **None**   This setting effectively disables automatic filtering. Settings on the Allow and Block lists are still respected, however.
- **Custom**   This setting enables parents to specify which types of material should be blocked.

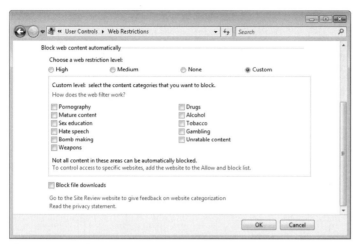

Figure 8-6   Selecting the Custom option for automatic Web filtering

Regardless of the option chosen, it is important to note that the Web filtering algorithms are not perfect and cannot always block all of a certain type of content. The Web Restrictions dialog box also enables parents to block file downloads for their children. This is often appropriate for security and privacy reasons because it prevents them from installing potential malware or unwanted programs.

Providing Site Reviews

Categorizing, rating, and filtering Web site content is a particularly difficult process. Because the definition of appropriate content is a subjective measure, site administrators, parents, and third parties (such as Microsoft and content rating companies) can disagree on whether certain content should be filtered. If parents or site administrators believe that content has been improperly classified, they can click the Go To The Site Review Website To Give Feedback On Website Categorization link. Figure 8-7 shows the Web site.

The site enables users to provide information about a particular URL and to specify why they feel that the content was improperly categorized. Microsoft staff members can then review reports and decide whether the content should be reclassified. Although the process is not immediate, it is a good way for concerned parents to help filter unwanted content for their children.

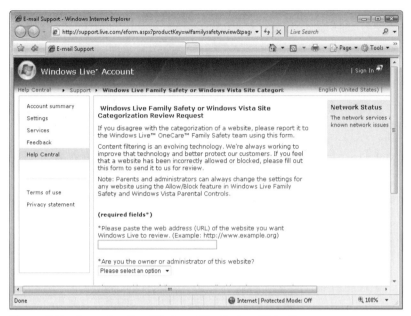

Figure 8-7   Accessing the Windows Site Review Web site

Attempting to Access Blocked Web Sites

When Web restrictions are enabled for a user account, all Web content that is accessed through a Web browser is automatically analyzed. When the content of a Web site is found to be inappropriate based on the Allow and Block lists or based on automatic filtering settings, children see the notice shown in Figure 8-8.

Parents can instruct their children to notify them to review blocked content. If the site is appropriate, then parents can use an Administrator account and make the appropriate changes to the settings. Although it is likely that adjustments will be needed periodically, the Web restrictions feature can help ensure the safety of children's online experience.

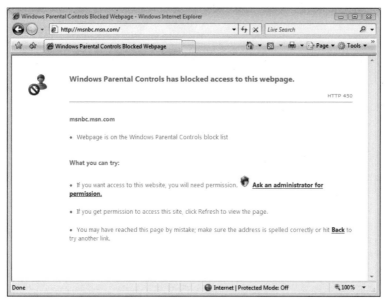

Figure 8-8 A message informing the user that certain content has been blocked

Using Internet Explorer Content Advisor

In addition to the standard Web restrictions settings that are available in Parental Controls, Internet Explorer includes a feature for advising users based on the type of content that is being accessed. Figure 8-9 shows an example of the available settings.

Each setting pertains to various types of content that can be detected through details reported by Web sites. It is important to keep in mind that the rating levels are often voluntary and might not agree with parents' filtering requirements. Internet Explorer also includes options for determining whether sites that do not include rating information can be viewed (see Figure 8-10). Further, it is possible to include additional ratings systems for use by Internet Explorer.

Lesson 2 covers more information about configuring this and other security features in Internet Explorer.

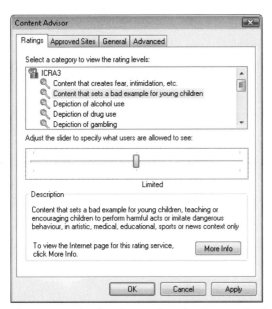

Figure 8-9   Configuring settings for Internet Explorer Content Advisor

Figure 8-10   Configuring general Content Advisor settings

Defining Computer Time Limits

Although computer use can be helpful to children who want to complete homework assignments and play games, parents might want to place limits on how much time their children spend doing these activities. The Time Limits link in the User Controls dialog box enables parents to define when the computer is accessible to children. Figure 8-11 shows the dialog box that enables defining days and times of the week during which children can log on.

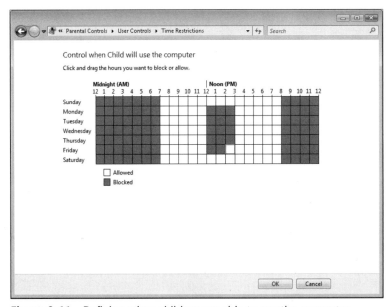

Figure 8-11   Defining when children are able to use the computer

When time limits are set, children that attempt to log on to the computer at times that are disallowed receive the message shown in Figure 8-12.

Figure 8-12 Viewing a message about logon times

Additionally, if a user is logged on to the computer when the end of an allowed time period is approaching, he or she is given a warning message. The user is then logged off of the computer automatically when a blocked time arrives.

Configuring Game Settings

Like other types of media, entertainment software such as games can contain a broad array of different types of content. Parents might feel that certain types of content are inappropriate for their children. Windows Vista Parental Controls provides the ability to define rating levels for games. Child accounts are restricted to running only those games that meet the requirements defined by their parents.

Choosing a Game Ratings System

Numerous third-party organizations have been created to help parents evaluate the content of entertainment software titles. As with other types of content ratings and filtering, reviews of content are subjective. Some settings might be affected by culture. Before defining game-related content restrictions, parents can first choose the type of ratings system that they want to use. This is done in the Parental Controls dialog box by clicking the Select A Games Ratings System link. Figure 8-13 shows an example of the available options.

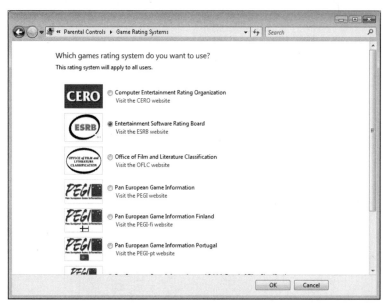

Figure 8-13   Selecting a game rating system for use with Parental Controls

For example, in the United States, the most commonly used game rating system is the Entertainment Software Rating Board (ESRB) system. Other standards organizations are also available to support other countries or methods of evaluating content. Parents can get more information about each system by clicking the links to visit the appropriate Web site. The selected system affects the options that are available for placing game-related restrictions.

Exam Tip   To support game restrictions, entertainment software must meet specific Windows Vista ratings requirements. Therefore, advise customers who are interested in enabling Parental Controls to look for the Games For Windows label on the box. Other entertainment titles are likely to include game ratings information on the box, but you cannot manage them through the Parental Controls feature.

Defining Game Restrictions

Use the Games link in the User Controls dialog box to define requirements for entertainment software. Figure 8-14 shows the available options.

Figure 8-14   Configuring Parental Controls settings for games

The first option determines whether game-related restrictions are enabled. If Yes is selected, parents can choose to block or allow games based on ratings. To do this, click Set Game Ratings. Figure 8-15 shows the available options for a computer that is configured to use the ESRB ratings system. The specific available options vary if other standards settings are chosen.

Figure 8-15   Configuring game restriction details

Although many games will submit to receiving ratings by standards organizations, some entertainment titles might not. The first set of options enables parents to determine whether games with no rating should be allowed or blocked. Next, parents can choose from the available ratings levels to determine which games can be played. It is also possible to add additional filtering based on types of content. These filters are enabled by selecting the appropriate check box. If a particular game contains one of these types of blocked content, the child is unable to play it (even if it is otherwise allowed based on its rating).

NOTE   Managing the online experience

Many modern games enable players to interact with others by playing online. Although most online players conduct themselves in an appropriate manner, there is always the possibility that children will be able to access unwanted game content or comments while playing online. For this reason, parents should supervise their children if they are allowed to play online-enabled games.

Allowing and Blocking Specific Games

In addition to configuring automatic restrictions based on games' rating levels, parents can also choose to block or allow specific games. This feature works by providing a list of games that have been installed and registered on the computer. Figure 8-16 shows an example.

Figure 8-16   Allowing or blocking specific games

There are three main options for each title that is available in the list:

- **User Rating Setting**   This option specifies that the current settings for allowed games will be used to determine whether the game is allowed. Therefore, this option does not allow or block the game explicitly.
- **Always Allow**   This setting specifies that the game title will always be accessible to the child, regardless of other game restriction settings.
- **Always Block**   This setting specifies that the game will never be allowed for the child, even if it meets the requirements of other game restriction settings.

It is important to note that the settings defined here override other rating-related settings. When a child attempts to run a game that is blocked, he or she sees the dialog box shown in Figure 8-17. Additionally, the Games folder displays blocked games with an icon that clearly shows that they are not allowed.

Figure 8-17   Viewing a message indicating that a particular game has been blocked

NOTE   **Managing access to games**

Some of the options related to blocking and allowing games on a computer running Windows Vista rely on the game to register itself with the operating system. In some cases, children might be able to download games from the Internet and run them directly. Game-related restrictions might not apply to these programs. As with many security and privacy features, it is important to use game ratings in conjunction with other Parental Controls options.

Managing Application Restrictions

In addition to game-related software, parents might want to restrict which programs a child can run. One example of a restricted application might be a financial management application. Although the product does not necessarily contain any inappropriate content, the program is generally not for use by children. Other examples might include e-mail, instant messaging, and other online-enabled tools. By default, application restrictions are disabled. To configure these settings, in the User Controls dialog box, click Allow And Block Specific Programs. Figure 8-18 shows the options that are available when you select the Child Can Only Use The Programs I Allow option.

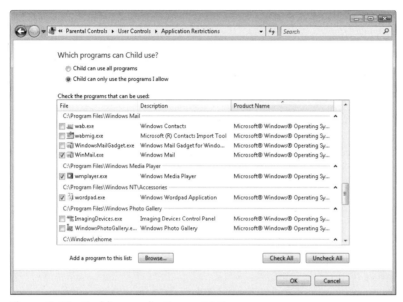

Figure 8-18   Enabling application restrictions

The complete list of programs is based on the executable program files registered with Windows Vista. Parents can click Browse to locate any programs that are not automatically included. When enabled, application restrictions work based on a list of allowed programs. For convenience, all of the items can be selected, and then certain programs can be removed from the list. When children attempt to run a program that is restricted, they receive an error message.

Reviewing Activity Reports

So far, you have learned about ways in which you can restrict the types of content and programs that children can access. Part of the process of ensuring that children are using the computer in approved ways is to review reports on their actual activity.

NOTE   Reviewing computer usage

It is important to keep in mind that the Windows Vista Parental Controls features are primarily designed to assist in managing children's access to content. It is not meant as a replacement for parental oversight. Activity reports provide an easy way for parents to review how their children are using a computer running Windows Vista.

In this section, you'll learn how to configure activity reporting and how to analyze the information shown in reports.

Configuring Activity Reporting

The activity reporting feature is designed to provide parents with an easy way to collect a wide variety of information about children's usage patterns. When Parental Controls are enabled, activity reporting is also enabled by default. To verify the setting, see the Activity Reporting section of the User Controls dialog box. When selected, the On, Collecting Information About Computer Usage option tells Windows Vista to keep track of which programs are accessed and which content is used.

System tray notifications can remind parents regularly to review activity reports. To configure this option, in the Parental Controls window, click Family Safety Options. Figure 8-19 shows the available options for notifications.

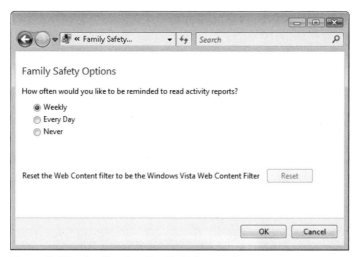

Figure 8-19 Configuring Family Safety options

The options enable parents to specify how often they will be notified to review activity reports. These settings do not, however, affect the actual collection of usage information. The Reset button is designed to help users reconfigure Web-based filtering if it has been replaced by a third-party program or other settings change.

Viewing Activity Reports

Windows Vista includes a convenient built-in method for reviewing users' activity based on Parental Controls settings. To access the report, select a child's user account, and then click View Activity Reports. Figure 8-20 shows an example of a typical report.

Figure 8-20   Viewing an activity report for a child account

The information is categorized based on the type of activity. It includes a wide variety of details, ranging from which Web sites were accessed to which games were played. Parents should review this information regularly to detect whether changes to current Parental Controls settings might be required. The report data itself is managed automatically, using features of Windows Vista, so there is no need to save the report files.

Quick Check

1. Which types of accounts should be created by a mother who wants to create Parental Controls restrictions for her two children?
2. What are two ways in which parents can restrict which Internet-based content children can access?

Quick Check Answers

1. Each child should be given a standard user account, and the mother should use an Administrator account.
2. Parents can filter Web content based on a list of allowed or blocked sites or by using automatic content-filtering options.

Practice: Configuring and Testing Parental Controls

In these practice exercises, you enable and configure Parental Controls settings for a child's user account. The steps in the exercise assume that you have access to a Windows Vista Administrator account and that you have created a standard user account for testing purposes. If children will be using the computer, create an additional test account to complete these exercises. The steps assume that Parental Controls have not yet been enabled or configured for the test standard user account.

▶ **Practice 1: Enable and Test Web Restrictions**

In this exercise, you enable and configure Web restrictions. Specifically, you configure the settings to block access to a specific Web site and to block content automatically, using a Web restriction level of High.

1. Log on to Windows Vista, using an Administrator account.
2. Open the Parental Controls window by accessing Control Panel and clicking Set Up Parental Controls For Any User in the User Accounts And Family Safety section.
3. Click the icon for the standard user account that you want to use for testing purposes. Subsequent steps refer to this account as the Child account.
4. In the Parental Controls section, select the On, Enforce Current Settings option.
5. Click Windows Vista Web Filter to access the Web restrictions settings.
6. Select the Block Some Websites Or Content option.
7. Click Edit The Allow And Block List.
8. In the Website Address text box, type **http://www.microsoft.com**. Click Block to add this to the list of blocked Web sites. Verify that the Only Allow Websites Which Are On The Allow List check box is cleared, and then click OK to save the settings.
9. In the Block Web Content Automatically section, select the High Web restriction level.
10. Click OK to save the Web restrictions settings. Click OK again to close the User Controls dialog box and save your changes.
11. On the Start menu, select Switch User. This command is located on the menu that is located next to the Sleep button and the Lock This Computer icon.
12. On the logon screen, select the Child account and provide the password (if required).
13. Open Internet Explorer and attempt to browse to *http://www.microsoft.com*. Note the error message that you receive because the site is blocked.
14. Attempt to navigate to a variety of different Internet sites and note which types of content are blocked by the High Web restriction filter.

15. When finished, log off the Child account, and then log back on to Windows Vista, using your Administrator account.

16. Optionally, you can review the Activity Report in the Parental Controls properties to see which actions were taken by the Child user.

▶ **Practice 2: Configure and Test Game Settings**

In this practice exercise, you configure restrictions on the built-in games that are provided with Windows Vista. Specifically, you configure rating settings and specify overrides that allow or block specific games.

1. Log on to Windows Vista using an Administrator account.

2. Open the Parental Controls options by accessing Control Panel and clicking Set Up Parental Controls For Any User in the User Accounts And Family Safety section.

3. Click Select A Games Ratings System to review the list of available options.

4. Select the Entertainment Software Rating Board (ESRB) option, and then click OK to save the setting.

5. Click the icon for the standard user account that you want to use for testing purposes. Subsequent steps refer to this account as the Child account.

6. In the Parental Controls section, select the On, Enforce Current Settings option.

7. Click Games to access the Game Controls dialog box.

8. Select Yes to allow the Child account to play games.

9. Click Set Game Ratings to specify game restrictions.

10. Select the Block Games With No Rating option.

11. Select Everyone in the list of ratings. Note that there are additional options available when you scroll down. When finished, click OK.

12. To create exceptions for specific games, click Block Or Allow Specific Games.

13. Select Always Allow for the Chess Titans game and select Always Block for the Minesweeper game. Keep the default of User Rating Setting for all other games. Click OK to save the settings.

14. On the Start menu, select Switch User.

This command is located on the menu next to the Sleep button and the Lock This Computer icon.

15. On the logon screen, select the Child account and provide the password (if required).

16. Click Start and select Games to view a list of games that are installed on the computer. Note that some icons appear with a red restricted mark. Attempt to launch a blocked game and note the error message.

17. Next, attempt to launch an approved game and verify that it runs properly.

18. When finished, log off the Child account, and then log back on to Windows Vista, using your Administrator account.

19. Optionally, you can review the activity report in the Parental Controls properties to see which actions were taken by the Child user.

Lesson Summary

- Parental Controls options can be enabled for standard user accounts.
- Web restrictions can be configured to allow or block specific Web sites or to determine restrictions automatically, based on content.
- Parents can place restrictions on when children can log on to the computer.
- Game restrictions can be based on reviews by a rating system or by specifically allowing or denying particular entertainment programs.
- Parents can restrict which applications a child can run on the computer.
- Activity reports can be viewed to provide details related to a child's usage of the computer.

Lesson Review

You can use the following questions to test your knowledge of the information in Lesson 1, "Configuring Parental Controls." The questions are also available on the companion CD if you prefer to review them in electronic form.

NOTE Answers

Answers to these questions and explanations of why each answer choice is correct or incorrect are located in the "Answers" section at the end of the book.

1. You are a Consumer Support Technician assisting a father with enabling Parental Controls for his daughter. He would like to prevent her automatically from accessing any Web site that includes specific types of inappropriate content. He would also like to prevent her from accessing Web sites that are not ratable based on automatic filtering. Which Web restriction level should he choose?

   A. High

   B. Medium

   C. None

   D. Custom

2. You are a Consumer Support Technician assisting a mother with configuring Parental Controls for her son. She would like to specify that he can play only games that have a rating of Everyone 10+. However, she would also like him to be able to play one specific game that does not meet this requirement. She has configured the computer to use the ESRB rating system. Which game restrictions settings should she choose? (Choose all that apply.)

   A. Allow games with no rating.

   B. Block games with no rating.

   C. Allow games only that are rated at up to Everyone 10+.

   D. Choose to block content that includes violence.

   E. Choose Always Allow for the specific game that should be accessible to the child.

Lesson 2: Securing Internet Explorer 7

In a relatively short time (even in computer terms), the Web browser has become one of the most frequently used applications on customers' computers. With the ability to access millions of different Web sites and related content on demand, the Web browser is practically indispensible for most users. Unfortunately, the popularity of the World Wide Web has brought with it numerous threats and challenges. Potential issues range from the merely annoying (such as pop-up ads) to seriously damaging (such as the installation of malware or collection of private information). These issues can reduce security, compromise privacy, and generally make accessing Web sites a potentially dangerous activity.

Microsoft has included numerous new security and privacy features in the Internet Explorer 7 browser that is included with Windows Vista. When enabled, these features can help reduce the risks related to browsing Web sites. As a Consumer Support Technician, you're likely to be asked for advice about how to enable, configure, and manage the many different options that are available. In this lesson, you'll learn about how you can take advantage of the privacy and security options of Internet Explorer.

After this lesson, you will be able to:
- Manage browser security settings by using security zones and associated options.
- Configure privacy settings to manage handling cookies.
- Use the Phishing Filter to verify Web sites automatically.
- Use certificates and encryption to create secure connections to Web sites.

Estimated lesson time: 60 minutes

Working with Internet Explorer 7

Windows Vista includes the Internet Explorer 7 browser as a built-in feature. Access it by using its program shortcut in the Start menu, by searching for the program, or through the default icon that appears in the toolbar. Most users who have Internet access are already familiar with using a Web browser. Internet Explorer 7 provides a wide range of enhancements over previous versions of the browser. For example, tab-based browsing can make accessing multiple Web sites significantly easier. The focus in this lesson is on ways in which you can configure the Internet Explorer security features. For more information about using Internet Explorer 7, see the Windows Internet Explorer Web page at *http://www.microsoft.com/windows /products/winfamily/ie/default.mspx*.

The default settings for Internet Explorer are designed to provide a significant level of security without hampering the Web browsing experience. For many users, these settings provide the optimal balance of privacy and usability. As a Consumer Support Technician, be aware of the purpose and function of each security implementation so that you can provide configuration and troubleshooting assistance. For example, in some cases, users might reduce security settings without understanding the implications, or their systems might have been compromised by malware.

Accessing Configuration Options

Although the basic user interface of Internet Explorer 7 might appear very simple, there are dozens of different options that you can configure to customize the browsing experience. To access the various configuration options for the browser, on the Tools menu, select Internet Options. Alternatively, you can open Control Panel, click the Security link, and then select the options in the Internet Options section of the page. Both of these methods launch the Properties dialog box that enables you to configure most of the available options (see Figure 8-21).

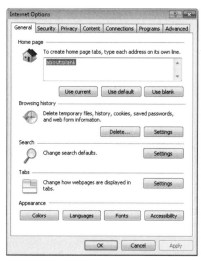

Figure 8-21   Viewing the Internet Options dialog box

Each tab of this dialog box includes collections of settings that pertain to usability, security, and related details. Although most settings can be modified while the Web browser is running, some changes might require a browser restart. That is, the browser must be closed and reopened for the settings to take effect.

Maintaining Web Security

Over time, security-related updates are often required to fix known vulnerabilities and to protect against recently discovered malware attacks. Because Internet Explorer is a default component of the Windows Vista operating system, it can be updated automatically, using the Windows Update feature. For more information about configuring Windows Update, see Chapter 7, "Using Windows Security Center."

Managing Browser Security Settings

Customers can use their Web browsers to access a wide variety of content from a broad range of different sources. The most common activity for most users is accessing public Internet sites. Although default settings work well for most of those sites, users might want to change security-related settings for some of them. Some Web sites might be allowed additional permissions because they are trusted. Others might be completely restricted because they are known to provide unwanted content or software.

To accommodate different types of settings, Internet Explorer includes a feature known as security zones. You can access these settings by opening Internet Explorer 7, clicking Tools, selecting Internet Options, and then clicking the Security tab. You can also access the properties by opening Control Panel, clicking Security, and choosing Change Security Settings. Figure 8-22 shows the default display.

Figure 8-22   Accessing the Security tab of the Internet Options dialog box

NOTE   **Practicing good security habits**

Although technical features can help reduce the likelihood of some types of computer problems, other issues require users' diligence. For example, you should always be careful to log off of your computer whenever it is not in use. This prevents others in the area from accessing all of your settings. Some convenience features (such as the Internet Explorer form-filling feature) can lead to security and privacy problems. Remember to protect your computer by using the Lock This Computer icon in the Start menu when it's not in use.

Understanding Zone Types

Four different types of security zones are included in the configuration settings. Each zone refers to a particular grouping of Web sites. Users can configure different security settings for each zone. The zone types are as follows:

- **Internet**   This is the default zone for all Web sites that do not belong to any of the other zones. For most users, this includes all public Internet Web sites. The default security level for this zone is Medium-High.
- **Local Intranet**   Some types of Web sites will be located on the computer's local network (also called an intranet). Examples include home media and networking devices that provide a Web-based administration interface and small-business environments that might include Web servers for sharing information. In general, these sites can be considered relatively trustworthy. Therefore, the default security level for this zone is Medium-Low. Users can further define which Web sites are part of their intranet.
- **Trusted Sites**   This zone initially does not include any sites, but it enables users to specify that a particular Web address is trusted. The default security level for trusted sites is Medium.
- **Restricted Sites**   In some cases, users know that accessing certain Web sites can be risky. The sites that are part of the Restricted Sites zone are accessed using the High security level. This helps reduce the risks in accessing the site.

Overall, security zones provide a simplified method of placing different types of sites into groups that can then be assigned various levels of permissions.

Managing Zone Settings

Whereas the Internet security zone is configured to provide a default collection of security settings, the other three types of zones can be further configured. The Local Intranet zone includes several options that assist Internet Explorer with determining which sites are part of the computer's local network. To access these settings, select the Local Intranet zone, and then click Sites. Figure 8-23 shows the available options.

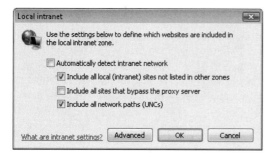

Figure 8-23   Managing options for the Local Intranet security zone

The default setting is for Internet Explorer to determine automatically whether a site is located on the intranet. This can be done by comparing the computer's network address with the address of the site. For more information about configuring network settings, see Chapter 9, "Configuring Windows Vista Networking." If the Automatically Detect Intranet Network check box is cleared, three additional options become available:

- Include All Local (Intranet) Sites Not Listed In Other Zones
- Include All Sites That Bypass The Proxy Server
- Include All Network Paths (UNCs)

In addition, you can click Advanced to specify manually which Web sites should be considered part of the Local Intranet zone. Customers who are working in a small-business environment might choose this option to simplify access to local servers that are not automatically detected.

The Trusted Sites and Restricted Sites zones also provide the ability to add specific sites manually. Figure 8-24 shows an example. Most commonly, a user adds a fully qualified URL for the site to the list. Whenever a Web site is accessed, Internet Explorer 7 searches the Trusted and Restricted Sites lists to determine whether special security settings should be used.

Figure 8-24   Adding sites to the Trusted Sites zone

Configuring Security Levels

So far, you have learned about the different security zones and how you can determine which Web sites belong in each. The main purpose of the zones is to facilitate the assignment of a variety of different levels of permissions. The easiest method of assigning security settings is to assign one of the built-in levels. The available levels include Low, Medium-Low, Medium, Medium-High, and High. For security reasons, not all levels are available for all different types of sites. You select levels by using the vertical slider control, and the dialog box provides an overview of the effects of each setting.

Each security level is actually a collection of settings that you can modify manually by clicking Custom Level. As shown in Figure 8-25, this shows a very long list of available security options. Examples of settings include determining how to deal with certain types of files (such as .pdf or .xps documents) and how users are notified about various actions that might affect security. Manually modifying settings is considered an advanced option and is recommended for use by knowledgeable end users who understand their effects.

Figure 8-25   Setting options for custom security levels

Depending on the specific security zone selected, various options include details about the recommended setting. When a user configures a setting to a potentially insecure value, Internet Explorer colors the option itself in red, and the associated text notifies the user (see Figure 8-26). Some items are marked with an asterisk (*) that signifies that the setting changes take effect only after the user restarts Internet Explorer.

If the user does not make setting changes carefully, it is easy to reduce the security of Internet Explorer significantly. The Reset To drop-down list and Reset button allow users to change all of the options quickly back to their default settings. Additionally, the Security tab of the Internet Options dialog box includes a Reset All Zones To Default Level button. This option is most appropriate when a user makes numerous changes to security settings or when troubleshooting specific problems with accessing Web sites. This command does not, however, change any configuration options related to which sites are located in which zones.

Figure 8-26   Viewing warnings for ActiveX control settings

Understanding Protected Mode

One of the most significant risks to overall security is when a malicious Web site installs unwanted software on a user's computer. In some cases, the software might perform functions such as accessing the file system or modifying data on the computer. Browsers often allow Web sites to launch programs, sometimes without users' consent. Although allowing Web sites to install programs can provide some useful functionality, this capability can also be used to cause serious system problems. The solution is to limit the ability of Web sites to run programs on the computer.

Protected Mode is a security feature that is available only in the Windows Vista version of Internet Explorer 7. It allows the Web browser to run in a limited security configuration. This prevents Web sites from launching external programs without the user's knowledge and can thereby avoid many types of unwanted actions. To enable Protected Mode for sites that are located in a zone, select the Enable Protected Mode check box. As the text in the dialog box notes, Internet Explorer must be restarted for changes related to enabling or disabling this option to take effect.

Summarizing Default Security Settings

When configuring and troubleshooting issues with accessing Web sites, it is often helpful to recall the default settings for each security zone. Table 8-1 provides a listing of each of the security zones, along with the available security levels and their initial settings.

Table 8-1   Internet Explorer Security Zones and Their Available and Default Settings

Security Zone	Allowed Security Levels	Default Security Level	Default Protected Mode Status
Internet	Medium Medium-High High	Medium-High	Enabled
Local Intranet	Low Medium-Low Medium Medium-High High	Medium-Low	Enabled
Trusted Sites	Low Medium-Low Medium Medium-High High	Medium	Disabled
Restricted Sites	High	High	Enabled

Configuring Privacy Settings

In the early days of the Internet, the vast majority of World Wide Web content was static in nature. All users would receive the same content, and Web activity was primarily read-only. Now, it's hard to find sites that do not allow users to log on and customize their experience. Activities such as placing items in a shopping cart and modifying personal preferences that are retained over time are common. The potential drawback, however, is that the same mechanisms that are used to enable this functionality can also be used to reduce users' privacy. In this lesson, you'll learn about ways in which you can configure Internet Explorer to address these concerns.

Understanding Cookies

A technical challenge related to providing customized Web experiences is the fact that the Hypertext Transfer Protocol (HTTP) is stateless. That is, HTTP does not include a built-in method of automatically keeping Web requests from a particular user or computer separate from other requests. Cookies are a method by which to overcome this limitation. Cookies work by sending information to the Web browser when a site is accessed. In some cases, the information might include a unique number that enables the Web site to track the user. It might also include additional information such as the contents of a user's shopping cart. Whenever a browser makes a request to a Web site, it also sends this data so the site can personalize the experience.

Usually, the process of requesting and managing cookies is automatic. Although this is helpful in the majority of cases, it can lead to potential privacy issues. For example, online advertising agencies often use cookie-based information to track sites that you have visited. This information might be used to present pop-up ads or other annoyances. From a security and privacy standpoint, cookies can be divided into these different types:

- **First-party cookies**   These cookies are issued by the site to which you are currently connected. They are used most commonly to maintain settings and options related to the usage of the site itself.
- **Third-party cookies**   These cookies are obtained from a Web site other than the one to which the user is connected. Commonly, these cookies are created by third-party marketing organizations to track site usage and to show targeted advertisements (such as pop-ups). For this reason, users might often want to prevent the use of third-party cookies.
- **Session cookies**   These types of cookies are designed to enable Web sites to identify visitors uniquely, generally by providing a number or some other token that does not contain personal information. Session cookies are automatically deleted after a certain period and are, therefore, usually not considered a significant security or privacy risk.

NOTE **Should you accept cookies from strangers?**

The issue of security often comes down to a tradeoff between privacy and usability. Many Web sites require the use of cookies to offer users the full benefits of customization. Usually, the sites have no method of collecting personal information unless users specifically provide it. In general, the act of performing common daily tasks (such as shopping) results in some loss of privacy (after all, people can see you when you enter a shopping mall, and you're usually faced with numerous advertisements). Most users find the tradeoff to be acceptable and should be satisfied with the default security options of Internet Explorer.

Managing Privacy Settings

The Privacy tab of the Internet Options dialog box enables users to customize the behavior of Internet Explorer (see Figure 8-27). The default setting is Medium, which allows certain types of cookies that can be identified as relatively safe.

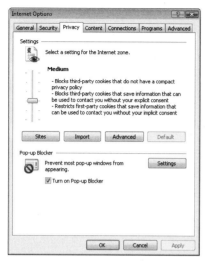

Figure 8-27   Configuring privacy settings in Internet Explorer

Table 8-2 lists the various privacy options and the associated descriptions for each level.

Table 8-2   Privacy Setting Levels and Their Effects

Privacy Level	Effects
Accept All Cookies	Saves cookies from any Web site. Cookies that are already on this computer can be read by the Web sites that created them.
Low	Blocks third-party cookies that do not have a compact privacy policy. (A compact privacy policy is a standard method by which Web site administrators can send information about how they use personally identifiable information to a Web browser.) Restricts third-party cookies that save information that can be used to contact you without your implicit consent.
Medium	Blocks third-party cookies that do not have a compact privacy policy. Restricts third-party cookies that save information that can be used to contact you without your explicit consent. Restricts third-party cookies that save information that can be used to contact you without your implicit consent.

Table 8-2   Privacy Setting Levels and Their Effects

Privacy Level	Effects
Medium High	Blocks third-party cookies that do not have a compact privacy policy. Restricts third-party cookies that save information that can be used to contact you without your explicit consent. Restricts first-party cookies that save information that can be used to contact you without your implicit consent.
High	Blocks all cookies from Web sites that do not have a compact privacy policy. Blocks cookies that save information that can be used to contact you without your explicit consent.
Block All Cookies	Blocks all cookies from all Web sites. Cookies that are already on this computer cannot be read by Web sites.

The settings that are chosen apply to all sites that are part of the Internet zone. Users can choose to create exceptions to this rule by clicking Sites. As shown in Figure 8-28, you can add specific Web sites to the list. You can configure the privacy settings to allow or block cookies from each site.

Figure 8-28   Allowing or blocking cookies for specific Web sites

In addition, the Privacy tab includes the ability to configure the handling of cookies manually by clicking Advanced. Figure 8-29 shows the available options for first- and third-party cookies as well as for session cookies.

Figure 8-29   Configuring advanced privacy settings

Configuring the Pop-Up Blocker

Minor annoyances are part of just about every type of shopping or commercial experience. Ranging from gaudy billboards to obnoxiously loud audio advertisements, they're hard to avoid in the real world. When browsing the Internet, pop-up ads can be significantly disruptive to the user's experience. They often interfere with the use of a site's features, and they require effort to close. To help alleviate some of these issues, Internet Explorer 7 includes a built-in Pop-Up Blocker feature. The main configuration setting specifies whether the feature is enabled. You can set this by using the Tools menu in Internet Explorer or by accessing the Privacy tab of the Internet Options dialog box.

Not all pop-up windows are unwanted, however. Many sites include pop-up windows to enable users to provide required information or to display additional information without forcing users to navigate to a new page. Internet Explorer attempts to determine whether a pop-up window was requested by using an automatic process. You can configure additional settings for the Pop-Up Blocker by clicking Settings. Figure 8-30 shows the available details.

You can add specific Web sites that should always be allowed to display pop-ups by providing the sites' URLs and clicking Allow. Additionally, users can specify whether a sound should be played whenever a pop-up is blocked. The Information Bar can also show details about a pop-up window that has been blocked and can allow users to choose to view it. Finally, you can modify the Filter Level setting. The available options include the following:

- High: Block All Pop-Ups (Ctrl+Alt To Override)
- Medium: Block Most Automatic Pop-Ups
- Low: Allow Pop-Ups From Secure Sites

Overall, these features can help minimize annoyances from unwanted windows.

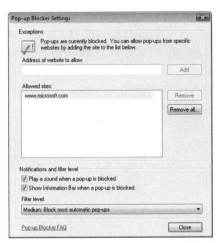

Figure 8-30 Configuring settings for the Pop-Up Blocker

Configuring the Phishing Filter

The theft of personal information has become increasingly sophisticated in recent years. Phishing is a method of obtaining sensitive information such as users' credit card numbers, national identification numbers, passwords, and other details. The term *phishing* is an allusion to the act of trying to use bait to trick unwary individuals into voluntarily providing information that could be used for unauthorized purposes. Generally, the process begins by sending e-mails that resemble official communications from financial institutions and similar companies that require a secure logon. Some messages are rather crude imitations of official communications, but others are very difficult to distinguish from authentic messages.

Users are usually directed to access the organization's Web site to perform a task such as verifying a password or other personal information. The associated Web site is designed to be almost indistinguishable from the official site it is trying to emulate. Unsuspecting people provide their logon information or other details. The site then captures this information and can use it for identity theft and other types of crimes.

To protect users against potential phishing Web sites, Internet Explorer 7 includes a feature called the Phishing Filter. In this section, you'll learn how you can use the filter to protect users.

Detecting Phishing Attempts

The primary goal of preventing users from being fooled by phishing Web sites is to identify those sites clearly when they are loaded. There are two primary methods by which the Internet Explorer Phishing Filter does this. First, the local computer contains a list of known phishing-related sites. These URLs are known to have been created to collect and misuse sensitive data.

Whenever a site is loaded in Internet Explorer, the URL is compared to the list. The second method of detecting phishing sites is to use various tests automatically to find characteristics that are common to those sites. By looking for certain terms and form fields, likely phishing sites can be identified.

When a known or suspected phishing site is detected, the address bar in Internet Explorer turns red, and the user sees the message shown in Figure 8-31. The recommended option is to close the Web page, but users can choose to continue. There is also a link at the bottom of the page that enables you to report that the site is not a phishing site. This sends a report to Microsoft and alerts the company to reevaluate the setting if enough such responses are received.

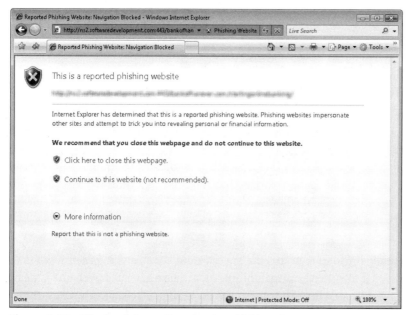

Figure 8-31   Viewing information about a phishing site

NOTE   Testing phishing functionality

If you would like to test the Internet Explorer Phishing Filter, you need to browse to a site that is a known phishing Web site. Several online databases provide links to known or suspected sites, and you can generally find them by doing a Web search. For example, the PhishTank Web site (*http:// www.phishtank.com/*) provides a database that enables viewers to submit and verify these Web sites. It goes without saying that, if you decide to visit one of these sites, be sure that you do not provide any personal information (no matter how tempting it might be).

Using Phishing Filter Options

You can perform various functions related to the Phishing Filter by using the Tools menu in Internet Explorer, which offers several different options. The Phishing Filter Settings option opens the Advanced tab of the Internet Options dialog box. Figure 8-32 shows the main options related to enabling or disabling the filter, as follows:

■ **Disable Phishing Filter**   Checking for Phishing Web sites can reduce system performance. Selecting this option can sometimes increase Web browsing performance, but it
is not recommended due to potential security risks.

■ **Turn Off Automatic Website Checking**   This option enables the Phishing Filter, but it
prevents Internet Explorer from automatically checking all loaded Web sites against the
Microsoft phishing database.

■ **Turn On Automatic Website Checking**   This option automatically verifies all URLs that
are loaded to test whether they are known or suspected phishing sites.

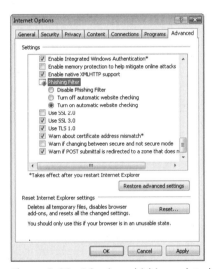

Figure 8-32   Viewing phishing-related settings in the Internet Options dialog box

The Internet Explorer Phishing Filter menu also provides the Turn On Automatic Phishing Filter (Recommended) option (see Figure 8-33). When enabled, this feature sends anonymous information to Microsoft to help detect phishing-related Web sites. The information sent is automatically stripped of any potentially sensitive information, and only the base URL is sent.

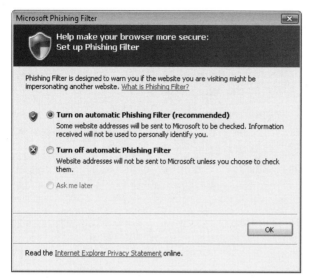

Figure 8-33   Configuring the automatic Phishing Filter

Manually Verifying and Reporting Web Sites

Customers can check the current Web site manually against the online phishing database from the Internet Explorer Tools menu by selecting Check This Website. This automatically sends the URL information to Microsoft and displays a phishing warning message to the user if the result comes back positive.

An important part of the fight against phishing is detecting quickly as many potentially dangerous sites as possible. All Internet users can help each other in this one area. An option displays in the Phishing Filter menu to report a specific site to Microsoft. Figure 8-34 shows the Web site that is loaded in a new browser window when this option is selected. For sites that do not generate a warning, users can report that they suspect it is a phishing site. If the current Web site is a suspected phishing site, you can report that it has been incorrectly identified.

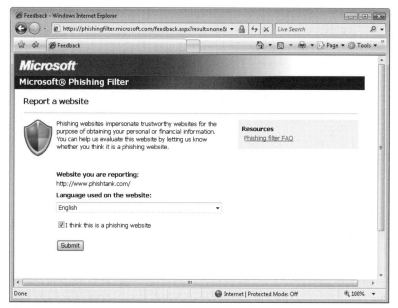

Figure 8-34   Reporting a potential phishing Web site to Microsoft

---

Real World

Anil Desai

It's a simple fact: many security and privacy violations that occur on peoples' computers are due to their own gullibility or a lack of adequate security settings. Actions such as visiting spoofed Web sites or downloading and installing software from unknown organizations are common sources of problems. As a Consumer Support Technician, your customers rely on you to help them fix the resulting problems. In some cases, the issues might be easy to fix. In others, it might require numerous time-consuming troubleshooting steps. All of this can lead to significant frustration for everyone involved.

When supporting end users, it's very easy to direct anger at the victim of a particular malware or security issue. After all, shouldn't the user have known better? Often, technical professionals use a condescending attitude toward the people who have encountered these problems. This creates a potentially hostile environment that isn't good for anyone. So what is a good Consumer Support Technician to do?

When dealing with situations in which user error (or lack of judgment) caused a problem, I strongly recommend that you put yourself in the user's position. Although you have the technical expertise to understand domain names and to be able to tell legitimate Web sites from malicious ones, many customers might be new to using the Internet and its annoyances and risks. The best approach is to explain the situation clearly without being accusatory.

There's a good chance that the customer is already embarrassed about the situation, and he or she already has to deal with resolving the problems. If appropriate, offer advice about how the problem can be avoided in the future. A particularly helpful Web site is the Windows Vista Help and How-To article titled "When to Trust a Website"(*http://windows help.microsoft.com/Windows/en-US/Help/dfe83943-3394-48fb-8a4b-406f0b479c331033 .mspx*). You might even go so far as to say that you've experienced the same problems before or that malicious Web sites are designed to trick users.

An important part of being a problem-solver for customer issues is your attitude and approach to resolving the problem and preventing it from occurring in the future. A good bedside (or computer-side) manner can make you a hero or heroine to users who are in need of your skills.

Other Internet Explorer Security Features

So far, you have learned about many different ways in which you can configure Internet Explorer to provide a safer Web experience. There are some other features included in Internet Explorer 7 that can help keep users protected. In this section, you'll learn about how they work.

Understanding the Internet Explorer Information Bar

There are times when Internet Explorer needs to inform the user of particular security-related situations. Common examples include when pop-up windows are blocked and when a Web site is attempting to install an application on the local computer. In these situations, the user might want to continue the action. The Internet Explorer Information Bar provides these messages by displaying them directly below the address bar in the browser (see Figure 8-35).

Figure 8-35   Viewing a message in the Information Bar in Internet Explorer

To respond to a message, users can click the Information Bar, and they are given options. For example, in the case of a pop-window that has been blocked, the user can choose to open it.

Using Secure Connections

By default, data that is sent over the Internet using HTTP is sent unencrypted. This means that the data itself potentially could be intercepted and decoded without significant effort. Although this is acceptable for some types of communications, other operations such as the transfer of credit card information and passwords should remain protected. Do this through the HTTP Secure (HTTPS) protocol. Sites that support HTTPS connections enable users' browsers to encrypt and decrypt data automatically that is transferred to the server. Internet Explorer clearly identifies when secure connections have been created by showing a lock icon next to the address bar (see Figure 8-36). This helps protect data from compromise during transit.

Figure 8-36   Accessing a Web site using a secure HTTPS connection

Understanding Certificates

A potential issue with Web-based security is ensuring the identity of a remote Web site. For example, how can you be reasonably sure that the servers hosted at *http://www.microsoft.com* actually belong to Microsoft? This is managed through certificates. Certificates are issued by trusted third-party organizations that perform research to ensure that organizations are who they claim to be. To obtain a certificate, a company must provide various pieces of information that are then validated. When accessing a Web site using a secure connection, users can view certificate details by clicking the lock icon and selecting View Certificate. Figure 8-37 shows the general information about a certificate.

Figure 8-37   Viewing general information about a certificate

To determine whether a site is trusted, Internet Explorer includes a list of recognized third-party certificate issuers. As long as all of the organizations in the trust chain are approved, the site should be safe. Figure 8-38 shows an example of a trust chain.

Figure 8-38   Viewing details about the certification path

If a certificate has expired or has not been issued by a trusted third party, the user is given a warning about trusting the site. Additionally, a warning is displayed if a particular Web page contains both secure and insecure content because this could result in the transmission of unencrypted data.

Managing Add-Ons

To expand on the functionality provided in Internet Explorer 7, users can download and install add-ons. Most add-ons must be installed manually on the computer by visiting a Web site and choosing to install them. In some cases, however, the add-on might cause unexpected problems (such as reporting on browsing activity). Alternatively, it might cause browser performance and stability problems. In these cases, the add-on should be disabled or removed. For more information about managing Internet Explorer add-ons, see Chapter 12, "Troubleshooting Windows Vista."

Deleting Browsing History

For convenience, Internet Explorer tracks various types of information as users browse Web sites. For example, it maintains a history of visited Web pages so that the user can go back to a specific site if needed. Additionally, temporary Internet files are stored to improve the performance of browsing. In some cases, users want to delete this information. Sometimes the data itself can contain data that can be misused. Deleting the browsing history is also useful in environments in which multiple users share a computer. To access these functions in Internet Explorer 7, click Delete Browsing History on the Tools menu. Figure 8-39 shows the available options.

Figure 8-39 Deleting browsing history information in Internet Explorer

Resetting Internet Explorer Settings

In this lesson, you have learned about many different configuration options that you can change to customize the behavior of Internet Explorer. In some cases, you might want to revert various settings to their original values. You can do so in the Internet Options dialog box.

Examples include using the option to reset security zone settings on the Security tab and using the Default button to revert to recommended settings on the Privacy tab.

The Advanced tab includes two options for restoring settings to the original values. Clicking Restore Advanced Settings sets all of the values on the Advanced tab to their original values.

The Reset Internet Explorer Settings section on the Advanced tab enables you to change all configuration values back to their defaults (see Figure 8-40). Use this option when other types of troubleshooting have failed because it can require users to reconfigure various preferences. When practicing for Exam 70-623, however, this can be a very helpful feature.

Figure 8-40   Viewing a confirmation about resetting Internet Explorer settings

---

Quick Check

1. How can you configure custom security settings for a group of public Internet sites?
2. How can you open a window that the Pop-Up Blocker has blocked automatically?

Quick Check Answers

1. You can add the sites to the Trusted Sites security zone and then configure the appropriate settings for that zone.
2. You can click the message in the Information Bar and choose to show the window. You can also hold down the Ctrl and Alt keys while clicking a link to disable the Pop-Up Blocker temporarily for that link.

Practice: Configuring Internet Explorer Security Settings

In this practice exercise, you enable and test the Internet Explorer security options. You need a computer that is running Windows Vista and configured to have Internet access to complete the steps.

▶ **Practice: Configure Security Zones**

This practice walks through the steps that are required to make changes to settings for security zones. Specifically, you place a Web site within the Restricted Sites zone and verify the effects that this has on Web browsing.

1. Open Internet Explorer and browse to the Microsoft Windows Downloads Web site at *http://www.microsoft.com/windows/downloads/*.

2. There are frequent changes to the contents of this site, but for this exercise, choose to download any file that is available on the site.

   You should see a dialog box that asks whether you want to save or open the file. For this exercise, click Cancel to avoid downloading the file.

3. In Internet Explorer, click the Tools menu and choose Internet Options.

4. Click the Security tab. Note the available security zones.

   By default, public Web sites are affected by the security settings for the Internet zone.

5. Select the Restricted Sites item, and then click Sites. In the Add This Website To The Zone text box, you should already have the current URL listed. If it is not, copy and paste the current URL from the browser's address bar. Click Add to add this site to the Restricted Sites security zone. Also, add the URL microsoft.com to the list.

   This is necessary because many download links redirect to other portions of the Web site.

6. Click Close to save the settings.

7. With the Restricted Sites zone still selected, click Custom Level to view the specific security settings for this zone.

8. In the Settings section, scroll down to the Downloads section. Verify that the File Download option is set to Disable (Recommended).

   This setting specifies that you are unable to download files from sites in this security zone.

9. Click OK to close the Security Settings dialog box.

10. Click OK to save the security zones settings and to return to the browser.

11. Attempt to download the file that you selected in step 2.

    You should receive a Security Alert dialog box stating, "Your current security settings do not allow this file to be downloaded."

12. Click OK to continue.

13. Remove the site from the Restricted Sites zone by clicking Tools, selecting Internet Options, and then clicking the Security tab. Click OK to save the settings, and then close Internet Explorer when finished.

Lesson Summary

- You can access security-related configuration settings for Internet Explorer by choosing Tools and selecting Internet Options.

- Security zones are designed to place Web sites into groups.

- You can configure security levels separately for the Web sites that are configured in each security zone.

- Internet Explorer Protected Mode is used to prevent Web sites from installing applications or accessing areas of the computer such as the file system.

- You can manage settings related to cookies on the Privacy tab of the Internet Options dialog box.

- The Pop-Up Blocker can be enabled to block unwanted advertisements and other browser windows automatically.

- The Phishing Filter is used to warn users automatically about sites that are attempting to trick them into providing sensitive information.

- Certificates and encryption can be used to create a secure connection between a Web browser and a Web site.

- Users can delete their browsing history to increase the security of their system.

- There are several ways to reset the security and configuration settings of Internet Explorer 7 to their default values.

Lesson Review

You can use the following questions to test your knowledge of the information in Lesson 2, "Securing Internet Explorer 7." The questions are also available on the companion CD if you prefer to review them in electronic form.

NOTE Answers

Answers to these questions and explanations of why each answer choice is correct or incorrect are located in the "Answers" section at the end of the book.

---

1. You are a Consumer Support Technician assisting a small-business owner with configuring security settings for several computers running Windows Vista. She would like to enable various browser options on these computers when they access the company's Web servers. For example, she would like to allow the automatic installation of ActiveX controls when accessing her company's Web-based applications. She would also like to maintain the recommended security settings when users of the computers running Windows Vista access any other sites. Which of the following is the easiest method of configuring these options?

   A. Disable Protected Mode for computers that are located in the Local Intranet security zone.

   B. Modify the settings for the Web sites that are in the Internet zone.

   C. Enable the appropriate options for the Local Intranet security zone.

   D. Place the server URLs in the Trusted Sites security zone, and then assign the appropriate permissions.

2. You are assisting a home user of Windows Vista who would like to remove all of the cookies that have been downloaded in the past from the computer. He would like to keep security-related settings at their recommended values. Which of the following options will meet these requirements?

   A. Configure the Phishing Filter to verify Web sites automatically.

   B. Change the setting on the Privacy tab to Medium-High.

   C. Change the setting on the Privacy tab to Block All Cookies.

   D. On the Tools menu, select Delete Browsing History and remove all cookies.

Chapter Review

To further practice and reinforce the skills you learned in this chapter, you can perform the following tasks:

- Review the chapter summary.
- Review the list of key terms introduced in this chapter.
- Complete the case scenarios. These scenarios set up real-world situations involving the topics of this chapter and ask you to create a solution.
- Complete the suggested practices.
- Take a practice test.

Chapter Summary

- The Windows Vista Parental Controls feature enables parents to define Web restrictions, computer-use time limits, game ratings restrictions, and application restrictions.
- Parents can use activity reports to review their child's activities on the computer.
- Internet Explorer 7 security zones can be used to specify different security options for Internet, intranet, and other Web sites.
- Internet Explorer 7 includes a Pop-Up Blocker, a Phishing Filter, and privacy settings to help maintain the security of the computer.

Key Terms

Do you know what these key terms mean? You can check your answers by looking up the terms in the glossary at the end of the book.

- activity reports
- certificates
- cookies
- Entertainment Software Rating Board (ESRB)
- game rating systems
- game restrictions
- Hypertext Transfer Protocol (HTTP)
- Hypertext Transfer Protocol Secure (HTTPS)
- parental controls
- phishing
- Phishing Filter
- Pop-Up Blocker

- Protected Mode, Internet Explorer
- security zones
- site reviews
- Time Limits (Parental Controls)
- Web restrictions
- Windows Vista Web Filter

Case Scenarios

In the following case scenarios, you apply what you've learned about configuring Windows Vista Parental Controls and Internet Explorer security features. You can find answers to these questions in the "Answers" section at the end of this book.

Case Scenario 1: Using Parental Controls

You are a Consumer Support Technician assisting a mother with configuring Parental Controls for her son. She would like to limit the amount of time that he spends on the computer. She would also like to ensure that he does not access inappropriate content on the Internet and that he can play games only with a Teen rating or below.

1. What types of user accounts should you create?
2. What steps should she take to limit the games most easily that her son can play?
3. What options does she have for configuring browser restrictions?

Case Scenario 2: Configuring Web Browser Security

You are a Consumer Support Technician for a new computer user. The customer is unfamiliar with security options for Internet Explorer. He would like to be protected against accidentally providing information to malicious Web sites and to prevent other common security issues. Wherever possible, you would like to set these security options to work automatically.

1. Which Internet Explorer feature will help prevent the user from accidentally sending sensitive information to a malicious Web site?
2. How can the user determine whether sensitive information is being transferred securely?
3. How can you ensure that the recommended security settings are being used for Internet Explorer?

Suggested Practices

To help you successfully master the exam objectives presented in this chapter, complete the following tasks.

Configuring Security Features

▶ **Practice 1: Working with Parental Controls**

Create a new standard user account on a computer running Windows Vista and enable Parental Controls. Experiment with using a wide variety of settings. Examples include the following:

1. Configure and test Web restrictions. Create and modify settings based on specific Web sites that are allowed or blocked. Also, configure Web restriction levels and note the difference between the High, Medium, and Custom options.

2. Enable application restrictions and allow only a few programs to be executed.

3. Configure game restrictions based on both ratings and allowed and blocked exceptions for particular titles.

4. Define logon time restrictions and test what happens when a user attempts to log on outside of these hours. Optionally, you can log on during valid hours and then verify that the user is automatically logged off of the computer when his or her time expires.

5. After you have made the configuration changes, log on to the computer, using the standard user account and verify the effects of the settings. The Windows Vista Switch User function (available in the Start menu) is a useful method of moving back and forth between the Parent (Administrator) and Child (Standard user) accounts.

▶ **Practice 2: Using Internet Explorer 7 Security Features**

Using the information you learned in Lesson 2, open Internet Explorer and test the effects of various security-related options. For example, add a test site to different security zones (such as Restricted Sites) and see the effects. For other types of changes, such as lowering security levels and installing add-ons, it is best to use a test computer. Also, be sure to reset all security options to their default values after you finish, especially if the computer will be used for browsing the Web.

Take a Practice Test

The practice tests on this book's companion CD offer many options. For example, you can test yourself on just one exam objective, or you can test yourself on all of the 70-623 certification exam content. You can set up the test so that it closely simulates the experience of taking a certification exam, or you can set it up in study mode so that you can look at the correct answers and explanations after you answer each question.

MORE INFO   Practice tests

For details about all the practice test options available, see the "How to Use the Practice Tests" section in this book's introduction.

Chapter 9

Configuring Windows Vista Networking

In the early days of desktop computing technology, it was most common for home and small office computers to be configured to run independently. Although networking technology was available, it was far from a standard option for most environments. Users often shared information by using removable media such as floppy disks. Accessing computers located outside of a home or a small office building was reserved for large corporations.

Now, most of us take network connectivity for granted. We expect to be able to access the Internet from our homes, offices, and even while traveling. We also rely on the ability to share media such as photos, music, and video between computers on our home networks. The underlying technologies that make this possible have changed and evolved over time, but the basic requirements for networking have remained the same. The goals include simplified setup of connections and maintenance of adequate security. Especially when using public networks such as the Internet, it's important that only authorized users are able to access information from a remote location. Convenience has significantly increased by wireless networking options, and it's usually just as easy for people to access Web sites from a coffee shop as it is for them to do so from home.

One of the major design goals for Windows Vista was to simplify the process of creating network connections. For a variety of reasons, there are significant complexities involved in creating secure wired and wireless connections. In this chapter, you'll learn details related to setting up and managing network connections in Windows Vista. Lesson 1, "Managing Network Protocols and Client Network Services," covers details of understanding and managing network protocols and services. Lesson 2, "Configuring Wireless Networking," focuses on configuring wireless network connections.

Exam objectives in this chapter:

- Configure and troubleshoot network protocols.
- Configure and troubleshoot network services at the client.
- Configure and troubleshoot wireless networking.
- Configure and troubleshoot Windows Vista by using the Network And Sharing Center.

Lessons in this chapter:

Before You Begin

It will be helpful for you to have a basic understanding of network connections and how they're used in typical home, home office, and small-business environments. Additionally, to complete the exercises in Lesson 1, you will need a network connection (either wired or wireless) correctly configured to access other computers or the Internet. You might also have a wired or wireless Internet router configured to enable multiple computers to share a single Internet connection. To complete the exercises in Lesson 2, you need to have installed a wireless network adapter that is compatible with Windows Vista.

Lesson 1: Managing Network Protocols and Client Network Services

When two people meet and need to communicate with each other, the first step is to determine a common language to use. When talking with friends and family members, you already know the best method to use. In the world of computers, there are several important standards that are commonly used to enable computers to communicate. By far, the most popular network protocol in the world is Transmission Control Protocol/Internet Protocol (TCP/IP). This protocol is the standard that is used on the public Internet, and it is the primary method of setting up network connections in wired and wireless homes and small businesses.

Customers expect you, as a Consumer Support Technician, to be able to explain to them the various standards and protocols that are available for communications. Furthermore, you need to be familiar with how you can set up and configure appropriate settings in Windows Vista, based on their requirements. In this lesson, you'll learn about networking improvements in Windows Vista, along with important protocols and settings. You'll also learn how to configure and troubleshoot network connections. Because all of the information in this lesson focuses on network protocols and services, it applies equally to both wired and wireless connections. Examples and exercises, however, are based on the use of wired network connections. In Lesson 2, you'll learn about information specific to setting up and managing wireless network connections.

After this lesson, you will be able to:

- Describe new features in the Windows Vista Next Generation TCP/IP Stack.
- List configuration information related to the IPv4 protocol, including IP address, subnet mask, default gateway, and DNS servers.
- Describe the benefits of the IPv6 protocol.
- Describe and manage DNS and DHCP settings on client computers running Windows Vista.
- Create and manage network connections using the Network And Sharing Center.
- Troubleshoot network connections.

Estimated lesson time: 60 minutes

Understanding the Next Generation TCP/IP Stack

Most operating system users rely on the ability to access public networks (such as the Internet) and to communicate with other computers in homes and offices. Because networking is such a critical part of common operations, Windows Vista includes numerous enhancements to the primary networking features of the operating system. The foundation of this functionality is the networking stack, a set of interrelated components that enable communication on the network.

As mentioned earlier, the most commonly used networking protocol is TCP/IP. Windows Vista includes a feature called the Next Generation TCP/IP stack. This term refers to a collection of technologies embedded in the core networking architecture of the operating system. All network-enabled applications, services, and features rely on this stack in one way or another. Although previous versions of Microsoft Windows include support for TCP/IP, Windows Vista includes numerous enhancements, including the following:

- **Automatic configuration** One of the most difficult parts of setting up a new computer (especially for novice users and customers) is configuring network settings. Microsoft designed Windows Vista to perform configuration options automatically wherever possible to avoid end-user confusion.

- **Performance enhancements** New TCP/IP components have been designed to support enhanced features that enable more efficient transfer of data based on a variety of different network conditions.

- **Extensibility** The Next Generation TCP/IP stack has been designed with the ability to add enhancements and new functionality in mind. Components of the network stack are segmented into logical divisions, making it easier for vendors and software developers to install updates.

- **Dynamic reconfiguration** Especially on modern notebook and portable computers, it's common to connect and reconnect frequently to various networks throughout the day. Microsoft designed the Windows Vista network stack to adapt to various configuration environments without requiring a reboot of the operating system.

- **Diagnostic features** Due to the complexity of network configuration, it's possible for various problems to prevent users from successfully connecting to other computers or to the Internet. When these problems occur, it can often be difficult to pinpoint the true source of the problem. The Windows Vista network stack includes diagnostic capabilities that can make it easier to diagnose and troubleshoot common problems.

- **Improved security** With the ability to connect to computers located around the world over the Internet come some potential security risks. Problems such as malware and malicious users can cause downtime, reduced performance, data loss, and security violations. The Next Generation TCP/IP stack has been designed to protect against common types of network-based attacks.

- **Support for multiple versions of the Internet Protocol (IP)** The networking features in Windows Vista enable support for current and future networking technologies based on the TCP/IP standard. Specifically, it provides support for both Internet Protocol version 4 (IPv4) and IP version 6 (IPv6), both of which you'll learn about in the next section. It also provides features to ease the transition between the protocols.

For the most part, all of these features work automatically whenever you create network connections. In typical use, you rarely have a reason to make modifications directly to the network stack. Now that you have an idea of the purpose and function of the basic network foundation, you can look at the different available protocols.

Understanding IPv4

The purpose of a network protocol is to specify the communications format and conventions that computers use when two or more networked devices need to send messages to each other. As mentioned earlier, Windows Vista supports two major protocol types: IPv4 and IPv6. In this section, you'll learn about the details of configuring IPv4. Specifically, you'll learn about the following settings:

- IP address
- Subnet mask
- Default gateway
- DNS server addresses

Exam Tip   Although network protocols other than TCP/IP are available, they're outside the scope of Exam 70-623 and the contents of this book. When taking the exam, you can safely assume that computers are configured to use TCP/IP. Keep in mind, however, that they might not be configured correctly, and you might need to determine how to resolve connection problems.

IP Addresses

By far, the most common version of IP in use at the time of the release of Windows Vista is IPv4 (usually pronounced "IP version 4"). This protocol is a portion of the TCP/IP standard that computers use to communicate on a local area network (LAN) and on the public Internet. A fundamental feature of networking is that each computer on a network must have a unique network address. IPv4 network addresses use a series of four numbers separated by dots. Each number must be between 0 and 254 (inclusive). The following are some examples of IP addresses:

- 10.0.1.1
- 192.168.0.10
- 207.46.232.182

Subnets

In some network environments, it's common for administrators to divide networks into smaller sections known as subnets. To identify which portion of the IP address refers to the network and which portion refers to the computer's address, computers use a subnet mask. Examples of commonly used subnet masks include the following:

- 255.255.255.0
- 255.255.0.0
- 255.0.0.0

Designing and calculating subnet details is beyond the scope of Exam 70-623, but it is important to understand that, in general, all of the computers that are required to be able to communicate with each other should be located on the same subnet. This means that they should all share the same subnet mask. Also, each computer should have a unique network address that is part of the same subnet. For example, the following computers will all be able to communicate with each other (assuming that other network settings are properly configured):

- 10.10.0.1 / 255.255.255.0
- 10.10.0.20 / 255.255.255.0
- 10.10.0.30 / 255.255.255.0

Note that in these examples, all of the subnet masks are identical, and each computer's host address is unique and located on the same subnet.

Default Gateways

Because you can place computers on separate isolated networks, it is often necessary for them to be able to communicate with each other. For example, if you launch Microsoft Internet Explorer and attempt to connect to *www.microsoft.com*, the specific computers that you are trying to access are obviously not located on your subnet. Your computer must then determine how to access that particular Web site.

This is the purpose of the default gateway setting. The default gateway is an IP address value that specifies the network address to which your computer sends all traffic if the traffic is not destined for the local subnet. For most home and small-business users, the default gateway address is the IP address of the router. A computer can use information from its own IP address and subnet mask together to determine whether a requested resource is on another network. If it is, the computer sends the network request to the default gateway. It is then the default gateway's responsibility to route the packets to another network to enable communications. For example, the infrastructure of the Internet is based on a large group of network devices that have the ability to send traffic to each other.

A valid default gateway address must be located on the same subnet as the computer that plans to use it. Typically, the default gateway is an Internet router when used in a home or small-business environment. This device is able to take network requests from computers on the LAN and forward them to other network devices on the Internet.

Managing IPv4 Settings

In most network environments, IP addresses, subnet masks, and default gateway settings are automatically assigned. For example, you can configure most home Internet routers to assign appropriate values automatically for computers on the network. The benefit is that users typically do not need to be concerned with managing the settings manually. You'll learn about how this is done later in this lesson.

Exam Tip   If you're relatively new to managing networking settings, you have probably noticed that there is a lot of information to know. You might be wondering how important it is to understand the underlying technical details of network protocols. In general, Windows Vista is designed to configure network settings whenever possible. However, when configuration or connection problems occur, it can be very useful to have a solid understanding of the actual communications mechanisms themselves. As with most technical topics, practicing common troubleshooting tasks can help you learn this information quickly and easily. If you've seen a particular networking problem before, you'll be well prepared to answer network-related questions when taking Exam 70-623.

Understanding IPv6

A newer version of the IP standard, IPv6, has been created to improve network-based communications. Although IPv4 has been able to adapt to widespread use throughout the Internet, it was never designed to support many millions of different types of devices. There are numerous limitations of the protocol, and it will eventually need to be replaced. Windows Vista includes full support for the IPv6 protocol, but it is important to note that the transition to the new version requires upgrades to all areas of networks and to the Internet before it is complete, a process that is expected to take many years.

MORE INFO   **What happened to IPv5?**

IP standards are defined by the Internet Engineering Task Force (IETF). This organization reviews submissions and ideas for future versions of network protocols, including IPv4 and IPv6. The standards themselves are named Request for Comments (RFC). You might wonder why there is little mention of the version that should come in between those. Initially, IPv5 was intended to be a new network protocol, but it was never made a widespread standard. For all practical purposes, IPv6 is the successor to IPv4. Although you won't be tested on these details on the exam, you can get more background information from the IETF Web site at *http://ietf.org/*.

The primary advantages of IPv6 include the following:

■ **Support for more addresses**   The total number of possible IPv6 addresses is enough to accommodate all of the network devices in the world for the foreseeable future. This expanded capacity allows literally every device in the world to have its own unique network address.

- **Simplified configuration**   Numerous network techniques are required to make IPv4 networks meet the needs of large networks such as the Internet. IPv6 simplifies the process of addressing devices and determining subnets.

- **Performance enhancements**   IPv6 includes features that enable it to adapt to a wide variety of different types of networks and workloads. It can automatically adjust the size of network packets and other settings to improve performance.

- **Security improvements**   A fundamental concern when transferring information over large networks is ensuring security. Only authorized computers should be able to access information during transit. To achieve the necessary encryption and authentication support, IPv6 includes a feature known as IPSecurity (IPSec).

The primary issue with using IPv6 is that computers and network devices must support this protocol to gain these advantages. In addition, operating system tools and software applications might need updates to use the newer version of the protocol. For these reasons, full-scale upgrades to IPv6 (especially on the public Internet) will take several years.

Understanding IPv6 Support in Windows Vista

Microsoft included full support for the IPv6 standard as part of the Windows Vista Next Generation TCP/IP stack. In addition to providing support for the newer version of IP, the stack is able to provide support for IPv4 at the same time. Therefore, a single computer can use IPv6 to communicate with computers that support it (such as other computers running Windows Vista) and use IPv4 to communicate with other computers and devices. Microsoft also provides support for the IPv6 protocol in Windows XP Service Pack 1 and in Microsoft Windows Server 2003. All future versions of the Windows client and server operating systems will support the protocol.

Although supporting IPv6 is an important feature, most of the network-related tools and application features of Windows Vista have been designed to work with the new protocol. For example, the Windows Vista networking features include graphical tools for configuring IPv6 details. You'll learn about specific examples later in this lesson.

Real World

Anil Desai

When IPv4 was initially developed (decades ago), it was not designed to sustain a worldwide network in which millions of computers require access. Through a variety of different technologies such as Network Address Translation (NAT), network administrators have been able to overcome some of these challenges. However, security, performance, and scalability needs are important considerations for moving forward.

The IPv6 protocol provides solutions to many of these problems, but it will not be a quick migration from IPv4. The primary reason for this is that many types of network devices and their interdependencies must be considered. The Windows Vista operating system is one example. Microsoft included full support for both the older and newer versions of IP in Windows Vista. Overall, however, Internet service providers (ISPs) and managers of networks throughout the world will need either to support IPv6 or implement methods to enable backward compatibility.

How does all of this affect you, as a Consumer Support Technician? First, you're likely to hear questions from customers about support for IPv6. The good news is that, for the most part, the default settings in Windows Vista are the most appropriate. It uses IPv4 when necessary and IPv6 when possible. In the future, however, it is important to keep an eye on the transition to IPv6 and to understand when new IPv6-enabled products are introduced. For recent updates, see the Microsoft IPv6 Web site at *http:// www.microsoft.com/technet/network/ipv6/default.mspx.*

Understanding IPv6 Addresses

IPv6 network addresses appear significantly more complicated than their IPv4 counterparts. The primary reason for this is that each network address must be unique, and a greater number of character combinations are required to make this possible. An example of an IPv6 network address is 2001:0:4136:e37a:2074:22b5:f5f5:ff99. Note that colons separate portions of the address. For most users, IPv6 network addresses and settings are configured automatically, and there is no need to configure them manually.

Exam Tip   The technical details of how IPv6 works can be complicated. For the sake of Exam 70-623, it's most important to understand the purpose and function of this protocol, along with how you can configure network settings in Windows Vista. For more detailed information about IPv6, see the Microsoft TechNet IPv6 Web site at *http://www.microsoft.com/technet/network/ipv6 /default.mspx.* Throughout the remainder of this chapter, the terms related to IP addresses focus on the IPv4 standard because this is the most commonly used version of the protocol and the one that is most emphasized on Exam 70-623.

Understanding Client Network Services

So far, you've learned about the basic rules for setting up network addresses for computers that are connected. In some ways, the basic rules are fairly simple: Each computer must have a unique IP address on the network and generally is located on the same subnet, which means that each computer must have the same network address as others on the same subnet. In some home and small-business environments, managing one or a few computers manually might be reasonable. However, when supporting additional computers, some automated methods for managing network services will be very helpful.

In this section, you'll learn how several network-related features of Windows Vista can help you manage settings such as IP addresses. Later in this chapter, you'll see how these settings can be defined when creating and managing network connections.

Exam Tip   This section and the corresponding Exam 70-623 objective that it covers mention the term *client*. With respect to Windows Vista, this term refers to desktop or notebook computers that are primarily used by individuals. In larger networked environments, it's common to refer to computers as either clients or servers. Because the focus of Exam 70-623 is on supporting Windows Vista for consumers, you will generally focus on the client side of network settings. Windows Vista includes the ability to use services such as Dynamic Host Configuration Protocol (DHCP) and Domain Name System (DNS) but not to function as a server for those protocols. Keep in mind, however, that the network services described here also have server-side components that must be configured properly for these features to be available. Additionally, most home and small-business routers also include built-in DHCP and DNS features. For more information, consult the product's documentation.

DHCP

When working in networked environments, users are able to provide custom IP addresses for their environments. As mentioned earlier, each computer must have a unique IP address and must be configured with other settings such as the subnet mask and default gateway address. Most consumers find it difficult to keep track of these settings. For example, a customer might need to write down the settings, and every time a friend or family member needs to add a new computer, he or she will have to provide the correct information. If two computers are accidentally configured with the same address, one or both might be unable to communicate on the network. Add in the requirement to support a virtually limitless number of wireless computers, and it can be very time-consuming to manage IP addressing. Clearly, there's room for improvement in this situation.

DHCP is designed to provide appropriate TCP/IP network addresses and related information automatically to computers when they first attempt to connect to a network. The process involves four main steps:

- **Discovery**   When a computer first initializes itself on the network, it does not have a valid network address. To obtain one, it sends a broadcast (a network message to all computers on the network) requesting an IP address.

- **Offer**   A DHCP server receives the broadcast request and responds by providing an IP address offer to the new computer. The specific address chosen is based on the configuration of the DHCP server's database. Most commonly, a range of IP addresses is configured for use on the network. Other details, such as the subnet mask and the IP address of the DHCP server, are also included.

- **Request** After the client receives the offer, it makes a request for the same IP address to the DHCP server. This step is required to ensure that the client actually needs to reserve the specific request. In some cases, for example, if the computer has received responses from more than one DHCP server, it might not need to make the request. Generally, DHCP clients make a request to the first DHCP server that has responded to a request.
- **Acknowledge** The DHCP server receives the request from the DHCP client and records that the offered TCP/IP address is now in use on the network. This address will be unavailable for assignment to other computers until it expires.

The assignment of a DHCP address is known as a lease, and there is typically a maximum amount of time that can elapse before the lease expires. For example, a typical DHCP server setting is to allow IP address leases to last for up to eight days. As the expiration of the lease approaches, the client computer sends a request to renew the address to the DHCP server. If the DHCP server approves the request, the client can continue using the address. This method helps ensure that computers that are no longer on the network are not taking up allocated IP addresses in the DHCP server's database.

The customers that you support as a Consumer Support Technician will generally enable DHCP services on their Internet router or other device. The specific administration methods and configuration options will vary based on the brand and model of the device, but the general process allows for enabling the DHCP server and configuring a valid range of addresses to assign. Some small business environments might include server computers that provide DHCP services. One example is Windows Server 2003, which includes a DHCP Server component. In these environments, it's simplest to configure only a single DHCP server to be active. If two are required, you must configure each with a different set of IP addresses to avoid potential duplication. Finally, if an environment does not have any DHCP server, users need to configure IP address settings on each networked computer manually.

Domain Name System

From a networking standpoint, the concept of unique IP addresses makes a lot of sense. One can quickly look at the number and determine details about which network it is using. However, when dealing with many computers, it can be difficult to remember which computers have which network addresses. When the millions of servers that are accessible over the Internet are taken into account, it's virtually impossible to keep track of the correct IP values.

Domain Name System (DNS) is designed to provide mappings between TCP/IP addresses and friendly DNS names. DNS names have multiple parts that are separated by a period (.) character. Examples of DNS addresses include the following:

- www.microsoft.com
- technet.microsoft.com
- MyComputer.local

You might recognize these names as similar to what you use to connect to public Web sites. The public structure of the Internet is configured with certain top-level domain names that identify computers that you can access from anywhere in the world. Several third-party service providers are able to make changes to the addresses used in the database. Due to the number of addresses, it's important for public DNS databases to be able to send requests to each other. When a client attempts to connect to another computer using a DNS name, the request is sent to one of the DNS servers that is configured as part of the IP addressing parameters on the client. The DNS server then attempts to resolve the requested name to its IP address by querying other DNS servers. After the IP address for the requested name is determined, it is returned to the client so that it can be used for transferring data. To improve performance, the client makes a temporary record of the address and uses it for subsequent requests.

Exam Tip   DNS is a standard on which the entire Internet is based. On the server side, there are many complexities and details that must be addressed to make this system work. For the sake of preparing for Exam 70-623, focus on troubleshooting client-side issues related to DNS. For example, a home computer might be able to connect to other computers on the local network and with an Internet router but not directly with Internet sites using a DNS address. In this case, it's likely that the DNS server IP information is incorrect.

Overall, the use of DNS names is a vital process for connecting to computers and services that are located on the Internet. It allows users to focus on meaningful computer and server names rather than difficult-to-remember IP addresses.

Firewalls

If there were no other restrictions placed on network traffic, it would be easy for all computers to communicate with each other. In some cases, this might be helpful. For example, many home and small-business users have more than one computer and want to share data such as documents, photos, and videos among them. A problem arises, however, when insecure or public networks are included. For example, when connecting to the Internet, it's helpful to be able to connect to any computer in the world through a device such as a router. However, for security and privacy reasons, you would not want unauthorized users and computers on the Internet to be able to access your private computers.

The purpose of a firewall is to divide networks by placing restrictions on communications between computers. In some cases, all traffic between two or more networks can be blocked. More commonly, most protocols are blocked while certain types of communications are allowed. For example, you can configure Windows Firewall to allow applications such as Internet Explorer to connect to Web sites using an outbound connection but to prevent other computers from using the same communications ports to connect to the local computer. For more details about working with the Windows Firewall feature in Windows Vista, see Chapter 7, "Using Windows Security Center."

In a typical home or small business environment, it's common for customers to use an Internet router or similar device that provides firewall functionality. Usually, the default settings of these devices enable computers to make outbound connections but prevent Internet-based users and computers from detecting local computers. The specific configuration steps and settings vary between devices from various brands and manufacturers, so it's important to consult the relevant documentation when assisting customers with setting up firewalls.

Configuring Network Connections

So far, the focus of this lesson has been on learning about IP addresses and related client network services. Understanding this information is important when creating, configuring, and managing network connections in Windows Vista. Generally, if you understand the basic concepts behind network protocols, you'll be able to make appropriate choices and resolve any issues that might arise. In this section, you'll learn how to configure network connections in Windows Vista.

Managing Network Settings

Windows Vista includes several different ways to access network-related settings and tools. One starting point is by clicking Network And Internet in Control Panel. As shown in Figure 9-1, various tasks and operations are available. From here, users can view details about current network settings and devices and set up and manage new connections.

Figure 9-1 Viewing options in the Control Panel Network And Internet group

You configure the majority of options by using Network And Sharing Center. This utility provides a central location from which users can view details about the local network. Figure 9-2 provides an example of the default view of the Network And Sharing Center section.

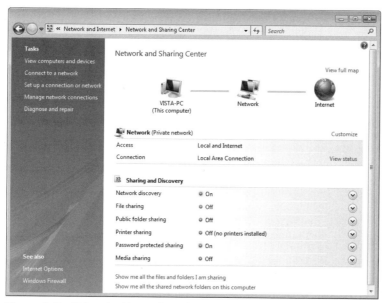

Figure 9-2   Using the Network And Sharing Center to view details about network connections

---

MORE INFO   Sharing network resources

The focus of this chapter is on creating and managing network connections to enable computers to communicate with each other. For more information about sharing network resources such as files, printers, and media, see Chapter 10, "Managing Network Sharing."

Viewing Network Information

When managing and troubleshooting network connections, it's often helpful to get an overview of current connections and how they're configured. Because network connections (and their relationships) can be confusing to customers, the Network And Sharing Center offers a Network Map feature. By clicking View Full Map, users can see the relationships between various network devices and services. Figure 9-3 shows an example. If the computer is connected to multiple networks (for example, a wired network and a wireless network), a drop-down list enables the user to choose which network is shown in the map.

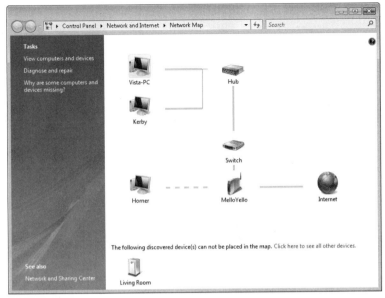

Figure 9-3   Viewing a network map on a desktop computer

You can view and modify information about various items in the network map by right-clicking them and viewing the list of available options. The type of network device determines which actions you can take. For example, you can access settings for a standard Windows Vista–based computer or view configuration details for a computer router or gateway device.

In addition to the Network Map feature, you can also view details about a particular network connection. The View Status link in Network And Sharing Center provides information about a particular network connection. Figure 9-4 shows an example.

Figure 9-4   Viewing status information about a wired network connection

The basic details specify whether the computer is currently connected to a network, whether the connection is enabled, how long the connection has been active, and the speed of the connection. In addition, the Activity section shows the number of bytes that have been sent by and received from the network connection. This information provides a good overview of the status of the connection.

In some cases, it can be helpful to view more details such as the specific TCP/IP configuration of the connection. You can click Details to open a dialog box that shows this information (see Figure 9-5). Specific information includes the network address, subnet mask, and information about DHCP and DNS servers. If the computer used a DHCP server to obtain the address information, details about the duration of the lease are also available.

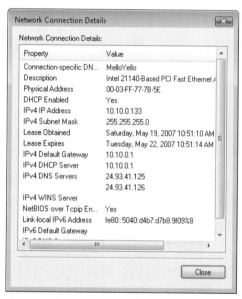

Figure 9-5   Viewing details for a network connection

Modifying Network Settings

The vast majority of networks today run a standard set of protocols and services. In most cases, Windows Vista is able to configure the appropriate setting for a network connection automatically. In some cases, however, it might be necessary to configure settings such as the IP address, subnet mask, default gateway, and DNS servers for a computer manually. It's most common to use a manual configuration when a DHCP server is either unavailable or not providing the correct information.

To access the properties of a network connection, open Network And Sharing Center and click View Status next to the relevant network connection. Then, click Properties (see Figure 9-6).

Figure 9-6   Viewing properties for a wired network connection

The specific list of items shown might vary based on the enabled services and protocols for the network. By default, new network connections include settings for both IPv4 and IPv6. You can uninstall or disable most of the items in the list. In general, it is recommended that you use the default options because they are required for certain types of functionality. For example, if you remove the File And Printer Sharing For Microsoft Networks feature, users will not be able to share or access files on other computers. It is also possible to install new services or protocols manually if they are required.

In addition to adding and removing services for a network connection, the primary settings that you can modify are related to the network connection and protocols. Clicking Configure in the Properties dialog box displays the details of the associated network adapter used by the connection. Most of the available properties are related to the settings for the hardware device itself. Many network adapters include advanced options that you can also modify if necessary (see Figure 9-7).

Figure 9-7   Viewing the Advanced tab of the Properties dialog box of a network adapter

Setting Network Location Details

Networked computers often have different security requirements based on the type of network to which they are connected. For example, within a typical home environment, it's likely that computers need to share information. Because the network is usually limited to authorized users and computers, it's safe to do this. When you connect the same computer to a public or insecure network (such as in an airport or other public place), it is recommended that you limit access to the computer. You can configure these settings by clicking Customize next to a network connection in the Network And Sharing Center. Figure 9-8 shows the typical options that are available.

Figure 9-8   Customizing network settings using the Network And Sharing Center

In addition to switching between the Public and Private options for network connection types, you can also change the name of the network. Windows Vista uses this setting to help you quickly identify the type of network that you are using. It is also possible to change the network icon. Finally, it is possible to merge or delete network connections. This option is useful when, for example, multiple network connections are defined on the computer that all use similar settings.

Manually Configuring TCP/IP Settings

The most commonly modified network connection settings are those related to the IPv4 and IPv6 network protocols. To access these settings, in the Properties dialog box for a network connection, select the appropriate protocol and click Properties. Figure 9-9 shows the properties that are available for the IPv4 protocol.

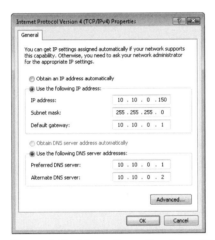

Figure 9-9   Manually configuring settings for the IPv4 protocol

By default, new network connections are designed to use DHCP for automatic assignment of settings. Using the Properties dialog box, however, you can manually specify information for several settings as follows:

- **IP Address**   The unique TCP/IP address of this computer
- **Subnet Mask**   The subnet mask that is used by all computers on the local subnet
- **Default Gateway**   The IP address of a router or other device that enables communications outside the local network
- **DNS Servers**   The IP addresses of a preferred and alternate DNS server

If DHCP is enabled, users also see an Alternate Configuration tab that enables them to define a second set of IP address information (see Figure 9-10). This information is most commonly used when you would like to leave the automatic settings to use DHCP, but you want to provide rules for which addresses should be used if a DHCP server is unavailable. The options include using an automatic private IP address (which is generated automatically by Windows Vista) or to provide specific IP address settings. This tab is also useful when a network connection is used at multiple locations. For example, if a customer uses a laptop computer at work and at home, he or she might need to assign different addresses for each environment manually.

Figure 9-10   Specifying alternate configuration options for a network connection

On the General tab of the Internet Protocol Version 4 (TCP/IPv4) Properties dialog box, the Advanced button enables further configuration of network details. Although these settings are not common for most consumers, it is possible to configure a single network adapter to use multiple IP addresses and subnet masks and to configure multiple gateways (see Figure 9-11).

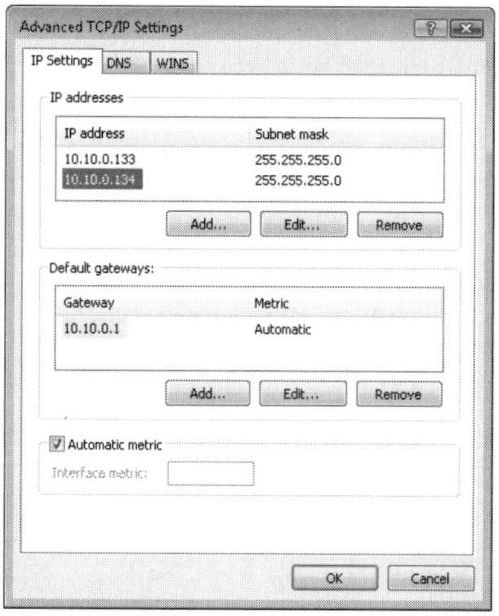

Figure 9-11   Configuring advanced TCP/IP settings for a network connection

In addition, there are advanced configuration options for DNS and Windows Internet Naming Service (WINS). Most home and small-business users use the default settings. In some business network environments, however, it might be helpful to change the default behavior of these protocols.

By default, the Properties dialog box of a network connection also includes details about the IPv6 protocol. As with IPv4 settings, the defaults are appropriate for most users. You can configure manual IPv6 addresses and other details by accessing the Properties dialog box of the protocol (see Figure 9-12).

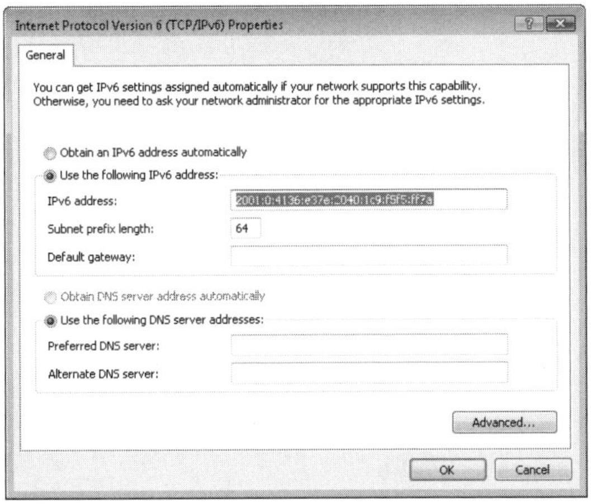

Figure 9-12   Configuring properties of the IPv6 protocol

Another method of configuring network settings is by clicking Manage Network Connections in the Network And Sharing Center. The resulting display shows all of the available network connections on the computer and enables the user to change the settings manually. This view is similar to the one that you see in previous versions of Windows such as Windows XP and Microsoft Windows 2000 Professional.

Creating a New Network Connection

The process of creating a new network connection is simple and can be performed by starting at the Network And Sharing Center. Clicking the Set Up A Connection Or Network link launches a dialog box that enables you to select the type of connection to create (see Figure 9-13).

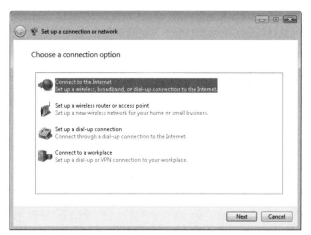

Figure 9-13   Setting up a new network connection by using the Network And Sharing Center

There are several different options, each of which provides a description of a typical usage scenario. For home and small-business users, the most common option is usually Connect To The Internet. The other network types include connecting to a workplace by using a virtual private network (VPN), creating a dial-up connection, or configuring a wireless router or access point. Each step of the process walks users through available options. The specific details are based on the type of network connection, whether other similar network connections have been defined, and the security requirements.

Troubleshooting Network Connections

As a Consumer Support Technician, you are likely to be asked for assistance with configuring customers' wired and wireless network connections. Common problems include having incorrectly configured IP address settings or trying to access remote resources when a network connection is disabled. Because the process of troubleshooting these types of problems usually follows a sequence of steps, Windows Vista includes an automatic method for resolving the most common issues.

Understanding the Network Diagnostics Framework

The process of troubleshooting network-related problems can be complicated, especially for customers with limited knowledge of the technical details. One of the most common errors that a user will report is receiving a "Page cannot be displayed" error in Internet Explorer. The root cause of the problem could be one of many different issues. For example, a network cable might be unplugged, or the computer might have failed to obtain a valid IP address from a DHCP server.

Windows Vista includes the Network Diagnostics Framework (NDF) to provide a method to determine the cause of a particular network problem automatically. It can then present options for resolving the issue, such as enabling a network adapter that is disabled. Behind the scenes, the NDF functionality looks at many different details related to network settings and uses a set of steps for determining the cause and potential resolution for the issue. The specific details might vary, for example, for wired and wireless network connections. This frees users and support staff from having to check multiple configuration settings to resolve the issue.

Diagnosing and Repairing a Connection

There are several ways to start the process of automatic troubleshooting for a particular network connection. One method is to right-click the system tray icon for the network connection (if it is available) and select Diagnose And Repair. Other options are to select the Diagnose And Repair option in the Status dialog box of a network connection or to use the Diagnose And Repair link in the Network And Sharing Center. Regardless of the method used, this starts the automatic repair process (see Figure 9-14).

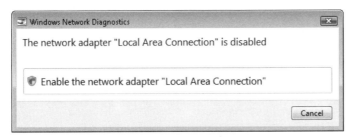

Figure 9-14   Automatically diagnosing and repairing a network connection

If a problem is detected, Windows Vista automatically attempts to resolve it. For example, if the computer is not currently configured with valid TCP/IP information, Windows Vista automatically attempts to release the current DHCP lease (if there is one) and obtain new IP address details. In some cases, Windows Vista might notify users that manual configuration changes might be required. Overall, the *Diagnose And Repair* function can help automatically resolve the most common types of connection problems without requiring expertise from users.

Using Network Troubleshooting Tools

When diagnosing and troubleshooting network connections, there are several different tools and techniques you can use to verify connectivity. In this section, you'll learn about several of the most commonly used tools. You run all of them from a command prompt, and they can return or change configuration details. For more information about a particular command, you can type the command followed by /?.

Windows IP Configuration

The Windows IP configuration (IPCONFIG) command provides a simple way to view and modify information for a network adapter. To view network details, you can use the command without any arguments or type **IPCONFIG /ALL** to view complete details about the configuration of the network connection and various protocol settings (see Figure 9-15).

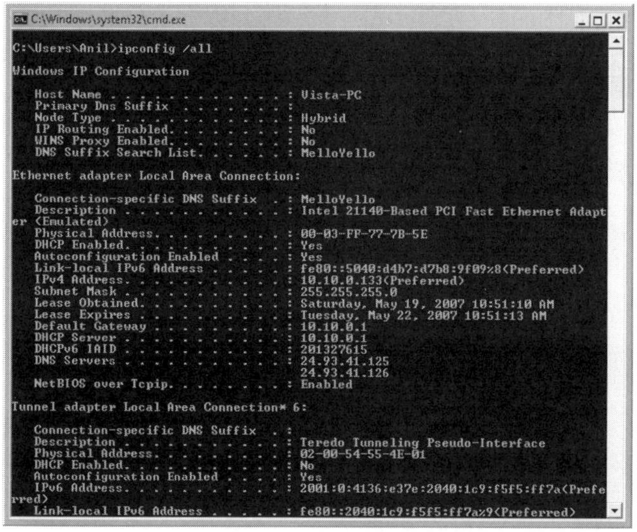

Figure 9-15   Viewing network configuration details by using IPCONFIG

In addition to viewing information about network connections, you can also release and renew DHCP addresses and perform DNS troubleshooting, using the IPCONFIG utility. Type **IPCONFIG /?** for more details on the specific command-line options.

PING

Often, when troubleshooting network connections, you want to test whether computers are able to communicate with each other without having to share files, printers, or other objects. The PING utility is designed to send a simple TCP/IP request to a remote computer and to return the response. Figure 9-16 provides an example.

In addition to determining whether another computer is reachable, the PING command returns the amount of time it took for a response to be received. Although this information is not intended to be used for performance monitoring, it does provide an indication of the speed of the network.

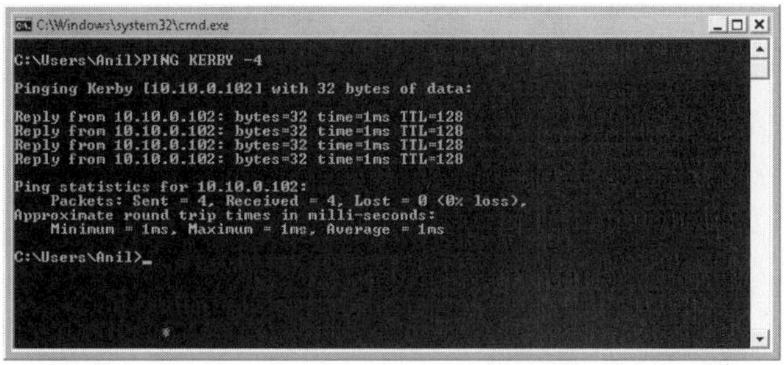

Figure 9-16 Performing a PING to verify IPv4 connectivity

NETSH

The NETSH command launches an interactive command-line application that enables viewing and modifying many different types of network settings. You can access the list of NETSH commands by typing **?** at the NETSH prompt. Common operations include viewing and modifying settings for a particular network interface, making firewall changes, and configuring protocol settings.

Quick Check

1. You would like to get a quick overview of the number and types of devices that are available on a customer's home network. What is the easiest way to do this?
2. What are the most important protocol settings related to an IPv4 connection?

Quick Check Answers

1. The Network Map feature that is available from within the Network And Sharing Center provides a graphical overview of all of the network devices that are present in the environment.
2. An IPv4 connection should include an IP address, a subnet mask, a default gateway, and DNS server addresses.

Practice: Configuring Network Settings

In these exercises, you will configure network settings in Windows Vista. The exercises assume that you currently have a wired network connection on a computer running Windows Vista and that you are able to access the Internet. It also assumes that you have obtained valid TCP/IP network information through a DHCP server. Internet access can be provided through a LAN, a home-based broadband router, or a direct broadband connection (using, for example, a DSL modem or cable modem). The steps in the exercise might result in temporary loss of your Internet connection.

▶ **Practice 1: Manually Configure IPv4 Settings**

In this exercise, you manually configure TCP/IP settings for a computer running Windows Vista. You use the current DHCP-assigned IP address information as a basis for determining the manually assigned address for the computer.

1. Open the Network And Sharing Center by right-clicking the system tray icon for your wired network connection and selecting Network And Sharing Center.

2. In the Network section of the user interface, click View Status for the wired network connection on the computer.

    You see details such as the speed of the connection, the duration of the connection, and the amount of activity for the adapter.

3. Click Details to view TCP/IP-related information for the network connection. Make a note of the following configuration settings:

    ❑ IPv4 IP Address: _____

    ❑ IPv4 Subnet Mask: _____

    ❑ IPv4 Default Gateway: _____

    ❑ IPv4 DNS Server (primary): _____

    ❑ IPv4 DNS Server (secondary): _____

4. Click Close to close the details of the network connection.

5. Click Properties to access information about the wired Internet connection.

6. In the list of network components, select Internet Protocol Version 4 (TCP/IPv4), and then click Properties.

7. On the General tab of the Properties dialog box, choose to assign TCP/IP information by selecting the appropriate options manually. Type the information you recorded in step 3 and then click OK to save the settings.

8. Click Close to close the network Properties dialog box, and then click Close again to return to the Network And Sharing Center.

9. Open Internet Explorer and browse to *http://www.microsoft.com* to verify that your Internet connection is working.

10. To return the system to its original configuration, click View Status for the wired network in the Properties dialog box of the TCP/IP connection. Access the Properties dialog box for IPv4 and specify that all information should be obtained from a DHCP server.

11. Close all open windows and close the Network And Sharing Center.

▶ **Practice 2: Diagnose and Repair a Connection**

In this practice exercise, you use the automatic network diagnostics of Windows Vista to troubleshoot a common network connection issue.

1. Right-click the system tray icon for your wired network connection and select Network And Sharing Center.

2. Click View Status next to the item for the wired connection.

3. Click Disable to disable the wired network adapter.

4. Open Internet Explorer and attempt to connect to *http://www.microsoft.com*. You should receive an error page stating "Internet Explorer cannot display the Web page."

5. On the Internet Explorer error page, click Diagnose Connection Problems. The Windows Network Diagnostics tool analyzes the connection.

6. The Windows Network Diagnostics dialog box shows that the network adapter is disabled. Click the relevant button to enable the network adapter. Click Close to verify the summary information.

7. Use Internet Explorer to attempt to connect to the same Web site you used in step 4. Verify that the page loads properly.

8. When finished, close Internet Explorer and close Network And Sharing Center.

Lesson Summary

- Windows Vista includes the Next Generation TCP/IP stack, which provides for improved performance, better security, and support for both IPv4 and IPv6.
- The IP address of a computer should be unique on a network.
- The subnet mask determines which addresses are part of a network.
- IPv6 provides a much larger range of addresses than IPv4, along with performance, security, and reliability enhancements.
- The Dynamic Host Configuration Protocol (DHCP) is used to assign TCP/IP settings to client computers automatically.
- The Domain Name System (DNS) is used to resolve friendly hierarchical names such as www.microsoft.com to TCP/IP addresses.
- The Network And Sharing Center can be used to create, configure, manage, and troubleshoot network connections.
- Additional TCP/IP troubleshooting tools include IPCONFIG, PING, and NETSH.

Lesson Review

You can use the following questions to test your knowledge of the information in Lesson 1, "Managing Network Protocols and Client Network Services." The questions are also available on the companion CD if you prefer to review them in electronic form.

NOTE Answers

Answers to these questions and explanations of why each answer choice is correct or incorrect are located in the "Answers" section at the end of the book.

---

1. You are a Consumer Support Technician assisting a home computer user with trouble-shooting a network-related problem. The user reports that he can connect to other computers on his network to share files, but one computer is unable to access the Internet. Which of the following IPv4 settings is most likely misconfigured?

    1. IP address
    2. Subnet mask
    3. Default gateway
    4. Network name

2. You are a Consumer Support Technician assisting a small-business owner with setting up a network for four Windows Vista–based computers. She would like to simplify the addition of new computers to the network and is unfamiliar with managing TCP/IP addresses. You have recommended that she purchase a network router for use in her office. Which of the following networking features will help the user meet her goal?

    1. DHCP
    2. DNS
    3. PING
    4. IPCONFIG

Lesson 2: Configuring Wireless Networking

In recent years, the thought of using a computer without access to the Internet has become hard to imagine for many consumers. Users rely on the ability to access information stored on their own networks or on computers located across the world quickly and easily. Although it is common to find network jacks in office locations, they are less likely to be found in home environments and some types of businesses. This makes the act of connecting to the Internet difficult and inconvenient. Fortunately, there's a better way.

In Lesson 1, you looked at details related to network protocols with a focus on managing wired network connections. The focus of this lesson is on examining the details of working with the convenience of wireless networks. For the most part, all of the information you learned in Lesson 1 applies equally to wired and wireless networks.

Although there are numerous benefits of using wireless technology, there are also some additional security and configuration-related concerns. As a Consumer Support Technician, you'll often be responsible for assisting users with configuring their wireless network adapters for use with Windows Vista. In this lesson, you'll learn about the basics of working with wireless networks, along with the details related to ensuring that these networks remain secure.

After this lesson, you will be able to:
- Describe potential security issues with using wireless network connections.
- Identify commonly used wireless network protocols.
- Describe the features and benefits of network security protocols such as WEP and WPA.
- Use the Network And Sharing Center to create and manage wireless network connections.
- Troubleshoot issues with wireless network connections.

Estimated lesson time: 45 minutes

Working with Wireless Networks

The benefits of using wireless networks are probably apparent to most end users and technical professionals. Not having to find and connect a network cable to a jack is a huge benefit in environments ranging from homes to public locations such as airports and restaurants. There are, however, several potential drawbacks to using wireless connections instead of wired ones.

First, there's the issue of physical security. With wired connections, it's often easy to determine who is connected to the network and to restrict access to a specific building. Due the nature of wireless communications, on the other hand, it is possible for users to connect to a network without having physical access to a building. Simply by enabling their wireless network adapters, it is possible to view network activity originating from other computers. The potential for intercepting data is high.

Additionally, there are technical issues such as finding the correct wireless network (especially in environments where multiple networks exist) and providing the proper security credentials to access it. Finally, there are numerous available standards and protocols related to wireless networks. This can make the process of selecting and configuring various devices complicated. Although standards are designed to provide for compatibility, there is still some potential for connection problems.

Understanding Typical Wireless Configurations

In most home and small-business environments, there are several required components that are necessary to create and use a wireless network. The first requirement is for a computer to have a wireless network adapter. Like a physical network adapter, a wireless adapter can be built into a computer (which is most common with portable devices such as notebook computers), or it can be added as a peripheral. Common examples of wireless network adapter types include universal serial bus (USB) and PC card–based devices. Desktop computer expansion cards are also available (for more information on installing new hardware devices, see Chapter 11, "Managing and Troubleshooting Devices.")

The network adapter provides the computer-side connection to the wireless network. Most commonly, the network itself is created by using a wireless router or access point. These devices can provide the ability to connect multiple computers through wireless connections. They usually include standard wired connection ports for supported standard LAN connections and for connecting to the Internet.

Other types of wireless networking hardware products are also available. For example, because the range of wireless devices is limited based on the strength of the signal, you can use network devices called repeaters to relay the signal to more distant locations.

Understanding Wireless Network Protocols

Regardless of the types of devices that are used, they generally must support the same wireless networking standards. The most commonly used wireless standards include 802.11a, 802.11b, 802.11g, and 802.11n. Each of these protocols differs in terms of the frequencies that are used, the data rate (speed), and the range. Table 9-1 provides a comparison of these values.

Table 9-1   Summary of 802.11 Networking Standards

Protocol	Initial Availability	Frequency Range	Data Rate (Typical)	Data Rate (Maximum)	Range (Indoor)
802.11a	1999	2.4–2.5 GHz	25 Mbit/s	54 Mbit/s	~50 meters

Table 9-1   Summary of 802.11 Networking Standards

Protocol	Initial Availability	Frequency Range	Data Rate (Typical)	Data Rate (Maximum)	Range (Indoor)
802.11b	1999	~5.0 GHz (multiple ranges)	6.5 Mbit/s	11 Mbit/s	~100 meters
802.11g	2003	2.4–2.5GHz	11 Mbit/s	54 Mbit/s	~100 meters
802.11n	2006 (draft)	2.4 GHz or 5 GHz	200 Mbit/s	540 Mbit/s	~250 meters

Exam Tip   When preparing for Exam 70-623, it's not necessary to memorize the different performance characteristics and details of various network protocols. Although the variations can have a significant effect on the types of products you recommend to customers, you configure all of the standard wireless networking features of Windows Vista similarly regardless of the network type.

In general, newer standards offer improved performance and improved range. Because the process of upgrading to newer standards often requires the replacement of numerous routers and network adapters, many wireless networking products support multiple protocols.

Understanding Wireless Security Options

As mentioned earlier, one of the security-related issues of transmitting information over a wireless connection is the risk of data interception by third parties. For example, if you are transmitting a document through e-mail while using a wireless connection in an airport, another wireless user might be able to collect this data without your knowledge. Also, in a home environment, the range of a wireless router or access point might make it possible for neighbors to connect to your network and access resources such as home computers or your Internet connection.

To address these concerns, you can protect data by using encryption technologies. The purpose of encryption is to scramble data into a format that is decipherable by only the intended recipient of the communication. Even if data is intercepted, it will be unusable by anyone who does not know the encryption key. There are several different methods by which you can implement encryption. The most common method is by using a shared secret, a password, or other information that is known only to authorized users of the network. In this section, you'll look at different ways in which you can help increase security.

Using Wired Equivalent Privacy

The oldest common wireless security method is known as the Wired Equivalent Privacy (WEP) standard. As its name implies, the goal of this security mechanism is to allow only authorized users to connect to a wireless network. Home and small-business users typically create a WEP key when they initially configure their routers and network adapters. The length of the key affects the level of security. More characters in the key make the system more difficult to compromise from a security standpoint. Key lengths are typically measured in bits, with some common strengths being 128-bit and 256-bit.

Using WEP security is clearly better than using no encryption, but this security protocol does have well-known vulnerabilities. Specifically, it is possible for unauthorized users to determine mathematically the value of the WEP key simply by monitoring a sufficient amount of networking traffic. Programs are available for automatically performing this task, and it can often be accomplished very quickly. Longer WEP keys make the process more difficult, but eventually, a knowledgeable user can break through the encryption.

Another security challenge is related to sharing WEP keys with authorized users. Although the problem is not specific to WEP, users must have a method of securely communicating the key. In home and small business environments, this can often be done by verbally transmitting the key, but in larger organizations, it can be a significant problem. Overall, WEP provides additional security, but it does not completely address all potential vulnerabilities.

Using Wi-Fi Protected Access

The goal of the Wi-Fi Protected Access (WPA) protocol is to provide for increased security over that of the WEP standard. WPA is generally seen as a replacement for the less secure WEP protocol, but WEP is still supported in operating systems such as Windows Vista for backward compatibility with devices that do not support it.

Like WEP, you generally configure WPA security on a wireless router or access point. To enable WPA, the network adapter and operating system must also support it. When creating a new connection, users are prompted to provide the appropriate WPA key (you'll look at the specific steps later in this chapter).

NOTE   Recommending wireless devices

Customers rely on your advice as a Consumer Support Technician when selecting wireless networking products. Most retail stores provide a wide array of options for adapters, routers, and other devices. When recommending products to use with Windows Vista, you should look for the Works with Windows Vista logo for the product. This information can help you determine that the product includes support for new features and standards used in the operating system. It also helps assure you that your customers will be able to get technical support and updated drivers if problems should arise.

Using Service Set Identifiers

When working with wired networks, it's often easy to tell to which network you're connecting. In a home or small-business environment, there is typically only one available network, and all of the connections enable computers to communicate (assuming that they have the proper permissions). In the world of wireless networking, it's possible for several different wireless networks to be available for access from a given location. For example, in a typical home environment, it might be possible to connect to neighbors' wireless networks.

The Service Set Identifier (SSID) is designed to assist users with finding and connecting to wireless networks that are available. The SSID is a name that is continually broadcast by a wireless access point device. The name of the wireless network (which you usually define when you initially configure an access point) is provided, along with details about whether the network requires security credentials. When a wireless network adapter is present in a computer, Windows Vista can automatically detect the available networks and identify them based on their SSID. Users can then choose to which network they want to connect (and, optionally, to provide security information).

NOTE Configuring SSIDs for usability and security

As a Consumer Support Technician, you'll likely need to answer customers' questions about setting up SSIDs. Most wireless network device vendors use a default SSID that does not contain descriptive information. Ideally, the wireless network name should be descriptive to the intended users of the network as well as unique. For example, "Office" might not be unique enough for a small-business network using office space that is shared with other businesses. Customers might also be tempted to disable SSID broadcasting as a method of increasing security. This practice is often known as "security through obscurity" and is generally not recommended. Nonbroadcast networks can still be detected but are more difficult for even authorized users to find (because they must know the exact name of the device). Overall, it is far better to rely on wireless encryption standards such as WPA to keep data secure.

Configuring Wireless Networks

In the past, end users have often found the process of connecting to wireless networks too complicated and unreliable. To address these issues, Windows Vista includes several different tools and methods for connecting to wireless networks. The goal is for these tools to remain consistent, regardless of the specific wireless protocols, security methods, and brands of network devices that are being used. In most cases, you can use the wireless network features to create a connection quickly, using minimal effort. In this section, you'll learn how to connect to a wireless network and manage wireless network settings. The content of this section assumes that you are already familiar with creating and managing standard network connections as described in Lesson 1 of this chapter.

Connecting to a Wireless Network

Unlike wired network connections, the process of connecting to a wireless network does not require a physical action such as plugging in a cable. Instead, users must choose to which wireless network they would like to connect from those that are within range. When you have installed and configured a wireless network adapter on the computer, the Network And Sharing Center shows the connection in the display. If the adapter is not currently connected to a specific wireless network, you can click the Connect To A Network link. The resulting dialog box (shown in Figure 9-17) shows all of the available wireless network connections within range, along with their signal strength.

Figure 9-17 Viewing a list of available wireless networks

The details also show whether the network is security-enabled or unsecured. You can click Connect to connect to a particular wireless network. If security information is required for the network (and it has not yet been stored on the local computer), Windows Vista prompts you to provide the necessary details (see Figure 9-18). Optionally, it is possible to provide network configuration information that is stored on a USB drive (if available).

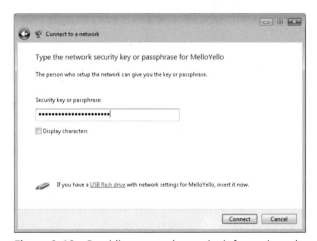

Figure 9-18 Providing network security information when connecting to a wireless network

If the connection is successful, you have the option to save the network settings. This option stores the security settings on the local computer running Windows Vista so that you do not need to provide the security details again in the future. If you save these settings, you can enable the option to connect automatically to this network connection when the computer is within range. If you enable this option, the user does not need to access the Network And Sharing Center manually to connect to the network when it is available.

It is also possible to access wireless network settings by right-clicking the wireless network icon in the system tray (if it is available) and choosing the Connect or Disconnect option. The Connect option automatically displays the wireless network connection screen. This method is useful if multiple wireless networks are available, and you would like to change connections quickly.

Configuring Wireless Ad Hoc Network Connections

It's most common in home and small-business environments to use a wireless router or access point for creating network connections. Often, these devices also provide access to other resources such as the Internet or computers that are located on other wired or wireless segments of the network. In some cases, however, it might be helpful for two or more computers to connect directly with each other to share files or perform sharing functions. Ad hoc wireless networks are designed to meet this need.

An ad hoc wireless network is connected directly between several different wireless-enabled computers without the use of a wireless access point. To create a new ad hoc wireless network, users can click Set Up A Connection Or Network in the Network And Sharing Center and choose the Set Up A Wireless Ad Hoc (Computer-To-Computer) Network option (see Figure 9-19).

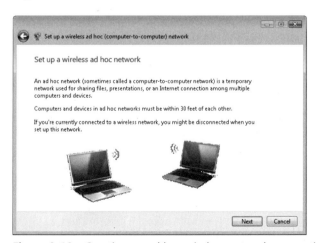

Figure 9-19   Creating an ad hoc wireless network connection

As indicated in the dialog box, it is not possible for the same wireless adapter to connect simultaneously to a standard wireless network and an ad hoc wireless network. Figure 9-20 shows the options that are available when setting up the new network.

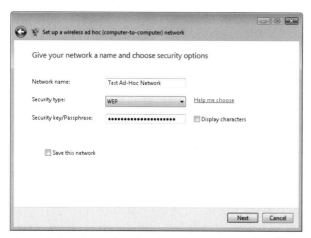

Figure 9-20   Providing details and security settings for an ad hoc wireless network

After you create the network connection, other users can connect to it as long as they are within range.

Viewing Wireless Network Connection Status Details

The speed of a wired connection is generally constant after a connection is made. With wireless connections, a variety of factors such as distance from the access point and the strength of the signal affect the performance of the connection. You can view the immediate status of the connection by clicking the appropriate View Status link in Network And Sharing Center. Figure 9-21 shows the details that are shown for a wireless connection.

The information that is unique to wireless connections includes the SSID, the speed of the connection, and the signal quality. Additionally, clicking Wireless Properties enables the user to set automatic connection and security-related settings for the connection (see Figure 9-22).

Figure 9-21   Viewing status details for a wireless network connection

Figure 9-22   Configuring security settings for a wireless network

Managing Wireless Network Connections

For most portable computers, it's common to work with wireless networks in several different environments. For example, a customer might use his or her laptop to connect to wireless networks at home, in a hotel, and at his or her office. Although the user could manually connect to each of these networks when they are in range, Windows Vista can simplify the process by storing the details of the connections on the local computer.

To manage settings for wireless networks, you can click Manage Wireless Connections in Network And Sharing Center. The management utility (shown in Figure 9-23) shows details about which wireless networks are currently configured on the local computer. The list shows the order of preference for wireless networks. Windows Vista tries to connect to networks that are listed higher in the list before attempting connections to the lower items. You can modify the preference order by selecting the item and using the Move Up or Move Down button.

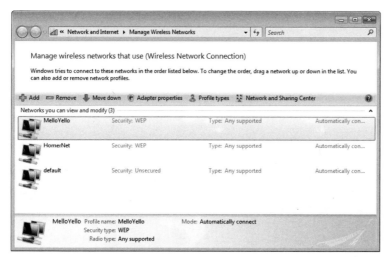

Figure 9-23   Using the Manage Wireless Networks dialog box

You can remove existing network connections if you no longer want the computer to connect to the network automatically. You can also add new wireless networks, using the Add button. Figure 9-24 shows the available options. If the wireless network you want to add is currently within range and is broadcasting its SSID, the first option is easiest.

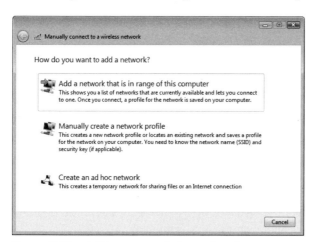

Figure 9-24   Adding a new wireless network

In cases in which the wireless network is not within range or the SSID is not being broadcast, you can use the Manually Create A Network Profile option. Figure 9-25 shows the details that you must provide.

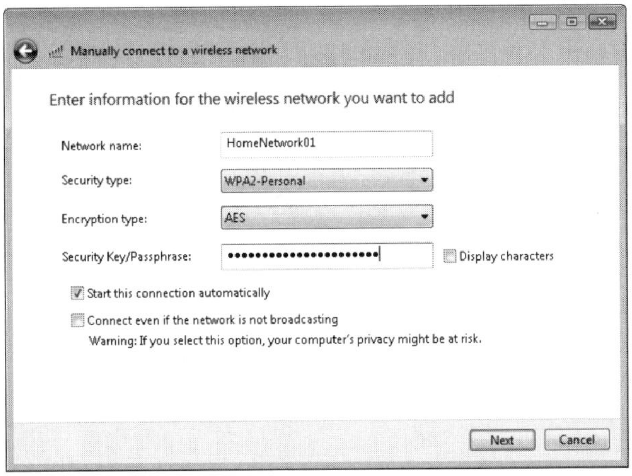

Figure 9-25   Manually connecting to a wireless network

Managing User Profile Types

In configurations through which multiple users regularly access the same computer, it might be helpful to control which users can connect to which networks. The Manage Wireless Networks dialog box provides the ability to configure the type of profile that Windows Vista uses for new wireless network connections. Figure 9-26 shows the available options.

Figure 9-26   Configuring default profile type settings for new wireless network connections

The Use All-User Profiles Only (Recommended) option is preferred, which specifies that all users on the computer share the same set of wireless network connection settings. If this is not desired for security reasons, you can enable per-user profiles, using the second option. When Windows Vista creates per-user profiles, users can create new network connections for only their own user accounts.

Troubleshooting Wireless Connections

Wireless networking technology does not always work flawlessly, and users might encounter issues with lost connections or intermittent problems. The general troubleshooting steps presented in Lesson 1 apply equally to wireless networks. For example, Windows Vista includes the ability to diagnose and repair wireless connections automatically. If the computer is not using a valid IP address for the network, the operating system can automatically attempt to obtain a new address through DHCP.

In addition to standard protocol-level troubleshooting, common wireless problems are related to the strength of the wireless network connection. Earlier in this lesson, you saw how to view the details in the Properties dialog box of the network connection. A quicker way to determine signal strength is to hover the mouse pointer over the wireless networking icon in the system tray. The resulting display (shown in Figure 9-27) shows currently connected networks, along with the quality of the connection.

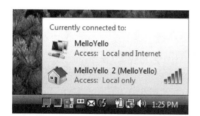

Figure 9-27 Viewing signal strength for a wireless connection, using the system tray

---

Quick Check

1. Which wireless security protocol provides the greatest level of security?
2. How would you connect to a wireless network that is not configured to broadcast its SSID?

Quick Check Answers

1. The Wi-Fi Protected Access (WPA) protocol provides increased security over the previous standard, Wired Equivalent Privacy (WEP).
2. Wireless networks that are not broadcasting SSID information can be connected to manually by using the Manage Network Connections list in Network And Sharing Center.

Practice: Managing Wireless Network Settings

In this practice, you will set up a new wireless network connection on a computer running Windows Vista. The exercise assumes that you currently have an active and functioning wireless network connection and that you have the appropriate information (including any security keys) required to connect to the network.

▶ **Practice: Connect to a Wireless Network**

In this practice, you disconnect from your current wireless network and then walk through the steps of adding the wireless network connection to the computer.

1. Right-click the icon for the current wireless network connection and click Network And Sharing Center.

2. In the Network And Sharing Center, click View Status to view information about the connection. Make a note of the SSID that the current connection is using, and then click Close to return to the Network And Sharing Center.

3. Click Disconnect next to the wireless network connection.

4. Next, click Manage Wireless Networks in the Network And Sharing Center. If the SSID that you recorded in step 2 is present in the list, right-click it and select Remove Network. Click OK to confirm the removal.

   This prevents Windows Vista from automatically connecting to the network when it is available.

5. Close the Manage Wireless Networks dialog box.

6. To create a connection to the wireless network, click Connect To A Network in the Network And Sharing Center.

7. Select the name of the SSID that you recorded in step 2, and then click Connect. Windows Vista attempts to connect to the network.

8. If prompted for security information for the connection, type in the security key or passphrase for the wireless network, and then click Connect.

9. If you would like Windows Vista to connect automatically to this wireless network connection in the future, select both check boxes in the final step of the connection process. If not, you can clear the Start This Connection Automatically and Save This Network check boxes. Click Close to return to Network And Sharing Center.

10. Open Internet Explorer and browse to a Web site to verify that the connection is working properly.

11. When finished, close Internet Explorer and close Network And Sharing Center.

Lesson Summary

- Wireless network connections typically involve the use of a wireless network adapter and a wireless router or access point.

- There are various wireless networking protocols available, each with a different combination of range and performance.

- The primary security protocols for wireless networks are Wired Equivalent Privacy (WEP) and the more secure Wi-Fi Protected Access (WPA).

- Ad hoc wireless networks are created between computers without requiring a wireless router or access point.

- Wireless networks can be created and managed using the Network And Sharing Center.

- Wireless network connection profiles can be created for all users or on a per-user profile basis.

Lesson Review

You can use the following questions to test your knowledge of the information in Lesson 2. The questions are also available on the companion CD if you prefer to review them in electronic form.

NOTE Answers

Answers to these questions and explanations of why each answer choice is correct or incorrect are located in the "Answers" section at the end of the book.

---

1. You are a Consumer Support Technician assisting a customer with configuring a wireless network. Specifically, the wireless network settings are working properly in her home environment. However, when she takes her notebook computer to her office, Windows Vista automatically connects to the incorrect wireless network. How can she resolve this problem?

    A. Reinstall the drivers for the wireless network adapter.

    B. Enable the wireless network adapter.

    C. Change the preferred network connection order, using the network map in the Network And Sharing Center.

    D. Configure the network connection order, using the Manage Wireless Networks option in the Network And Sharing Center.

2. Which of the following methods enable you to view the current signal strength for a wireless network connection? (Choose all that apply.)

    A. View the status of a wireless network in the Network And Sharing Center.

    B. Generate a network map in the Network And Sharing Center.

    C. Click Set Up A Connection in the Network And Sharing Center.

    D. Click the system tray icon for the wireless network connection.

Chapter Review

To further practice and reinforce the skills you learned in this chapter, you can perform the following tasks:

- Review the chapter summary.
- Review the list of key terms introduced in this chapter.
- Complete the case scenarios. These scenarios set up real-world situations involving the topics of this chapter and ask you to create a solution.
- Complete the suggested practices.
- Take a practice test.

Chapter Summary

- The Next Generation TCP/IP stack of Windows Vista supports both IPv4 and IPv6.
- Computers that are using IPv4 can be configured to use a DHCP-assigned address. Users can also manually set the IP address, subnet mask, default gateway, and DNS server address(es) for the computer.
- Windows Vista includes built-in tools for connecting to wireless networks and managing wireless network functionality.
- Windows Vista supports the Wired Equivalent Privacy (WEP) and Wi-Fi Protected Access (WPA) wireless security standards.

Key Terms

Do you know what these key terms mean? You can check your answers by looking up the terms in the glossary at the end of the book.

- ad hoc wireless network
- default gateway
- Domain Name System (DNS)
- Dynamic Host Configuration Protocol (DHCP)
- Internet Protocol v4 (IPv4)
- Internet Protocol v6 (IPv6)
- IP address
- local area network (LAN)

- Service Set Identifier (SSID)
- subnet mask
- Wi-Fi Protected Access (WPA)
- Wired Equivalent Privacy (WEP)

Case Scenarios

In the following case scenarios, you apply what you've learned about configuring Windows Vista networking. You can find answers to these questions in the "Answers" section at the end of this book.

Case Scenario 1: Adding a New Computer to a Network

You are a Consumer Support Technician assisting a customer with configuring a new wired network connection in his home. In the past, you assisted him with setting up a home network connection. The network currently does not have any method of automatically assigning network addresses. The IPv4 information you used on the original computer includes the following:

- IPv4 Address: 10.10.0.120
- Subnet Mask: 255.255.255.0
- Default Gateway: 10.10.0.1
- DNS Server Address (Primary): 10.10.0.1

The other computer is working properly and can access the Internet. He would like the new computer to be able to access the Internet and to be able to communicate with the other computer. There are no other computers on the network.

1. What IP address should you assign for the new computer?
2. What value should you use for the subnet mask of the new computer?
3. How can you manually configure the network settings for the TCP/IPv4 protocol on the new computer?
4. How can you simplify the process of managing network address information for future computers that are added to the network?

Case Scenario 2: Managing Wireless Network Connections

You are a Consumer Support Technician assisting a customer with configuring a wireless connection for use in multiple scenarios. The customer states that she frequently travels between multiple locations and wants to use the features of Windows Vista to connect to wireless networks quickly and easily when they are available. Examples of typical locations include the customer's home, her local office, coffee shops, airports, and hotel rooms. In some locations, such as her local office, multiple wireless network connections are available, but the customer would like to connect automatically to only one of these. Occasionally, she will share her laptop computer with a co-worker who already has an account on the computer.

1. For security reasons, the customer would like to be prompted for a key or passphrase whenever she connects to a new wireless network. How can you configure this?
2. How can you specify an order of preference for wireless network connections that are available at the customer's local office?
3. How can the customer configure some connections to connect automatically for only her user account?

Suggested Practices

To help you successfully master the exam objectives presented in this chapter, complete the following tasks.

Managing Network Connections in Windows Vista

The following practices help you become familiar with various methods of working with wired and wireless network connections in Windows Vista.

- **Practice 1: Configure Network Connections**   Choose several different computers running Windows Vista and examine their network configurations. If possible, attempt to connect new computers to a test wired or wireless network and keep track of the settings that you have decided to use. Use the Network Map feature of the Network And Sharing Center to gain an overview of all of the available computers in the environment.

- **Practice 2: Troubleshoot Network Problems**   Choose a computer running Windows Vista that has either a wired or wireless network connection. Manually make various changes to TCP/IPv4 settings, such as the IP address, subnet mask, default gateway, and DNS servers. Choose values that might not be compatible with the current network. Then, use the Diagnose and Repair options to try to troubleshoot the problems automatically. Additionally, use command-line tools such as IPCONFIG, PING, and NETSH to help determine the source of problems and to correct them.

Take a Practice Test

The practice tests on this book's companion CD offer many options. For example, you can test yourself on just one exam objective, or you can test yourself on all of the 70-623 certification exam content. You can set up the test so that it closely simulates the experience of taking a certification exam, or you can set it up in study mode so that you can look at the correct answers and explanations after you answer each question.

MORE INFO Practice tests

For details about all the practice test options available, see the "How to Use the Practice Tests" section in this book's introduction.

Chapter 10
Managing Network Sharing

One of the most useful features of working in a networked environment is the ability to share data between computers. The various scenarios can range from a home environment to a small business to interacting on the Internet. It's common for home and small-business users to need to keep track of and share data such as documents, music, photos, and videos.

For example, in a home environment, a user might want to access his or her photo library from a desktop computer, from a server, and from his or her Windows Media Center extender device. In work environments, it's often useful for groups of users to be able to access the same files from a central location. Regardless of the particular use case, the ability to share files quickly and easily must also engender security considerations. Only authorized users should have access to view and modify data stored on other computers.

In the past, it was difficult to configure the appropriate permissions and settings to share files. Users might have been unable to set up resource sharing in a networked environment and might have resorted to sending files through e-mail or placing them on removable media. Alternatively, they would set up sharing with permissions that were far too generous (possibly inviting malicious or unwanted access to their sensitive information). Clearly, there was room for improvement in setting up file sharing functionality.

Windows Vista includes numerous new and enhanced features that enable sharing resources between computers and other devices located on the network. As a Consumer Support Technician, you're likely to encounter customers who need help setting up various levels of file and resource sharing in their home or small-business environments. They'll want recommendations and assistance in making sure that their data remains available and secure.

In this chapter, you'll learn about different ways in which you can enable and manage data sharing between computers. You'll also see how there are several different ways to configure and manage security permissions based on users' needs.

Exam objectives in this chapter:
- Configure Windows Vista Security.
    - ❏ Configure Windows Firewalls.
- Configure, Troubleshoot, and Repair Networking
    - ❏ Configure and troubleshoot Windows Vista by using the Network and Sharing Center
    - ❏ Troubleshoot file and print sharing

Lessons in this chapter:

Before You Begin

The lesson content and practice exercises in this chapter focus on working with file, printer, and media sharing in a networked environment. To work through the exercises and follow along with the content, you should have access to at least two computers that are connected to the same network. The connections can be wired or wireless (Internet access is not required). For more information about configuring, managing, and troubleshooting network connections, see Chapter 9, "Configuring Windows Vista Networking."

MORE INFO   Using virtual machines to simulate a network

To follow the content in this chapter and to complete the practice exercises, you will need to have a network environment with at least two separate computers running Windows Vista. Although the use of physical computers is preferred, it is also possible to set up a virtual machine (VM) on a single computer to simulate a network environment. Microsoft Virtual PC is a free product that enables you to set up virtual networks and VMs quickly and easily. For more information, see *http://www.microsoft.com/windows/products/winfamily/virtualpc/default.mspx*.

Lesson 1: Using the Network and Sharing Center

When sharing files such as music, photos, video, and documents, one of the most important concerns is related to ensuring that only intended users can access the data. In a home network environment or within a small business, this might be less important. Generally, family members and co-workers are authorized to access at least some data using the network. The primary consideration is in determining which data is available to which users.

In other network environments, it is often appropriate to exercise more caution. A common example is one in which a notebook computer is connected to a shared wireless network environment in a public place such as an airport. In such cases, it's important to limit which types of information can be accessed from other computers.

The networking features of Windows Vista are designed to take into account the type of network connection that you create (for example, a public or private connection) when specifying defaults. In general, the basic settings are focused on limiting the amount of exposure to unwanted access. For this reason, many file and resource sharing features are disabled by default. In this lesson, you'll learn about ways in which you can change configuration settings based on your specific sharing and security requirements.

After this lesson, you will be able to:
- Describe the types of resources that you can share across a network and how users can access them.
- Enable network discovery to find computers located on the network easily.
- Configure file, folder, printer, and media sharing, using the Network And Sharing Center.
- Configure permissions and related settings for file sharing.

Estimated lesson time: 60 minutes

Working with Network Resources

Before you learn more about setting up and accessing shared information in Windows Vista, some background information will be helpful. In this section, you'll learn about the networking locations of Windows Vista and how you can access resources on remote computers by using network paths and mapped network drives. This information is the foundation for managing and working with sharing data among Microsoft Windows-based computers.

Understanding Network Locations

Computers are often used in a variety of different environments, ranging from relatively secure home and small office environments to public locations such as airports, coffee shops, and hotels. To accommodate different default settings for these environments, Windows Vista enables users to specify the type of network to which they're connecting when they configure a new network connection.

The available options include the following:

- **Home Or Work**   If the computer is connected to a home or work network, this option enables standard file sharing and network discovery functionality. It is assumed that only known authorized computers and users are able to connect to the network, so the risk of misuse is lower. It is very important to keep in mind that the network itself must be secure. For example, if the user is connecting to a wireless network, it is highly recommended that you or the user enable wireless security.

- **Public Place**   In public locations, a large number of different types of users are able to connect to the network. In these situations, it is important to limit network access to the computer. When you configure a new connection for a public location, Windows Vista disables many settings by default, and its focus is on limited access to other resources. For example, file and printer sharing, public folder sharing, and media sharing are all disabled by default when you connect to a public network. This option is also most appropriate when a computer will be running by itself in a network environment (for example, in a single-computer home that uses the network primarily for Internet access). When in doubt, advise customers to use the public network location because it is most secure.

After you create a network connection, it is possible to change the type of network. For example, if a home environment uses a wired network connection in potentially insecure hotel rooms, the settings can be modified accordingly. To change the setting, click Customize next to the appropriate section in the Network And Sharing Center (see Figure 10-1). For more information about creating and managing network connections, see Chapter 9.

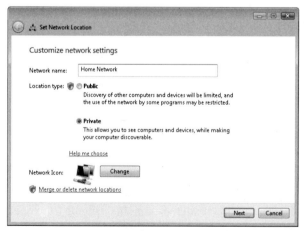

Figure 10-1 Changing security location information for an existing network connection

The default settings that Windows Vista uses for sharing information are based on the type of network that you choose. Examples include whether network discovery is enabled and whether file sharing is turned on. Additionally, Windows Firewall is configured differently for public and private connections. You can modify the specific details using tools such as the Network And Sharing Center.

Understanding Network Paths

When connecting to resources such as files on the local computer, the physical path names generally start with the drive letter of a logical volume on the computer. For example, you might want to access files that are located in the C:\Download folder. When accessing files and other resources that are stored on other computers, it is also necessary to include information about the name of the computer to which you want to connect. The Universal Naming Convention (UNC) standard was developed to provide a consistent method for accessing data that is stored on other computers.

UNC paths begin with two backslash characters. This is followed by the name of the computer or device to which the path refers and then the name of the shared resource. Examples of UNC paths include the following:

- \\Notebook01\Music
- \\Notebook01\Photos
- \\Notebook01\Public\Shared Documents
- \\Desktop01\Data\Download\SampleFile.doc

There are several different ways in which you can use UNC paths in Windows Vista. The first is through the Start menu. You can launch the Run command by clicking Start, All Programs, and then Accessories (or, you can use the shortcut Windows Key + R). This enables you to type or paste the full UNC path into the Open text box and click OK to open the appropriate location. Similarly, you can enter a UNC path directly into the Address bar in a Windows Explorer window. Finally, you can also embed a link to a UNC file or resource in a way that is similar to embedding an Internet-based URL or hyperlink. This can be useful for sending paths through e-mail. (You'll see a specific example later in this lesson.)

You use UNC paths as a shortcut to connecting to remote resources, and it works the same way as using the graphical tools of Windows Vista (such as the Network view in the Start menu). To connect successfully to remote resources, users must have the necessary permissions. Another important point to remember is that the UNC path must be surrounded by quotes if it contains a space. Overall, the use of UNC paths can simplify the process of accessing files stored on other computers.

Mapping Network Drives

Although the process of using UNC paths is fairly simple, it can be tedious and time-consuming to type these locations each time you require a remote file or resource. Users might prefer to make certain network locations as readily available as local devices. That is the purpose of mapping network drives. A network drive mapping enables you to assign an available drive letter to a particular UNC path. For example, a home user might map his or her P drive to the UNC path \\Desktop01\Photos. After this mapping is created, the user can access the P drive as if it were a local device, and all read and write operations occur over the network. The network connection and remote computer must be available to access the data.

You can create new network device mappings by browsing to a shared folder by using the Network item on the Start menu. You can then right-click a shared folder and select Map Network Drive to open the Map Network Drive dialog box. Additionally, you can create drive mappings by right-clicking the Network item on the Start menu and selecting the same option. Figure 10-2 shows the available options.

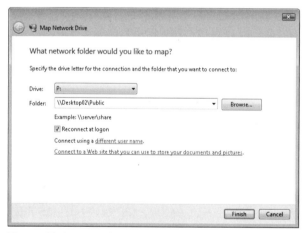

Figure 10-2 Mapping a network drive to a UNC path

There are several available options, beginning with the drive letter that should be used for the mapping. You can choose any available drive letter. You use the Folder text box to specify the UNC path to the shared folder. You can enter this value either directly, by typing the path, or by using the Browse button. By default, Windows Vista uses drive mappings only for the current user session, but there is an option to reconnect automatically to the network share at logon. This makes the mapping semipermanent, although the remote computer must be available on the network to access the relevant files. For security purposes, there is also an option that enables specifying a different user name and password for connecting to the shared folder.

Configuring Network Discovery

Windows Vista users often want to find a simple method of making information available to other computers in their network environments. They might also want to get a quick overview of which types of data are being shared and who can access it. In Chapter 9, you learned about using the Network And Sharing Center to create, configure, and troubleshoot both wired and wireless network connections.

As its name implies, the Network And Sharing Center is also the primary tool for configuring details related to various networking features that enable sharing information between other computers in the environment. Figure 10-3 provides an example of the settings that can be managed in the Network And Sharing Center.

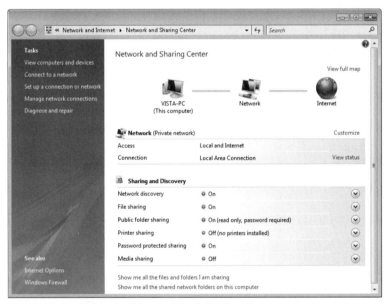

Figure 10-3   Using the Network And Sharing Center to manage sharing and discovery

In this section, you'll learn about ways in which you can configure and manage the types of information that are made available to other computers and users in a network environment.

Accessing Shared Files and Folders

Windows Vista makes the process of accessing shared files, folders, and printers simple by integration with the Start menu and the Windows Explorer shell. Perhaps the most common method of accessing resources over the network is by clicking Network on the Start menu. The resulting display shows the various computers that are available on the network (see Figure 10-4).

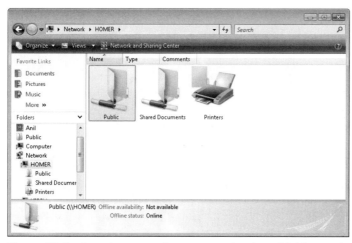

Figure 10-4 Browsing network computers for shared folders and printers

The process of accessing data is similar to that of navigating local files and folders. For example, double-clicking a remote folder opens it and shows a list of files (assuming, of course, that you have the necessary permissions). Later in this lesson, you'll see how you can specify which users can connect to which resources and how permissions can be defined.

Configuring the Computer Name and Related Settings

Windows Vista includes several computer-specific settings that you can configure to make computers on the network easier to identify. You can view and modify these settings by right-clicking the Computer item on the Start menu and selecting Properties. In the Tasks section of the computer's System window, click Advanced System Settings and then click the Computer Name tab (see Figure 10-5) in the displayed System Properties dialog box.

The primary detail that you can modify here is the computer description. This is a friendly description that specifies the purpose or use of the computer. It is not directly used for network identification, but the information is available to users who are browsing the network for computers and other devices.

You can click Change to modify the name of the computer and to specify a workgroup (see Figure 10-6). The name of the computer is the primary method that users use to connect to it over the network. In general, it is best either to use a short descriptive name for the computer or to identify the person to whom the computer belongs. The Workgroup setting is a name that you can use to group collections of computers logically. For the purpose of finding and connecting to other computers on a network, all computers should be using the same workgroup identification.

Figure 10-5   Viewing computer name and description information

Figure 10-6   Changing the name and workgroup setting for a computer

Certain editions of Windows Vista also include the ability to connect to a network domain. A network domain is designed to provide for centralized security management in a network environment that supports many computers. It requires dedicated server computers and configuration expertise to set up and maintain. For these reasons, domain-based security is outside the scope of Exam 70-623 and the contents of this training kit.

Managing Network Discovery Options

When working in a networked environment, it can be very helpful to know the names of other computers that are available. For example, in a home that contains several computers, users might often forget the specific name of each computer when attempting to access files. The network discovery feature of Windows Vista is a method by which computers can report their presence on the network. Other computers can also do the same. You can see the computers that Windows Vista has discovered by selecting Network on the Start menu (see Figure 10-7). Windows Vista also uses network discovery to create a network map, using the Network And Sharing Center, as shown in Figure 10-8. Both methods make finding other resources simpler.

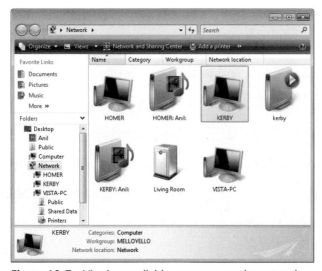

Figure 10-7   Viewing available resources on the network

On shared or insecure networks, it is often desirable to limit network discovery. When other users are unaware of the presence of a computer, they are less likely to try to access it accidentally or maliciously. For these reasons, network discovery is disabled by default for public network locations and is enabled by default for home or work-based network locations.

You can manage settings for the network discovery feature, using the Network And Sharing Center. Figure 10-9 shows the available options. The two primary options are Turn On Network Discovery and Turn Off Network Discovery.

Lesson 1: Using the Network and Sharing Center

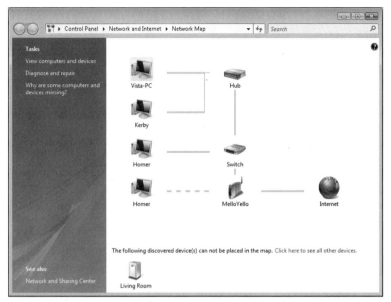

Figure 10-8 Viewing a network map using the Network And Sharing Center

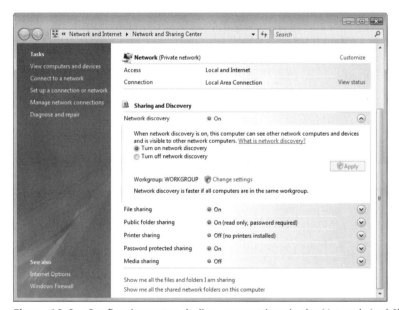

Figure 10-9 Configuring network discovery settings in the Network And Sharing Center

Configuring File and Folder Sharing

The underlying technology involved in making shared resources available to other computers is fairly complex. Details include determining which data is being shared and security settings that restrict who can access the information. Although some users might need to create detailed sets of information to share, the vast majority of home and small business customers simply want to make data available quickly and easily. In this section, you'll learn about different ways in which you can make files and folders available for use by other users and computers.

NOTE **Sharing data with other operating systems**

The focus of this chapter and Exam 70-623 is on sharing resources between multiple computers that are running Windows Vista. Many of these same features are available in previous versions of the Windows operating system platform, although the specific steps required to share files and other types of information might vary. Additionally, other types of operating systems might be able to access or share data with computers running Windows Vista. More information is generally available in the respective operating systems' help files or documentation.

Public Folder Sharing

The simplest method of sharing information on a computer running Windows Vista is through the use of a built-in feature called the Public folder. The Public folder is designed to enable multiple users on the same computer to share files with each other. By default, it is not available to network users. From the viewpoint of the file system, the Public folder is located within the C:\Users folder on the local computer. Only a single Public folder is created for use by all users on the system. In the file system, this folder is similar to any other folder. Files can be moved and copied into it, and local users can access the files to share documents between them.

Users typically move or copy files that they want to make available into the Public folder. Because files must reside within this folder, one potential drawback is that users must make multiple copies of the information. For example, if a user has a large number of music files in his or her user-specific Music folder, he or she must copy all of those files to the Public folder to make them available to others. Additionally, if the user changes the "primary" copy of his or her files and folders, he or she needs to make the same changes manually within the Public folder. The path to the Public folder on the local computer is C:\Users\Public. By default, the Public folder includes several folders that you can use to store certain types of information (see Figure 10-10). In addition, users can delete these folders and create their own to organize shared data.

Figure 10-10   Viewing the default set of folders created within the Public folder

The primary benefit of using the Public folder is that it is quick and easy to set up. The first step is to open the Network and Sharing Center and expand the Public Folder Sharing section (see Figure 10-11).

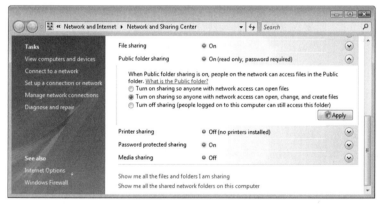

Figure 10-11   Configuring settings for Public folder sharing in the Network And Sharing Center

There are three main options in this section:

- Turn On Sharing So Anyone With Network Access Can Open Files
- Turn On Sharing So Anyone With Network Access Can Open, Change, And Create Files
- Turn Off Sharing (People Logged On To This Computer Can Still Access This Folder)

The description of each option is largely self-explanatory and should meet the needs of most typical users. For example, if a small-business customer would like to enable others to view certain documents on his computer, he or she can select the first option and then copy the relevant files into the Public folder. Alternatively, if several different family members would like to update a single calendar document over the network, the Public folder can be set up with the second option.

The security permissions that Windows Vista applies to the files and folders in the Public folder are the same for all users who connect to it. Although it is possible to override these settings manually or to create new shares based on these folders, the primary purpose of the Public folder is to make the process of securing shared data as easy as possible. Overall, using the Public folder is a simple way to make information available to other users on the network.

Configuring Password-Protected Sharing

From a security standpoint, all local users on the computer are able to access the contents of the local Public folder. When attempting to access the folder over the network, however, you can determine whether Windows Vista requires users to have an account and password to access the contents of the Public folder. You define this setting by using the Network and Sharing Center.

When you enable password-protected sharing, users must have an account and password to log on to the local machine. Whenever a network user attempts to access the files, he or she is prompted to provide authentication information. When you disable password-protected sharing, users are potentially able to access resources without providing authentication information.

Configuring File Sharing

Although enabling access to the Public folder is a quick process, there are several cases in which users might want to share other files and folders that are located on their computers. The primary reasons for this are to avoid making and maintaining copies of files in the Public folder and for providing different security permissions for different users. For example, if a small-business owner requires several users to access and update a large set of files, he or she might find himself or herself frequently copying those files to and from the user-specific Documents folder. Additionally, the owner might want some employees to be able to make changes to those files and restrict other employees to just viewing them.

To accommodate these needs, Windows Vista includes a File Sharing feature. You can turn this feature on or off using settings in the Network and Sharing Center (see Figure 10-12). It is important to know that the Turn On File Sharing and Turn Off File Sharing options enable only users of the local computers to share files. They do not, by default, share any particular data.

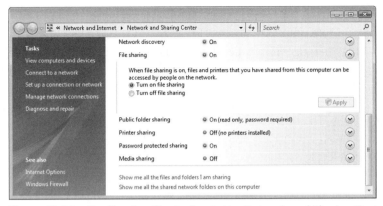

Figure 10-12 Configuring file sharing in the Network and Sharing Center

After you enable file sharing, users can specify which files and folders should be made available to network users. Additionally, they can specify permissions related to which users will be able to access the information and what specific operations they can perform. You can start the process of setting up a new shared folder by selecting a folder, using Windows Explorer and then either right-clicking it and choosing Share or by clicking the Share button in the command bar. Figure 10-13 shows the default display for a new shared folder.

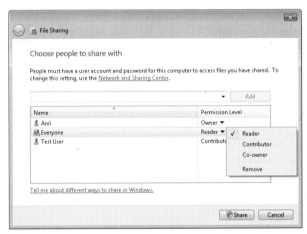

Figure 10-13 Creating a shared folder

To enable additional user accounts to access the shared folder, you must add them to the list. You can do this by typing the name of the user you want to add or by selecting the user from the drop-down list. You can also create a new user account by using the Create A New User option. For more information about creating and managing user accounts, see Chapter 6, "Configuring Windows Vista Security."

Three main permissions are available when setting up file and folder sharing:

- **Reader** Users who have Reader permissions can view lists of files and open them, but they cannot make changes to the files themselves. For example, if a user has Reader permissions on a Microsoft Word document, he or she can open it but cannot save changes to it. That user can, however, make a copy of the file to another location and modify the copy.

- **Contributor** A user who is a Contributor can read all of the files in the shared folder. Additionally, a Contributor can add new files to the shared folder and can later make changes to or delete those files, as needed.

- **Owner/Co-Owner** The default owner of a file or folder is the user who created that folder. By default, every shared folder has a designated owner who has full permissions on it. The Owner can perform all of the operations of the Contributor and can change security permissions. You can add additional owners as Co-Owners, so that you can give them the same permissions.

One special logical group of users that you can add to the permissions set is Everyone (All Users In This List). Users often do this when the folder does not contain sensitive documents, and it is acceptable for any network user to access it. For example, a small business might store the company holiday schedule or related information in a shared folder and grant permissions to the Everyone group. The permissions that an actual user has on the shared folder is the sum of all of the permissions assigned. For example, if you have given the Everyone group Reader permissions, but you have also given a specific user account Contributor permissions, the user effectively has Contributor permissions on the contents of the shared folder.

After you have added users and set their permissions, you can click Share to create the new shared folder. Figure 10-14 shows an example of the confirmation dialog box.

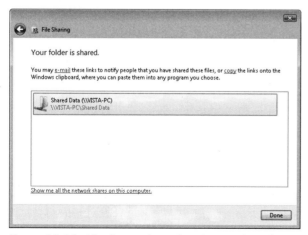

Figure 10-14 Viewing options after the creation of a new shared folder

The dialog box shows the UNC network path for the new shared folder. It also provides the ability to create a new e-mail that you can use to send information about the shared folder to other users as well as a link to copy the shortcut to the clipboard (so you can manually paste it into a document or message). Figure 10-15 shows an example of the default e-mail format. To complete the process, click Done.

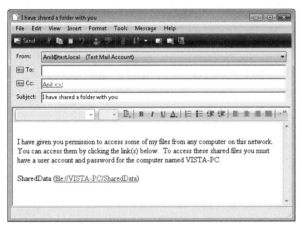

Figure 10-15   Sending a shared-folder notification e-mail

Windows Explorer now shows the folder with a special overlay that indicates that it is being shared. You can change the sharing settings by right-clicking the shared folder and clicking Share or by clicking the Share button in Windows Explorer. Figure 10-16 shows the two available options. You can change the permissions, or stop sharing the folder.

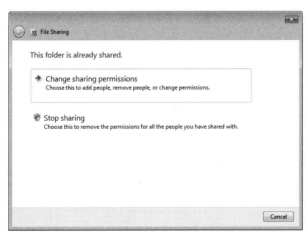

Figure 10-16   Changing settings for a shared folder

Managing Shared Folders

Some Windows Vista users will likely need to create numerous shared folders on the computer. Sometimes, it can be difficult to remember which folders are shared. One way to find out which resources are available is to use the Network item in the Start menu and to double-click the local computer. This shows you which folders and printer objects are available based on the permissions of the current user.

Another method of obtaining the same details is to use the Network and Sharing Center. Two links are available at the bottom of the dialog box:

- **Show Me All The Files And Folders I Am Sharing**   This link starts a search that returns a list of the actual shared contents. This is often useful when trying to determine whether a particular set of files is available in any shared location on the computer.
- **Show Me All The Shared Network Folders On This Computer**   This function is similar to browsing to the local computer and viewing a list of shared folders and printers. You can then use standard Windows Explorer features to open various shares and view their contents.

From a security standpoint, it is important for users to keep track of which information is available to users on the network. As a Consumer Support Technician, advise home and small-business users to review the list of shared files regularly.

Sharing Printers and Media Resources

In addition to sharing files and folders, Windows Vista makes it possible to share other features of the local computer. In this section, you'll learn about printer sharing and media library sharing.

Printer Sharing

In networked environments, it can often be helpful to share printers between computers. This enables, for example, a remote computer to send a print job over the network and to have it output by the printing device. The Network and Sharing Center provides two options related to printer sharing:

- Turn On Printer Sharing
- Turn Off Printer Sharing

When you enable printer sharing, users who browse to the local computer can access printers on the local computer. If you have enabled password-protected sharing, users need to have an account and password on the local computer to print. Assuming they have the appropriate permissions, they can right-click the printer object and select Connect to create a local printer connection. They then see the remote printer as an option when choosing the Print function from common applications.

After you have enabled printer sharing in the Network and Sharing Center, you can make specific printer devices available to network users. The process involves accessing the Printers item in Control Panel. To access the relevant properties, right-click the printer and select Sharing. Figure 10-17 shows the available options.

Figure 10-17 Configuring settings for a shared printer

The available options include the following:

- **Share This Printer**   This check box determines whether the printer is available for connection from remote computers.
- **Share Name**   This is the name potential network users of the printer see when they browse this computer. It is a good idea to make the printer name descriptive of its location and type.
- **Render This Print Job On Client Computers**   The process of rendering a print job involves converting the actual data that is to be output into a language that the print device can understand. When you select this check box, the rendering process (which can consume significant system resources) is performed on the machine that sends the print job. This option helps reduce the performance impact to the local computer, especially when numerous users access it over the network.
- **Additional Drivers**   For remote computers to be able to send a print job to a device, they must have the appropriate drivers installed. This dialog box allows users optionally to install drivers for other operating system versions on the computer so that they can be automatically installed over the network.

To create the shared printer, click OK after you have made the appropriate configuration settings.

Media Library Sharing

It is increasingly common for users to share media files such as pictures, music, and video between different devices. Although it is certainly possible to make the files available via the Public folder or through shared folders, these methods are often limited in the types of operations that are enabled. The media sharing features of Windows Vista provide numerous benefits, including the ability to stream media to devices such as the Xbox 360. It also enables you to configure Windows Media Player to access and manage files on a remote computer.

NOTE   **Finding compatible media players**

Numerous manufacturers have created devices that are compatible with Microsoft Windows Media Player and media library functionality. It can sometimes be difficult to identify and recommend the right devices, however, because some can provide similar functionality without integrating with Windows. To help identify devices that have been designed to take advantage of these features, Microsoft has developed a Plays for Sure designation. More details and a list of compatible products can be found at *http://www.playsforsure.com.*

The Network and Sharing Center contains a media library section that you can use to configure sharing settings. Figure 10-18 provides an example of the configuration options.

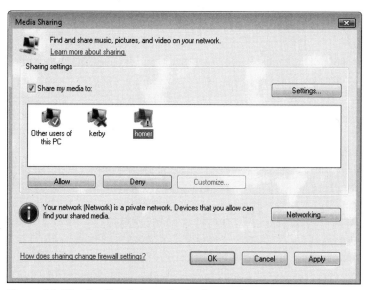

Figure 10-18   Configuring media sharing options

The list shows the specific network devices that you can give access to media stored on the local computer. Generally, Windows Vista detects the available network devices automatically (if you have enabled network discovery). For each device, you can choose to allow or deny access. In addition, there are default settings that you can use when making media files available (see Figure 10-19). There is also an Allow New Devices And Computers Automatically (Not Recommended) option. Although this can reduce security, it can be convenient in a secure network environment such as a home.

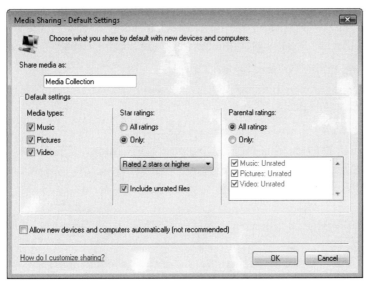

Figure 10-19   Configuring media sharing settings

The methods for accessing shared media vary based on the type of program or device that requires access. Overall, however, media sharing is a great way to avoid creating and managing copies of music, video, photos, and other files.

Quick Check

1. What are some ways in which you can access a shared folder on a remote computer running Windows Vista?
2. What are some limitations of using the Public folder to share files?

Quick Check Answers

1. You can access files on remote computers by using Windows Explorer or the Network item on the Start menu, or by typing UNC path locations manually.
2. Files must physically be located within the Public folder to be available to network users. Generally, permissions for all of the files in the Public folder are the same for all users.

Practice: Sharing Files and Folders

In these practice exercises, you walk through the process of making shared files and folders available to computers on the network. You do this using both Public folders and the file sharing options. To complete these exercises, you will need two computers that are connected on the same network. The steps assume that the network location is set to Home Or Work and that you are using the default settings in the Network and Sharing Center.

▶ **Practice 1: Enabling Public Folder Sharing**

In this practice exercise, you enable sharing using the Public folder. You also see the effects of Public folder permissions settings.

1. Open the Network and Sharing Center and the first test computer.
2. Expand the Public Folder Sharing section and choose the Turn On Sharing So Anyone With Network Access Can Open Files option.
3. Expand the Password-Protected Sharing section and turn off this feature (if it is currently enabled).
4. Open the Public folder by clicking Show Me All The Shared Network Folders On This Computer.
5. Double-click the Public folder and verify that default subfolders such as Public Documents and Public Downloads appear in the list.
6. Create a new blank text file by right-clicking the blank space within the Public folder (in the right side of the Windows Explorer view), selecting New, and then clicking Text Document. Name the file **Test**. You should now see a new text document created within the Public shared folder.
7. Log on to the second computer and attempt to access the Public share on the first computer. Do this by opening the Network item in the Start menu, double-clicking the name of the computer, and then opening the Public folder. Note that you are not required to provide a logon and password to access this folder.
8. Double-click the Test.txt file to open it. This verifies that you have permissions to open the file.
9. Return to the original computer and open the Network and Sharing Center.
10. Change the public folder sharing option to Turn On Sharing So Anyone With Network Access Can Open, Change, And Create Files.
11. Turn on the password-protected sharing option.
12. From the test computer, again attempt to connect to the Public folder. Note that you are prompted to provide logon information to connect.

13. Create a new text document within the Public folder to verify that you have permission to create files.

14. When finished, close all open windows on both computers. Optionally, you might want to disable Public folder sharing on the source computer for security reasons.

▶ **Practice 2: Configuring File Sharing**

In this practice exercise, you use the file sharing feature of Windows Vista to make a shared folder accessible to users on the network. You can either create a new folder to share or choose to share an existing one. This exercise assumes that you have at least two users defined on the local computer (for more information on creating user accounts, see Chapter 6).

1. Open the Network and Sharing Center.

2. Expand the file sharing section and select the Turn On File Sharing option if necessary; then click Apply to save the setting.

3. Turn on the password-protected sharing option by expanding the relevant section and selecting the Turn On Password Protected Sharing option. Click Apply.

4. Open Windows Explorer and right-click the folder you would like to share. Select the Share command from the shortcut menu.

5. Note the default permissions settings for the share. If you have more than one user defined on the local computer, add the user to the list of user accounts and then assign the user the Reader permission level. Make a note of the user names and their associated permission levels. Click Share to save the settings.

6. In the confirmation dialog box, make a note of the UNC path to the Shared Folder you have created. Click Done to close the confirmation dialog box.

7. Log on to the remote computer and open the Network item on the Start menu.

8. Double-click the name of the source computer and then double-click the name of the new shared folder that you created in step 5. If logon information is required, you are prompted to provide authentication information. Provide the user name and password for the account that has Owner permissions on the shared folder.

    Note that if you have created accounts that use the same user name and password on both computers, Windows Vista automatically connects you to the shared folder without requiring you to provide logon information.

9. Verify that you can access, create, and delete documents stored in that location. When finished, close any open windows.

10. Return to the source computer. Open Windows Explorer, right-click the shared folder you created earlier, and select Share.

11. Choose the Stop Sharing option to stop sharing the folder.

12. On the remote computer, verify that the shared folder is no longer available on the network.

Lesson Summary

- Network paths that access remote computers use the Universal Naming Convention (UNC) format.
- Users can map network drives to attach a drive letter to a UNC path.
- The network discovery feature enables Windows Vista to detect other computers and network devices automatically that are attached to the network.
- Public folder sharing provides a simple way to set up sharing for a set of files and folders.
- File sharing enables users to share file system data directly and to set specific security permissions for different users.
- Printer sharing enables remote computers to send print jobs to the local computer for output on a print device.
- Media library sharing enables files such as photos, music, and videos to be accessed by other Windows computers or compatible network devices.

Lesson Review

You can use the following questions to test your knowledge of the information in Lesson 1, "Using the Network and Sharing Center." The questions are also available on the companion CD if you prefer to review them in electronic form.

NOTE   Answers

Answers to these questions and explanations of why each answer choice is correct or incorrect are located in the "Answers" section at the end of the book.

1. You are a Consumer Support Technician assisting a small business owner with configuring file and folder sharing in Windows Vista. The customer would like to share five different files with all of the users on his office network. Currently, six employees in the office require access to the files. The customer would like all users to be able to read the files and wants them to be able to access the files without providing a user name and password. He would like to configure sharing using the simplest method available. Which of the following options should he enable in the Network And Sharing Center? (Assume that all other features are set to Off.)

   A. File sharing

   B. Public folder sharing

   C. Password-protected sharing

   D. Media library sharing

2. You are providing support for a home user who is complaining that it often takes a long time for Windows Vista to find other computers on her home network. The user frequently connects to networks on other computers, and her computer was originally configured by personnel at her office. You have verified that network discovery is enabled for the network connection. Which of the following methods is most likely to improve the performance of network discovery?

    A. Disable network discovery on the computer.

    B. Change the type of the network location to Public Place.

    C. Change all of the home computer's workgroup settings to use the same value.

    D. Rename all of the computers on the network.

    E. Disable Windows Firewall.

3. A customer recently purchased Windows Vista Ultimate and an Xbox 360 game console. He would like to use features of the Xbox 360 to stream music from the computer running Windows Vista. He also wants to ensure that no other computers or devices on the network can access the music files, even if they have logon credentials for the local computer. Which of the following options in the Network and Sharing Center will enable him to do this most easily?

    A. Enable Public folder sharing.

    B. Enable password-protected sharing.

    C. Enable media library sharing.

    D. Enable file sharing.

Lesson 2: Troubleshooting File and Print Sharing

As a Consumer Support Technician, you're likely to be called on when an operating system feature or function is not working as expected. The process of configuring shared resources such as files, folders, and printers is straightforward. Windows Vista includes numerous other tools that have hidden the underlying complexity of settings such as security permissions. For example, managing settings for the Public folder and enabling printer sharing can be performed using standard operating system tools.

However, in some cases, technical issues can prevent networked computers from accessing the resources that they require. In this lesson, you learn about ways in which you can troubleshoot various problems that might be preventing shared resources from being properly shared.

After this lesson, you will be able to:

■ Troubleshoot resource sharing issues that are related to the configuration of shared folders or permissions.

■ Troubleshoot resource sharing problems that are related to network settings or features such as network discovery and firewalls.

Estimated lesson time: 35 minutes

Troubleshooting Resource Sharing Issues

When working in an environment involving multiple computers, it's necessary to consider several different potential causes of a file, folder, printer, or media sharing problem. Common sources of issues include the configuration of resource sharing settings. In this section, you'll learn about different ways in which you can troubleshoot common configuration issues that can affect these features.

Verifying Sharing and Discovery Settings

When you or a customer you are supporting is experiencing a problem with sharing or accessing data over the network, a good first troubleshooting step is to start with the Network and Sharing Center. The Sharing And Discovery section provides a quick overview of which features are enabled and which are either disabled or not configured. For example, if a user is having problems sharing a printer device with another computer, the cause of the problem might simply be that printer sharing is disabled in the Network and Sharing Center.

Verifying Shared Resource Settings

When troubleshooting, think of the settings in the Network and Sharing Center as master switches that control a specific feature. That is, turning on a feature such as file sharing provides the ability only to share folders; it does not explicitly share any data. As mentioned earlier, the specific data that is shared (and the associated permissions) must be configured separately.

There are several ways to verify that a particular resource is being shared. The details vary based on the type of data being provided by the source computer, but some examples include the following:

- **Network discovery**   Verify that Network Discovery is enabled in the Network and Sharing Center. Also, note that the type of network location that is configured affects the status of the network sharing service.

- **File sharing**   Verify that the File Sharing feature is enabled in the Network and Sharing Center. To find specific files and folders that are shared on the computer, you can click Show Me All The Files And Folders I Am Sharing and Show Me All The Shared Network Folders On This Computer. Additionally, you can right-click a folder, using Windows Explorer, and select Share to verify whether a folder is shared and to set its permissions.

- **Public folder sharing**   Verify that the settings in the Network and Sharing Center enable access to files stored in the Public folder. Also, verify that the Public folder exists and that the expected contents are present within the folder.

- **Printer sharing**   Verify that the Printer Sharing option is enabled in the Network and Sharing Center. If it is enabled, use the Printers item in Control Panel to ensure that the desired printers have been shared. In cases in which multiple print devices are available, it can be helpful to verify the name of the shared printer.

- **Media sharing**   Verify that Media Sharing is enabled in the Network and Sharing Center. Using the default settings, you must explicitly allow devices to access media over the network. You can configure these settings in the Media Sharing dialog box. The default settings control which media files are available, but device-specific settings can override these values.

Usually, verifying settings in the Network and Sharing Center takes only a short time, but it can help ensure that the basic settings are configured properly.

Troubleshooting Shared Folder Permissions

When troubleshooting problems in which users can see shared resources on the network but cannot access them, one of the likely causes of the problem is security permissions. A good starting point for troubleshooting shared files and folders is to verify the permissions that are defined for the shared resource. When working with the Public folder, it is also important to ensure that no file or folders in the Public folder location have different sets of permissions. All of this can be done in Windows Explorer by right-clicking the appropriate file or folder and selecting Share.

In addition to checking permissions on the resource itself, the Password Protected Sharing option in the Network and Sharing Center determines whether users must log on to the local computer to access data. If this setting is enabled, users must provide the appropriate authentication information if accessing the resource from another computer. Finally, troubleshooting might include verifying user accounts and passwords to ensure that they are set as expected. For more information about managing user accounts, see Chapter 6.

Verifying File System Permissions

When users attempt to access files and folders across the network, security permissions are actually checked at two different levels. The first set of permissions is configured at the level of the shared folder. These settings apply to users who attempt to access the resource over the network.

Files and folders also have security settings that you can define from within the file system itself. File system permissions apply to both local users and network users who are attempting to access the files. These permissions are also referred to as NTFS permissions because they are available only on file systems that use the NTFS format. You configure these permissions by right-clicking the appropriate object in Windows Explorer, selecting Properties, and then clicking the Security tab. Figure 10-20 shows the available options.

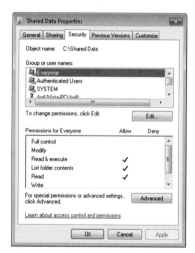

Figure 10-20   Configuring file system permissions for a folder

Configuring file system permissions is considered an advanced method of managing security because there are numerous complexities related to the inheritance of settings from parent to child folders. In general, home and small-business users do not need to make changes manually at this level. The primary types of file system permissions available for a folder include the following:

- Full Control
- Modify

- Read & Execute
- List Folder Contents
- Read
- Write

For network users to be able to access files, they must have the appropriate share and file system permissions. Whichever permissions are more restrictive determine the effective permissions for the user. For example, if the shared folder permissions enable the user to modify files but the file system security permissions enable for reading files only, the user effectively has only read access on those files. Therefore, when troubleshooting a problem in which shared folder settings appear to be configured properly, it is often useful to verify the file system permissions as well.

MORE INFO   Checking for encrypted files

Although it is not within the scope of Exam 70-623, one potential cause of permissions issues is that files might be protected using the Windows Vista Encrypting File System (EFS). EFS is designed to provide a higher level of security than simple permissions because it cannot easily be bypassed by other users of the system. There is, however, one major risk related to using EFS: if the encryption key information is lost, the encrypted data will be unrecoverable. For more information about EFS, see *http://www.microsoft.com/technet/security/smallbusiness/topics/cryptographyetc/protect_data_efs.mspx*.

Troubleshooting Network-Related Sharing Issues

When working with network resources, it's important to keep in mind network settings that might be preventing computers from communicating. To access shared files, folders, printers, and media successfully, the computers must be able to send and receive information. Additionally, network security settings should be configured to enable the necessary types of traffic to pass. In this section, you'll learn how to troubleshoot network-related issues that might prevent resource sharing.

Verifying Computer Settings

In a networked environment, computers running Windows are generally identified through the name of the computer. The default settings for a computer might have been defined during the setup process or by the computer manufacturer. Often these names are not descriptive, and you should modify them. When troubleshooting network-related issues, be sure to verify the name of a particular computer by right-clicking the Computer item on the Start menu, selecting Properties, and then clicking Advanced System Settings. The Computer Name tab provides details related to the current configuration.

In addition to the name of the computer, a description can sometimes be helpful. For example, in a home office or small-business environment, you might specify the primary user of the computer or its physical location (if it is a desktop computer). Also, verify the workgroup to which the computer belongs. Although it is not absolutely necessary for the workgroup to be the same for all computers, it is generally easier to find shared resources when computers are members of the same workgroup.

Verify Network Connectivity

The first step in troubleshooting network-related sharing issues is to verify that the local computer is connected to the network. This is easiest to do from within the Network and Sharing Center or by inspecting the appropriate system tray icon for the network connections. Tools such as the Network and Sharing Center network map, and command-line utilities such as PING, can be helpful for isolating connection-level issues. Also, the Windows Vista Diagnose and Repair functionality can be helpful for resolving common problems. For more information about performing general network troubleshooting, see Chapter 9.

Assuming that the computer is connected to the network, it is also useful to verify the status of the Network and Sharing Center Network Discovery feature. If it is turned off, the names of other computers in the environment might not be visible. If you know the name of a particular computer, you can attempt to use a UNC path to connect to it. Often, you can use the network map feature of the Network and Sharing Center to help you identify connectivity problems (see Figure 10-21). This can help isolate which computer in a home or small-business network environment is the cause of the lack of network connectivity.

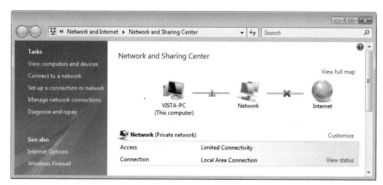

Figure 10-21   Identifying network connectivity problems, using the network map feature

Testing Shared Resources on the Local Computer

In some cases, it can be helpful to verify that shared resources are properly configured by accessing them on the local computer. This is easy to do by clicking the Network item on the Start menu and then double-clicking the name of the local computer. When you do this, you should see a view that is similar to what network users see (see Figure 10-22).

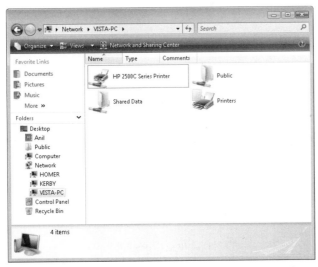

Figure 10-22   Testing shared resources by connecting from the local computer

Although the resources are physically located on the local computer, you can also access them using a UNC path or Windows Explorer. Keep in mind that this level of testing can help identify shared resource configuration issues, but it is usually not helpful for troubleshooting security permissions for networked users.

Verifying Firewall Configuration

Firewall technology is designed to keep unwanted network traffic away from a particular computer. Usually, these features are based on filtering both incoming and outgoing data on the network. By default, Windows Firewall is automatically configured using the Network and Sharing Center. For example, when network discovery functionality is enabled, the appropriate ports on the firewall are opened. You manually verify Windows Firewall settings on the Exceptions tab of the Windows Firewall Settings dialog box (see Figure 10-23). For more information about working with Windows Firewall, see Chapter 7, "Using Windows Security Center."

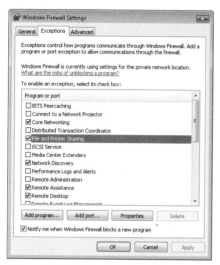

Figure 10-23   Viewing firewall exceptions using the Windows Firewall tool

When using a third-party firewall product, inbound and outbound filters might not be created and managed automatically. For example, you might need to enable traffic on specific ports after enabling file and folder sharing or network discovery features. More information about the specific protocols and ports that must be enabled is available in the Windows Help and Support documentation. The details of creating firewall exceptions will vary based on the specific product used, so consult your vendor's documentation to find the process for enabling exceptions.

Real World

Anil Desai

When working in real-world networked environments, I'm often faced with trouble-shooting complex issues. For example, computers might be unable to talk to each other when everything seems to be configured properly. Often, there are numerous potential sources for the problem, ranging from network connections to network devices to operating system configuration. The goal is usually to fix the problem as quickly as possible with minimal disruption to the environment. Less experienced technical professionals often attempt to resolve the issue by randomly making changes and hoping that the problem will be resolved. Although the root cause of the problems can vary, I've found that the most useful technical troubleshooting skill is to use an organized troubleshooting approach.

Before diving into the technical details of troubleshooting issues with resource sharing, it's often useful to get an idea of the actual symptoms of the problem. Sometimes, it's tempting to jump in and start making configuration changes that might actually make the problem worse. Ask yourself questions such as these:

- **What is the intended configuration?** Sometimes customers are unsure of what exactly they're trying to do. Rather than using the simplest method of sharing resources (such as enabling sharing of the Public folder), they might make unnecessary permissions changes. Therefore, it's important to determine your goals before you start troubleshooting.

- **Which computers are affected?** If there is only one computer that can't connect to several other machines, that computer is likely to have a problem. Alternatively, if no computers can access shared data, the issue is probably on the remote computer that is acting as a server.

- **When did the problem occur?** In some cases, the resource sharing configuration might never have worked properly. In that case, it's likely that an operating system setting or permissions issue is the problem. In other cases, everything might have worked properly until recently. In that case, it can be helpful to track down any changes that might have been made.

Based on this information, you can begin to devise an organized troubleshooting plan that can help resolve the issue. Often, there are several configuration settings that might be causing the problem. Keep in mind that you should generally make only one change at a time and then retest to see if that change resolved the issue. Overall, through the use of solid troubleshooting practices, you can quickly and easily isolate the source of even complex issues.

Quick Check

1. What are some likely causes of computers failing to appear in the Start menu Network section?
2. How can you verify the permissions on a shared folder?

Quick Check Answers

1. It is most likely that either network connectivity is unavailable between the computers or that the network discovery feature is disabled on one or more of the computers.
2. You can verify settings for a shared folder by right-clicking it in Windows Explorer and choosing Share.

Practice: Troubleshooting File and Print Sharing

In this practice exercise, you see the effects of making various file and print sharing configuration changes. The goal is to become more familiar with common problems that might prevent the successful sharing of file and print resources on the network. The steps assume that you are familiar with the process of creating and configuring shared folders, as covered in Lesson 1 of this chapter.

▶ **Practice: Troubleshooting Network Discovery**

This practice exercise involves making changes to the file and folder sharing configuration on the local computer and testing the results. You will need two computers running Windows Vista that are connected to the same network to complete these steps. The steps refer to these computers as the source computer (the one that is sharing resources) and the remote computer (the one that is attempting to access shared resources). Additionally, verify that the computers are able to communicate with each other before starting this exercise.

1. Open the Network and Sharing Center and disable the Network Discovery feature. Before beginning, make a note of the initial configuration settings for the sharing and discovery options.

2. To allow access to the Public folder, enable Public Folder Sharing and choose the Turn On Sharing So Anyone With Network Access Can Open, Change, And Create Files option.

3. Disable Password Protected Sharing.

4. From the remote computer, verify that you can connect to the Public folder on the source computer.

5. On the source computer, turn on the password-protected sharing option.

6. Connect to the Public folder over the network to verify that you are prompted for logon information. Provide the necessary information to access the shared files and folders.

7. In the Network and Sharing Center on the source computer, expand the Public Folder Sharing section and select Turn Off Sharing (People Logged On To This Computer Can Still Access This Folder).

8. Try to connect to the Public folder from the remote computer and verify that it is no longer available.

9. Return to the source computer. Click the View Status link next to an active network connection and then click Disable.

10. On the remote computer, verify that you can no longer access the computer over the network.

11. Finally, on the source computer, re-enable the network connection and return all Network and Sharing Center options to the default settings you recorded in step 1.

Lesson Summary

- Enable Network Discovery to allow computers to connect easily to each other in a network environment.
- Shared folder settings such as the share name and permissions can affect whether users can access data over the network.
- Connectivity between computers can be verified using the network map in the Network and Sharing Center.
- Details related to which files and folders are shared can be determined using the Network and Sharing Center or by connecting to the local computer using the Network item in the Start menu.
- Windows Firewall is automatically reconfigured when changes are made in the Sharing And Discovery section of the Network and Sharing Center.
- It might be necessary to configure exceptions in third-party firewall applications manually when troubleshooting resource sharing issues.

Lesson Review

You can use the following questions to test your knowledge of the information in Lesson 2, "Troubleshooting File and Print Sharing." The questions are also available on the companion CD if you prefer to review them in electronic form.

NOTE Answers

Answers to these questions and explanations of why each answer choice is correct or incorrect are located in the "Answers" section at the end of the book.

1. You are a Consumer Support Technician assisting a home user with configuring a shared folder for use by other members of the family. The user would like to configure the Public folder to require all users to provide a user name and password to access the files in this location. Currently, users can access and modify files without being prompted for password details. How can he most easily resolve this issue?

    A. Change the settings for Public Folder Sharing in the Network and Sharing Center.

    B. Disable Network Discovery.

    C. Change the passwords for all user accounts on the local computer.

    D. Enable Password Protected Sharing.

2. You are assisting a customer with troubleshooting a network issue in a home network environment. The customer currently has four computers that are connected to the environment. They are named Home01, Home02, Home03, and Home04. When she attempts to use the Start menu Network item on Home01, only three of the computers are present in the list. Home04 does not appear. She would like to see the fourth computer appear in the list. What is the most likely cause of the problem?

   A. Network Discovery is disabled on Home01.

   B. Network Discovery is disabled on Home04.

   C. Windows Firewall is incorrectly configured on Home01.

   D. The network location for Home04 is set to Private.

Chapter Review

To further practice and reinforce the skills you learned in this chapter, you can perform the following tasks:

- Review the chapter summary.
- Review the list of key terms introduced in this chapter.
- Complete the case scenarios. These scenarios set up real-world situations involving the topics of this chapter and ask you to create a solution.
- Complete the suggested practices.
- Take a practice test.

Chapter Summary

- The Network and Sharing Center can be used to share files, folders, printers, and media with other computers in the environment.
- Troubleshooting shared resources involves verifying network connectivity, Network and Sharing Center configuration details, and permissions.

Key Terms

Do you know what these key terms mean? You can check your answers by looking up the terms in the glossary at the end of the book.

- computer description
- computer name
- mapped network drives
- media library sharing
- network discovery
- network locations
- password-protected sharing
- permissions
- printer sharing
- Public folder
- Shared folder
- Universal Naming Convention (UNC)
- workgroup name

Case Scenarios

In the following case scenarios, you apply what you've learned about configuring, managing, and troubleshooting shared resources. You can find answers to these questions in the "Answers" section at the end of this book.

Case Scenario 1: Choosing Folder Sharing Options

You are a Consumer Support Technician assisting a small business owner with setting up file and folder sharing for her network environment. The customer would like to set up her own computer to provide a set of shared files to other members of the business. There are more than 1,000 files that she wishes to share, many of which are very large. She would like some users to be able to modify these files and add new ones, whereas others should be able only to view them. All users should be required to provide logon information when attempting to access shared files. The customer would also like to simplify the setup process for configuring sharing of data. All computers are running Windows Vista Business Edition.

1. Which options in the Network and Sharing Center should you enable to meet these requirements?

2. How should you configure the workgroup setting for the computers in the office environment?

3. How should the customer define permissions for shared folders?

Case Scenario 2: Working with Public Folder Sharing

You are a Consumer Support Technician assisting a home user with configuring sharing options in a home environment. The home currently contains one standard desktop computer that stores numerous photos, video, and music files. The customer would like a simple way to make some of these files available over the network for use by his children. He does not want the shared files to be modified. He wants to perform a minimal amount of configuration. He would also like to make photos and music available for access with his Xbox 360 game console. For files and folders that are shared, the user does not want his children to be required to provide logon information. You have verified that the customer's computer has plenty of available hard disk space.

1. Which options in the Sharing And Discovery section of the Network and Sharing Center should you enable to meet these requirements?

2. Which permissions settings should he use for this shared folder?

3. Which Network and Sharing Center options should be enabled to provide data to the Xbox 360?

Suggested Practices

To help you successfully master the exam objectives presented in this chapter, complete the following tasks.

Configuring and Troubleshooting Resource Sharing

These practice exercises will help you become more familiar with setting up shared resources and troubleshooting common problems that might occur. All practice exercises require at least two different computers running Windows Vista that are configured on the same network.

- **Practice 1: Setting Up Resource Sharing**   Configure one computer running Windows Vista to use file sharing and another to use Public folder sharing. Simulate various usage scenarios in which one would be more useful than the other. For example, determine which method would be most useful for sharing a large number of files to many different users who should have different permissions. Then, configure the shared folders and permissions accordingly and test the settings, using different user accounts.

- **Practice 2: Troubleshooting Network Resource Sharing Issues**   Configure two or more computers running Windows Vista to share files and folders and verify that the shared resources can be accessed over the network. Then, simulate various situations that might prevent resource sharing and notify the effects on the functionality. Examples might include unplugging one of the computers from the network, disabling network discovery, and changing file system permissions.

- **Practice 3: Configuring Media Sharing**   Enable media sharing to allow remote computers running Windows Vista to access your music library. On another Windows Vista–based computer, connect to the remote music files and play them to verify connectivity. If you have an Xbox 360 console available, access and play back the music from the source computer.

Take a Practice Test

The practice tests on this book's companion CD offer many options. For example, you can test yourself on just one exam objective, or you can test yourself on all of the 70-623 certification exam content. You can set up the test so that it closely simulates the experience of taking a certification exam, or you can set it up in study mode so that you can look at the correct answers and explanations after you answer each question.

MORE INFO   Practice tests

For details about all the practice test options available, see the "How to Use the Practice Tests" section in this book's introduction.

Chapter 11

Managing and Troubleshooting Devices

One of the greatest benefits of working with modern computers is the ability to choose from a wide variety of different hardware devices. Product designers understand the potential benefits of enabling customers to perform a wide variety of tasks while such devices are connected to their computers. For example, portable music players have limited storage space and often cannot access the Internet directly. By connecting them to a computer, users can download music and transfer data to the devices, using familiar software. Similarly, there are many different methods for performing input and output. Printers, scanners, fax devices, and related technologies provide a good way to interact with other forms of media.

In the past, the process of installing new devices on a computer was tedious, complicated, and unreliable, primarily because many hardware vendors did not follow standards for designing the required software. Device drivers are often a major source of frustration and can lead to system performance and reliability issues. Windows Vista provides numerous advances that can help make this process easier and more reliable. For example, customers who purchase devices that are certified to work with Windows Vista should be able to install and use the product easily. This process is simplified because much of the functionality that was provided by device manufacturers is now included directly in the operating system itself. In some cases, however, there's a need to troubleshoot installation and configuration issues.

In this chapter, you'll learn about ways in which you can install and troubleshoot devices in Windows Vista. In Lesson 1, "Installing and Managing Media," you'll learn about working with media-related devices such as scanners, printers, digital cameras, and fax capabilities. Windows Vista includes several enhancements over previous versions of the Windows platform to make working with these types of devices easier. In Lesson 2, "Working with Mobile Devices," you'll learn about mobile devices and ways in which you can synchronize information between them and your computer running Windows Vista.

Exam objectives in this chapter:
- Install, configure, and troubleshoot devices.
  - ❏ Connect peripherals to Windows Vista.
  - ❏ Install, configure, and troubleshoot mobile devices.

❑ Install, configure, and troubleshoot digital cameras and camcorders.

❑ Install, configure, and troubleshoot media devices.

❑ Install, configure, and troubleshoot printers, fax machines, and copy devices.

Lessons in this chapter:

Before You Begin

The focus of this chapter is on working with many different types of devices in Windows Vista; however, several of the sections cover features that are not available in Windows Vista Home Basic. (For more details about features in each edition, see Chapter 1, "Preparing to Install Windows Vista.") To test all of the hardware-related features in Windows Vista, you need access to the following types of devices:

■ A printer that connects to the computer, using a direct or network connection

■ A scanner that is supported by Windows Vista

■ A portable music player that is compatible with the Windows Vista Sync Center

■ A digital camera device that is supported by Windows Vista

■ A modem that is capable of sending and receiving faxes

■ Devices that connect to the computer using infrared and Bluetooth wireless connections

■ A Windows Mobile device (such as a personal digital assistant) that is compatible with Windows Vista

Because this is a long list of requirements, wherever possible, the practice exercises use steps that you can perform with limited access to all of these devices. Detailed requirements are included in the introduction to each practice exercise.

Lesson 1: Installing and Managing Media Devices

Computers have gone from being isolated devices designed for specific tasks to an integral component of a user's typical day. As a Consumer Support Technician, you'll need to assist customers in using devices such as printers, digital cameras, scanners, and fax functionality. Customers want to know how they can perform tasks such as receiving faxes and transferring pictures from their digital cameras to their computers.

Real World

Anil Desai

In working in consumer support and roles as well as in consulting, I've learned some valuable lessons related to determining the best solution to a particular problem. Perhaps the most useful of these is that what people ask for is not always what they want or need. Additionally, it's easy to focus on specific solutions first and then to try to fit them to the original problem. For example, imagine a situation in which a customer asks for a better mousetrap. Although providing a more efficient and user-friendly trap might be helpful, the real goal for the customer is to rid his or her house of pests. When you look at it in that way, there might be several superior solutions that don't involve the use of traps at all. The technology itself is just a method of reaching the real goal.

The same logic can apply to working with computer solutions. In your role as a Consumer Support Technician, your goal should be to provide the best solution for accomplishing a particular task. This usually involves collecting and analyzing various pieces of information about the real problem or desired capabilities. Customers are often subjected to advertising that makes them feel that a product will improve their lives magically and automatically. Ranging from music players to digital cameras to multifunction printing and scanning devices, all of these products offer benefits. The goal for you (and for customers) is to determine how and why they want to use the product.

For example, if a customer primarily is looking for a method to print out traveling directions, a basic printer device will likely meet his or her needs. Alternatively, if a small-business owner needs to scan documents frequently, such as packing slips, multifunction devices might make more sense. Overall, when helping customers implement products and technology, be sure you understand the big picture of what the customer is really trying to do instead of focusing on a particular detail or technology.

After this lesson, you will be able to:
- Use Device Manager to view and manage devices and device drivers in Windows Vista.
- Install scanners and digital cameras.
- Use Windows Fax and Scan to send and receive faxes, using an analog modem.
- Install and manage local and network-connected printers.

Estimated lesson time: 45 minutes

Managing Hardware Devices

One of the first steps you might need to perform when working with computers running Windows Vista is to determine what hardware is already installed in the system. For example, a customer might state that she would like to be able to send and receive faxes from her computer. You first need to verify that the computer has an installed fax-capable modem. Windows Vista supports many different types of hardware devices. The primary location for working with hardware is the Hardware And Sound Control Panel item. Figure 11-1 shows some of the available options.

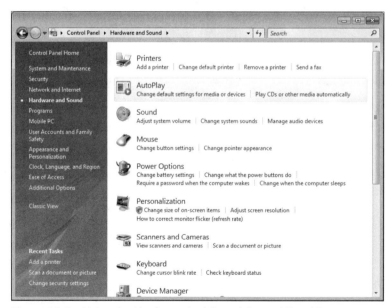

Figure 11-1 Using the Hardware And Sound Control Panel item

Later in this chapter, you'll learn about working with many of the different types of available devices and options.

Using Device Manager

The primary Windows Vista tool for viewing details about hardware components is Device Manager. To launch this utility, in the Hardware And Sound section of Control Panel, click Device Manager. The default view includes a list of the many different types of hardware devices supported by Windows Vista. Figure 11-2 shows an example of the types of information that you can obtain.

Figure 11-2   Viewing devices by type in Device Manager

You can expand each section to view the devices associated with that category. Some categories might not be present if a certain type of device is not installed. For example, if the computer does not have a modem installed, the Modems section does not appear.

In addition to viewing details based on the default view in Device Manager, the View menu includes other options for accessing the same information. The available views are as follows:

- Devices By Type
- Devices By Connection
- Resources By Type
- Resources By Connection

In general, the default view, Devices By Type, is the most intuitive way to collect device-related details. The Resources views can be helpful for troubleshooting earlier hardware and for detecting conflicts with some types of devices. Usually, these details are not necessary for normal operations.

Configuring Device Settings

Apart from viewing information about devices, Device Manager provides the ability to access properties for various devices. It also enables you to manage and update device drivers. To access the properties of a particular hardware device, right-click it and select Properties. The specific tabs that are displayed vary based on the type of device, and some types of devices might not include configuration options. Figure 11-3 shows options for one type of device.

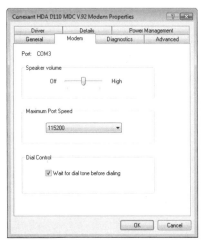

Figure 11-3 Viewing options related to a modem device

There are several other functions that you can perform within Device Manager, which you'll learn about next. In addition to the features and commands available in Device Manager, it is also helpful to note that several of the functions are also available by using links in the Control Panel Hardware And Sound section.

Detecting Hardware

Legacy hardware is the term used to describe products that are not Plug and Play–compatible. Generally, these are older devices. You can add them from the Action menu by selecting Add Legacy Hardware. This launches the Add Hardware Wizard, which walks the user through the steps of selecting and connecting a device (see Figure 11-4). The Wizard offers the ability to search automatically for devices that are connected to the computer, or you can select and configure the device manually.

For the vast majority of devices, Windows Vista can detect automatically when the item is added. If new devices have been connected to the computer but do not appear automatically in Device Manager, you can check for changes manually. To do this, from the Action menu, select Scan For Hardware Changes. Windows Vista then scans the system for compatible Plug and Play devices.

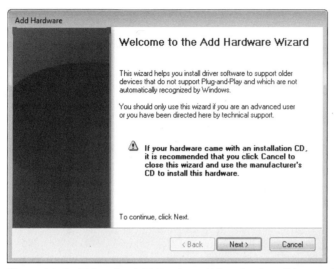

Figure 11-4   Using the Add Hardware Wizard to install legacy devices

Managing Device Drivers

Device Manager provides a starting point for performing various operations related to managing device drivers. To access these options, right-click a device and select the appropriate command. The Properties option accesses details related to the device and associated device driver. Figure 11-5 shows the Driver tab for a device, which includes information about the version number of the driver and the date it was created. It also provides several other functions for managing drivers.

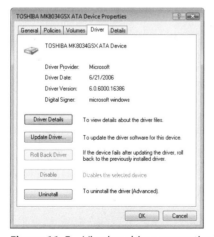

Figure 11-5   Viewing driver properties for a hard disk drive

Perhaps the most common operation is attempting to update driver software. You can start this process by selecting Update Driver Software from the shortcut menu for a device (see Figure 11-6). The first method of finding driver updates is to search automatically for them. This process tells Windows Vista to look through the local and online driver databases for newer versions of drivers. The other option is to specify the location of device drivers manually. This is useful for updates that you have downloaded manually or that are available on removable media such as a CD-ROM.

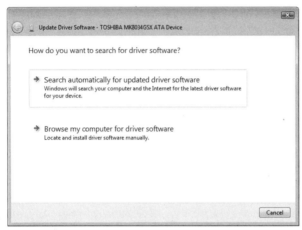

Figure 11-6   Updating device driver software

Sometimes, installing an updated driver might cause the device to stop working. This most commonly occurs due to poorly written driver software or when the incorrect driver has been chosen manually. After a driver has been updated, you can click Roll Back Driver to revert to an earlier version of the driver.

Although these functions are not usually required, it is possible to disable a hardware device or to uninstall device drivers. Both commands are available by right-clicking the device in Device Manager or by accessing the Driver tab of the device's Properties dialog box. Disabling a device makes it unavailable for use in Windows Vista. You can sometimes do this if you know that the device is not needed or if it is not working properly. For example, if a customer has no need for a modem, you can disable the device. Uninstalling a device removes its drivers from Windows Vista. For Plug and Play devices, Windows Vista attempts to redetect the device automatically, either immediately or after a reboot of the computer.

Device Manager is an extremely useful utility for viewing and modifying settings related to hardware devices and their associated device drivers. Keep these functions in mind as you learn about working with different types of devices in Windows Vista.

Working with Scanners and Digital Cameras

The ability to store, modify, and access digital content is one of the main features of Windows Vista. In Chapter 4, "Configuring Windows Features," you learned about many different media-related tools in Windows Vista, including Windows Photo Gallery. Scanners and digital cameras are two ways in which users can add digital images to their computer. A scanner is a device that is typically used for capturing physical content ranging from documents to photographs. Software and hardware work together to create digital picture files that are stored on computers. Digital cameras provide a similar function for taking photographs and then storing them on internal media, which can then be transferred to a computer.

Installing Scanners and Cameras

You typically install digital cameras and scanners by using a universal serial bus (USB) or FireWire connection. From a hardware standpoint, the computer must support the appropriate connection type, either internally or through an expansion card. In most cases, Windows Vista is able to detect automatically when you connect one of these devices to the computer. Windows automatically launches a process for detecting the hardware and attempting to install the appropriate drivers. This is the preferred method for configuring cameras and scanners.

In some cases, Windows Vista might not include the drivers that are required for a particular device. Sometimes, additional software is also required to provide the necessary functionality. For example, some scanner manufacturers use their own software for configuring capture settings. To view and configure these devices manually, click the Scanners And Cameras link in the Hardware And Sounds Control Panel window. Figure 11-7 shows the main dialog box.

Figure 11-7   Manually installing scanners and cameras

Click Add Device to start the process of finding the appropriate drivers. The first step in the process provides a list of manufacturers and models that are currently supported by the system. If the desired model is not listed, users can click Have Disk to provide the location of the drivers.

Using a Scanner

After the appropriate device drivers have been installed, users are able to use them to transfer data to the computer. The process can vary depending on the capabilities of the device. For scanners, the most common operation is to scan a new document using the Windows Fax and Scan application. Clicking the New Scan button displays a dialog box for specifying scan settings. More details about using this application are provided later in this lesson.

Using a Digital Camera

Because they are portable devices, digital cameras are configured most commonly with built-in internal memory, a removable media card, or both. There are two main ways in which pictures can be transferred from a digital camera to the computer. The first is by directly connecting the digital camera to the computer. As long as the camera device drivers are installed, it is automatically detected. Generally, users can access their pictures by opening the Computer item in the Start menu. The storage from the digital camera device appears as if it were a removable media device. Many cameras create some type of folder structure within which pictures are stored. They also use a unified format for the photo files themselves. You can move or copy the files from the device as if you are accessing a standard hard disk drive.

It is also possible to use the Windows Photo Gallery application to import pictures from a digital camera. To do this, open the application and, from the File menu, select Import From Camera Or Scanner. Figure 11-8 shows an example of the available options. When the files are being transferred, you also have the option of adding a tag, so you can identify the pictures easily later.

Figure 11-8   Importing pictures with Windows Photo Gallery

The other method of transferring pictures from a digital camera involves the use of a media card reader device. Media card readers are sometimes installed in desktop and laptop computers. They are also available as add-in devices for desktop computers (they often fit into an available drive bay) or as a USB-connected device. Most media card readers support a wide variety of media formats, such as Compact Flash, Secure Digital, and Smart Media.

Transferring data by using this method involves removing the storage card from the camera and placing it in the media reader. The media should then appear in Windows Explorer, enabling files to be moved and copied. The advantage of using a media card reader is that it is often more convenient to insert a storage card into a reader than it is to connect the camera physically to the computer, using a cable. Additionally, this method saves battery power on the camera because no additional power is required while files are being read and written.

Using Windows Fax and Scan

Before the rise in popularity of the Internet and the availability of e-mail, a common method of transferring documents was by fax machine. These machines used an analog phone line to transfer data. Although the transmission speed and quality of faxed documents are not ideal, they do offer advantages over alternatives (such as physically printing and mailing a document).

The functionality of a fax machine is similar to the combined functionality of both a printer and a scanner. You use the scanner component to convert a paper document to a digital format for storage or transmission. You use the printer component to do the opposite: based on a digital source, you output the file to paper. Additionally, an analog modem device is necessary to connect to a phone line. Many different types of devices that perform these functions are available today. A stand-alone fax machine is able to perform scanning, printing, and transmission functions without the need for a computer. These are still found commonly in business environments.

Working with Windows Fax and Scan

Many Windows Vista users occasionally need to send and receive faxes. They might not want to invest in a dedicated device for this purpose because of the cost and space requirements. Windows Vista includes faxing capability. The Windows Fax and Scan program allows users to perform the most common operations through an analog modem that is connected to a phone line. Additionally, if a user has installed a scanner device, he or she can use it to scan paper documents and then use a printer to create a hard copy of a received fax.

You can launch Windows Fax and Scan from the Start menu or in Control Panel by clicking Hardware And Sound and then clicking the Scan A Document Or Picture link in the Scanners And Cameras section. Figure 11-9 shows the default user interface of the program.

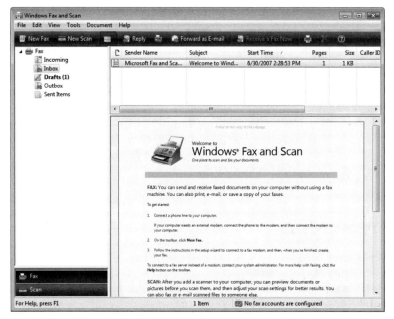

Figure 11-9   Using Windows Fax and Scan

The primary window layout of Windows Fax and Scan is similar to that of the Windows Mail application (which you learned about in Chapter 4). The left side of the interface includes several folders:

- **Incoming**   The location of new fax items when they are received
- **Inbox**   The location of Windows Fax and Scan items that have been imported
- **Drafts**   A folder for temporarily storing documents that have not yet been sent
- **Outbox**   The location of documents that are pending delivery (such as an outbound fax that is currently being transmitted)
- **Sent Items**   The location in which a copy of all sent items is stored

The bottom of the left panel also enables you to select whether you want to work with Fax documents or Scan documents. The latter option enables importing documents into the computer, as described earlier in this lesson.

Setting Up a Fax Account

Before you can send a fax by using Windows Fax and Scan, you must configure a fax modem. The process is known as setting up a fax account because it contains all of the settings that enable a user to send and receive faxes. The first step is to verify that the computer has an analog modem with fax capabilities installed and configured. You can do this by using Device

Manager, as described earlier in this lesson. In addition, the fax modem should be connected to an analog phone line.

MORE INFO   **Digital phone lines**

Some small-business environments might use digital phone systems rather than standard analog lines. Although the plug connector might look identical to that of an analog phone line, it is possible to damage a modem by incorrectly plugging it into a digital wall socket. Be sure to verify the type of connection before you attempt to connect a modem.

To begin the process of setting up a fax modem, click New Fax. If a device has not yet been configured, you have the option of doing it at this point (see Figure 11-10).

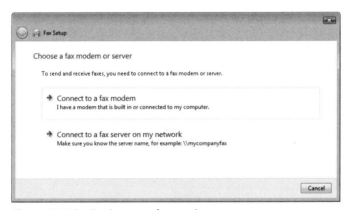

Figure 11-10   Setting up a fax modem

The first option is to connect to a fax modem that is installed locally on the computer. The second option involves connecting to a fax server that is located on the network. This process is similar to connecting to a network printer (a topic covered later in this lesson). When you choose to use a local modem, you'll be able to provide a logical name for it. This option is useful if there are multiple fax-capable devices installed on the computer.

The next step enables you to configure settings for the receipt of faxes when using a local modem (see Figure 11-11). The options are as follows:

- **Answer Automatically (Recommended)**   This option automatically answers incoming phone calls after five rings and starts the fax receipt process. If the phone is answered before five rings, Windows Fax and Scan does not attempt to receive the fax.
- **Notify Me**   This option enables the receipt of faxes, but the user must manually select the option to start receiving. If the phone line is used for both voice and fax communications, this option can be helpful. The typical process is for the user first to answer the phone. If a fax beep is heard, he or she can then start the receive process. Note that if a user is not present, faxes are not received automatically.

■   **I'll Choose Later; I Want To Create A Fax Now**   This option effectively disables the receipt of faxes until the settings are changed at a later time.

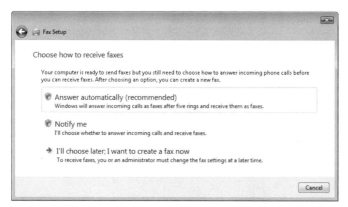

Figure 11-11   Configuring receive options for a fax modem

You can add or remove fax accounts by clicking Fax Accounts from the Tools menu (see Figure 11-12). You'll learn how you can configure other settings later in this section.

Figure 11-12   Managing fax account settings

Creating a New Fax

The screen for creating a new fax appears similar to that of an e-mail message (see Figure 11-13). You use the *To* field to specify the recipient of the fax. You can provide this either by using an item from the Windows Contacts list (assuming that the contact has a fax number) or by typing the number manually.

Figure 11-13   Creating a new fax

When sending a fax, the exact dialing rules can vary. Sometimes, you must enter a number to access a line that can dial out. In other cases, you might need a country code or area code for long-distance calls but not for local ones. You can enter the exact number to use, including prefixes and options, manually. Alternatively, you can choose to create a new dialing rule (see Figure 11-14). The specific options might also vary based on the regional version of Windows Vista being used.

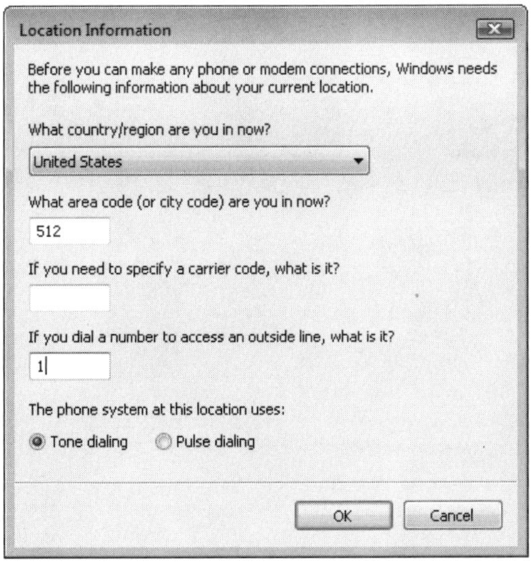

Figure 11-14   Creating new dialing rules settings

The text entered in the body of the fax is included on the cover page. You often want to use the Insert menu to attach a file or document to send. The options include the following:

- File Attachment
- Picture
- Text From File
- Pages From Scanner

You can also change the options for when a fax is sent from the Tools menu by clicking Options. Figure 11-15 shows the available settings. To send the fax, click Send. Windows Fax and Scan automatically attempts to dial the number and transmit the fax. During this time, the item appears in the Outbox folder. After it has been sent successfully, it is moved to the Sent Items folder.

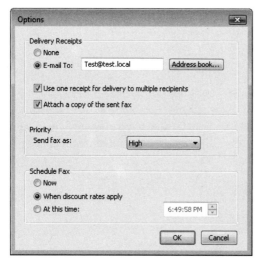

Figure 11-15   Configuring options for a new fax

Configuring Fax Settings

Windows Fax and Scan provides several different options that you can use to configure how and when faxes are sent. To access the options, from the Tools menu, click Fax Settings. Figure 11-16 shows an example of the options. The available tabs are as follows:

Figure 11-16   Configuring fax settings

- **General**   This tab includes settings for whether faxes can be sent through a device and whether faxes should be received automatically. The More Options button enables you to specify station identifiers (which are included in the fax header data) and to choose whether faxes should be printed or saved automatically.
- **Tracking**   This tab includes various settings for viewing progress and notifications related to sending and receiving faxes.
- **Advanced**   This tab shows configuration options for the file system location in which faxes are stored. There are also settings for redial options and for defining times during which the phone line has discount rates.

■ **Security** This tab enables administrators of the computer to configure which actions are available to which users. The security permissions include Fax, Manage Fax Configuration, Manage Fax Documents, and Special permissions (see Figure 11-17).

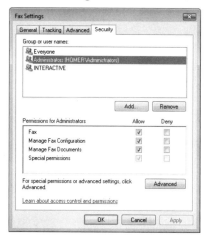

Figure 11-17   Configuring security settings for Windows Fax and Scan

Installing and Managing Printers

Most computer users are very familiar with printers. Although increased computer use has generally decreased the need for paper, it is hard to eliminate it completely. For example, it's common to print a hard copy of a map or directions when traveling to a new location. In addition to being able to output standard black-and-white documents, many printers can output color documents and photographs. There are several different types of printers available on the market:

■ **Wired printers** These printer devices are designed to connect directly to a computer. Older printers commonly use a parallel port (also called an LPT port) connection. Most new wired printers connect using a USB port on the computer.

■ **Network printers** A standard wired printer requires a computer to be able to output documents. In some cases, many users want to share a printer without placing a dependency on one of the computers. Network-enabled printers are able to connect directly to a wired network. They include functionality for enabling users to connect directly to the device over the network.

■ **Wireless printers** Some stand-alone printers include a built-in wireless network interface or support for standards such as infrared and Bluetooth connections. Bluetooth is a low-range wireless network connection method that requires the computer to have a Bluetooth receiver. Infrared connections are often included on portable computers such as notebooks and personal digital assistants (PDAs). Wireless printer options are helpful in homes and small-business environments when users might need to connect to many different output devices quickly or when portable print devices are used.

■ **Multifunction devices**   Some printer-related devices provide a wide range of different functionality in a single physical device. For example, they might include a scanner, internal memory, a printer, and an analog fax-capable modem. They can be wired or wireless devices and can be shared directly on the network.

MORE INFO   Evaluating printer costs

Customers are likely to ask you, as a Consumer Support Technician, for recommendations about printers. The most common question is often, "Which is the better option, an inkjet printer or a laser printer?" Inkjet printers might be cheaper to purchase (they're often sold at a loss by retailers), but the costs for purchasing ink cartridges can add up quickly. Laser printers often provide better quality and provide reduced costs over the life of the device. Be sure to take into account the long-term costs in addition to the initial purchase price when recommending a type of printer to customers.

Installing Local Printers

Windows Vista includes a large database of available printer drivers. In most cases, the process of plugging in a wired printer results in the automatic installation of the appropriate drivers. When installing multifunction devices or wireless printers, users should refer to the documentation that came with the device. Often, specific settings must be configured on the device itself. For example, network printers require you to configure Transmission Control Protocol/Internet Protocol (TCP/IP) address information. (For more details about configuring network settings, see Chapter 9, "Configuring Windows Vista Networking.")

It is also possible to add a printer device manually. This is necessary when Windows Vista does not detect a connected printer device automatically. It is also the process by which users can connect to a printer that is located on another computer or that is directly accessible on the network. To start the process, open Control Panel, click Hardware And Sound, and then click the Add A Printer link. Figure 11-18 shows the main options.

When adding a local printer, you have the option of specifying the port to which the printer is attached (see Figure 11-19). Options include printer (LPT) ports, serial (COM) ports, USB ports, and any other virtual device ports that might be configured. Known TCP/IP network printer ports are also included. Some types of software applications are able to install virtual printer devices that users can use to output documents to files or to other types of programs. For example, users can use virtual print devices to generate XML Paper Specification (XPS) or Adobe Portable Document Format (PDF) files from any program that is capable of sending output to a printer.

Figure 11-18   Manually adding a new printer

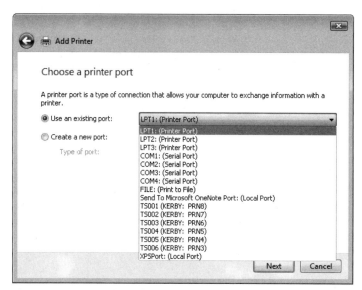

Figure 11-19   Configuring ports for a locally attached printer

After you choose the printer connection type, you have the option of choosing a printer from the list of known manufacturers and models. You can also click Have Disk to provide drivers manually. Finally, the Windows Update command enables you to look for driver updates online automatically.

Adding a Network, Wireless, or Bluetooth Printer

Some printer devices are designed to be shared using a standard network connection, a wireless connection, or a Bluetooth connection. Because these devices are not connected to a computer port directly, you generally must configure them manually. When you choose the Add A Network, Wireless, Or Bluetooth Printer option in the Add Printer Wizard, Windows Vista automatically attempts to locate available shared or wireless printer devices on the network (see Figure 11-20) by using network discovery features. (For more information about configuring network sharing, see Chapter 10, "Managing Network Sharing.") It is important to understand that you add printers that are connected directly to a network by using a TCP/IP connection, using the Add A Local Printer option.

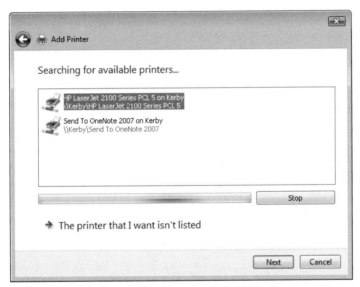

Figure 11-20   Viewing a list of available network printers

If Windows Vista does not detect the printer automatically, click The Printer That I Want Isn't Listed.

Managing Printer Settings

Most printers have options that you can use to manage how they output print jobs. For example, some printers have multiple paper size options and the ability to print on both sides of a page (a feature known as duplexing). To access the properties of a printer, click the Printers link in the Hardware And Sound section of Control Panel. Then, right-click the printer and choose Properties to open the printer's Properties dialog box. The specific available tabs differ based on the capabilities of the printer (see Figure 11-21).

Figure 11-21   Configuring advanced settings for a printer

In addition, users can choose one of the printers to be the system default. This is the printer to which Windows Vista sends documents unless another device is chosen, using the Printer Options dialog box.

Sharing Printers

To be able to send data for output to a printer, the computer must have information about its settings, options, and data format requirements. The printer driver provides these details. For locally attached printer devices, the drivers are typically loaded automatically on the computer. They are either included with Windows Vista or are provided by the hardware manufacturer. In the case of connecting a network printer, Windows Vista automatically attempts to download the available drivers from the network printer.

Users of Windows Vista can also share their printers on the network to enable others to use them. To enable printer sharing, users must first enable it by using the Network and Sharing Center. (For more information, see Chapter 10.) To share a printer, right-click the printer object and select Sharing. Figure 11-22 shows an example of the available settings. The Share Name specifies the specific name that users use to access the printer. The full network path has the \\ComputerName\PrinterShareName format. It is a good practice to include details about the owner or location of the printer in the share name. One potential disadvantage of sharing a printer is that the computer to which the printer is connected can be bogged down by preparing printed documents to be sent to the printer device (a process that is referred to as rendering). When selected, the Render Print Jobs On Client Computers check box requires print processing to occur on the client computer, thereby offloading some of the overhead on the computer that is sharing the printer.

Figure 11-22   Sharing a printer for use over a network

Because users can connect to a network printer by using a variety of different operating systems, it is also possible to add additional drivers to the configuration by clicking Additional Drivers and selecting which platforms the printer should support. The specific list of operating system options is based on the capabilities of drivers that are provided by device manufacturers or that are included with Windows Vista. If drivers are not available over the network, users need to use the Windows Vista built-in driver for the device (if one is available) or manually provide the driver during the printer installation process.

Quick Check

1. How can you determine which types of media devices are currently installed on the computer?
2. What are the options for configuring fax receipt settings in Windows Fax and Scan?

Quick Check Answers

1. The Windows Vista Device Manager provides a list of all of the connected devices, along with details about how they're configured.
2. You can configure Windows Fax and Scan to receive faxes automatically, to ignore faxes, or to be available for receiving faxes manually. You can also configure the number of rings after which the fax device automatically answers the phone.

Practice: Working with Media Devices

In these practice exercises, you gain familiarity with the fax and printer features of Windows Vista.

▶ **Practice 1: Send a Fax with Windows Fax and Scan**

This exercise involves performing the initial configuration of Windows Fax and Scan and sending a test fax document. To complete the steps in this exercise, your computer should have an analog modem connected to a phone line. The steps in the exercise assume that you have not yet created a fax account using Windows Fax and Scan. If you have already created a new account, you can delete it using the Fax Accounts item from the Tools menu. To test the receipt of the fax, you need the phone number of a fax machine or another computer that is configured to receive faxes. If your computer does not have Windows Vista installed, you can still perform the initial configuration steps (although no fax is actually sent).

1. Open Windows Fax and Scan by searching for it in the Start menu.

2. To start the process of configuring a fax account, click New Fax.

3. In the first step, choose Connect To A Fax Modem.

4. In the second step, enter **Test Fax Modem** for the name of the device. Click Next.

5. In the Fax Receive Options step, select I'll Choose Later; I Want To Create A Fax Now.

6. If you are prompted to make changes to the Windows Firewall configuration, choose the Unblock command. This is necessary to allow network-enabled features such as sending e-mails. (For more information on configuring Windows Firewall, see Chapter 7, "Using Windows Security Center.")

7. In the Cover Page drop-down list, select the Generic option. You are prompted to add Sender information. Click Yes, and then select the Use The Information For This Fax Only check box. Enter any contact information you would like the recipient to see, and then click OK.

8. In the *To* field, type the full phone number of the fax recipient, including the area code and any dialing prefix that might be required.

9. In the Subject text box, type **Test Fax – Please Ignore**. Repeat this text in the Cover Page Notes section and in the body of the fax message.

10. Optionally, you can attach a file to this fax if you have one available. To do this, from the Insert menu, select File Attachment. Browse to and select the file you want to attach. Generally, this is an image file or a document such as one created in Microsoft Office. When you have selected the file, click Attach.

11. To see how the fax will appear to recipients, from the View menu, select Preview.

12. When finished composing the fax, click Send. If prompted for Location Information details, enter your area code and other settings. Click OK to continue. Then, in the Phone And Modem Options dialog box, click OK to verify the settings.

13. In the main Windows Fax and Scan view, select the Outbox folder to verify that the fax appears there. Note that if you do not have a modem installed in the computer, the fax remains here. You can delete it manually if necessary. After the fax has been sent, you can select the Sent Items folder to access it.

14. When finished, close Windows Fax and Scan.

▶ **Practice 2: Set Up and Share a Printer**

In this practice exercise, you walk through the steps of installing and sharing a locally connected printer. The steps actually install a printer driver for a printer that is connected to the LPT1 port, even if there is no printer attached to this port. Therefore, you can perform the steps of this exercise without having a printer attached to the computer. For the sake of this practice exercise, the steps assume that there is no printer attached to the computer. To test the printer sharing feature without requiring another computer or network access, you create a network-based printer connection to the same computer.

1. Open Control Panel, click Hardware And Sound, and then click Add A Printer in the Printers section. This launches the Add Printer dialog box.

2. Click Add A Local Printer.

3. In the printer port step, select Use An Existing Port, and then select LPT1: (Printer Port) from the drop-down list. Click Next.

4. From the list of printers, for the Manufacturer, choose Generic. In the Printers list, select Generic/Text Only. Note that you can click Windows Update if you have an Internet connection and would like to view which drivers are available online. Click Next to continue.

5. For the Printer Name, leave the default setting of Generic/Text Only. Clear the Set As The Default Printer check box. Click Next.

6. Windows Vista automatically installs the necessary printer driver. When this is finished, you should see the Printer Sharing step. Select the Share This Printer So That Others On Your Network Can Find And Use It option. For the share name, enter **Test Printer**. For the location, you can enter a description of the printer's physical location optionally. For the comment, enter **Generic test printer**. Click Next to save the settings and continue.

7. Note that you have an option to print a test page. Because no printer is actually attached to the computer, click Finish to complete the process.

8. In the Hardware And Sound Control Panel window, click the Printers link to see all of the printers that have been configured on the computer.

9. Right-click the Generic/Text Only printer and select Properties. Click through the various settings and options that are available.

10. In the next steps, you create a network printer connection to this shared printer on the same computer. On the Hardware And Sound Control Panel page, click the Add A Printer link.

11. Select Add A Network, Wireless Or Bluetooth Printer. Windows automatically searches the network and the local computer for available shared printers.

12. Select the generic printer you created earlier, and then click Next.

13. For the Printer Name, enter **Test Shared Network Printer**, and then click Next.

14. Click Finish to complete the setup process for the network printer.

15. On the Hardware And Sound Control Panel page, click the Printers link. Because you have chosen to connect to a printer that is configured automatically on the same computer, you do not see the new shared printer that you created. If you had performed this operation from another computer, however, it would appear in the list.

16. Delete the generic test printer by right-clicking it and selecting Delete.

17. When finished, close all open windows.

Lesson Summary

- The Windows Vista Device Manager enables you to view which devices are connected to the computer and to update, remove, or disable device drivers.

- Windows Vista can install many different types of printers, digital cameras, and scanners automatically.

- The Camera and Scanner Installation Wizard can be used to install devices that were not automatically detected by Windows Vista.

- Windows Fax and Scan can be configured to send and receive faxes, using an analog modem device.

- Windows Vista provides the ability to access wired, network, wireless, and multifunction printer devices.

- Users can share printers for use by other computers on the network.

Lesson Review

You can use the following questions to test your knowledge of the information in Lesson 1, "Installing and Managing Media Devices." The questions are also available on the companion CD if you prefer to review them in electronic form.

NOTE Answers

Answers to these questions and explanations of why each answer choice is correct or incorrect are located in the "Answers" section at the end of the book.

---

1. You are a Consumer Support Technician assisting a customer with setting up a new computer running Windows Vista Home Premium. The customer would like to be able to send paper documents to her work fax machine, using Windows Fax and Scan. She would like to receive faxes for viewing on the computer. Which of the following types of hardware are required to enable this functionality? (Choose all that apply.)

   A. A fax-capable analog modem device

   B. A wired printer connected directly to the computer

   C. A scanner that is compatible with Windows Vista

   D. A network connection on the local computer

   E. Access to an analog phone line

2. You are assisting a small-business owner with setting up printing functionality in his office. The customer has attached a new printer to his own computer running Windows Vista. You have assisted him with installing the device drivers and in sharing the printer using the name Office Printer. He would like two other computers in the environment to connect to the shared printer over the network. He would also like to minimize the performance impact on his local computer. Which steps should he take? (Choose two.)

   A. Create separate shared printer devices for use by other users on the network.

   B. Enable the Keep Printed Documents option on the Advanced tab of the printer's Properties dialog box.

   C. Select the Render Print Jobs On Client Computers check box.

   D. Enable the Print Directly To The Printer option on the Advanced tab of the printer's Properties dialog box.

   E. On each computer that wants to use the printer, choose Add A Printer and select the appropriate printer device.

Lesson 2: Working with Mobile Devices

In the early days of mobile computing, so-called portable devices were extremely heavy and were limited to performing a few basic computer functions such as word processing or managing spreadsheets. Times have changed significantly, and now very powerful devices are often as small as a deck of cards. Many home and small-business users select notebook computers for their convenience and portability, and it's not uncommon for users to have multiple computers. For example, a small-business owner might use a laptop at work, a desktop computer at home, and other devices while traveling. Although these devices allow flexibility in computer use, they do pose challenges.

Ideally, all of the types of mobile devices that consumers use are able to exchange information. For example, if you update a friend's phone number on your PDA, you would like the same change to be reflected on your home and work computers. It can also be very helpful to transfer document updates automatically between computers for backup and convenience purposes. Although users can perform these tasks manually, users of Windows Vista and mobile devices are likely to ask you for an easier way to manage their distributed information.

Windows Vista includes numerous features for making the process of working with and managing mobile devices quicker, easier, and more reliable. In this lesson, you'll learn about tools such as Windows Mobility Center, which can help users have a consistent experience with notebooks, PDAs, and other compatible devices. You'll also learn how Windows Sync Center can be used to keep information up to date in multiple locations.

After this lesson, you will be able to:

- Describe how you can install and configure compatible mobile devices for use by Windows Vista.
- Use Windows Mobility Center to manage settings that are commonly accessed on mobile computers running Windows Vista.
- Describe the ways in which Windows Sync Center can be used to coordinate information between multiple devices and computers.
- Set up Offline Files to keep information synchronized between multiple computers.

Estimated lesson time: 30 minutes

Working with Mobile Devices

There are many different types of mobile devices available today. They range from relatively simple single-function devices such as music players to fully capable PDAs that enable users to run complex applications. In the past, managing these types of devices has been complicated. Hardware vendors were often required to create their own tools and utilities to enable synchronizing between different applications. Users often needed to install and configure multiple applications, each of which had different user interfaces. In this section, you'll learn about features in Windows Vista that are designed to simplify the process of working with mobile devices.

MORE INFO Evaluating mobile devices

When recommending mobile devices to your customers, you are likely to consider the primary features of the device. For example, more memory, a faster processor, and better built-in functions are all useful benefits. However, you should also keep in mind the convenience and quality of the included software. Users who plan to synchronize their information with their computers running Windows Vista should look for the logos that indicate Windows Vista compatibility. Better yet, devices that are based on the Microsoft Windows Mobile operating system have been designed to provide a consistent experience with the Windows platform.

Installing Mobile Devices

The first step in allowing a mobile device to work with Windows Vista involves connecting it to a computer. The connection allows the computer to send and receive data to and from the device. There are several common methods by which mobile devices can connect to computers running Windows Vista, as follows:

- **USB**   These wired connections are available on most computers and can be a convenient way to plug devices into a computer. Some mobile devices have built-in USB connectors. Others require connection through a cradle or other device.

- **Infrared**   These connections work over small distances, using the same method used by a traditional television remote control. Infrared connections are relatively slow but do enable wireless transfer of information with a compatible computer.

- **Bluetooth**   The Bluetooth wireless standard provides connectivity with nearby computers and other devices. To connect to a Bluetooth-compatible mobile device, a computer must have a Bluetooth receiver. Some notebook computers come with this functionality included. For other computers, external Bluetooth receivers (which usually connect to a USB port) are required. To associate a Bluetooth device with the computer, you must configure the passkey for the device. This process enables users to determine which devices should be able to communicate when multiple Bluetooth-enabled receivers are present.

- **Serial cables**   Serial connections are an old but reliable standard. They are typically much slower than other connection methods and are most often found on legacy devices.

- **Wireless network connections**   Some mobile devices provide compatibility with the 802.11 wireless network standard. These devices can be configured to connect to a wireless network and communicate with other computers. For more information about configuring wireless networking, see Chapter 9.

Because mobile devices vary greatly in their connection methods, you need to refer to the documentation for the device to determine the specific connection steps. Some mobile devices require users to enable features such as wireless connections or Bluetooth.

Installing Windows Mobile Device Center

Windows Mobile is the Microsoft operating system standard for mobile devices. Several versions of the platform are available. When you connect a Windows Mobile–based device to a computer running Windows Vista, users are prompted to download and install Windows Mobile Device Center (see Figure 11-23). This program is the primary method by which users can access various functions of their mobile devices from their computers.

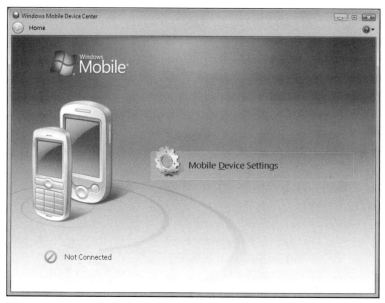

Figure 11-23   Using Windows Mobile Device Center

In addition to connecting to a mobile device, Windows Mobile Device Center includes drivers that enable other features. For example, you can use Windows Sync Center (covered later in this lesson) to coordinate data modifications between devices. The specific available capabilities vary based on the specific type of device that is being connected.

MORE INFO   **Working with Windows Mobile Device Center**

The mobile device industry changes much more rapidly than even the desktop and notebook markets. For up-to-date information on mobility features and compatible devices for Windows Vista, see the Windows Mobile Web site at *http://www.microsoft.com/windowsmobile/*.

Using Windows Mobility Center

Portable devices such as notebook computers provide many useful features for customers who travel often or who work at multiple locations. In the past, the major challenge related to working with these computers was learning the various hardware-related features and utilities that enabled access to all of the functionality. Usually, each manufacturer of portable computers would include its own utilities for managing screen settings, battery usage, wireless network settings, and other details. End users often had to install and learn these different components for each computer they used.

Exam Tip   Although the names are very similar, be careful not to confuse Windows Mobility Center with the Windows Mobile Device Center. Windows Mobility Center is designed to provide functionality for notebook computers and other similar devices that run the full Windows Vista operating system. The Windows Mobile Device Center is used to communicate with devices that run the Windows Mobile operating system.

Windows Vista includes numerous mobility-related features as part of the base operating system. This provides consistency and the ability to access the most common functions easily when using a notebook computer. In addition, it provides a way for notebook manufacturers to include their own branding and additional utilities that might be unique to those systems. Figure 11-24 shows an example of the Windows Mobility Center interface. Note that the top section includes built-in components that are standard to the application, whereas the bottom portion includes manufacturer-specific utilities and features.

Figure 11-24   Using Windows Mobility Center on a Dell notebook computer

Windows Mobility Center has been designed to be accessible quickly on notebook computers. The easiest way to access it is by right-clicking the battery meter icon and selecting Windows Mobility Center. You can also open the application by searching for it in the Start menu.

MORE INFO **Shortcut keys**

Many computer manufacturers provide an even easier method of accessing commonly used note-book computer features. Settings such as speaker volume and screen brightness can often be accessed using dedicated keys or by using a keyboard combination. For more information, consult the computer's documentation.

The default sections of Windows Mobility Center include the following:

- **Display Brightness** This option provides a slider bar to change the brightness of the display quickly. Users often modify this setting based on the external lighting, available battery charge, and personal preferences. You can change the default options for brightness by clicking the icon (see Figure 11-25).

Figure 11-25 Adjust Display Brightness settings

- **Volume** These settings enable you to mute the computer's speakers and to change the master volume. Clicking the icon launches the Sound Control Panel page.
- **Battery Status** This section shows the current amount of available battery charge. It also enables changing quickly between the various power profiles that are listed in the drop-down list. Clicking the icon loads the Power Options Control Panel page.

- **Wireless Network**   This section displays the status of the current wireless network connection (connected or disconnected). Clicking the Network Center button launches the Network and Sharing Center, which can be used to connect to wireless networks.

- **External Display**   If an external display device is connected to the computer, this icon enables you to configure the screen resolution options. Notebook users who commonly connect to external monitors or to projector devices can use this option to find associated configuration settings.

- **Sync Center**   This button shows the status of any synchronization partnerships that have been defined on the computer (if applicable). More information about using Windows Sync Center is covered later in this lesson.

- **Presentation Settings**   When giving a presentation, users often want to make temporary changes to their computer settings. For example, they might want to choose an alternate desktop background, change the speaker volume, disable the screen saver, and suppress various notifications such as new e-mails. Figure 11-26 shows the options that are available by clicking the Presentation Settings icon in the system tray when presentation settings are enabled.

Figure 11-26   Adjusting presentation settings on a mobile computer

Providing these commonly accessed settings in one place means users do not need to search through the Control Panel to find mobile device settings.

Using Windows Sync Center

Keeping data synchronized between multiple devices can be a particularly difficult and frustrating task. When done manually, users must keep track of which files are modified on which device. They must then remember to move, copy, or delete the appropriate files from all of the devices that they use. Forgetting to do this can result in out-of-date information or loss of data. Even when this process is managed carefully, users often have to remember different path locations for their files on different computers. Clearly, this is a task that could benefit from automation.

Windows Sync Center is designed to enable multiple computers and mobile devices to keep important information synchronized. It supports any computer that is running Windows Vista, as well as mobile devices that are running the Windows Mobile platform. In this lesson, you'll learn how to set up and use Windows Sync Center.

MORE INFO **Using Windows Briefcase as an alternative**

An alternative method of keeping files synchronized between computers has been available on the Windows platform for years: Windows Briefcase. Briefcase is still functional in Windows Vista, but it lacks many of the capabilities of Windows Sync Center. For more information about creating and managing Briefcase, see the Windows Vista help file.

Accessing Windows Sync Center

Windows Sync Center can be launched in several different ways. Earlier in this lesson, you saw how users can monitor and access this feature using Windows Mobility Center. The program can also be launched by searching for it in Control Panel or in the Mobile PC section of Windows Sync Center. Figure 11-27 shows the main screen of this utility. The available tasks are listed on the left side of the interface.

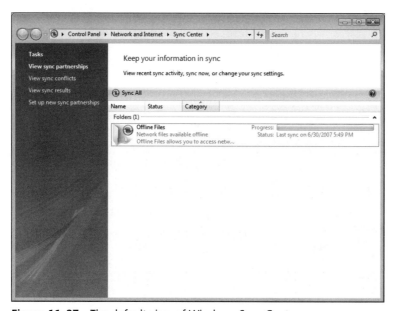

Figure 11-27 The default view of Windows Sync Center

Understanding Sync Partnerships

Windows Sync Center is configured and managed through sync partnerships, which are relationships between two devices that automatically enable consistency of data. To define a new partnership, click the Set Up New Sync Partnerships link (see Figure 11-28).

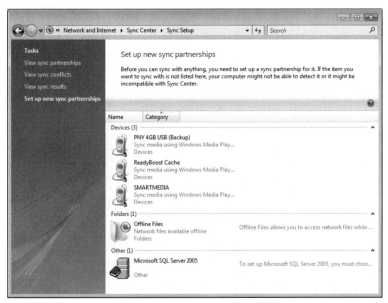

Figure 11-28   Creating new sync partnerships in Windows Sync Center

The different sections of the user interface show the devices that are currently connected to the computer. For example, if a device running the Windows Mobile operating system is connected and configured, it appears in the list. In addition, certain applications (such as Microsoft SQL Server 2005) provide their own components for working with Windows Sync Center. For more information about application-specific features, see the program's documentation.

There are two main types of sync partnerships. One-way sync partnerships enable copying files from a network location to a mobile device. They do not provide a method by which changes are sent back to the original source location. Two-way sync partnerships allow either computer to make changes to file contents and can make the corresponding changes automatically when the computers are connected.

Setting Up Offline Files

The most commonly used feature on a mobile computer is the ability to make network-based files available even when the computer is disconnected. For example, a small-business owner might store his or her work-related documents in a shared network folder. When the owner is disconnected from the network, he or she would still like to access and modify those documents. Additionally, users might not want to depend on the network to access their important documents. For example, if a network connection becomes unavailable, they would still like to be able to work. Finally, constantly accessing files across a slow connection can be a time-consuming process. Accessing a local copy is much more efficient in those cases. The Offline Files feature provides a solution to all of these problems.

You actually perform the process of setting up an offline files partnership independently of Windows Sync Center. To do this, use Windows Explorer to connect to a shared folder that is located on the network. Then right-click the folder and select Always Available Offline. Windows Vista automatically begins to make a local copy of the files in that location (see Figure 11-29). The icon then appears with a green synchronization icon when viewed in Windows Explorer.

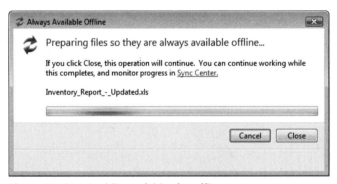

Figure 11-29   Enabling a folder for offline use

After you enable the Offline Files feature for a folder, you can access the Offline Files tab in the folder's Properties dialog box to view settings. The settings allow for enabling or disabling the Offline Files feature. A button for manually starting a synchronization option is included.

You can repeat the offline folders setup process on as many folders as you need. Whenever the computer is disconnected from the network, you are still able to access that folder, using the exact same path that you used to configure it. Files can then be moved, added, deleted, or changed.

Managing Offline Files

Although the majority of the work happens automatically when using Offline Files, there are several configuration options that can be useful. First, the files that are made available offline take up disk space on the local computer. To view details about the location of these files, open the Offline Files application by searching for it in the Start menu. Figure 11-30 shows the default display.

Figure 11-30   Viewing Offline Files settings

The General tab provides the option to enable or disable the Offline Files feature. It also enables opening Windows Sync Center to view details related to synchronization status. The View Your Offline Files button opens a special folder to view locally stored content. You can perform most file-related tasks by accessing the relevant network folders. Additionally, you can right-click a folder on which Offline Files is enabled and select Delete Offline Copy.

The Disk Usage tab provides important details related to how much space is being used by all of the offline files on the computer (see Figure 11-31). Clicking Change Limits enables you to specify the maximum amount of disk space this feature can use. Offline Files also uses temporary files to keep track of data that is stored on computers that are part of a sync partnership. You can reclaim this space by clicking Delete Temporary Files.

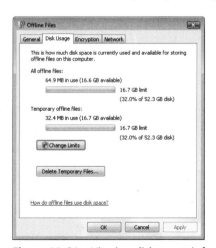

Figure 11-31   Viewing disk usage information for offline files

By default, offline files are stored in a format that is identical to the original files for performance reasons. You can, however, choose to encrypt the files so that they remain secure on the mobile computer. The Encrypt and Unencrypt options are available on the Encryption tab. Finally, the Network tab in the Offline Files dialog box enables users to configure the offline version of files to be used automatically when connecting over a slow connection.

Managing Synchronization Settings

You can use the View Sync Partnerships link in Windows Sync Center to view all of the folders configured for offline use. When clicked, the Sync All button automatically attempts to synchronize data stored in all folders that are available on the network. If a network connection is unavailable, then the contents of those folders are not synchronized.

Although manual synchronization is a useful option, it depends on users' ability to remember to perform the operation. Forgetting to synchronize files before disconnecting from the network can cause users to miss important file updates. To help reduce this problem, users can choose to schedule automatic synchronization settings for a partnership. To access these settings, right-click a sync partnership and select Schedule For Offline Files. The two main options enable synchronizing at a specific time or for basing synchronization on specific events (see Figure 11-32). Figure 11-33 shows the event options for synchronization.

Figure 11-32   Configuring synchronization schedule settings

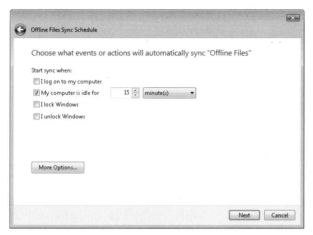

Figure 11-33 Enabling synchronization based on specific events

Verifying Synchronizations

To view details related to the status of file synchronizations, click the View Sync Results link. Figure 11-34 shows an example of the available events and status details.

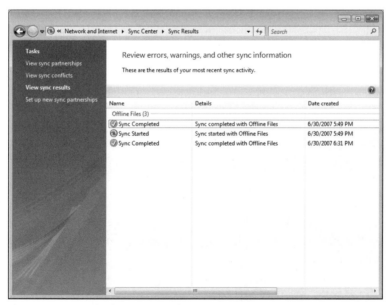

Figure 11-34 Viewing sync results

Although the majority of changes can be performed automatically, there are certain situations in which a conflict might occur. For example, if you choose to modify an offline file when you are disconnected from the network and another user modifies the online version of the file, Windows Sync Center is unable to determine which version of the file to keep. To make a decision, you can click the View Sync Conflicts link. Items that require manual decisions to be made are listed along with the possible options.

Overall, Windows Sync Center and Offline Files folder provide a great way to keep data on multiple computers and devices consistent and available over time.

Quick Check

1. What is the primary utility for working with Windows Mobile devices in Windows Vista?
2. How can you create a new Offline Folders sync partnership?

Quick Check Answers

1. The Windows Mobility Device Center replaces previous utilities, and it is the primary method of working with Windows Mobile devices.
2. To create a new sync partnership, right-click the network folder you want to include, and then select Always Available Offline.

Lesson Summary

- Mobile devices can be connected to Windows Vista using a variety of methods, including wireless networks, Bluetooth, infrared, and USB connections.
- The Windows Mobile Device Center is the primary method of working with devices that run the Windows Mobile operating system.
- Windows Mobility Center provides a central location for settings that notebook users commonly access.
- Windows Sync Center provides a way to manage and monitor sync partnerships between computers and mobile devices.
- The Offline Files feature enables users to synchronize data automatically that is stored in network locations.

Practice: Using Windows Sync Center

In this practice exercise, you use Windows Sync Center to set up a new sync partnership. To complete the steps, you must have access to two computers running Windows Vista that are configured to communicate on the same network.

▶ **Practice: Set Up Offline Files**

This exercise involves accessing a folder over the network and configuring it to be available offline. To complete these steps, you must have first created a shared folder on one of the two computers running Windows Vista. For more information about setting up shared folders, see Chapter 10. The shared folder should include at least a few editable files that are not important or that are copies. (Some of the files might be deleted or modified as part of the exercise.)

In the exercise, the computer with the shared folder contains the files that are to be synchronized with the other computer. All steps should be performed on the other computer.

1. From the Start menu, select Network.

2. Double-click the name of the computer that contains the shared folder.

3. Right-click the shared folder object and select Always Available Offline.

   Windows Vista automatically begins the process of copying files from the network location. The amount of time that this takes is based on the total number and size of the files located in the shared folder. When the process is finished, note that there is a small sync icon next to the folder icon.

4. After the initial sync process is complete, close any open windows.

5. Disconnect the computer from the network. If you are using a wired network, you can physically unplug the network cable. If you are using a wireless network, you can open the Network and Sharing Center and disable the appropriate connections.

6. From the Start menu, search for and start the Offline Files application.

7. Click the Disk Usage tab to view information about how much space the offline files are using.

8. Click the General tab, and then click View Your Offline Files.

   This opens a Windows Explorer window that enables you to access the files even though you are not connected to the network.

9. Double-click Computers, and then double-click the name of the computer on which the offline folders were created.

10. You can see the name of the shared folder that you chose to make available offline. Open the folder and verify that the contents of the folder are available. Make several test changes to the contents of the folder. For example, change the data that is stored in a file, delete a file, and move a file to another subfolder (if one exists). When finished, close all open windows and dialog boxes.

11. Open Windows Sync Center by searching for it in the Start menu. Note that the Offline Files item appears in the View Sync Partnerships task.

12. Reconnect the computer to the network by reversing the actions you performed in step 5.

13. Select the Offline Files item in Windows Sync Center, and then click Sync. Windows Vista automatically connects to the network location and attempts to synchronize the files. Wait for the process to finish before continuing to the next step.

14. Click the View Sync Results link to view a summary of the actions that were taken.

15. To remove the Offline Files settings, in the Start menu, click Network. Navigate to the shared folder you had selected for storing offline files. Right-click it and select Always Available Offline to disable offline files.

    Your local copies of the files are deleted, but the shared folder on the other computer still contains the most recent versions of those files.

16. When finished, close all open windows, including Windows Sync Center.

Lesson Review

You can use the following questions to test your knowledge of the information in Lesson 2, "Working with Mobile Devices." The questions are also available on the companion CD if you prefer to review them in electronic form.

NOTE Answers

Answers to these questions and explanations of why each answer choice is correct or incorrect are located in the "Answers" section at the end of the book.

1. You are assisting a small-business owner with configuring her computer running Windows Vista to synchronize data with her Windows Mobile PDA. She has connected the mobile device to her computer by using a USB connection. When she goes to Windows Sync Center, she does not see any options related to synchronizing with the device. Which of the following is most likely to resolve the issue?

    A. Installing a Bluetooth adapter in the computer

    B. Modifying the network settings of the computer running Windows Vista

    C. Downloading and installing the Windows Mobile Device Center

    D. Resolving sync conflicts in Windows Sync Center

2. You have set up an Offline Folders sync partnership, using Windows Sync Center. You plan to use this feature to synchronize files between two computers running Windows Vista. Which of the following options helps increase the security of this configuration?

    A. Changing the security permissions on the local offline files folder

    B. Encrypting the Offline Files data

    C. Configuring a one-way synchronization for the partnership

    D. Changing the security permissions on the shared network folder

    E. Enabling Windows Firewall

Chapter Review

To further practice and reinforce the skills you learned in this chapter, you can perform the following tasks:

- Review the chapter summary.
- Review the list of key terms introduced in this chapter.
- Complete the case scenarios. These scenarios set up real-world situations involving the topics of this chapter and ask you to create a solution.
- Complete the suggested practices.
- Take a practice test.

Chapter Summary

- Device Manager is the primary method for viewing and managing devices and device drivers.
- Windows Fax and Scan enables sending and receiving faxes, using an analog modem.
- Windows Vista can connect to local or remote network printers.
- The Windows Mobile Device Center and Windows Mobility Center provide ways to work with portable computers and devices.
- Windows Sync Center and Offline Files enable users to synchronize their data automatically with information stored on networked computers.

Key Terms

Do you know what these key terms mean? You can check your answers by looking up the terms in the glossary at the end of the book.

- Bluetooth
- Compact Flash card
- Infrared Data Association (IrDA)
- legacy hardware
- mobile device
- personal digital assistant (PDA)
- scanner
- Secure Digital (SD) card
- trusted device
- Windows Mobile (OS)

- Windows Mobile Device Center
- Windows Mobility Center
- Windows Sync Center

Case Scenarios

In the following case scenarios, you apply what you've learned about working with media devices and mobile devices. You can find answers to these questions in the "Answers" section at the end of this book.

Case Scenario 1: Managing Mobile Devices

You are a Consumer Support Technician assisting a user who has recently purchased a notebook computer that is running Windows Vista Home Premium. The customer also owns a PDA that is running the Windows Mobile operating system. She would like to share contacts and documents between the two devices. The customer also frequently uses her notebook computer to give presentations when at work.

1. Which utility should she use to enable Windows Vista to exchange information with the PDA?
2. How can the customer specify which data is transferred between her notebook computer and her PDA?
3. How can the customer most easily configure settings for giving presentations, using her notebook computer?

Case Scenario 2: Configuring Media Devices and Features

You are assisting a small-business owner whose organization has five computers running Windows Vista. Two of the computers are configured with scanners. The business frequently takes pictures of products to place on its Web site. The customer has recently purchased a USB wired printer for use by all of his employees, but he has not yet installed or configured it. One of the users would like to have the ability to send and receive faxes.

1. What steps should the customer take to configure the printer to meet his requirements?
2. What are the additional requirements for enabling users to send and receive faxes?

Suggested Practices

To help you successfully master the exam objectives presented in this chapter, complete the following tasks.

Managing Media and Mobile Devices

■ **Practice 1: Working with Scanners, Digital Cameras, and Faxes**   Obtain a digital camera device and use Windows Photo Gallery to import new pictures into the computer. Obtain a scanner and install it for use with Windows Vista. Scan in new documents by using Windows Photo Gallery and Windows Fax and Scan. Using a computer that has a fax-capable modem and access to an analog phone line, practice the entire process of scanning a paper document, creating a new fax message, receiving a fax message, and, finally, printing a hard copy of the document.

■ **Practice 2: Synchronizing Data**   Practice using the Windows Sync Center and Offline Files features to keep data consistent between multiple computers and devices. For example, enable Offline Files on a shared folder. Attempt to make different types of changes to see which ones are managed automatically during a synchronization operation. Generate a sync conflict by modifying the same file on two different computers while they are disconnected. Use Windows Sync Center to view and resolve conflicts.

If available, install and configure a Windows Mobile PDA device in Windows Vista. Download and install the Windows Mobile Device Center and use Windows Sync Center to set up a sync partnership for various types of data (such as contacts or documents). Make changes to the data on both devices and synchronize them automatically.

Take a Practice Test

The practice tests on this book's companion CD offer many options. For example, you can test yourself on just one exam objective, or you can test yourself on all of the 70-623 certification exam content. You can set up the test so that it closely simulates the experience of taking a certification exam, or you can set it up in study mode so that you can look at the correct answers and explanations after you answer each question.

MORE INFO   Practice tests

For details about all the practice test options available, see the "How to Use the Practice Tests" section in this book's introduction.

Chapter 12
Troubleshooting Windows Vista

As a Consumer Support Technician, one of the most valuable skills you can provide to customers is the ability to troubleshoot problems. When things go wrong, home and small-business users will likely turn to you for a resolution. These users depend on their computers and their operating systems to be stable, reliable, and ready to perform a wide variety of tasks. One of the most frustrating computer-related issues for users occurs when there is a problem on the system, and they don't know how to resolve it.

Although Microsoft designed Windows Vista with numerous reliability features, there is always the possibility of technical issues. In some cases, such as the failure of a hard disk or other physical computer component, the problem is not easily avoidable. In other cases, poorly written device drivers might cause system instability. There's always the ever-present threat of malware, such as viruses and spyware, that can also prevent users from getting tasks done.

One of the most important aspects of troubleshooting Windows Vista involves understanding the various tools and operating system features that are available to resolve problems. Ranging from help files to system utilities, each of these tools has its own purpose and benefits. The focus of this chapter is on troubleshooting a wide array of different problems that can occur on computers running Windows Vista. First you'll learn about tools and approaches that can be used to determine the root cause of particular types of problems. You'll also learn how to resolve them. Then, you'll learn how to troubleshoot a particularly common challenge, identifying and removing malware.

Exam objectives in this chapter:
- Configure Windows Vista Security.
    - Configure Windows Defender.
- Troubleshoot and repair Windows Vista.
    - Diagnose a specified issue.
    - Remove malware from a client system.

Lessons in this chapter:

Before You Begin

The explanations and exercises in this chapter are based on ways in which you can detect problems with computers running Windows Vista. Some of the potential resolution steps can make permanent system changes. It will be helpful to have a computer running Windows Vista that you do not rely on for general use to carry out some of these steps. Virtual machines provide another useful option for performing various troubleshooting steps.

Lesson 1: Diagnosing Issues in Windows Vista

The first step in troubleshooting is to attempt to diagnose the root cause of a problem. When working with complex operating systems such as Windows Vista, there are numerous potential sources for any given symptom. Technical professionals are often tempted to jump quickly into making changes without clearly determining the issue. The first step in successful troubleshooting is to diagnose the problem. After you have a good idea of the problem, you'll need to identify the most appropriate resolution method. You often have several different options of tools and operating system settings to modify, and your job as a Consumer Support Technician is to choose the combination that will resolve the problem most quickly and completely.

In this lesson, you'll learn about numerous ways in which you can diagnose and resolve common issues in Windows Vista. The best approach to solving common problems varies depending on the type of the problem. That makes it important to understand all of the different resources you have available. To that end, you'll learn about numerous tools and features that are included with Windows Vista as well as how and when they should be used.

After this lesson, you will be able to:
- Use Event Viewer to monitor items that are stored in the Windows event logs.
- Use the System Restore feature to revert the configuration of the computer to an earlier state.
- Run the Windows Memory Diagnostics Tool to test for problems related to physical memory.
- Troubleshoot startup problems by using Safe Mode and other boot options.
- Use advanced startup options such as boot logging and the Last Known Good Configuration.
- Use the Repair process to correct boot problems and other issues with the operating system.
- Use the Problem Reports and Solutions utility to find resolutions to application and system problems.

Estimated lesson time: 75 minutes

Monitoring Windows Event Logs

The Windows Vista operating system ships with dozens of features and applications. In addition, it provides one of the most flexible platforms for installing new hardware and applications. All of these components of the system might need to send messages and notifications to users. Examples include warnings, error messages, and status messages. In some cases, graphical programs might have their own user interface for displaying messages. Some programs can use system tray notifications to get attention. However, many components of Windows Vista do not have user interfaces at all.

The Windows event logs enable operating system features, drivers, applications, and services to record important information that users might need to review. Application developers can create their own event logs or write to existing ones.

Using the Event Viewer

It is not uncommon for the Windows operating system to have thousands of messages that might provide some useful types of information. Clearly, using a method such as text files would make it difficult for you to find information that is of interest. To help resolve this potential information overload, Windows Vista includes an updated Event Viewer console that enables users and support technicians to access and review relevant event-related information quickly.

NOTE   Using the Event Viewer console

For more information about using the Event Viewer console to detect performance-related problems, see Chapter 5, "Optimizing Windows Vista Performance."

You can launch Event Viewer through the Administrative Tools program group or by searching for it using the Start menu. Figure 12-1 shows an example of the information available in the Event Viewer user interface.

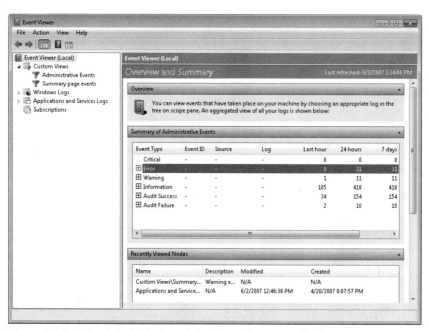

Figure 12-1   The default display of the Event Viewer application

Viewing Events by Event Types

One of the more challenging aspects of monitoring system-related messages such as those stored in the Windows event logs is filtering out unwanted details. Event Viewer automatically performs several different types of grouping. In the Administrative Events section under the Custom Views grouping, Event Viewer displays items based on the type and importance of the message. The default event types you see in all event logs include the following:

- **Critical** Serious system-related issues that could cause downtime or data loss. Review these items immediately.
- **Error** Application-related or service-related error reports.
- **Warning** Informational messages that can identify potential situations of which users should be aware.
- **Information** Messages that provide details but are not necessarily warning or error conditions.
- **Audit Success and Audit Failure** Events that are generated based on auditing options you enable.

You can obtain an overview of items in each category by expanding the relevant section. You can get more details about a specific item by double-clicking it in the list. Figure 12-2 shows a network-related warning. The General tab provides basic information about the event, including when it occurred and a text description. You can obtain additional information about the event by clicking the Details tab.

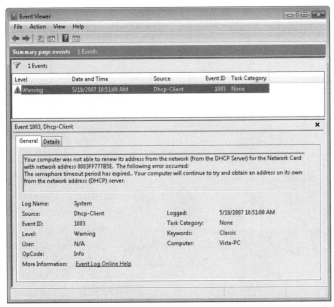

Figure 12-2 Viewing details for a warning message, using Windows Event Viewer

When troubleshooting a computer running Windows Vista, a good first step is to access Event Viewer and then examine a list of the critical and error-related events (if any). A good starting point for getting an overview of important events is to select the Administrative Events item in the Custom Views folder. You can easily identify a wide range of issues, from application problems to hardware-related configuration details, in this section.

Viewing Specific Event Logs

Another method by which Windows Vista categorizes event information is based on the actual event log itself. The primary types of Windows event logs include the following:

- Application
- Security
- Setup
- System

Numerous additional logs are available within the Applications And Services Logs section in Event Viewer. Figure 12-3 shows some examples. Each of these logs is specific to a particular application, service, or operating system function. For example, there are logs related to various diagnostics such as networking and disks.

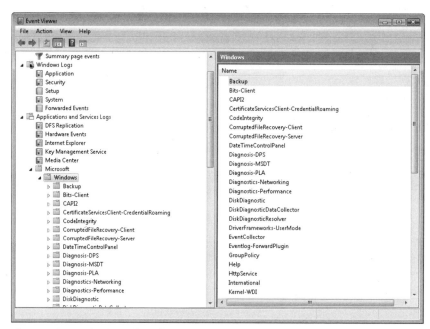

Figure 12-3   Viewing a list of available event logs

Overall, Event Viewer can provide a great starting point for detecting specific problems or errors that are occurring on the system. In fact, users should monitor these messages regularly, even if the system appears to be running properly.

Real World

Anil Desai

Over time, operating systems and applications have become increasingly complicated. Platforms such as Windows Vista include dozens of features and options that you can configure based on users' settings. There's always the potential for some of this functionality to stop working correctly. That's when the process of troubleshooting is required.

In the past, there have been frustrating technical problems in which I resorted to making seemingly random system changes in an attempt to resolve the issue. Although it's often tempting to attempt to make haphazard changes to a system and measure the effects, this is rarely the most efficient route to correcting a problem. In some cases, you might get lucky, but there's almost always a better approach.

Perhaps the single most important aspect of troubleshooting complex issues is developing a logical process. Some examples of steps include the following:

- **Identify the issue** Before beginning the troubleshooting process, it's important to have a clear picture of the issue you need to resolve. In some cases, the problem might be apparent. For example, if Windows Vista does not boot properly, the symptoms are clear. In other cases, the problems might be more difficult to detect. For example, a customer might mention that his or her computer has slowed down significantly over time. There are numerous potential causes of this problem.

- **Collect details about the problem** The most common cause of technical issues is change. When troubleshooting operating system issues, some important questions to ask revolve around when the problem started. Generally, you'll often find that the user has installed new software or hardware on the computer or changed the configuration of a feature. It's important to note that this isn't always the case; for example, hardware failures can crop up seemingly instantly and cause serious issues.

- **Develop a troubleshooting plan** Often, there are numerous ways in which you can attack a particular problem. Your goal should be to combine information about the likelihood of a solution and its difficulty. For example, it's quite likely that reinstalling the operating system from scratch will resolve many common issues. However, the time-consuming process of reinstalling and reconfiguring applications should make this option a last resort. Using malware scanners such as Windows Defender and other system utilities might be more likely to resolve the problem and require less effort.

> - **Verify the solution**   It probably goes without saying that you should retest to verify that the issues you identified in the first step have been resolved.
>
> When working in the role of a Consumer Support Technician, you might find yourself resolving problems for the customer. To prevent future problems, it's often worthwhile to educate the user about the source of the problem and how he or she might avoid the problem in the future. This can significantly help improve the end-user experience and reduce the amount of support you'll need to provide in the future.
>
> For experienced technical professionals, these steps might seem like common sense. However, many different approaches to solving problems are available. To use an analogy from the medical profession, an important directive is "First, do no harm." Some types of troubleshooting steps (such as wiping the hard disk and doing a complete reinstallation) might be excessive. They're roughly analogous to curing the disease by killing the patient. The overall key is to remember to follow an organized process when troubleshooting simple and complex problems and to use the most efficient (and least harmful) method of resolution.

Using System Restore

The most common sources of system-related issues are stored in startup and configuration files and in the Windows Registry. Often, when problems occur, it is useful to revert these files to their previous state. For example, if the installation of a new hardware device causes system instability, the first step might be to try uninstalling the program. What if the uninstall operation is unsuccessful? It would be useful to be able to roll back the system configuration to a previous point in time.

Windows Vista provides an automatic method of backing up important system configuration data. The feature is called System Restore. The System Restore process is enabled by default within Windows Vista. It works by periodically creating new restore points on the system. By default, Windows Vista automatically creates restore points at specific times. For example, Windows Vista automatically creates a new restore point whenever you install new programs or device drivers. Because these types of operations are potentially risky from a system stability standpoint, automatically created restore points are created before the changes are made. You can also manually create System Restore points in Windows Vista, as described in the next section. In some cases, you might want to do this before making an operating system configuration change or performing other types of actions that you might need to roll back.

Although you can use restore points to roll back system configuration changes such as operating system settings and installed applications, they do not affect users' data files (such as documents, photos, music, and videos). This makes the rollback process a safe and easy way to recover from many types of common problems caused by configuration changes or the installation of new drivers or software.

Configuring System Protection

The settings that define how and when restore points are created are called System Protection. You can configure these settings by clicking System Protection (which is described in the next section) in the System window of Control Panel. You can access these settings from the Start menu by right-clicking Computer and selecting Properties. Then, click System Protection in the Tasks section. Figure 12-4 shows the options that are available.

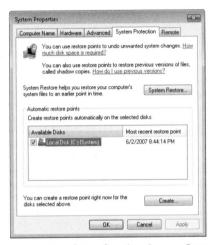

Figure 12-4   Configuring System Protection settings

The Automatic Restore Points section of the user interface specifies for which disks Windows Vista will create the system restore point. It is highly recommended that you configure Windows Vista to create restore points for at least the operating system volume. The utility also shows the date and time of the most recently created restore point.

You can also manually create restore points by clicking Create. You are prompted to provide a description of the restore point so that you can easily identify it later. You usually want to specify the purpose of creating the restore point (for example, "Before installing new scanner drivers").

Restoring System Settings

The System Restore Wizard is designed for reverting the configuration of Windows Vista to an earlier point in time. You can launch the program by searching for System Restore in the Start menu. Figure 12-5 shows the Restore System Files And Settings page of the System Restore Wizard.

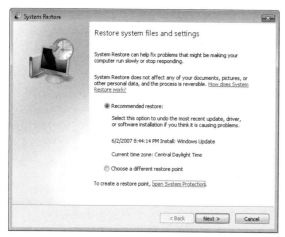

Figure 12-5 Using the System Restore Wizard

The default option is to choose to restore from the most recent restore point. The page shows the date and time at which the restore point was created, along with a description. In some cases, you might want to revert to an earlier restore point. For example, you might have made numerous sets of changes to the system, and reverting to the newest restore point might not resolve the problem. Figure 12-6 shows the options that are available when choosing to revert to an earlier configuration.

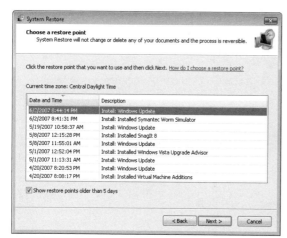

Figure 12-6 Choosing a specific restore point using the System Restore Wizard

After you select the appropriate restore point, you can click Finish to begin the restore process. Because System Restore must replace important system files, the computer is automatically restarted to complete the operation. Overall, the System Restore process provides a quick and easy method of resolving common configuration and installation problems.

Performing Windows Memory Diagnostics

Modern operating systems such as Windows Vista rely heavily on the use of system memory to speed up common operations. Random access memory (RAM) chips are a very reliable component of the computer's architecture. Because they have no moving parts, they're not as likely to fail as other components such as fans or hard disks. However, memory-related issues can cause a variety of problems on the computer. Symptoms can range from application crashes to a complete shutdown or restart of the operating system. The results could include data loss and reduced system reliability.

During normal operations, Windows Vista attempts to detect memory-related errors. For example, if an application has crashed or an operating system feature stops working correctly, the detection process might determine that physical memory is a potential cause of the problem. In this case, Windows Vista displays a notification icon in the system tray, recommending that the user run a diagnostic test.

Starting the Memory Diagnostics Tool

The Memory Diagnostics Tool is designed to test the physical memory installed in the computer. Because the analysis process requires direct access to memory hardware, you must run this utility before you start the operating system. There are two main ways to instruct the system to perform a memory diagnostic test. The first is to choose this option during the boot process (see Figure 12-7). To access boot options, press F8 prior to the system startup process. When the boot menu appears, the user can select the appropriate startup menu option to launch the utility. To access that option, press the Tab key, select Windows Memory Diagnostic, and press Enter. This method is most appropriate when the operating system is not running (or will not boot), and you suspect that the root cause of the issue is the physical memory in the system.

In other cases, you might currently be running Windows Vista and either receive a memory-related alert or want to perform a memory diagnostic. In this case, you can launch the Memory Diagnostics Tool by using a shortcut in the Administrative Tools program group or by searching for it using the Start menu. Figure 12-8 shows the available options.

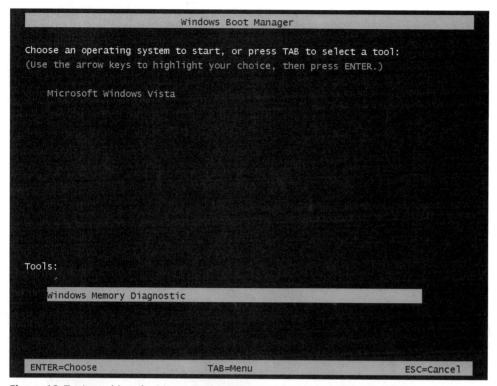

Figure 12-7   Launching the Memory Diagnostics Tool during system startup

Figure 12-8   Scheduling the Memory Diagnostics Tool to run during the next reboot

Both options have the same effect: they instruct Windows Vista to boot into the Memory Diagnostics Tool automatically when the system restarts. The first option automatically performs a restart immediately, whereas the second option specifies that the diagnostics should run whenever the computer is restarted.

Performing Memory Diagnostic Tests

Regardless of the method used to launch the Memory Diagnostics Tool, the system boots to a text-based user interface. A standard memory test begins to run automatically, as shown in Figure 12-9. Two test passes are executed, each of which runs many different operations to verify that the system's physical memory is working properly. For the majority of cases, the default test options are appropriate.

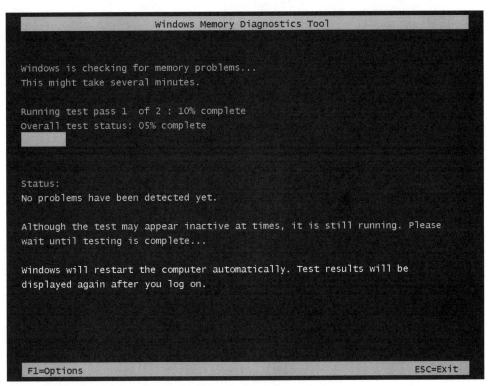

Figure 12-9   Using the Windows Memory Diagnostics Tool

If you want to run specific tests or change diagnostic settings, you can press F1 to access memory diagnostics options (see Figure 12-10). Use the arrow keys to make settings changes within a section and the Tab key to move between the sections.

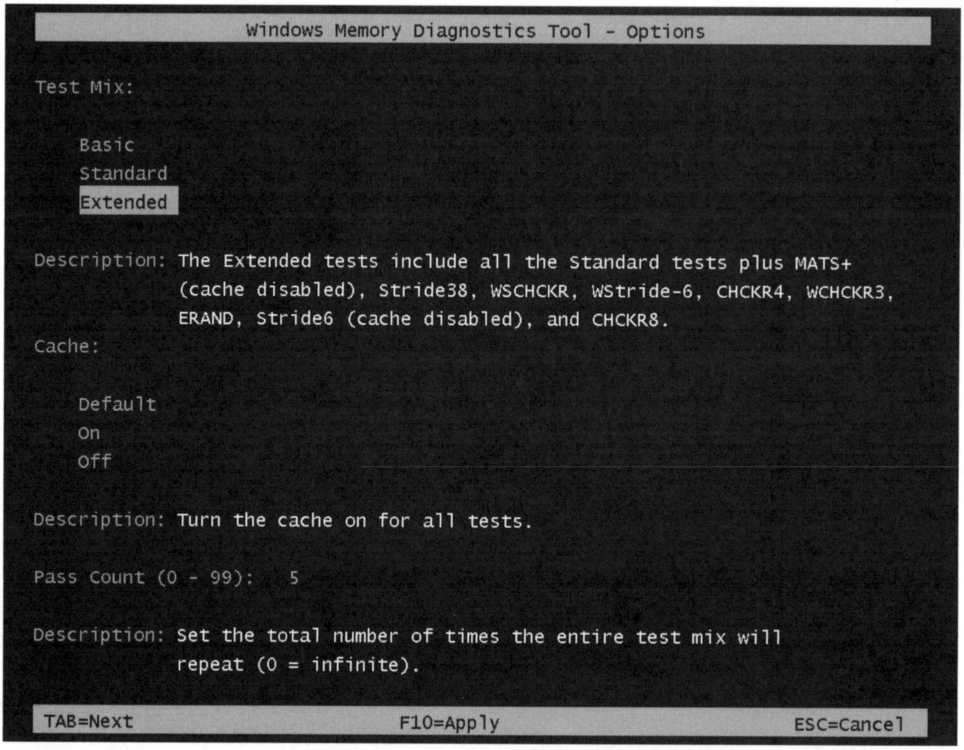

```
                    Windows Memory Diagnostics Tool - Options

 Test Mix:

    Basic
    Standard
    Extended

 Description: The Extended tests include all the Standard tests plus MATS+
              (cache disabled), Stride38, WSCHCKR, WStride-6, CHCKR4, WCHCKR3,
              ERAND, Stride6 (cache disabled), and CHCKR8.
 Cache:

    Default
    On
    Off


 Description: Turn the cache on for all tests.


 Pass Count (0 - 99):   5


 Description: Set the total number of times the entire test mix will
              repeat (0 = infinite).


 TAB=Next                        F10=Apply                        ESC=Cancel
```

Figure 12-10 Changing Windows Memory Diagnostics options

The available options include the following:

- **Test Mix (Basic, Standard, or Extended)**   These settings control which tests the tool runs to analyze physical memory. The Basic test runs more quickly than the default (Standard) option, and the Extended test takes more time but performs a more rigorous diagnostic.

- **Cache**   The Windows Memory Diagnostics Tool can use memory caching options to improve performance. Various operations in the selected test mix might automatically enable or disable cache settings. Therefore, the Default setting enables each test to use its recommended settings. You can also choose to enable or disable the cache for all tests, regardless of the default settings.

- **Pass Count**   The final option specifies how many test passes the Windows Memory Diagnostic process executes. Because memory-related problems can be intermittent (that is, they might occur relatively rarely), you might want to configure the tests to run many times to be reasonably sure that the system memory is performing adequately. The available values are 0 to 99. The value of 0 specifies that the memory test runs continuously until you manually interrupt the process.

When you have chosen the options that you wish to use, press F10 to apply the settings and start running the tests.

Viewing Memory Diagnostics Results

You can view the progress of the memory test as it is running by using the text-based user interface. The Status section reports any errors the tool finds. The Memory Diagnostics Tool automatically restarts the system as soon as it completes testing. The next time a user logs on to Windows Vista, a notification is displayed providing the results of the last memory diagnostic test (see Figure 12-11).

Figure 12-11   Viewing the results of a successful Memory Diagnostics test

If the system did detect a problem, the Memory Diagnostics Tool might provide additional details. In general, any errors that are indicated will be based on a physical hardware problem. To resolve the issues, users should contact their computer manufacturers or technical support personnel for information on how to resolve the issue.

Troubleshooting Startup Problems

When the Windows Vista operating system encounters problems during the startup process, the symptoms are usually apparent. The system might not display a startup screen at all, or a startup screen is shown, but the computer does not boot to a logon screen or the Windows desktop. In some cases, the computer might spontaneously reboot during the startup operation. Regardless of the symptoms, the goal is to enable Windows Vista to boot normally again.

The most frustrating part of troubleshooting startup problems is that there is generally no available operating system with which to interact. Without the Windows Vista user interface, it's not possible to launch standard graphical programs. To assist in troubleshooting these problems, Windows Vista includes numerous startup modes that you can use to try to regain access to the system. Users can access the Advanced Boot Options menu during the startup process by pressing F8. Figure 12-12 shows the available options.

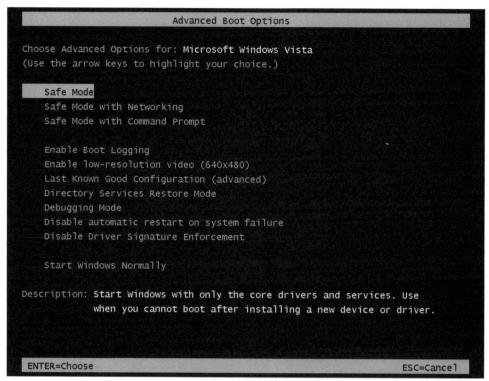

Figure 12-12 Viewing Advanced Boot Options for Windows Vista

Each option has its own particular purpose for resolving a potential problem. Table 12-1 provides a listing of each option and its associated description.

Table 12-1 Advanced Boot Options for Windows Vista

Advanced Boot Option	Description
Safe Mode	Starts Windows with only the core drivers and services. Use when you cannot boot after installing a new device or driver.
Safe Mode With Networking	Starts Windows with core drivers, plus networking support.
Safe Mode With Command Prompt	Starts Windows with core drivers and launches the command prompt.
Enable Boot Logging	Creates Ntbtlog.txt, which lists all drivers that load during startup, including the last file to load before a failure.
Enable Low-Resolution Video (640x480)	Sets or resets the display resolution. Starts Windows in low-resolution display mode (640x480).
Last Known Good Configuration (Advanced)	Starts Windows, using settings from last successful boot attempt.

Table 12-1   Advanced Boot Options for Windows Vista

Advanced Boot Option	Description
Directory Services Restore Mode	Starts Windows in Directory Services Repair Mode (for Windows domain controllers only).
Debugging Mode	Enables Windows kernel debugger.
Disable Automatic Restart On System Failure	Prevents Windows from automatically rebooting after a crash.
Disable Driver Signature Enforcement	Allows drivers containing improper signatures to be loaded.
Start Windows Normally	Starts Windows with its regular settings.

Exam Tip   When taking Exam 70-623, keep in mind that the best troubleshooting options are usually those that are quick and easy to perform and that have the least negative impact on the system. When choosing startup options, keep in mind that features such as Safe Mode are designed for performing troubleshooting operations and for avoiding more time-consuming operations such as reinstalling the operating system.

The descriptions provide an overview of the type of startup option. In this section, you'll learn how you can use the various options to troubleshoot common problems.

Understanding Safe Mode

The most common types of problems that can prevent Windows Vista from starting up normally include the installation of new device drivers or system-related applications or services. If these programs are incorrectly configured or are of poor quality, they can cause the startup process to fail entirely. To help troubleshoot these problems, Windows Vista includes a Safe Mode feature.

When booted in Safe Mode, the operating system startup process loads only a minimal set of device drivers and settings. It also enables various other troubleshooting features. For example, Figure 12-13 shows how the startup process displays a list of drivers and Windows-related files that are automatically loaded.

The goal of Safe Mode is to prevent device drivers and other software from interfering with the startup process. For example, because only basic display adapter drivers are loaded, you can use Safe Mode to avoid common problems caused by video drivers. There is, however, an associated disadvantage: some operating system features and functionality are unavailable in Safe Mode. The most noticeable difference is that the screen resolution and color depth are usually set to low values, and the system might appear to be operating much more slowly than normal. Figure 12-14 shows an example of logging on to Windows Vista while running in Safe Mode. Note that the words "Safe Mode" are displayed in the corners of the screen, and then a Windows Help And Support window automatically opens.

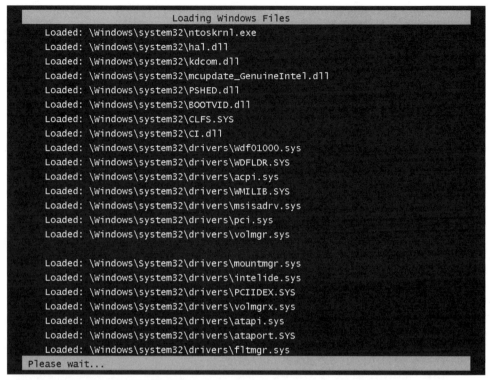

Figure 12-13 Viewing a list of device drivers when performing a Safe Mode startup

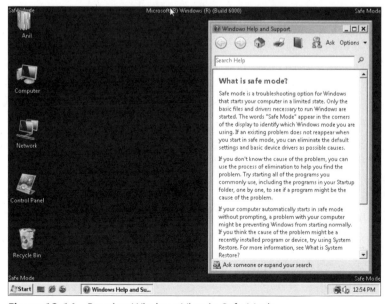

Figure 12-14 Running Windows Vista in Safe Mode

In addition to the standard Safe Mode boot options, users can choose from related options. Safe Mode with Networking loads a minimal set of drivers but also loads network drivers. This option is helpful because it allows troubleshooters to connect to the Internet to obtain updated drivers or more information about the problem. The Safe Mode with Command Prompt option automatically launches the command window for performing text-based operations. This option is most appropriate when system problems are preventing Windows Explorer from properly starting.

Safe Mode is intended to be a temporary startup option designed to perform troubleshooting. Common operations might include uninstalling new software or removing or disabling hardware devices. After the troubleshooting process completes, users should choose to restart the computer. On the next boot operation, Windows Vista automatically attempts to perform a normal boot.

Using Windows Error Recovery

Startup problems can occur due to a variety of different problems on the system. In some cases, the addition of new hardware or faulty device drivers might prevent the computer from starting up normally. In other cases, a hardware failure or corruption of boot-related files might have occurred. It's also possible that there was a temporary problem, such as a power failure.

Windows Vista is able to detect startup-related failures automatically. If the operating system failed to boot successfully during its last attempt, the boot manager automatically displays the Windows Error Recovery screen (see Figure 12-15).

This screen informs the user that there was a potential problem with startup and that there might be a hardware-related error. The available boot options include the following:

- Safe Mode
- Safe Mode With Networking
- Safe Mode With Command Prompt
- Last Known Good Configuration (Advanced)
- Start Windows Normally

Although it is certainly possible that a hardware-related issue might require restarting the computer by using the installation disc or by using one of the other options, it is also possible that a simple power failure caused the screen to appear. Therefore, it is generally a good idea to try using the Start Windows Normally option unless the problem occurs repeatedly.

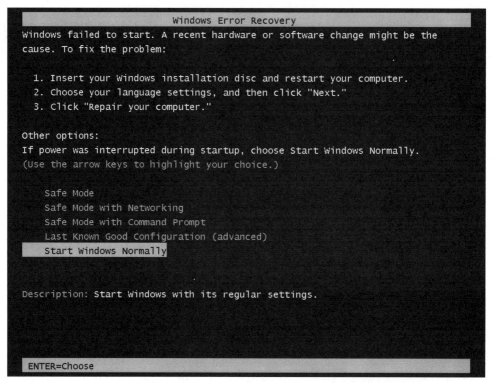

Figure 12-15   Using the Windows Error Recovery screen during the boot process

Using Boot Logging

One potentially challenging aspect of troubleshooting startup problems is identifying the source of the startup problem. Windows Vista loads dozens of drivers and services during a typical startup process, but which one is causing the problem? The purpose of the Boot Logging startup option is to instruct Windows Vista to create a text file automatically that contains a list of the operations it performs during the boot process. To enable boot logging, during the startup process, from the Advanced Boot Options menu, select Enable Boot Logging. Generally, the last item in the list is the source of the startup problem.

The log file itself is a text file named Ntbtlog.txt located within the Windows folder (usually C:\Windows), which you can open using Notepad or command-line utilities such as Type. Figure 12-16 shows an example of the information that you can find in the file.

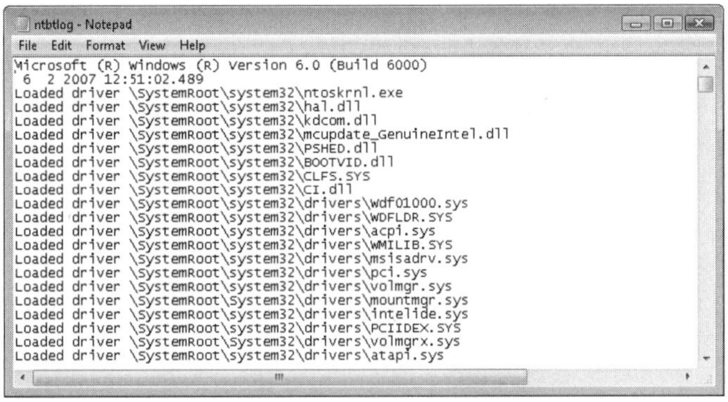

Figure 12-16 Viewing the contents of the Ntbtlog.txt file

Using the Last Known Good Configuration

Sometimes, when performing troubleshooting operations, you might find yourself wishing for a way to revert the system configuration automatically to a previous state. That's the purpose of the Last Known Good Configuration startup option on the Windows Error Recovery screen. When Windows Vista successfully completes a boot operation, it makes a backup of the important startup-related files and settings. If a problem occurs during the startup process, the system can use the previous "known good" set of startup files.

Although this option can simplify troubleshooting, there is a potential drawback to consider: if new applications were installed or system settings were recently modified, it's likely that other system problems might occur. For example, if a newly installed application required system Registry changes to occur, it might not run properly when reverted to an older configuration. In this case, it might be necessary to reinstall the program. Because of these potential issues, the Last Known Good Configuration boot option is considered an advanced process and is not recommended as an initial troubleshooting step.

Configuring Startup Options with MSConfig

In some cases, the Windows operating system might boot properly, but you want to change the way in which the system starts up the next time you restart it. You can use the System Configuration (MSConfig) utility to specify various startup options. Figure 12-17 shows the General tab of the System Configuration dialog box.

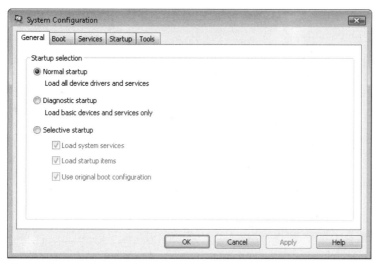

Figure 12-17 Viewing the General tab of the System Configuration dialog box

The Startup Selection options include the ability to specify Normal Startup (the default option) or to perform a Diagnostic Startup. The latter option specifies that the computer should run with a minimal set of devices and services. It is useful when trying to resolve issues that might have been caused by the installation of new software or devices to the system. The last option, Selective Startup, offers the ability to enable or disable the following boot operations:

- Load System Services
- Load Startup Items
- Use Original Boot Configuration

When you select modified startup options, Windows Vista informs the user of this during the next boot of the computer. Users can then return to the MSConfig utility to make changes to the computer's startup configuration. Generally, you should use these settings only when troubleshooting a specific problem. It is not recommended that computers run using modified startup operations for general use because certain operating system features and applications might fail to work properly.

NOTE Troubleshooting startup problems

For more information about using MSConfig to troubleshoot issues with startup programs and services, see Chapter 5.

In addition to the settings on the General tab, the System Configuration dialog box includes a set of startup options on the Boot tab (see Figure 12-18). These options enable users to specify which mode Windows Vista should use when they restart the system. For example, you can select the Safe Boot check box to boot the system into Safe Mode automatically without requiring input from the user.

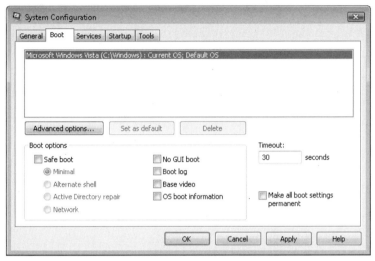

Figure 12-18   The Boot tab of the System Configuration utility

Repairing Windows Vista

Thus far, the content of this lesson has focused on troubleshooting common operating system problems by using a variety of tools and techniques. In some cases, however, it's possible that none of these methods works. For example, if critical system files have been deleted or there has been severe file system corruption, these issues might not be easily resolvable. If there's an issue related to startup configuration, you might not be able to access the startup menu to perform further troubleshooting.

One potential resolution is for you to reinstall the entire operating system. Although this strategy will most likely work (except in the case of physical hardware failures), it can lead to a lot of additional effort. For example, you will need to reinstall all applications, add all drivers and system updates, and reset operating system configuration options. Fortunately, there's a better option that can resolve many common issues.

Accessing System Repair Options

You can access the Windows Vista Repair options by booting the computer, using the Windows Vista installation media. Home and small-business users usually receive this media from either their computer manufacturer (if the operating system came preinstalled) or with their retail purchase of the product. Note that, in some cases, users might need to change the boot preference order in their system basic input/output system (BIOS) or press a specific key during the system startup process to boot from the installation media.

The initial screen that loads provides options related to installing Windows Vista. If you wish to start a reinstallation of the operating system, you can do so using the steps described in Chapter 2, "Installing Windows Vista." To access repair-related options, click Repair Your Computer. The System Recovery Options dialog box is displayed (see Figure 12-19). The program attempts to locate automatically any existing Windows Vista installations on the local computer.

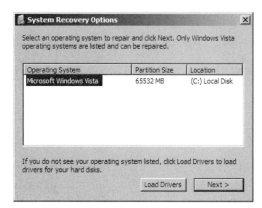

Figure 12-19   Viewing the System Recovery Options dialog box

If no Windows Vista installations can be found, there are two likely causes. The first is that you must load additional drivers for the storage controller or hardware. You can do so by using the Load Drivers command. The other possibility is that the hard disk itself has failed or that the data has been severely corrupted and cannot be read. In these situations, it is likely that you first need to resolve the hardware-related issue and then reinstall Windows Vista.

If the operating system does appear in the list, select it and click Next to access additional troubleshooting and repair options. The next dialog box displays a list of available troubleshooting commands and options (see Figure 12-20).

The System Restore and Windows Memory Diagnostic Tool options were described earlier in this lesson. The Windows Complete PC restore functionality is covered in Chapter 13, "Protecting Data and Repairing Windows Vista." The two main troubleshooting options are Startup Repair and Command Prompt.

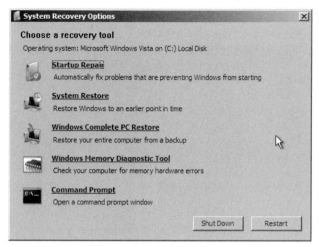

Figure 12-20   Viewing troubleshooting options in the System Recovery utility

Using Startup Repair

There are several common causes of startup-related issues for Windows Vista. Some of the most common ones involve the deletion of critical boot-related files or improperly configured startup options. The Startup Repair operation can automatically detect and repair these common configuration issues.

The actual tests performed include the following:

- Check for updates
- System disk test
- Disk failure diagnosis
- Disk metadata test
- Target OS test
- Volume content check
- Boot manager diagnosis
- System boot log diagnosis
- Event log diagnosis
- Internal state check
- Boot status test

The most common types of issues, if encountered, can generally be repaired automatically without any additional user input. Figure 12-21 shows an example of the results displayed when no configuration problems are detected.

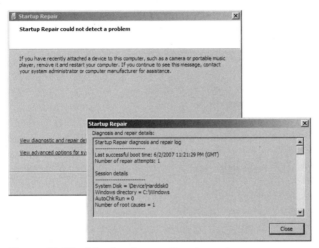

Figure 12-21   Viewing Startup Repair results

Using the Command Prompt

The Repair installation process does not include a full operating system, but it does include a basic command prompt feature that enables you to perform a variety of operations. Examples of commands include the ability to list, move, copy, or rename files. Additionally, it is also possible to use the DiskPart utility to create and manage disk partitions (see Figure 12-22) and the bcdedit command to modify boot-related settings. Another useful command is the chkdsk utility, which you can use to detect file system errors on the computer.

MORE INFO   The Windows Recovery Console

Earlier versions of the Windows platform (including Microsoft Windows 2000 Professional and Windows XP) include a Recovery Console option. This feature enables users to access a command prompt for performing various troubleshooting options. These features are now available to you by using the Repair option when booting from the Windows Vista installation media.

For more information about the specific commands that are available, see the Command-line reference for IT Pros page on the Windows Vista Web site at *http://windowshelp.microsoft.com /Windows/en-US/Help/4e7cd306-e9b0-4296-9528-9121d4f9bd111033.mspx*.

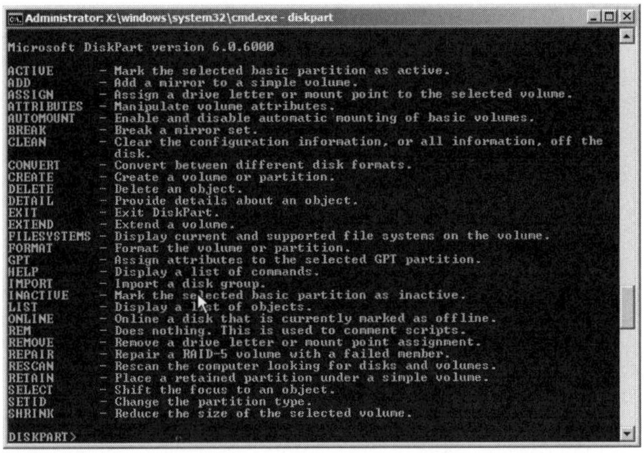

Figure 12-22 Viewing available commands for the DiskPart utility at the command prompt

Using Other Diagnostic and Troubleshooting Tools

In addition to the troubleshooting tools that you've learned about in this lesson, there are some other utilities in Windows Vista that can help in diagnosing and resolving common errors. In this section, you'll learn how to use them.

Registry Editor (RegEdit)

The Windows Registry is a centralized database that is used to store a wide variety of information related to the configuration of the operating system and the applications and services it supports. Examples of information stored in the Windows Registry include the following:

- Hardware details
- Operating system configuration details
- Software registration information
- User-specific settings

In most cases, users should try to use the built-in tools and features of Windows Vista to manage various system settings. For example, when removing software, it is safest to use the uninstall features that are available in Control Panel. When making changes to programs such as Microsoft Internet Explorer 7, it is best to use the configuration Properties dialog boxes.

Sometimes, you will need to make specific configuration changes for which there is no user interface or graphical method for changing settings. In these cases, it might be necessary to make changes directly to Registry values. You can launch the Windows Registry Editor (RegEdit) program by clicking regedit in the Start menu. Figure 12-23 provides a view of the Registry Editor interface.

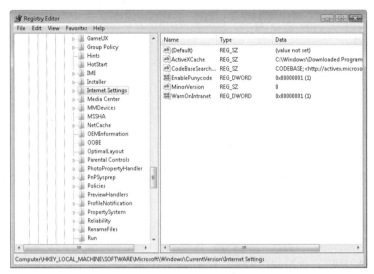

Figure 12-23 Viewing Registry settings by using the Registry Editor

A typical Windows Registry includes thousands of keys and values, organized based on the types of settings. For example, there are sections of the Registry that are computer-specific and others that are user-specific. You can change values by double-clicking an item and entering the new value. It is highly recommended that you make a backup copy of the Registry before making any changes because some types of changes might prevent the system from properly booting. For more information about backing up the Registry, see the topic entitled "Back up the Registry" in the Windows Vista Help and Support documentation.

Exam Tip Although it is a good idea to be familiar with the RegEdit utility and its purpose, you generally won't have to know any specific Registry settings when taking Exam 70-623. It is possible that, as a Consumer Support Technician, you might need to make manual Registry changes based on instructions from application or hardware vendors.

Problem Reports and Solutions

When applications and operating system features fail to function properly, they often result in an error message. Usually, users cannot do much to resolve the problem, other than to search manually for an update that might resolve the issue. Often, that process can be tedious because it might involve going to several different Web sites to find the correct update (assuming that one exists).

Microsoft included Problem Reports and Solutions as part of the Windows Vista operating system to make this process easier. You can access this feature through Control Panel by first clicking System And Maintenance. There are several useful aspects of automated problem reports. The first is error reporting itself. You can configure this feature to send error reports automatically to Microsoft for analysis. This can help identify which applications, services, features, or drivers are causing the most system errors. Ideally, Microsoft could then notify the program vendor to create relevant updates.

The other major benefit is that the Problem Reports and Solutions utility can automatically search for potential problem resolutions. For example, if an unstable driver is causing reliability issues, the utility can provide a direct link to a location from which you can obtain an updated driver. This method can save a significant amount of time for end users and can help to resolve common problems.

Figure 12-24 shows the main interface of the Problem Reports and Solutions Control Panel item. The default display provides information related to any known solutions for existing problems as well as to reports of other issues.

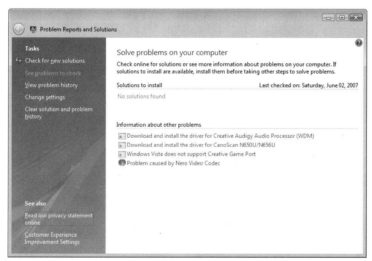

Figure 12-24 Using the Problem Reports and Solutions Control Panel utility

The Tasks pane provides several useful features for managing problem reports. The first item is to check for new solutions. This process automatically uploads relevant problem information to Microsoft and downloads any updates that might resolve those issues (see Figure 12-25). The See Problems To Check link provides a list of existing error reports that will be verified.

Figure 12-25 Checking for new solutions with the Problem Reports and Solutions utility

To view a list of problems that have been collected and reported in Windows Vista, click View Problem History. Figure 12-26 provides an example of the types of information that are available.

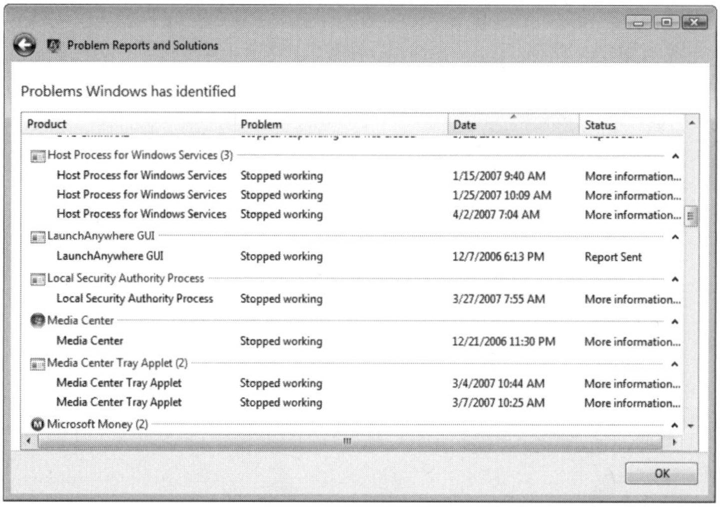

Figure 12-26 Viewing a problem history in the Problem Reports and Solutions utility

You can get more information about a particular problem by right-clicking it and selecting View Problem Details. Figure 12-27 provides an example of the details that are available.

Finally, it is possible to change the default settings to determine how and when the computer sends problem reports to Microsoft. Figure 12-28 shows some of the available options. In some cases, such as on software developers' test computers, it might be advisable to disable error reporting (at least for particular programs). In such cases, a large number of automatic error reports might decrease system performance.

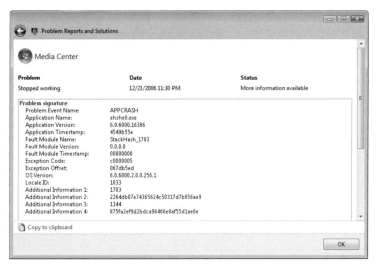

Figure 12-27   Viewing details about a particular Windows problem item

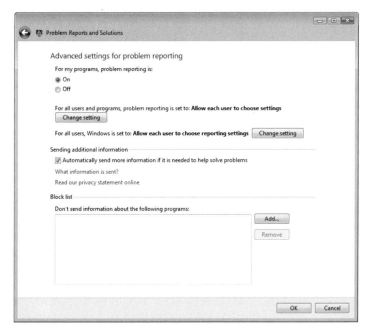

Figure 12-28   Viewing Problem Reports and Solutions advanced settings

The final task in the Problem Solutions and Reports utility enables you to clear the entire solution and problem history. This can be a quick way to remove all older items from the list and start collecting new problem and solution information.

NOTE Using the Performance and Reliability Monitor

To get an overall idea of system reliability, you can use the Reliability Monitor utility. Chapter 5 provides details related to working with this tool. When troubleshooting, it's useful to consult this utility to get an idea of when problems first started occurring and to collect clues about the types of changes that have occurred on the system.

Quick Check

1. How does choosing Safe Mode affect the Windows Vista startup process?
2. What are two ways in which you can launch the System Restore utility?

Quick Check Answers

1. When running in Safe Mode, Windows loads only a minimal set of device drivers and operating system services.
2. You can launch System Restore from within Windows Vista or by choosing the Repair option when booting from the Windows Vista installation media.

Practice: Diagnosing and Troubleshooting Windows Vista Issues

In these practice exercises, you use various diagnostic and troubleshooting features of Windows Vista to resolve simulated problems.

▶ **Practice 1: Using System Restore**

In this practice exercise, you create a new restore point on a computer running Windows Vista. You then make a simple operating system change and use the System Restore feature to revert the computer to its original state.

1. Log on to Windows Vista.
2. On the Start menu, right-click Computer and select Properties.
3. In the Tasks pane of the System Properties window, click System Protection.
4. In the Automatic Restore Points section of the System Properties dialog box, verify that the check box is selected for the hard disk that contains the Windows Vista operating system. (The System Properties dialog box displays [System] after this hard disk in the Available Disks list.)
5. Click Create to create a new restore point manually.
6. Type the description **Windows Vista System Restore Test**, and then click Create. Wait until the restore point has been created before moving to the next step.
7. Click OK to close the System Protection message box, and then click OK again to close the System Properties dialog box.

8. Change the Windows desktop background to use a different wallpaper than the current setting. (If you need more information about completing this step, see Chapter 3, "Configuring and Customizing the Windows Vista Desktop.")

9. Open the System Restore Wizard from the Start menu. On the Restore System Files And Settings page, click Next.

10. On the Choose A Restore Point page, select the manual restore point that has the description of Windows Vista System Restore Test, and then click Next.

11. Verify the information on the Confirm Your Restore Point page, and then click Finish to start the restore process. Click Yes when asked to confirm the process.

12. After Windows Vista restarts, log on to the computer and verify that the system settings have changed so that the original desktop wallpaper is now being used for the system.

13. When finished, log off Windows Vista.

▶ **Practice 2: Using Safe Mode**

In this practice exercise, you boot the computer to Safe Mode to view the effects this has on system settings. These steps do not make any permanent changes to the system, although it is possible that desktop icons will be rearranged.

1. If the computer is currently running, choose to restart it. If it is not running, power on the computer.

2. During the startup process, press the F8 key to access the Advanced Boot Options menu.

3. Select the Safe Mode option, and then press Enter to start the boot process.

4. Note the differences in the boot process, including the fact that Windows Vista now displays a list of device drivers as it loads them.

5. Verify that the words "Safe Mode" appear in the corners of the display and that you see the Windows Help and Support Center window. Also, note that the display is using lower resolution and color depth than your standard display settings.

6. Launch Internet Explorer 7 and attempt to connect to a Web site. Note that this operation fails because Windows Vista did not load network support.

7. When finished, reboot the computer and verify that it performs a normal startup.

▶ **Practice 3: Performing a Repair Operation**

In this practice exercise, you use the Windows Vista Repair option to see how you can resolve startup problems. Although it is assumed that the computer currently does not have any startup problems, the steps that you perform are identical to those you should perform when troubleshooting a real startup failure problem. You need the Windows Vista installation media (most commonly on DVD-ROM) to complete these steps:

1. Place the Windows Vista installation media into the appropriate drive and either restart or power on the computer.

2. If necessary, change the boot options in the system's BIOS settings to boot from the DVD-ROM device. The detailed steps for doing this should be available in your system documentation.

3. When prompted, press a key to boot from the Windows Vista installation media. You should see a progress bar and the message "Windows is loading files."

4. At the Install Windows step, verify that the appropriate language and location settings are chosen, and then click Next.

5. Click Repair Your Computer to start the Repair process.

6. On the System Recovery Options screen, select the Windows Vista installation, and then click Next. Note that, on some systems, you might need to use the Load Drivers command to install storage drivers.

7. Make a note of the various recovery options that are available. Click the Startup Repair link to start the automatic boot troubleshooting process.

8. In the Results screen, click View Diagnostic And Repair Details to view details and which tests were performed.

9. When done, click Finish.

10. Remove the Windows Vista installation media from the appropriate drive, and then click Restart to reboot the computer. Windows Vista should reboot normally.

Lesson Summary

- You use Event Viewer to monitor messages that are written to the Windows event logs.

- You can use System Restore to roll back the configuration of the computer to an earlier point in time.

- You use the Memory Diagnostics Tool to verify that physical memory on the computer is functioning properly.

- Windows Vista automatically detects startup problems and provides users with a list of alternate boot options.

- The Safe Mode option enables you to boot Windows Vista, using a minimal set of drivers and services to facilitate troubleshooting.

- You can correct many types of boot problems by using the Repair option in Windows Vista Setup.

- The Problem Reports and Solutions utility can be used to track, report on, and find fixes for Windows application errors.

Lesson Review

You can use the following questions to test your knowledge of the information in Lesson 1, "Diagnosing Issues in Windows Vista." The questions are also available on the companion CD if you prefer to review them in electronic form.

NOTE Answers

Answers to these questions and explanations of why each answer choice is correct or incorrect are located in the "Answers" section at the end of the book.

1. You are a Consumer Support Technician assisting a small-business owner with troubleshooting a startup problem. The customer reports that, after updating the drivers for his display adapter, Windows Vista no longer boots properly. Before shutting down the computer, he made numerous changes to application and operating system settings, and he does not want to redo the changes manually. Which of the following options is most likely to enable the computer to boot for troubleshooting without making permanent system changes? (Choose all that apply.)

    A. System Restore

    B. Safe Mode

    C. Safe Mode With Networking

    D. Memory Diagnostics Tool

    E. Last Known Good Configuration

2. You are attempting to resolve a problem with a computer running Windows Vista on behalf of a customer. The computer powers on, but does not start the Windows boot process. You are unable to access the startup menu. Which of the following options is most likely to help you resolve the issue?

    A. Safe Mode

    B. Safe Mode With Networking

    C. Last Known Good Configuration

    D. System Repair

3. You are assisting a customer with installing a program that is unsupported on Windows Vista. She has stated that another of her coworkers had mentioned having problems uninstalling the program, but that others have found that they are able to complete the uninstall process properly on Windows Vista. Which of the following methods should you use to provide a way to test the application safely?

    A. Create a new restore point before installing the program.

    B. Create a new restore point after installing the program.

    C. Use MSConfig to specify a selective startup for the next reboot of the computer.

    D. Use the Registry Editor to change program installation settings.

Lesson 2: Removing Malware from Windows Vista

An unfortunate fact of working on modern computers is the risk of the installation of malicious software. Often collectively referred to as *malware,* these programs range from merely annoying to seriously damaging. One of the primary opportunities for these types of attacks is that users commonly are connected to a global network through which just about anyone can create threats to others' computers. In some cases, the primary motivations are financial gain. In other cases, they're simply a matter of mischief that benefits no one.

Regardless of the goal, as a Consumer Support Technician, your advice can help users keep their computers clear of malicious software. In the event that malware infections do occur, you'll need to know how to remove them. Fortunately, Windows Vista includes numerous features that are helpful in detecting and removing malware. In this lesson, you'll learn ways in which you can diagnose and remove malware.

MORE INFO   Preventing malware installations

Windows Vista includes numerous features that can help prevent, detect, and remove malware. The focus in this lesson is on detecting and removing malicious programs. For more information on how User Account Control (UAC) can protect against malware installations, see Chapter 6, "Configuring Windows Vista Security." For details on security-related features in Internet Explorer 7, see Chapter 11, "Managing and Troubleshooting Devices." Chapter 9, "Configuring Windows Vista Networking," covers network protection features such as Windows Firewall. Finally, for details on detecting and removing startup programs, see Chapter 5. When used together, all of these technologies significantly reduce the risk of malware infections.

> **After this lesson, you will be able to:**
> - Describe various types of common malware, including their sources and potential effects on users' computers.
> - Detect and remove malware by using Windows Defender.
> - Identify options for dealing with detected malware.
> - Describe the purpose and benefits of joining the Microsoft SpyNet community.
> - Troubleshoot Web browser malware issues by using built-in features of Internet Explorer 7.
> - Describe other methods for repairing malware-infected computers.
>
> **Estimated lesson time: 45 minutes**

Understanding Common Malware Issues

One of the unique challenges that you'll face as a Consumer Support Technician is that of dealing with software that you have likely never seen before. Before you can adequately defend a computer against typical types of malware, you must first understand issues related to how malware works. Often, understanding the methods by which spyware and other unwanted software is installed can be a good start. Additionally, recognizing the effects of malware installations can be helpful in quickly diagnosing and troubleshooting problems. In this section, you'll learn about malware and how it works.

Types of Malware

There are numerous different types of malware that can be installed on users' computers. Although each type of malware has some unique characteristics, all of these types of programs have one thing in common: they perform unwanted actions on the user's computer. Examples of types of malicious software include the following:

- **Spyware**   The fundamental purpose of spyware is to monitor and collect information from the computer on which it is installed. For example, a spyware program might keep track of which files you open or even record the typing of logon information and passwords. The spyware can then transmit this information to other computers over the Internet. For example, an individual or organization might attempt to create databases of users' credit card information or passwords.

- **Adware**   Advertising is almost unavoidable on the Internet, but users are fairly familiar with encountering it when visiting Web sites. The revenue obtained from placing ads often helps support the creation and distribution of the content. Adware, on the other hand, is designed to be installed on a computer to present commercial advertisements. This might take the place of random pop-up ads that appear whether or not the user is using a Web browser or other Internet tool.

- **Viruses**   Viruses are malicious software programs that have the ability to spread. The virus code itself can perform a wide variety of different functions. Some are annoying, such changing system settings or displaying unwanted messages on the computer. Others can be completely devastating and can target specific files or entire hard disks. Like biological viruses, they tend to multiply and spread to other computers in a network environment. For example, a virus might automatically detect other computers in a small-business environment and copy itself to those computers.

- **Root kits**   This type of unwanted software is designed to access a computer and then gain full permissions on it. These are sometimes referred to as Trojan horses, in reference to the story from Greek mythology. After the program is able to run with complete access to the system, it can either perform specified instructions or carry out operations that might be sent over the Internet. Root kit infections can often do extensive damage to the local computer.

- **Other unwanted software**   There are numerous other types of software that perform malicious or unwanted actions. In many cases, these programs are included as part of an Internet download. Sometimes, licensing agreements provide a limited description of the purpose of the program. In other cases, there is no warning whatsoever that the additional software is being installed. Regardless of the way in which these programs are installed, most users would want to remove them.

One important point to keep in mind is that the definition of which software is truly malware might be subjective. A few programs might have legitimate uses that appeal to a relatively small number of computer users. Perhaps a "free" Internet program might require users to install additional software to use the product legally. In these cases, users might choose to keep the installed software on their computers. Later in this lesson, you'll see ways in which users can identify and remove potential malware.

Sources of Malware

The original source of the installation of malware can include many different avenues. Examples include the following:

- **Software installations** Some software products include additional functionality that might perform unwanted actions on the computer. This is often true of programs downloaded from the Internet. For example, a screen saver or other product might be available at no charge, but the program itself might include the installation of software that randomly displays advertisements on the user's computer, or the program itself might collect and transmit information without requiring the user's consent.

- **Web sites** Internet Web sites can contain a large number of different types of files and content that can affect the local computer. Usually, reputable Web sites clearly inform users before they install new programs on users' computers. In some cases, however, malicious sites can make changes to browsers and operating systems, resulting in the installation of malware.

- **Data files** It is possible for office productivity files to include viruses or other malicious content. For example, documents created using Microsoft Office can contain macros, sets of programmatic code that can perform a wide array of operations. Macros can be configured to access other files on the computer and make system changes. Although Microsoft Office contains numerous safeguards against these types of operations, users can disable these safeguards and leave their machines vulnerable.

- **E-mail** The presence of unsolicited commercial bulk e-mail (also known as spam) is extremely common among Internet users. Malicious e-mail messages might include attachments that, when installed on the computer, can cause data loss or reduced performance.

Unfortunately, new types of malware are continually being developed. Often, the user is required to take some kind of action, but he or she might do so based on limited knowledge of the exact effects of the program.

Effects of Malware Installation

After malware is installed on users' systems, a wide range of different actions can be performed, including the following:

- Changes to system or application settings (such as the configuration of the Internet Explorer home page or toolbars).

- Changes to application behavior. For example, a command or function that used to perform one task might now redirect the user to a specific Web site.

- The addition of new programs or features on the computer. This can often be seen in new programs that appear in the Start menu or that automatically load when a user logs on to the computer.

- System performance slowdowns. Examples include general application performance decreases and increased startup times for the operating system. Users might also notice significant hard disk or network activity that cannot be explained based on user activity.

- The automatic display of advertisements even when the user is not actively using the Internet.

It is important to note that sophisticated malware developers can be considerably clever when designing their products. Some of the most malicious pieces of software might work without providing any noticeable effects on the computer. Therefore, the absence of any of the symptoms just listed does not necessarily imply that the computer is free of malware. Regardless, it is important to remove malicious and unwanted software from customers' computers quickly.

Real World

Anil Desai

Although you cannot reasonably prevent some types of malware infections without the use of additional detection and removal software, you can prevent many of them through user education. A common method by which malware is installed on computers is by tricking users. Operating systems such as Windows Vista and Internet-enabled applications such as Internet Explorer include numerous security-related features that attempt to warn users of the potential dangers of installing a new application. Although this can help reduce the frequency of malware installations, it cannot protect users from themselves. For example, if a customer believes that he or she can dramatically improve system performance by downloading and installing an application, the user is very likely to ignore or bypass any warnings.

It is tempting to blame users for most of these actions, but there are also cases in which it is understandable that someone would be fooled by malware authors. After all, it is the business of these authors to dupe unsuspecting visitors to Web sites and other locations. How can you help prevent these problems? The best approach is end-user education. Here are some useful pointers to provide to customers in an effort to reduce the likelihood of unwanted software installation:

- **Consider the source**   When shopping in the physical world, individuals often have a way of determining the validity of a claim or a vendor. On the Internet, it's much more difficult to do the same. In general, users should be suspicious of exaggerated claims and programs that are available "completely free." They should ask themselves why a company would offer this product and how the company benefits. Often, the inclusion of adware or spyware is the answer.

- **Don't be too trusting**   Malware vendors are experts at building Web sites that appear to be reputable. They might use other organizations' logos and ask for private information. In general, users should avoid giving out personal information or details like credit card numbers unless they are sure of the source of the request. Often, official e-mail messages include details such as the user's account number to help ensure its authenticity.

Although the presence of malware will continue for the foreseeable future, it's important for Consumer Support Technicians to realize that technology is only one part of the solution. By educating the users you support, you can help reduce this deceptive business practice and the harm that it can cause. It can also help give you more time to focus on other, more interesting, technical challenges!

Removing Malware by Using Windows Defender

It's no secret that malware installations can cause significant frustration for end users and technical professionals alike. Computer users should certainly use some form of defense against the installation of unwanted programs. Windows Defender is the primary method of combating malware in Windows Vista. It is included with every edition of the operating system, and Microsoft designed it to prevent, detect, and remove malicious software programs.

Windows Defender includes a combination of different technologies that are designed to work together to keep users' systems free of unwanted software. For example, it has the ability to detect malware based on various "signatures" that are stored within its definitions database. It uses this information to monitor for system modifications, downloading of new files, and running of applications. It also periodically scans the file system for known malware programs. Because new types of malware are constantly being developed, it also integrates with the Windows Update feature (covered in Chapter 5) to download new definitions regularly.

Windows Defender is enabled by default and includes basic configuration settings that should meet the needs of most users. In this section, you'll learn how you can use this program to identify and remove malware.

Working with Windows Defender

During general operations, Windows Defender is designed to run without any specific input from users. It runs constantly in the background on computers and attempts to detect any unwanted software installations or activities. It also monitors for potentially risky modifications to system settings or the presence of known malware files.

Windows Defender also offers several features and settings that you can modify based on users' specific requirements. You can launch Windows Defender from the Start menu or by double-clicking the Windows Defender icon in the system tray (if it is present). Figure 12-29 shows the default display of the program.

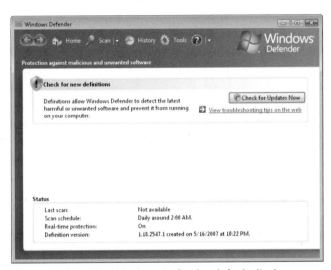

Figure 12-29   The Windows Defender default display

The screen provides details related to the last time a scan was run as well as an overview of current Windows Defender settings. It can also provide information that might require the user to perform a task. For example, if the Windows Defender definitions file is outdated, the user is prompted to download and install updates.

NOTE **Keeping systems protected**

Although users can choose not to use Windows Defender, it is highly recommended that they enable some type of antivirus and antimalware program on the computer. Numerous third-party products are available. When making recommendations as a Consumer Support Technician, verify that these programs are designed with Windows Vista in mind. For more information on how anti-malware and antivirus products can integrate with Windows Security Center, see Chapter 7, "Using Windows Security Center."

Scanning for Malware

One of the most common operations that users perform with Windows Defender is scanning for malware. Although the program is initially configured to perform a regular scan, as a Consumer Support Technician, you might want to run a new scan to detect recently installed malware. You can start the process of performing a standard Quick Scan by simply clicking the Scan button in the toolbar. This instructs Windows Defender to start scanning the most common locations in which malware might be located (see Figure 12-30). These locations include the Windows Registry (including locations in which startup programs are defined) and commonly used file system locations (such as user-specific folders). It also performs a scan of the Windows operating system folder.

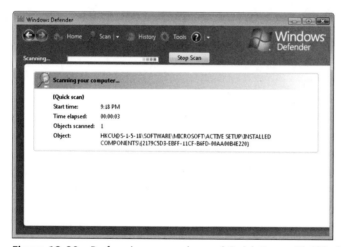

Figure 12-30   Performing an on-demand Quick Scan with Windows Defender

In addition to the Quick Scan, there are two other options. You can access both by clicking the arrow next to the Scan button. The Full Scan option performs all of the operations of the Quick Scan, but it also inspects all areas of the computer's file system. The process can take a significant amount of time (especially on computers with many files), but it is the most reliable way to detect any potential malware on the computer.

Another option is to perform a Custom Scan. This option enables users to specify a particular hard disk volume or folder to search for malware, which can be useful when you suspect that recently downloaded files stored in a specific location might be malware. Any results that are found are immediately displayed on a results screen.

Responding to Malware Alerts

When Windows Defender encounters potentially malicious software on the computer, it might need to notify the user to determine what to do. In most cases, users should disable or remove the software. Sometimes, the software might be legitimately required and should be given permission to perform its tasks. For this reason, Windows Defender can notify users of the issue by using the system tray icon. If there is an issue that requires attention, the icon changes to include either a yellow exclamation mark or a red stop sign. Additionally, Windows Defender can display system tray notification messages or pop-up windows (see Figure 12-31).

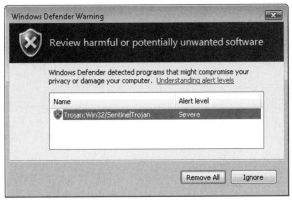

Figure 12-31   Viewing a notification about potential malware

The potential danger of certain pieces of malware can range significantly, based on type and design. Using information stored in its definition files, Windows Defender can determine the importance of a particular piece of suspected malware and can present details to users. The potential alert levels are as follows, in order:

- Severe
- High
- Medium
- Low
- Not yet classified

Typically, items that are marked with Severe or High alert levels should be removed immediately from the computer. Figure 12-32 shows the action options that are available when malware has been detected.

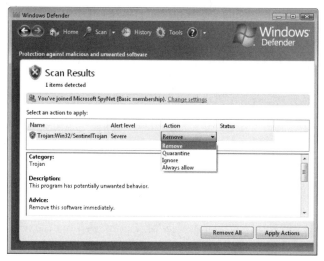

Figure 12-32   Responding to a malware alert in Windows Defender

The user is given several different options to determine how the problem should be resolved, as follows:

- **Remove**   This option automatically removes the malware. Often, this includes deleting any files that were detected and changing any system settings that might have been modified. For example, this might involve removing the program from the list of startup items.

- **Quarantine**   In some cases, users might not know whether to allow the program and, therefore, will not want to delete it. The purpose of the quarantine feature is to move the software to a safe location on the computer. It will no longer be able to run automatically, but it will not be permanently deleted. If users find that they do indeed want to run the program, they can choose to remove it from quarantine.

- **Ignore**   This option does not perform any actions based on the detection of malware. If a program has been configured to run automatically, it will continue to run. Users will continue to be notified of the detection of the program on future scans.

- **Always Allow**   This option is designed to allow certain programs to continue running on the computer without generating any future warnings. In general, users should select this option only if they are completely sure that they trust the program and are aware of its capabilities.

Additional details are often available by selecting a specific item from the list. To make decisions easier for users, each alert level can have a corresponding default action. You'll look at those details later in this section.

Exam Tip   When studying for Exam 70-623, you might want to install a piece of known malware purposely to practice responding to it. Installing malware is potentially risky because it can often result in data loss or unwanted system configuration changes. One way to reduce this risk is to use a product such as Microsoft Virtual PC to run a copy of Windows Vista on a virtual machine. One of the most useful features is the ability to use undo disks to revert the virtual machine to its initial configuration after you're done testing. For more information about Microsoft Virtual PC, see *http:// www.microsoft.com/windows/products/winfamily/virtualpc/default.mspx.*

Viewing the Windows Defender History

Over time, it is likely that Windows Defender will detect multiple pieces of malware. As a Consumer Support Technician, you might want to review this list. For example, if a user reports that he or she is missing several important data files, it is possible that malware might have moved or deleted them from the computer. To access these details, click the History button on the Windows Defender toolbar. Figure 12-33 shows an example of the types of information that might be available.

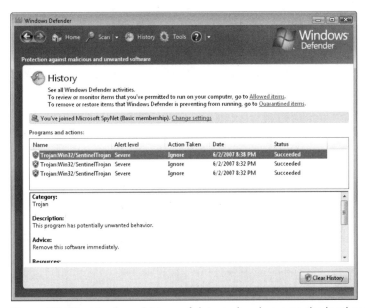

Figure 12-33   Viewing a history of detected malware on the local computer

Viewing Quarantined and Allowed Items

Earlier in this lesson, you learned about the option to place malware items in a quarantine location. This is a useful option when you are unsure whether you should allow a specific program, but you don't want to enable it immediately. Later, you might want to review the items in this location to make a determination about whether you should enable or remove them from the system. You can view the quarantine location by clicking the Tools button in Windows Defender and then selecting Quarantined Items. When you select an item, you can decide what should be done with it.

Similarly, Windows Defender keeps track of which items the user allows to run on the computer. As a Consumer Support Technician, you might want to verify that a user did not unknowingly enable a malicious program to run on the computer. You can access this list by clicking Allowed Items on the Tools page in Windows Defender.

Joining Microsoft SpyNet

One of the most challenging technical issues in the battle against spyware is detecting new malicious programs. Malware authors are constantly making changes to existing programs and creating new ones to circumvent definitions used by programs like Windows Defender. To react more quickly to new malware, Microsoft has created a system that enables users to report these programs automatically. The resulting online community is known as Microsoft SpyNet. You can configure membership options by using the Microsoft SpyNet link in the Tools window in Windows Defender (see Figure 12-34).

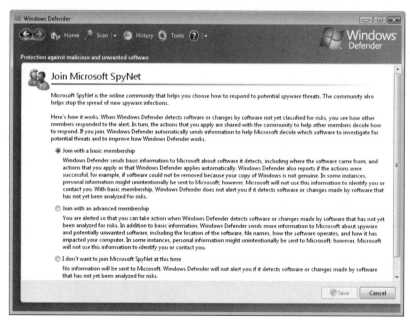

Figure 12-34   Configuring SpyNet membership options

There are three options for these settings. The first option is Join With A Basic Membership. This is the default setting, and it allows Windows Defender to send information about detected malware to Microsoft. As the text notes, there is a possibility that the report might contain personal information. However, Microsoft states that it will not use this information in any way. The primary limitation of this setting is that it does not protect users from items that are defined as not yet classified.

The second option is Join With An Advanced Membership. This option enables Windows Defender to collect and transmit information about unclassified potential spyware. Windows Defender can collect numerous technical details to help analyze whether the program is indeed malicious. Apart from helping detect malware more quickly, this setting also configures Windows Defender to present alerts for unclassified malware that it detects.

The final option is I Don't Want To Join Microsoft SpyNet At This Time. In most cases, the basic and advanced memberships will be most useful for customers. No special registration process is required, and Microsoft guarantees that user-specific information will remain confidential if it is included with a malware report.

Configuring Windows Defender Options

Windows Defender includes numerous basic and advanced options that you can configure based on users' specific needs. You access these settings in Windows Defender by clicking Tools and then clicking Options (see Figure 12-35). The main sets of options that are available include the following:

Figure 12-35   Viewing Windows Defender configuration options

- **Automatic Scanning**   These settings specify whether automatic scanning is enabled. If it is, the user can choose the frequency and time at which Windows Defender performs the scans. Additionally, there is an option to download updated definitions automatically before performing the scan.

- **Default Actions**   This section allows users to specify actions that Windows Defender automatically takes when it detects malware. The default settings specify that the recommendations that are included in the definition files should be used. This is often the most appropriate setting for users. Other options include specifying whether items of a certain alert level should be automatically removed or ignored.

- **Real-Time Protection Options**   Windows Defender includes numerous features that are useful for automatically preventing against common malware installation methods. This section, shown in Figure 12-36, enables users to specify which types of actions Windows Defender should monitor. The most secure setting is to leave all of the check boxes selected. For performance or testing reasons, however, you might want to disable one or more of the items.

Figure 12-36   Viewing real-time protection options in Windows Defender

- **Advanced Options**   This section includes several settings related to which files Windows Defender scans, along with specific behaviors such as automatically creating restore points. You can click the Add button to specify files or locations that Windows Defender should not scan (see Figure 12-37).

- **Administrator Options**   This section enables you to specify whether Windows Defender is enabled and whether other users on the computer can make changes to its configuration.

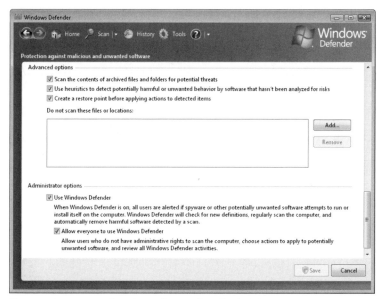

Figure 12-37   Configuring advanced and administrator options in Windows Defender

Overall, Windows Defender includes a large number of options for customizing the behavior for malware detection and removal.

Troubleshooting Internet Explorer

Although the Internet provides numerous benefits to computer users, it also provides a method for malware authors to distribute and collect information from users' computers. A common target of malware is the Web browser. To protect against common attempts to install malicious software on customers' computers, the Windows Vista Internet Explorer 7 Web browser contains numerous security features. For more details about configuring security for Internet Explorer 7, see Chapter 8, "Configuring Parental Controls and Browser Security."

Malware that targets Web browsers is often designed to make configuration changes. Examples include the following:

- Changes to existing bookmarks or the addition of new ones
- Automatically redirecting users to other Web sites
- Changing security levels for specific sites
- Automatically downloading and installing adware, spyware, or other unwanted software
- Installation of Browser Helper Objects
- Accessing operating system files and user data
- Collecting sensitive personal information such as logons, passwords, and credit card numbers

- Creating or adding new toolbars
- Tracking users' browser behavior

Features included in Internet Explorer 7 have been designed to prevent many of these types of unwanted changes. However, to maintain compatibility with advanced Web-based user features, it is possible for users to agree unknowingly to install potentially malicious software. For example, the browser's home page might be changed, or the user might start receiving an extremely large number of pop-up ads.

Deleting Browser History

When troubleshooting the installation of malware, there are ways to remove or undo unwanted changes. A quick and easy first step in troubleshooting browser-related issues can be to use the Delete Browsing History command on the Tools menu. As shown in Figure 12-38, this option enables you to remove files such as cookies that have been stored on the computer.

Figure 12-38   Using the Delete Browsing History feature in Internet Explorer

Managing Add-Ons

Another option for managing unwanted programs is to view and verify the list of browser add-ons that have been installed on the computer. Software vendors create legitimate add-ons to improve the browsing experience. They might add useful features and functionality to the browser or, perhaps, tasks that can make working with Web sites easier. Unfortunately, malware authors can misuse the same features to present advertisements or make changes to browsing behavior.

To obtain a list of add-ons that are installed in Internet Explorer 7, click the Tools menu, select Manage Add-Ons, and then select Enable Or Disable Add-Ons. Figure 12-39 shows the Manage Add-Ons dialog box.

Figure 12-39   Managing Internet Explorer add-ons

There are four main options in the Show drop-down list that specify which items are shown, as follows:

- Add-Ons That Have Been Used By Internet Explorer
- Add-Ons Currently Loaded In Internet Explorer
- Add-Ons That Run Without Requiring Permission
- Downloaded ActiveX Controls (32-Bit)

As a Consumer Support Technician, you should examine the list of items to identify potential malware. This can be difficult, however, because the names of some items might be missing, incomplete, or confusing. The Manage Add-Ons dialog box also provides the ability to enable and disable the listed items. Disabled items are prevented from running, but they can also be easily reenabled in the future. The Delete button in the Delete ActiveX section provides a way to remove controls permanently that have been downloaded to the system.

Resetting Internet Explorer Options

In some cases, you might find that standard troubleshooting steps are unable to resolve the problems that a user is experiencing. An example might include the installation of malware that caused numerous changes to search settings, the default home page, add-ons, and other configuration details. Alternatively, users might have made numerous changes to their security settings, and it is difficult and time-consuming to change them back. For those situations, Internet Explorer 7 includes a feature that enables you to reset all of the browser settings to their default values.

To reset the Internet Explorer settings, click Internet Options in the Tools menu of the browser. Click the Advanced tab. In addition to a long list of advanced options, the bottom of the dialog box offers a Reset button. When you click this button, a message box outlines the changes that occur if you start the process (see Figure 12-40).

Figure 12-40   Using the Reset Internet Explorer Settings option

As the warning message notes, this option is designed for use when other standard trouble-shooting methods have failed. The primary reason for this is that users might have made numerous useful changes to their browser settings, and some of those revert to their original values. However, in some cases, performing a reset of all of the settings might be the quickest and easiest method of restoring proper operations.

NOTE   Modifying customers' computers

As a Consumer Support Technician, customers trust you to detect and resolve problems that are preventing their systems from running correctly. They should also be able to assume that you will not make changes without their permission. When performing operations that could result in an inconvenience to the user, always attempt to explain the situation and obtain his or her approval first. This way, you can verify that it's a team decision.

Other Methods of Removing Malware

So far in this lesson, you've looked at ways in which you can use features of Windows Defender and Internet Explorer to resolve malware issues. In addition to these tools, there are some other ways in which you can combat malicious software. In this section, you'll learn about these methods.

Uninstalling Programs

Sometimes, the most obvious solutions are the ones technical professionals look to last. When troubleshooting malware, consider accessing the Uninstall a Program item in Control Panel. The display returns a list of installed programs and provides the ability to remove unwanted applications.

It's unlikely that the author of a malicious program went through the effort to design a proper installer and removal utility. However, many pieces of software that might be considered adware or spyware by some users are designed to remove themselves properly. For example, if an Internet-based freeware download included unwanted software, the uninstall process might provide the option to remove it. Although attempting to uninstall programs won't solve all malware-related issues, it does provide a simple way to remove some of them.

Reinstalling Windows Vista

Although this situation should be exceedingly rare, there might be cases in which you choose to reinstall the Windows Vista operating system completely. For example, some business environments might find that it is too time-consuming to perform in-depth troubleshooting. Some small businesses might not have the expertise required to clean malware from computers. In these cases, the organization might opt to perform a reinstallation of Windows Vista. For more information about reinstalling Windows Vista, see Chapter 2.

CAUTION   Choosing to reinstall

In most cases, consider choosing to reinstall the entire operating system due to a malware problem a last resort. Apart from losing configuration settings, users might have to spend a significant amount of time reinstalling and customizing their applications. In some cases, this potential solution might be worse than the problem. Always try to use all of the other troubleshooting methods at your disposal before deciding to reinstall Windows Vista.

An alternative to performing a full reinstallation is to use other standard diagnostic and troubleshooting tools. For example, you can attempt to boot the computer to Safe Mode to prevent unnecessary startup programs from running, as covered in Lesson 1 of this chapter. Finally, another option might be to perform a Complete PC restore operation, as covered in Chapter 13.

Keeping up with Security Details

Although you might not like their products, malware writers do often spend significant amounts of time coming up with ingenious ways of installing software on users' computers. Consumer Support Technicians can provide a valuable service to their customers by remaining up to date on the latest security issues. A useful starting point is the Microsoft Security At Home Web site, which is available at *http://www.microsoft.com/athome/security/spyware/software/isv/default.mspx*. Additionally, numerous third-party vendors and independent security researchers on the Internet keep computer users up to date on potential fraudulent activities.

> ### Quick Check
>
> 1. Which Windows Defender response option should a user select if she is unsure of whether she wants a program to run on her computer?
> 2. How can a user quickly remove an unwanted toolbar add-on in Internet Explorer?
>
> ### Quick Check Answers
>
> 1. Usually, the most appropriate option is to quarantine the item to prevent any unwanted actions. She can later choose to reenable the application, using Windows Defender.
> 2. The Manage Add-Ons dialog box (which is accessible from the Tools menu) allows for enabling, disabling, and removing add-ons.

Lesson Summary

- Common types of malware include viruses, root kits, spyware, and adware, which can be installed without providing notification to the user.
- Windows Defender is configured to scan for and detect malware by default.
- Users can choose to remove, quarantine, ignore, or allow potential malware programs.
- Windows Defender offers numerous real-time monitoring options that can be disabled.
- Internet Explorer 7 provides features for deleting browsing history, managing add-ons, and resetting all browser settings to their initial states.
- Some types of malware can be removed by uninstalling associated programs, using Control Panel.

Lesson Review

You can use the following questions to test your knowledge of the information in Lesson 2, "Removing Malware from Windows Vista." The questions are also available on the companion CD if you prefer to review them in electronic form.

NOTE Answers

Answers to these questions and explanations of why each answer choice is correct or incorrect are located in the "Answers" section at the end of the book.

---

1. You are a Consumer Support Technician assisting a customer with a malware-related issue on his computer. You have performed a full scan of the system, using Windows Defender, and one malware item has been detected. After consulting the customer, you are unsure of whether the detected program is actually required on the computer. However, you want to prevent the computer from being modified by the program. Which of the following actions should you choose to meet these requirements?

    A. Remove

    B. Ignore

    C. Quarantine

    D. Allow

2. A customer recently downloaded and installed a new Internet Explorer utility application. She initially found it to be useful, but now she would like to permanently remove it from her computer. She has asked you to remove the item without making additional changes to the system. Which of the following options provides the simplest method to do this?

    A. Use the Reset Internet Explorer Settings command.

    B. Use the Delete Browsing History command.

    C. Run a scan in Windows Defender to detect and remove the item.

    D. Use the Manage Add-Ons dialog box.

Chapter Review

To further practice and reinforce the skills you learned in this chapter, you can perform the following tasks:

- Review the chapter summary.
- Review the list of key terms introduced in this chapter.
- Complete the case scenarios. These scenarios set up real-world situations involving the topics of this chapter and ask you to create a solution.
- Complete the suggested practices.
- Take a practice test.

Chapter Summary

- Windows Vista includes numerous tools for diagnosing and troubleshooting system problems. Options include the Windows Event Viewer, System Restore, Windows Memory Diagnostics, and Problem Reports and Solutions.
- The Windows Vista Repair process can help resolve problems that prevent Windows Vista from booting.
- You can use Windows Defender to scan for and remove malware from a computer running Windows Vista.
- Internet Explorer contains numerous features for preventing malware and reverting to default configuration settings.

Key Terms

Do you know what these key terms mean? You can check your answers by looking up the terms in the glossary at the end of the book.

- boot logging
- Event Viewer
- Last Known Good Configuration
- malware
- Problem Reports and Solutions
- registry
- Registry Editor (RegEdit)

- Repair command prompt
- restore points
- Safe Mode
- Selective Startup
- Startup Repair
- System Protection
- System Restore
- Windows Error Recovery
- Windows event logs
- Windows Memory Diagnostics

Case Scenarios

In the following case scenarios, you apply what you've learned about troubleshooting, repairing, and removing malware from Windows Vista. You can find answers to these questions in the "Answers" section at the end of this book.

Case Scenario 1: Diagnosing and Troubleshooting Startup Problems

You are a Customer Support Technician assisting a Windows Vista user with troubleshooting a system startup problem. The user recently installed several new programs on the computer, along with drivers for two new devices: a USB-based scanner and a USB-based digital camera. He also recently upgraded the physical memory on his computer. He then attempted to reboot the computer, but the operating system would not load. He is currently able to get to the Advanced Boot Options screen.

1. You want to attempt to boot Windows Vista using a minimal set of drivers so that you can download a particular file from the Internet. No other computers are available at this location, so which boot option should you choose?

2. How can you determine whether the physical memory is causing a startup problem?

3. How can you determine which program or device driver is causing the startup problem?

Case Scenario 2: Working with Windows Defender

You are a Consumer Support Technician assisting a new Windows Vista user with configuring her computer. The customer is a small-business owner who would like to ensure that her employees' computers remain free of malware. In the past, she has seen several types of malware installed on a computer named Workstation01. The malware has since been removed from the computer. The customer's office has reliable Internet connectivity.

1. How can the customer make sure that Windows Defender remains up to date?
2. How can all of the computers in the business be protected against potential malware programs that have not yet been classified?
3. How can the customer determine which spyware products were previously installed on Workstation01?

Suggested Practices

To help you successfully master the exam objectives presented in this chapter, complete the following tasks.

Troubleshooting Windows Vista

These practice exercises assist you with troubleshooting common Windows Vista issues. In general, you can carry out these exercises without creating specific problems on computers running Windows Vista. However, it is highly recommended that you perform these tasks on a test computer because changes can affect the functioning of Windows Vista.

- **Practice 1: Troubleshooting startup problems**   Assume that a computer running Windows Vista fails to start normally. Access the Advanced Boot Options menu during startup and use the Safe Mode With Networking option. Also, enable boot logging and view the resulting Ntbtlog.txt, using Notepad.

- **Practice 2: Repairing Windows Vista**   Assume that you are troubleshooting a computer running Windows Vista that is unable to start up and does not display the Advanced Boot Options menu. Access the Windows Vista Repair process by booting from the installation media. Use the System Restore, Command Prompt, and Startup Repair features and determine the effects.

- **Practice 3: Removing malware with Windows Defender**   If available, find a computer that has potential malware programs installed (it is also possible to download sample malware from various Internet sites). Use Windows Defender to detect the item, and then choose to place it in quarantine. Permanently remove the item, and then verify that it shows up in the Windows Defender History. Also, configure Windows Defender to join Microsoft SpyNet with an advanced membership.

Take a Practice Test

The practice tests on this book's companion CD offer many options. For example, you can test yourself on just one exam objective, or you can test yourself on all of the 70-623 certification exam content. You can set up the test so that it closely simulates the experience of taking a certification exam, or you can set it up in study mode so that you can look at the correct answers and explanations after you answer each question.

MORE INFO   **Practice tests**

For details about all the practice test options available, see the "How to Use the Practice Tests" section in this book's introduction.

Chapter 13

Protecting Data and Repairing Windows Vista

Consumers typically rely on data stored on their computers for a wide variety of purposes. In some cases, the information itself is important for work or business purposes. For example, users often use accounting information and personal financial data files to keep track of expenses. Other types of information might include e-mails, photos, videos, music files, and documents. Although the exact nature of the data itself might vary, there's often one common overall aspect: data loss can be extremely frustrating. Even if the data can be manually re-created, it is a tedious and error-prone process.

The primary causes of data loss can range from technical issues (such as the failure of a physical hard disk) to user error (for example, the accidental deletion of an important file). The clear solution to these types of problems is to make copies of the information itself and to store them securely in case they're needed. Fortunately, modern operating systems include tools for protecting users' important data. Windows Vista includes features that make setting up and performing backups simple for even end users with limited knowledge. As a Consumer Support Technician, your customers rely on your expertise to help them decide what information needs to be protected and how to do so.

In the case of a hardware failure or a serious corruption of the operating system, it might become necessary to resort to reinstalling the operating system. One approach is to delete all data completely and start from the beginning. However, this method will result in the loss of users' system settings, data, and application installation information. Windows Vista includes features that make the process of performing a complete restore of the entire PC a simpler process.

In this chapter, you'll learn about ways in which you can use the backup and recovery features of Windows Vista to protect important information on the computer. You'll also learn about ways in which you can repair a nonworking operating system, using a minimum amount of time and effort. All of this is valuable information that you'll need to know to help customers deal with protecting and recovering important information.

Exam objectives in this chapter:

- Configure Windows Vista Security.
    - ❏ Protect data.
- Troubleshoot and Repair Windows Vista.
    - ❏ Repair a corrupted operating system.

Lessons in this chapter:

Before You Begin

The text and practice exercises in this chapter focus on ways in which you can perform backups and use backups to restore important information. You can perform the majority of these operations using a single computer running Windows Vista. Note, however, that there's a chance for some data and settings to be lost when you perform a restore operation. For that reason, it's highly recommended that you use a test computer (or a virtual machine) when following along with the steps described. In addition, have adequate disk space available for performing a backup of the entire computer. Generally, the requirement is to have greater than 50 percent free disk space remaining on the system. Additional requirements are described as needed.

Lesson 1: Using the Backup and Restore Center

It seems to be part of human nature to rely on certain technologies, and computers are no exception. We tend not to notice the importance of technology until it is no longer available. Computer users often tend to rely on their notebooks, desktops, and other computing devices for managing a variety of different types of information. In general, they expect this data always to be available. They often neglect to think about the potential ramifications of the loss of the information.

Modern computers are complex devices that have numerous components. The failure of any one of these components can lead to issues such as data loss or a computer that is completely unusable. Although it is not possible to protect against every kind of failure, it is possible to make backup copies of important information. If the primary copy of the data becomes unavailable, users should be able to access their backups.

Of course, the ability to restore data is based on the presence of a backup. Users often neglect to create backups of their important information for several reasons. First, they might never have thought about the potential for a hard disk or other computer component to fail. They might not realize that components in their computers could malfunction with little or no warning. Additionally, they don't think about the very real potential of accidentally deleting, overwriting, or modifying an important file. Second, assuming that users want to perform backups, they're often unsure of which files and content to select. They sometimes need assistance with setting up the backup process. Finally, to protect data, users must keep track of where backups are being stored. This information might be required if there is a need to restore information or the entire computer itself.

Windows Vista includes several features that are designed to make the process of creating and managing backups simpler for end users. In this lesson, you'll learn about how you can use the Backup and Restore Center to protect data on users' computers.

After this lesson, you will be able to:
- List factors that should be considered when planning for backups.
- Identify different types of backup destinations.
- Use the Backup and Restore Center to define and schedule new backup jobs.
- Perform manual file backups and manage backup files.
- Restore files from a backup.
- Restore older copies of files using the Previous Versions feature.

Estimated lesson time: 45 minutes

Planning for Backups

Before you learn about the technical details of working with backup-related functionality in Windows Vista, it is helpful to identify some of the requirements for performing backups. In this section, you'll learn about several important concepts to keep in mind when helping customers plan for backups.

Reasons for Performing Backups

As mentioned earlier, users often fail to recognize the importance of performing backups until a problem occurs. There are several different reasons for performing backups, and all focus on protecting against data loss. Common sources of problems include the failure of hardware components such as a disk controller or hard disk drive. Because hard disk drives have moving components, they're often one of the most vulnerable aspects of the computer itself.

Although hardware failures can and do occur, they are often relatively rare compared to another data-related danger: user error. For home and small-business consumers, it's likely that they'll accidentally delete or overwrite important information at some time. When this happens, they'll want to recover the file or revert it to an earlier version.

Finally, the threat of viruses and other types of malware can put users' information at significant risk. Some types of malicious software can directly access files and make changes to their contents or delete them altogether. In the worst cases, it might become necessary to recover the files from a backup. For more information about troubleshooting malware-related problems, see Chapter 12, "Troubleshooting Windows Vista."

Selecting Files to Back Up

When planning for backup operations, it's important to identify which types of files and information must be protected. Computers contain a wide variety of important data that is often stored in different locations on the computer. With Windows Vista, some important types of data to back up include the following:

- Data files (documents, photos, video, music, and so on)
- Operating system settings
- Application settings

In the case of data loss, all of this information is difficult to re-create, if it is possible at all. In addition to settings and data, there are other types of files that are required for proper operations of the computer. For example, the Windows Vista operating system itself includes thousands of different files necessary for proper operation. Additionally, applications such as those included with Microsoft Office can contain large numbers of files.

Although all files are important, in the case of complete data loss, it is usually possible to reinstall programs or the operating system from installation media. (You'll learn about the process of repairing Windows Vista in Lesson 2, "Using Windows Complete PC Backup and Restore," of this chapter.) In some cases, you might want to advise users to perform a complete backup of all data and files on their computer. In other cases, technical limitations (such as the amount of available disk space) will make this impossible.

Scheduling Backups

Another important consideration related to planning for backups is determining how often the data should be copied. The optimal answer varies based on the ways in which customers use their computers. For example, if a home user primarily uses the computer for accessing Web sites and Web-based e-mail, a weekly backup might be suitable. On the other hand, a small-business owner who relies on an accounting system and customer project files might want to back up files daily or even several times per day.

Backups can be performed manually, but users should set up a scheduled backup process. This helps ensure that users do not forget to perform regular backup operations based on their requirements. Ideally, backups should be performed when the user is not actively using the computer. It is possible to perform various tasks while backups are running, but the process can reduce performance. A typical schedule is to run a backup operation in the evening or night, when users are less likely to be using their desktops and notebooks.

There is one additional scheduling consideration: for backup operations to be performed, the computer must be on. Home and small-business users who rely on desktop computers might choose to keep computers running when they are finished using them. You can use the standard power management options in Control Panel to ensure that systems use minimal energy when not in use. Users of portable computers must also ensure that their computers are connected to a power source for backups to be performed. The reason for this is that the backup process itself can place a significant load on the hard disk and other components of the system. This can lead to the battery draining very quickly, often, before the backup process is complete.

Real World

Anil Desai

For many technical professionals, there's a tendency to focus on technology solutions before the problem is properly defined. The process of implementing backups is no exception. I sometimes find myself implementing a variety of backup operations on users' computers without first taking the time to determine what is actually needed. First and foremost, it's important to recognize that the goal of performing backups is to provide the ability to restore data.

So how can you determine the restore requirements? As a Consumer Support Technician, perhaps the most important aspect of the process is to listen to your customers when they tell you how they use their computers. Some questions you should be thinking of include the following:

- What types of information would be difficult to replace in the case of a complete data loss? Usually, this includes users' important data and media-related files. In some cases, databases or other types of applications might include additional information that must be protected.
- How often does data change on the computer, and how important are the changes? For users who do most of their work online or those that rarely modify system settings and applications, less frequent backups might make more sense.
- What are the technical constraints within which you must work? Often, disk space limitations and the amount of time it takes to perform a backup will be important factors.
- How quickly does the user need to restore the system, assuming a complete loss of all data? In some cases, it might be acceptable for the user to reinstall the operating system and applications manually. Other types of users, such as small-business owners, might find that downtime is extremely costly.
- What is the total amount of acceptable data loss? In a worst-case scenario, users should be able to determine how much information they can stand to lose. Occasional computer users might find that the loss of a week's worth of information is not a significant concern. Others might see a high cost related to losing even a few hours' worth of information.

Only after you've determined customers' requirements should you start working on the technical details of implementing, scheduling, and testing the backup process.

Choosing Backup Destinations

When planning to perform backups, consider your customers' hardware resources. It's important to determine where backups can be stored. Common examples of backup destinations include the following:

- **Hard disks** The backup utilities of Windows Vista enable storing backups on the hard disk. The backups themselves can be stored to any local hard disk volume, but it is highly recommended that they be stored on a separate physical disk drive from the primary copy. This helps prevent the loss of the original data and the backup in the case of hardware failure.

- **Removable media**   One of the most common methods for storing backups is the use of writable CD- or DVD-based media. The primary advantage of this approach is that blank discs are inexpensive and can be easily stored in a secure location. Ideally, an entire backup will fit on a single piece of media. If multiple discs are required, a user needs to change them manually during the backup process. To perform a restore operation, all of the discs that are part of a backup set are required. If one or more discs are missing, however, it is usually possible to restore some data from the remaining media.

- **Network devices**   It is possible to store backup information over the network. This is most useful when an environment contains multiple computers that are connected to the same network or when a network-based storage device is available. The speed of the network connection can affect backup performance, and it is important to ensure that the network connection is reliable. Also, keep in mind that the destination device or computer must be online and available for the backup process to occur.

- **Removable memory devices**   Memory devices typically plug in to a computer's universal serial bus (USB) port. In general, they provide a quick and easy method for storing backup information. Often, however, the capacity of the device is smaller than that of other backup media options. This makes them more suitable for backups of smaller sets of files.

- **External hard disk drives**   These devices contain a hard disk or other storage device that generally attaches to the computer through a USB or FireWire connection. Because the drives are external, they can be removed and stored in a safe location after the backup completes.

For more information about installing new hardware devices, see Chapter 11, "Managing and Troubleshooting Devices."

NOTE   Protecting backup data

It's common for users to store sensitive personal or financial information on their computers. Keep in mind that when you make a backup, you're creating a copy of all of this information. For this reason, you should protect backups by storing them in a secure location that is accessible only to authorized individuals. Home users might choose to store them in a locked safe or filing cabinet or another location (such as at their workplace). Small-business owners might consider investing in an off-site backup service that automatically stores media in another location.

NOTE   Backups using the Internet

There are numerous online services that allow users to store backup copies on remote servers by using the Internet. The benefit is that the backups are automatically and securely stored on a remote server. Although this is not a feature that is specifically supported by Windows Vista, it can be a helpful option for home and small-business consumers.

Using the Backup and Restore Center

The primary data protection tool in Windows Vista is the Backup and Restore Center. You can launch it from the Start menu by searching for the name of the program, or you can click the Backup And Restore Center link from within the System And Maintenance section in Control Panel. Figure 13-1 shows an example of the main screen of the Backup and Restore Center utility.

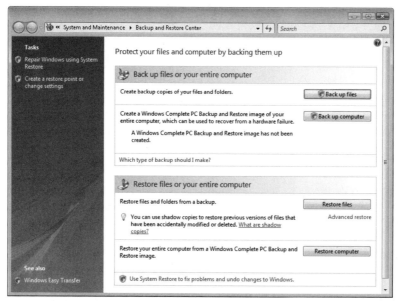

Figure 13-1   Using the Backup and Restore Center

The two main sections of the program divide the functionality into backup and restore operations. Windows Vista automatically keeps track of which backups have been performed and reports on the details. The main approaches to performing are either to back up specific files or to perform a Complete PC backup. In the following sections, you'll learn how to create file-based backups. In Lesson 2 of this chapter, you'll learn how to back up and restore data using Complete PC backups.

Performing File Backups

The process of backing up files and folders involves making a copy of users' data and other types of information. This information is stored in a backup location and can later be used to recover information, if necessary. The primary goal of this approach is to enable users to identify easily which information is important. A file backup does not, however, include operating system files.

Defining and Scheduling a New Backup

To start the creation of a new backup process, in the Backup and Restore Center window, click Back Up Files. The first step asks you to specify the destination location for the backup (see Figure 13-2).

Figure 13-2   Choosing a backup destination

The first option displays a drop-down list that includes all of the available local backup destinations. This includes local hard disk volumes, removable memory devices, external hard disks, and writable CD- and DVD-based devices. The Windows Vista operating system hard disk does not appear in the list, because it is not possible to back up system-related information to this disk. The list also shows how much space is available on each of these devices.

The second option allows you to specify a network location to which the backups will be stored. You can enter the information by typing a Universal Naming Convention (UNC) path name to the destination folder or by using the Browse button. For more information on working with network locations, see Chapter 10, "Managing Network Sharing." After you select a backup destination, click Next.

The second step of the backup process involves selecting which disks should be backed up (see Figure 13-3). By default, all of the disks that are available for backup purposes are listed. If you selected a specific volume or disk in the previous step, it does not appear here because Windows Vista does not enable performing a backup to the same disk. The operating system disk is automatically added to the backup set, and you cannot remove it. You can specify which additional storage devices should be backed up by selecting or clearing the check boxes for each item.

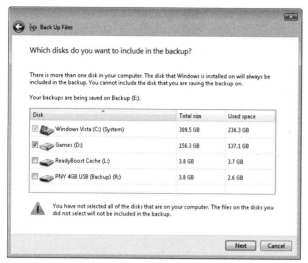

Figure 13-3   Selecting which disks should be backed up

The next step involves specifying which types of files should be backed up (see Figure 13-4). Table 13-1 lists the available options and the associated category details as listed in the Backup and Restore Center.

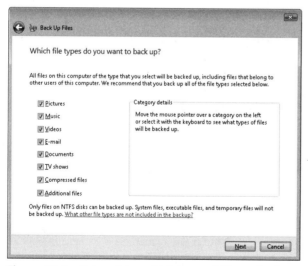

Figure 13-4   Determining which types of files to back up

Table 13-1 Backup File Categories and Their Descriptions

Category	Category Details
Pictures	Digital photographs, clip art, drawings, scanned pictures, faxes, and other image files, including .jpeg and .png files.
Music	Music, play lists, CD tracks, and other audio files, including Windows Media Audio and MP3 files.
Videos	Videos and movies, including Windows Media Video, .mpeg, and .avi files.
E-mail	E-mail messages and contact lists, including .pst and .eml files. E-mail that is stored online only will not be backed up.
Documents	Documents, such as work processing files, spreadsheets, and presentations, including .pdf and .xps files.
TV Shows	TV shows recorded from Windows Media Center.
Compressed Files	Compressed, image, and archive format files that contain other files, such as .zip, .cab, .iso, .wim, and .vhd. This category also includes compressed folders.
Additional Files	Any files that do not fit in the other categories. System files, program files, and temporary files are never backed up.

Assuming that the backup destination has sufficient space, it is ideal to select the check boxes for all of these types of files. In many cases, however, the backup destination might not have enough space to store all of the file types. In that case, users can choose to exclude some file types. For example, TV shows recorded by Windows Media Center can be large and might not be considered critical from a backup and restore standpoint.

The next step is to specify the schedule for the backup process (see Figure 13-5). The main option is the frequency of the backup operation. The settings include Daily, Weekly, and Monthly. Based on this selection, the other options specify the details for when the backup process begins.

If you have not yet created a backup of the system, you see a notice at the bottom of the screen specifying that a new full backup will be created immediately. Click Save Settings And Start Backup to begin the operation. Figure 13-6 shows the progress information display for a backup.

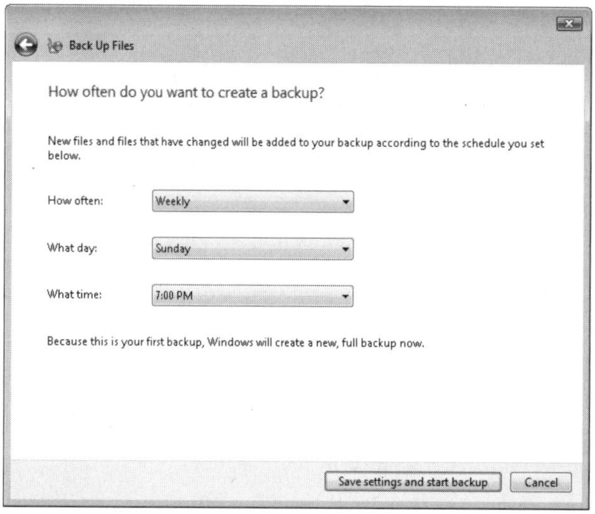

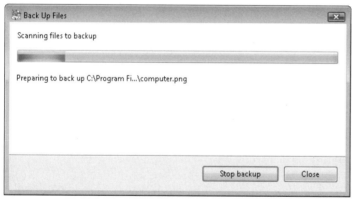

Figure 13-5   Specifying a backup schedule

Figure 13-6   Viewing progress for a backup job

While the backup is running, users can continue to access the computer and can even make changes to files. Windows Vista uses a file system feature known as shadow copy to access files while they are in use. Files that are modified during the backup process are copied during the next backup operation. The backup job is also scheduled to run based on the settings that were chosen.

Performing Manual Backups

After you create a scheduled backup process, you can view details about it in the Backup and Restore Center. As shown in Figure 13-7, the details include the date and time of the last backup and the scheduled time for the next backup operation.

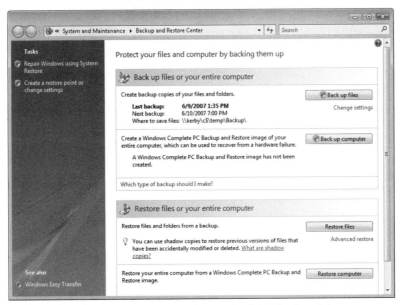

Figure 13-7 Viewing details related to a scheduled backup job

The Change Settings link enables you to launch the Backup Status And Configuration window (see Figure 13-8). You use this window to verify settings and locations for backup operations and to perform several different operations.

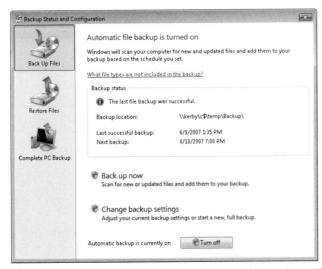

Figure 13-8 Using the Backup Status and Configuration utility

You can click Change Backup Settings to make modifications to the current backup job. This is useful if you want to change the backup destination, which files are copied, or the backup schedule. You also have the ability to turn off automatic backups altogether.

In general, users should create and schedule a regular backup process. In some situations, however, it is useful to perform a manual backup. This might be important, for example, when a large number of files has been created or modified on the system, and the user does not want to wait until the next scheduled backup operation to protect those files. Clicking Back Up Files in the Backup and Restore Center launches this process. Files are automatically copied to the destination location. You can view the progress of the backup by clicking the backup system tray icon.

One approach to performing a new backup would be to copy all of the selected data files. The drawback, however, is that this would require a lot of time and a significant amount of disk space. Usually, only a few files will have changed since the last backup operation. Windows Vista automatically tracks which files have been backed up and can detect which files have been created or modified since the last backup operation. When performing subsequent backup operations, only changed and added files are copied to the destination location. This makes the process significantly faster than performing a full backup and uses a much smaller amount of backup space.

Managing Backup Files

The Backup and Restore features in Windows Vista are designed to create backup-related files and folders automatically as needed. Over time, however, you might want to delete older backups or move backups to a different storage location. You might want to move a set of backups to another computer to restore the data there.

The standard folder structure that is used in the backup location begins with a folder name based on the name of the computer that is backed up. Within this folder, there is a backup set subfolder that is named based on the date and time at which the backup was run (for example, Backup Set 2007-06-09 132923). Each Backup Set folder also includes one or more folders that start with the name Backup Files. Figure 13-9 shows an example.

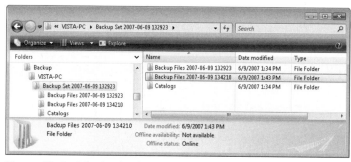

Figure 13-9 Viewing backup-related files

Subsequent backup operations include new folders within the Backup Set folder. The backed up data itself is stored within a compressed (zipped) folder. Its contents can be accessed manually to restore specific files. In addition, there is a Catalogs folder that includes an index of all of the files that have been backed up. This information is used by the Windows Vista restore utilities to find files quickly without searching through all of the data.

Restoring Files from a Backup

So far, you have focused on the process of performing backup operations on a computer. Of course, the primary purpose of creating backups is to enable restores. The process of restoring data is most easily started by clicking Restore Files in the Backup and Restore Center. Figure 13-10 shows the initial screen of the Restore Files process.

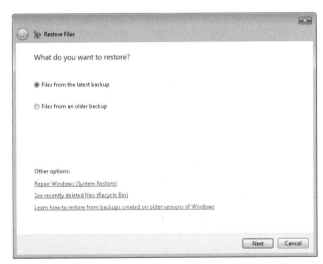

Figure 13-10   Starting the Restore Files process

Performing a Restore Operation

The first step is to determine whether you want to restore from the latest backup or from an older backup. Because Windows Vista automatically keeps track of backup operations on the local computer, there's no need to provide additional information. If, however, you want to restore from an earlier backup, you can choose the date and time of that backup (see Figure 13-11). Later in this lesson, you'll learn how you can restore from backups that do not appear in the list.

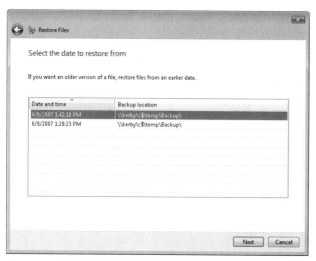

Figure 13-11   Selecting an older backup from which to restore

After you choose the backup from which you want to restore, you'll need to specify which data should be copied back to the computer. If you know specifically which files and folders you want to recover, you can choose to add them using the Add Files and Add Folders buttons. Another useful option is to use the Search button to find particular files or types of files. Regardless of the method you use, the Restore Wizard shows which files will be restored (see Figure 13-12).

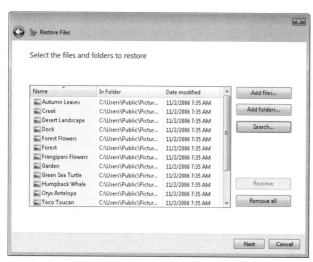

Figure 13-12   Selecting files and folders to restore

The next step requires you to specify the destination for the restore operation (see Figure 13-13). In many cases, you will want to restore files over their original copies. For example, if you accidentally delete a Microsoft Word document, you probably want it to be restored to the same location.

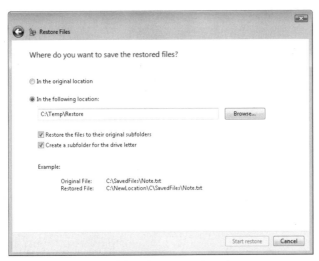

Figure 13-13   Specifying the restore location

In other cases, however, you might want to choose an alternate location. This is useful when you want to compare the backup copy of the file with the current version, or if you want to reorganize the way in which the files are stored. The options allow you to specify or browse to the destination path location. You can also choose whether you want to create subfolders. Selecting this option re-creates the directory structure of the original files. Finally, if multiple hard disks were backed up, it can be helpful to create a separate top-level subfolder for each hard disk. The Example section provides information about how the resulting files will appear.

Click Start Restore to begin copying the files to the destination location. Figure 13-14 shows the progress display of the restore operation. When the operation is complete, click Finish. You can then use Windows Explorer to view the recovered data.

Exam Tip   In general, the process of creating backups is fairly simple. However, the real goal is to be able to perform restore operations. When preparing for Exam 70-623, be sure to spend some time simulating various restore scenarios. This will help you understand the complete data protection and recovery process. It will also help you significantly when supporting customers who have experienced data loss. The home and small-business users who rely on you will be significantly more confident in your skills if you've performed various restore operations in the past.

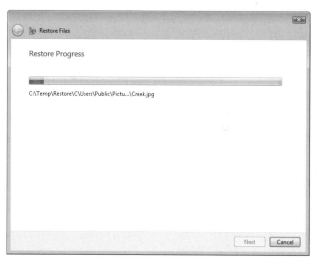

Figure 13-14   Viewing the progress of a restore operation

Using Advanced Restore

Although the standard restore process works well for most standard operations, there will be cases in which you need to perform different actions. For example, you might need to restore files from a backup that was stored on another computer. You can access this option by clicking Advanced Restore in the Backup and Restore Center. This launches the Backup Status and Configuration window. If necessary, click Restore Files (see Figure 13-15).

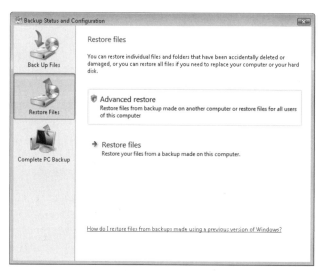

Figure 13-15   Using the Restore Files options in the Backup Status and Configuration utility

Clicking Advanced Restore enables you to choose a new option in the first step of the restore process: Files From A Backup Made On A Different Computer. When you click Next, you'll have the option of manually specifying the location of the backup set from which you want to restore (see Figure 13-16). Options include choosing from a local storage location or specifying the path to a shared folder on the network.

Figure 13-16   Manually providing restore-related information

After you locate a valid backup set, the restore process identifies dates and times. You can then carry out the restore process as described in the previous section.

Using Previous Versions of Files

Generally, the process of creating backups is useful for ensuring that your data remains protected. It provides an easy way to restore large numbers of files in the case of a large amount of data loss. What about simpler situations? For example, suppose you've made some changes to a Microsoft Word document on your computer, and you want to undo those changes. In this case, it can be a time-consuming process to access the Backup and Restore Center, find the relevant backup set, and then choose the files you want to restore. Fortunately, there's a much better way.

Using Windows Explorer, you can right-click any file or folder on your computer and click the Previous Versions tab of the item's Properties dialog box (see Figure 13-17). You can also right-click a file or folder item and select Restore Previous Version. The list might include numerous previous versions of the file. The total number of versions depends on various settings, including how often you modified the file. In this section, you'll learn about how the Previous Versions feature works.

Figure 13-17   Viewing the Previous Versions tab for a file

Sources of Previous Versions

There are two main methods by which Windows Vista stores previous versions of files on the computer. The first is based on backups that you create using the Backup and Restore Center. For example, if you configure a backup job that runs nightly on your computer, a previous version of the file is available based on the time of that backup. New versions of the files apply only if the contents of the file have changed. In this example, if you modify the file daily (and perform backups every night), you should see a previous version for each of the backups. Alternatively, if you don't modify the file, the backup process does not create another copy of it, and a previous version will not be available for that time period.

The second source of previous versions of a file or folder is through the System Restore feature. In Chapter 12, you learned about how you can use System Restore to troubleshoot problems with the state of the computer. Whenever a new restore point is created on the computer, changes to data files are also recorded. Although you do not directly configure the dates and times of the creation of restore points, you can create one manually from the Start menu by right-clicking Computer, selecting Properties, and then clicking the System Protection tab (see Figure 13-18). The Create button enables you to generate a new restore point. By default, Windows Vista automatically creates new restore points daily. Restore points are also created when system changes (such as the installation of new software or device drivers) are performed. For more information on System Restore, see Chapter 12.

Figure 13-18   Viewing System Protection configuration information

Over time, as backups and restore points are deleted to save disk space, previous version information might also be removed. Therefore, it is a good idea to keep multiple previous versions of backups for historical reasons. Overall, the Previous Versions feature and System Restore are not replacements for standard backup procedures.

Restoring Previous Versions of Files and Folders

The primary benefit of using the Previous Versions feature is that it enables you to access earlier versions of data easily simply by using standard file properties. From the Previous Versions tab of a file or folder, you can sort the list of versions based on name, modification date, or location of the file. You have three main options for choosing how to work with earlier copies of the files.

The first is to click Open on the Previous Versions tab of the file or folder's Properties dialog box. This opens an earlier version of the file or folder and enables you to view it as it existed at a previous point in time. For example, if you open a version of a Microsoft PowerPoint document that was created the previous week, you'll see only the slides and content that were in the file at that time. Similarly, when you open a previous version of a folder, you'll see all of the files that existed within that folder at the time the previous version was created.

The second option is to click Copy to copy a previous version of a file or folder to another location. When you click this button, you are prompted to provide the destination file system location for the item. The older version of the file or folder is then copied to that location (see Figure 13-19). The copy feature is useful when you want to compare an older copy of a file with a newer one or if you're not sure which version you want to restore.

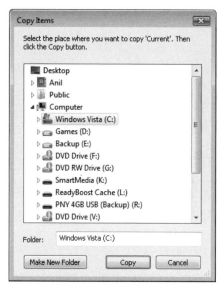

Figure 13-19   Using the Copy command to restore a file to a different location

In some cases, you want to replace the current version of the file with an earlier version. You can do that by clicking Restore on the Previous Versions tab of the file or folder's Properties dialog box. A dialog box prompts you for confirmation of this operation (see Figure 13-20). It is important to note that when you choose to restore a file or folder, you are no longer able to change it to a later version. Therefore, if you are unsure of whether you want to roll back permanently to a previous version of the item, it's best to copy it to another location and then overwrite it later.

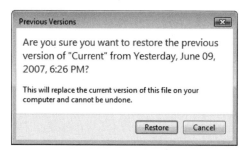

Figure 13-20   Restoring to a previous version of a file

Restoring Deleted or Renamed Files

So far, the focus has been on ways in which you can restore to previous versions of files or folders. The process involves clicking the appropriate file and accessing the Previous Versions tab of its Properties dialog box. What about files that have been deleted or renamed? In those cases, the original file is no longer present, so you cannot select it and display its properties to access the Previous Versions tab.

Fortunately, there's a way to restore these files as well. You need to know the location of the item that you are trying to recover. To restore the file or folder, access its parent folder, and then choose to open a previous version. You should then be able to see the file or folder you want to restore. After you have located the item, you can again copy it back to its earlier location. The Previous Versions feature in Windows Vista makes the process of restoring files and folders quick and easy.

Quick Check

1. What are typical scheduling options that are available when creating new backup jobs?

2. What are two ways in which you can restore a copy of a file that has been corrupted?

Quick Check Answers

1. New backup jobs can be scheduled to occur daily, weekly, or monthly. You can also specify the particular date and time at which the process will run.

2. You can restore a file using the Previous Versions tab or by clicking Restore Files in Backup and Restore Center.

Practice: Creating and Restoring File-Based Backups

In these practice exercises, you perform the steps that are required to create a new file-based backup. Then, you restore the backup files to test the complete process. It is recommended that you perform these steps on a test computer running Windows Vista (or within a virtual machine) because important files could be overwritten. Also, if the computer is currently configured with backup jobs, you should make note of the settings if you want to change them back after completing the exercises.

▶ **Practice 1: Create a New Backup Job**

In this practice exercise, you create a new nightly backup job on a computer running Windows Vista. To complete this exercise, you must have sufficient space to make a backup of user data files. The destination can be a network share, an external hard disk, or removable media.

1. Open the Backup and Restore Center and click Back Up Files.

2. For the backup destination, choose a network share, a local hard disk, or an external storage device. Make a note of the device and location that you choose. Click Next to continue.

3. Now, you need to select which types of files you want to back up. If you have adequate storage space, leave the default settings of having all check boxes selected. If you have limited backup storage space, clear one or a few of the check boxes. Note that the Category Details section provides you with information about which types of files will be included. Click Next to continue.

4. For the backup schedule, choose to perform the backup operation nightly at 9:00 p.m. Alternatively, you can change the schedule to fit the needs of the computer (for example, you can choose to perform the backups weekly or monthly).

5. Click Save Settings And Start Backup. Note that a full backup of the files begins immediately. Monitor the progress of the backup.

   The process starts by creating a shadow copy of the files that are required. You can continue to use the computer while the backup process is running.

   When the backup process is complete, click Close.

6. To verify that the backup was created, open the backup destination device and location.

   You should see a folder structure that starts with the name of the computer and includes additional folders for backup sets and backup files. You will use these files in the second practice exercise.

7. Verify that the Backup and Restore Center now shows the date and time of the last backup. Also, note that it shows the scheduled time for the next backup operation.

8. When finished, close the Backup and Restore Center.

   You can optionally turn off the backup job by accessing the Backup Status and Configuration utility. You can also reset the backup job settings to their initial configuration (if backups were enabled before you began this exercise).

▶ **Practice 2: Restore from File-Based Backups**

In this practice exercise, you restore the files that you backed up in Practice 1. You store the restored files to an alternate location to avoid overwriting the current versions of those files.

1. Open the Backup and Restore Center and click Restore Files.

2. On the first page of the Restore Files Wizard, select Files From An Older Backup. Click Next.

3. Notice that you can see a list of the dates and times of any backup operations that were performed on this computer. You can also see where the backup has been stored. If you created earlier backups prior to performing the steps in Practice 1, they appear here. Select the backup that you created in Practice 1, and then click Next.

4. Specify that you want all .jpg picture files to be restored by clicking Search and searching for JPG.

5. Click Select All to specify that all .jpg picture files should be restored.

6. Click Add to add the items to the selection list. Note that you can also add specific files and folders by using the appropriate buttons. Click Next to continue.

7. Choose the second option to save the restore files to an alternate path on your computer. Specify the full path to a folder on the local computer. Make a note of this path.

8. Select the Restore The Files To Their Original Subfolders and Create A Subfolder For The Drive Letter check boxes.

9. Click Start Restore to begin copying the files to the alternate location.

10. When the restore process is complete, click Finish.

11. Use Windows Explorer to open the file system location that you specified in step 7. Note that you will see a folder based on the drive letter(s) of the content. Within that folder, you should see any folders that contained .jpg files (along with the files themselves).

12. When finished, close Windows Explorer and close the Backup and Restore Center.

Lesson Summary

- When planning for backups, consider which data must be backed up and how frequently you should perform backups.
- Backups can be stored to local hard disks, removable media such as CDs and DVDs, external hard disks, or to a network location.
- The Backup and Restore Center provides a method for accessing backup and restore commands.
- File-based backups can be configured to make copies of certain types of files, based on users' requirements.
- Files can be restored from backups by using the Backup and Restore Center.
- Windows Vista makes previous versions of files available based on restore points and backups.
- You can restore previous versions of files and folders by right-clicking an item and clicking the Previous Versions tab.

Lesson Review

You can use the following questions to test your knowledge of the information in Lesson 1, "Using the Backup and Restore Center." The questions are also available on the companion CD if you prefer to review them in electronic form.

NOTE Answers

Answers to these questions and explanations of why each answer choice is correct or incorrect are located in the "Answers" section at the end of the book.

1. You are a Consumer Support Technician helping a new Windows Vista user protect her data. The user is a small-business owner who wants to make sure that her data is backed up nightly to another computer on her network. Which of the following is the easiest method of doing this?

    A. Create a Complete PC backup and choose to store the files to a network location.

    B. Create a file-based backup job and choose to store to files to a network location.

    C. Configure System Restore to copy data to a remote network location.

    D. Create a file-based backup job and choose to store the files to an external hard disk. Periodically move the external hard disk to the other computer.

    E. Create a file-based backup job and choose to store the files to a local hard disk. Create a job to copy the backup set to a network location.

2. You are a Consumer Support Technician helping a Windows Vista user with a backup-related issue. The customer recently made an accidental modification to a large number of Microsoft Word documents and wants to use a previous version of the files. The System Restore feature is enabled, and a backup job is configured to run every evening at 6:00 p.m. He is unsure of which version of the files he wants to restore. Which of the following commands should he use?

    A. Restore the latest previous version of the folder that contains the Word documents.

    B. Restore the first previous version of the folder that contains the Word documents.

    C. Copy previous versions of the folder containing the documents to a different location.

    D. Open the most recent previous version of the folder containing the documents.

3. You are assisting a customer with restoring her personal document files to a new installation of Windows Vista. When she clicks Restore Files in the Backup and Restore Center, she does not have the ability to select the appropriate backup set. How can you restore data from the backup set?

    A. Manually create a new restore point, using System Protection.

    B. Use the Restore Computer command to restore the backup.

    C. Use the Back Up Files command and specify the location of the existing backup set.

    D. Use the Advanced Restore command.

Lesson 2: Using Windows Complete PC Backup and Restore

File-based backup and restore operations are designed primarily to protect users' important documents and files. This can help minimize the size of backups and reduce the time it takes to create them. Although it does not include operating system information or applications, the idea is that you can recover these files and programs, using installation media.

The problem, however, is that it can take a significant amount of time to recover from the failure of an entire hard disk. The typical steps required in the case of complete data loss begin with the reinstallation of the Windows Vista operating system. Users then need to install device drivers, reinstall applications, update the operating system, and make all of the necessary configuration changes. Although complete data loss should be very rare, the recovery process can take several hours to complete. In this lesson, you'll learn how the Complete PC Backup and Restore feature of Windows Vista can simplify this process.

After this lesson, you will be able to:
- Describe the purpose and function of the Complete PC Backup and Restore feature.
- Create a Complete PC backup, using the Backup and Restore Center.
- Perform a Complete PC restore, using the Windows Recovery environment.

Estimated lesson time: 35 minutes

Understanding Complete PC Backup and Restore

The Windows Vista Complete PC Backup and Restore feature is designed to simplify the process of recovering an entire operating system. The backup that is created includes the entire operating system, installed programs, user-specific and system-specific settings, and data files. This provides a simplified method of restoring an entire computer.

There are some drawbacks, however. For example, you are unable to specify which files and folders are restored. For that reason, customers should use file-based backups for regularly protecting their data files. They can periodically make Complete PC backups to help recover from a serious system issue.

Creating a Complete PC Backup

You can start the process of creating a Complete PC backup from within the Backup and Restore Center by clicking Back Up Computer. The first step of the process enables you to select the backup destination location. The first set of options includes a list of locally attached hard disk drives (see Figure 13-21). For this option to be available, the computer must contain at least two separate hard disks. This is required because you cannot store a Complete PC backup on the same disk as the operating system.

Figure 13-21   Choosing the backup location for a Complete PC backup

The other destination option is to use one or more DVDs. This option is available if the computer has a device that is capable of writing to DVDs. The total space required for the entire backup can be very large, so users should keep in mind that multiple DVDs might be required. The Complete PC backup process attempts to estimate how many disks might be required.

NOTE   Complete PC backup storage limitations

Unlike standard file-based backups, it is not possible to make a Complete PC backup to some types of removable media devices such as USB memory drives. Storing the backup in a network location is also not supported. The primary reason for this, as you'll learn later in this chapter, is that the Complete PC restore process runs within a limited recovery environment that does not include additional network support or device drivers.

When you click Next, you are prompted to confirm the backup settings (see Figure 13-22). The backup requires you to include the entire Windows Vista system volume in the backup set. An estimate based on the amount of required disk space is also made.

To begin the backup process, click Start Backup. The Windows Complete PC Backup dialog box shows the progress of the backup (see Figure 13-23). You can continue to use the computer while the backup is being created, but system performance is decreased due to the additional disk activity. The process typically takes a long time because all of the files, programs, and data on the system hard disk need to be copied.

Figure 13-22   Confirming the backup settings for a Complete PC backup

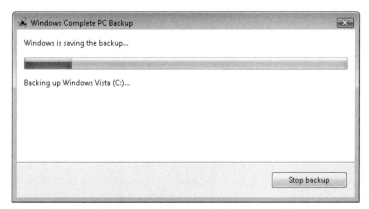

Figure 13-23   Viewing the progress of a Complete PC backup operation

Performing a Complete PC Restore

In the event of hard disk corruption or significant data loss due to hardware failure, the best method of getting up and running might be to restore the complete operating system as well as all user programs and data files. Consider this approach when other resolution methods have failed. (For more information about diagnosing and troubleshooting Windows Vista, see

Chapter 12.) Assuming that a valid backup is available, the Complete PC restore process enables users to perform a relatively pain-free recovery of the operating system. At the end of the process, applications, settings, data files, and all other contents of the system hard disk should be recovered to the point in time of the backup. Users also have the option of including nonsystem volumes in the backup.

Unlike the restore process for standard file-based backups, performing a Complete PC restore requires you to reboot the computer into the special recovery environment. This is necessary because operating system files, application settings, and other data cannot be restored while the operating system is running. It is also helpful because the actual reason for performing the restore might be that Windows Vista is unable to boot properly.

Starting the Restore Process

When you click Restore Computer in the Backup and Restore Center, you see a message box that provides details about how to proceed (see Figure 13-24). It is important to note that the entire system is effectively rolled back to the point in time of the backup, and there are no options for choosing which files are restored. If the system is still accessible and you have files that were created or modified since the last Complete PC backup, it is a good idea to create a new backup of those files before proceeding.

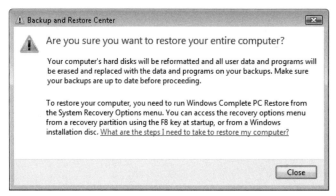

Figure 13-24   Viewing instructions and a warning related to the Complete PC restore process

---

NOTE   Combining Complete PC backups and file backups

File-based backups provide several advantages for protecting data: they're quicker to perform, and they use less disk space. This means that users can back up files fairly often. Complete PC backups take a large amount of disk space and are designed to be run less frequently. Fortunately, you can use both methods together. A complete recovery process might begin with restoring from a Complete PC backup and then performing a file-level restore to recover any files that were added or modified since the complete backup.

You can launch the Complete PC Restore process in two different ways. The first is to boot the computer, using the Windows Vista installation disc. The Windows Complete PC Restore option displays in the list of available options when you choose the Repair option (see Figure 13-25). The other method is to press the F8 key during the boot process to access the Advanced Boot Options menu. Of course, this option is available only if the computer is able to boot to this point. Clicking Repair Your Computer allows you to start the restore process. For more information on both of these methods, see Chapter 12.

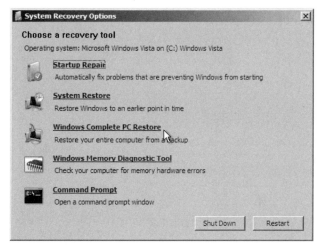

Figure 13-25   Selecting the Windows Complete PC Restore option from the Windows Recovery environment

Selecting Restore Options

When you click Windows Complete PC Restore, the recovery environment automatically attempts to locate an available backup. If the backup is available on another hard disk connected to the computer, Windows Vista should be able to find it automatically. It then populates the display with the relevant information (see Figure 13-26).

If multiple backups are available, you have the option to choose a specific backup by selecting Restore A Different Backup. Figure 13-27 shows the information that is available for the Complete PC backups.

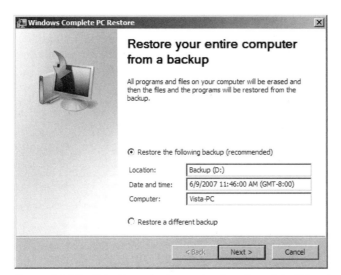

Figure 13-26   Selecting a backup set, using Complete PC restore

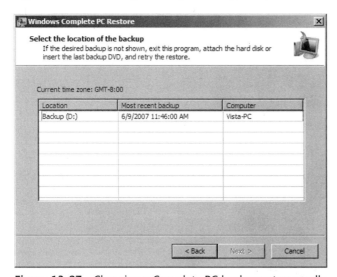

Figure 13-27   Choosing a Complete PC backup set manually

After you have chosen the appropriate backup set, you see details and options related to what you want the restore process to do. Figure 13-28 shows an example of the screen. The available information includes the following:

■ **Location**   The source location for the Complete PC backup files.

- **Date And Time**   The date and time at which the backup was created. It's important to note that the time is displayed in Greenwich Mean Time (GMT), so adjustments might be required if the computer is in a different time zone.
- **Computer**   The name of the computer running Windows Vista. For more information on configuring the computer name, see Chapter 9, "Configuring Windows Vista Networking."
- **Disks To Restore**   This is a listing of which hard disks were included in the backup. If multiple logical or physical volumes were selected, they appear here.

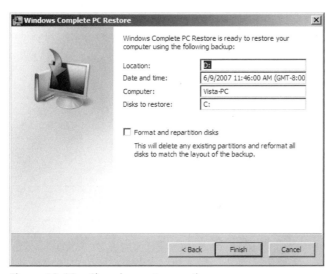

Figure 13-28   Choosing restore options

The Format And Repartition Disks check box enables you to specify whether you want the restore process to repartition local hard disks automatically to match the configuration of the backup. This is a useful option when you are attempting to restore to a completely new hard disk on the computer. If you leave the check box cleared, the recovery process keeps the existing partitions intact.

Completing the Restore Process

To begin the restore process, click Finish. You receive one final confirmation warning. When you click OK, the restore operation begins (see Figure 13-29). Depending on the size of the hard disk and the data you restore, the process might take a long time to complete.

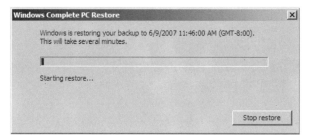

Figure 13-29   Performing a Complete PC restore

After the restore operation completes, the computer automatically reboots, and Windows Vista should appear just as it did at the time when the Complete PC backup was created.

NOTE Restoring system settings

The System Restore feature in Windows Vista enables you to restore system settings without affecting data or requiring a reinstallation of the entire operating system. This is often useful when troubleshooting startup problems, device driver issues, or the installation of unwanted software. For more information about using System Restore, see Chapter 12.

Quick Check
1. What types of files and information are included in a Complete PC backup?
2. How can you perform a Complete PC restore after replacing a failed hard disk?

Quick Check Answers
1. A Complete PC backup includes the entire system volume, including operating system files, user data, program files, and related information.
2. You can boot from the Windows Vista installation media and choose the Repair option to access the Complete PC restore feature.

Practice: Performing a Complete PC Backup and Restore

In this practice exercise, you create a Complete PC backup on the local computer. You then restore the computer, using the Windows Complete PC restore process. Because some operating system changes or settings might be lost between the times you perform the backup and restore operations, you should perform this exercise on a test computer. Additionally, you need sufficient disk space to perform a Complete PC backup. You should use a second physical hard disk in the computer for the destination, but you might choose to use DVD media if necessary. The amount of storage space required is approximately the size of the current system volume. You also need a copy of the Windows Vista installation media for the computer.

▶ **Practice: Create and Restore a Complete PC Backup**

1. Open the Backup and Restore Center and click Back Up Computer.

2. Choose the destination for the Complete PC backup. The preferred method is to store the backup on a local hard disk, if it is available. Otherwise, choose to use DVD media. Click Next.

3. On the disk selection screen, verify that check box for the System volume is selected. Clear any check boxes for other available disks to minimize backup space and time. Click Next.

4. Make a note of the backup location and the amount of estimated disk space that is required. Click Start Backup to begin the Complete PC backup process.

5. Monitor the backup process. Because all of the data on the System volume is being copied, the process might take a long time. When finished, close the Complete PC Backup dialog box.

6. To provide a way to test the effects of the Complete PC restore process, make some changes to the current operating system. For example, change the desktop wallpaper or install new applications.

7. In the Backup and Restore Center, click Restore Computer. Note the instructions that are provided.

8. Place the Windows Vista installation media in the appropriate drive and reboot the computer. Choose to boot the computer from the CD/DVD device. If you are not prompted for this, consult your computer's documentation for information about changing the order of preference for boot devices.

9. After the setup process has loaded, select your regional settings on the first screen and click Next.

10. Select the Repair Windows Vista option and click Next.

11. Make sure that the installation of Windows Vista you want to recover is selected, and then click Next.

12. Choose the Windows Complete PC Restore option from the System Recovery Options menu.

13. The recovery process attempts to locate any Complete PC backups that are available on local hard disks. Select the appropriate backup, and then click Next.

14. Verify the settings for the restore. Generally, you should leave the Format And Repartition Disks check box cleared because the disks should already be properly partitioned.

15. Click Finish, and then confirm that you want to perform the restore operation.

16. Wait for the Complete PC restore process to finish, and then reboot the computer. Remove the Windows Vista installation media from the device.

17. Log on to Windows Vista normally and verify that the system reverted to its settings prior to the modifications you made in step 6. You should now be able to boot and use Windows Vista normally.

Lesson Summary

■ The Complete PC Backup and Restore feature is designed to provide users with a quick way of restoring an entire computer in the case of a serious failure or disk corruption.

■ Users cannot specify which files or settings are restored when using a Complete PC backup.

■ You can create a Complete PC backup, using the Backup and Restore Center.

■ Complete PC backups must be stored on a local hard disk or on removable DVD media.

■ The restore process for Complete PC backups involves restarting the computer, using Windows Vista installation media, and accessing the Repair option.

■ The Complete PC restore operation can automatically partition and format a new hard disk.

Lesson Review

You can use the following questions to test your knowledge of the information in Lesson 2, "Using Windows Complete PC Backup and Restore." The questions are also available on the companion CD if you prefer to review them in electronic form.

NOTE Answers

Answers to these questions and explanations of why each answer choice is correct or incorrect are located in the "Answers" section at the end of the book.

---

1. You have recently replaced a failed hard disk in a customer's computer with a new hard disk. The customer had previously created a Complete PC backup, and you have verified that it is present on the computer's second hard disk drive. Which of the following is the first step you should perform to restore the computer as quickly as possible?

    A. Boot the computer, using the Windows Vista installation media, and choose the Repair option.

    B. Boot the computer using the Windows Vista installation media and choose to reinstall the operating system.

    C. Boot Windows Vista into Safe Mode and launch the Backup and Restore Center.

    D. Boot Windows Vista normally and launch the Backup and Restore Center.

2. You are a Consumer Support Technician assisting a customer with setting up backups for his computer. The customer would like to minimize the amount of time it takes to recover the computer in the case of a hard disk failure. He would also like to make frequent backup copies of his data files. He currently has a limited amount of disk space available on a second hard disk. How can he meet these requirements? (Choose two.)

   A. Schedule a Complete PC backup to occur every month.

   B. Schedule a file-based backup to occur every month.

   C. Schedule a file-based backup to occur every evening.

   D. Schedule a Complete PC backup to occur every evening.

Chapter Review

To further practice and reinforce the skills you learned in this chapter, you can perform the following tasks:

- Review the chapter summary.
- Review the list of key terms introduced in this chapter.
- Complete the case scenarios. These scenarios set up real-world situations involving the topics of this chapter and ask you to create a solution.
- Complete the suggested practices.
- Take a practice test.

Chapter Summary

- The Backup and Restore Center provides the ability to create file-based backups and Complete PC backups.
- You can perform a Complete PC restore by booting from the Windows Vista installation media and choosing the Repair option.
- Previous versions of files are automatically stored when a restore point or a file-based backup is performed. You can access earlier versions of files and folders by using the Previous Versions feature.

Key Terms

Do you know what these key terms mean? You can check your answers by looking up the terms in the glossary at the end of the book.

- Advanced Boot Options
- Advanced Restore
- Backup and Restore Center
- backup catalogs
- backup files (folder)
- backup set (folder)
- Complete PC backup
- Complete PC restore
- hard disk, external

- Previous Versions
- restore point
- shadow copy
- Windows Complete PC restore

Case Scenarios

In the following case scenarios, you apply what you've learned about file-based backups and the Complete PC Backup and Restore process. You can find answers to these questions in the "Answers" section at the end of this book.

Case Scenario 1: Evaluating Restore Options

You are a Consumer Support Technician helping a Windows Vista user restore data on his computer. The customer had configured a backup job to run nightly on his computer at 9:00 p.m. He has verified that all of the backups were created and that they are available on an external hard disk drive. You have also verified that System Protection is enabled and configured properly. In addition, the customer created a Complete PC backup several months ago after installing and configuring numerous new applications. Recently, the customer's hard disk experienced a complete physical failure and failed to boot. He has purchased a new hard disk drive, and you have helped him install it in the computer. The customer would like to recover as much data as is possible.

1. What is the easiest way to make the computer bootable again?
2. How can the customer recover the latest backups of his data files?
3. How can the user verify that the Previous Versions feature will be available for his data files?

Case Scenario 2: Evaluating Restore Options

You are a Consumer Support Technician working in a retail environment. A customer is planning to upgrade several of the computers running Microsoft Windows XP in her small-business environment to Windows Vista Home Premium. In the past, she has experienced data loss due to accidental deletions or modifications of files and the failure of hard disk drives. When hard disks have failed, it has often taken her several hours to repair the computer and reinstall applications. Therefore, one of her primary concerns is ensuring that backups are being regularly performed. For ease of maintenance, she would like to have all backup files stored centrally on a single computer. The customer would like to achieve all of these goals without requiring significant training for users of these computers.

1. How can the customer ensure that files are being regularly backed up on each computer?

2. Where should the backups be stored?

3. How can the customer minimize the amount of time it would take to recover from a hard disk failure?

4. How can she verify the date and time of the most recent backup on a particular computer running Windows Vista?

Suggested Practices

To help you successfully master the exam objectives presented in this chapter, complete the following tasks.

Practicing Backup and Recovery Procedures

The practice items in this section enable you to practice the process of creating backups and restoring data.

- **Practice 1: Working with backup options**   Create a new backup job on a computer running Windows Vista and use various backup options. For example, if you have the available hardware, back up to a local hard disk, an external hard disk, and to removable DVD media. Also, change several of the file selection options to change the size of the backup. For all of the backups, view the collection of backup sets and backup files created. Open various compressed folders to see which files were included and how they were organized.

- **Practice 2: Test restore options**   Based on the backups created in Practice 1, recover data to the computer running Windows Vista. In some cases, you might be able to use the standard file-based restore process. In other situations, you might need to use the Advanced Restore command to find the backup-related files.

- **Practice 3: Working with previous versions**   On a test computer running Windows Vista, practice using the Previous Versions feature to look at earlier copies of files and folders. Make manual changes to a file, and then create a new restore point by using the System Protection feature. Verify that a new previous version is available in the properties of the file. Finally, delete a file and restore it using the Previous Versions feature.

- **Practice 4: Testing the complete PC backup process**   On a test computer running Windows Vista, create a new Complete PC backup. Make several changes to the computer, including installing new programs and changing operating system settings such as the desktop wallpaper. Then, perform the Complete PC restore process by booting from Windows Vista installation media. After the system is rebooted, verify that all system settings appear as they did at the time the backup was created. Alternatively, if you have an extra available hard drive, physically replace the original Windows Vista system disk with a blank drive. Then, perform the Complete PC restore process to the new hard disk drive.

Take a Practice Test

The practice tests on this book's companion CD offer many options. For example, you can test yourself on just one exam objective, or you can test yourself on all of the 70-623 certification exam content. You can set up the test so that it closely simulates the experience of taking a certification exam, or you can set it up in study mode so that you can look at the correct answers and explanations after you answer each question.

MORE INFO   Practice tests

For details about all the practice test options available, see the "How to Use the Practice Tests" section in this book's introduction.

Answers

Chapter 1: Lesson Review Answers

Lesson 1

1. **Correct Answer: A and B**
   - **A.** **Correct:** Windows Aero is included in Windows Vista Home Premium.
   - **B.** **Correct:** Windows Media Center is included in Windows Vista Home Premium.
   - **C.** **Incorrect:** Windows Vista Ultimate is the only consumer-focused edition of Windows Vista that includes BitLocker Drive Encryption.
   - **D.** **Incorrect:** Windows Vista Business and Windows Vista Ultimate include support for advanced backup features such as scheduling.

2. **Correct Answer: B and C**
   - **A.** **Incorrect:** Windows Vista Home Basic does not support Windows Aero and does not include Windows Media Center.
   - **B.** **Correct:** Windows Vista Home Premium includes both Windows Aero and Windows Media Center. The customer can disable Windows Aero if he chooses.
   - **C.** **Correct:** Windows Vista Ultimate includes both Windows Aero and Windows Media Center. The customer can disable Windows Aero if he chooses.
   - **D.** **Incorrect:** Windows Vista Business includes support for Windows Aero but does not include the Windows Media Center feature.

Lesson 2

1. **Correct Answer: A and D**
   - **A.** **Correct:** At least 128 MB of video memory is required.
   - **B.** **Incorrect:** Support for 32-bit color depth meets the requirements for enabling Windows Aero features.
   - **C.** **Incorrect:** Support for the WDDM meets the requirements for enabling Windows Aero features.
   - **D.** **Correct:** The video adapter must provide support for DirectX 9 or later.

2. **Correct Answer: B**

   A. **Incorrect:** Although the Windows Vista Capable logo specifies that the computer can be upgraded to Windows Vista, it does not specify that the computer supports advanced features such as Windows Aero.

   B. **Correct:** A computer bearing the Windows Vista Premium Ready logo provides support for advanced features of the Windows Vista operating system.

   C. **Incorrect:** The Certified for Windows Vista logo is available only on new computers that were shipped with Windows Vista preinstalled.

   D. **Incorrect:** The Works with Windows Vista logo is designed for ensuring that individual software and hardware devices are compatible with Windows Vista. It does not indicate that an entire system is compatible.

3. **Correct Answer: D**

   A. **Incorrect:** The Works with Windows Vista logo is designed to specify hardware and software compatibility, but it does not ensure that an entire system can be upgraded.

   B. **Incorrect:** Although contacting hardware manufacturers could provide useful information, it is not the quickest and easiest way to obtain upgrade information because the user might need to contact several different vendors.

   C. **Incorrect:** The Windows Vista Upgrade Advisor is designed to evaluate the hardware and software configuration of a local computer before the upgrade process.

   D. **Correct:** The Windows Vista Upgrade Advisor will be able to evaluate the current system, including hardware, software, and device drivers, prior to the upgrade process.

Chapter 1: Case Scenario Answers

Case Scenario 1: Evaluating Windows Vista Upgrade Options

1. Windows Vista Ultimate includes all three of these features. Windows Vista Home Premium does not include support for BitLocker, and Windows Vista Home Basic does not provide any of the three features.

2. Both the Windows Vista Capable and Windows Vista Premium Ready logos would indicate that the computer could be upgraded to Windows Vista.

3. The customer should download, install, and run the Windows Vista Upgrade Advisor to test the system for compatibility.

Case Scenario 2: Verifying Hardware and Software Compatibility

1. The Certified for Windows Vista logo indicates that a hardware device has undergone extensive testing to ensure that it is compatible with and optimized for Windows Vista. It's often much easier to look for this logo than it is to compare the technical specifications of each graphics adapter.

2. The customer should look for the Certified for Windows Vista logo to ensure compatibility.

3. The customer should look for the Games for Windows logo. Entertainment software titles that contain this logo have been designed to meet several standards related to the installation and use of the product.

Chapter 2: Lesson Review Answers

Lesson 1

1. **Correct Answers: C and D**
   A. **Incorrect:** Windows Vista Home Basic supports only a clean installation if Windows XP Professional is already installed.
   B. **Incorrect:** Windows Vista Home Premium supports only a clean installation if Windows XP Professional is already installed.
   C. **Correct:** Windows Vista Business supports an in-place upgrade of Windows XP Professional.
   D. **Correct:** Windows Vista Ultimate supports an in-place upgrade of Windows XP Professional.

2. **Correct Answer: A**
   A. **Correct:** A clean installation replaces the existing version of Windows.
   B. **Incorrect:** Performing an in-place upgrade to an edition of Windows Vista that will result in a loss of functionality is not supported. For example, you cannot upgrade from Windows XP Media Center Edition to Windows Vista Home Basic.
   C. **Incorrect:** A multiboot installation enables Windows Vista to coexist with a previous version of Windows.

Lesson 2

1. **Correct Answer: B**
   A. **Incorrect:** A clean installation will overwrite the customer's existing applications.
   B. **Correct:** An in-place upgrade retains the customer's existing applications.
   C. **Incorrect:** A multiboot installation will allow the customer to retain his or her applications, but they will not be installed on Windows Vista.

Lesson 3

1. **Correct Answer: B**
   A. **Incorrect:** This keeps themes from being applied to menus but does not affect the entire application.
   B. **Correct:** This corrects jagged or improperly rendered applications.
   C. **Incorrect:** This disables special effects such as the transparency feature.
   D. **Incorrect:** The graphical appearance of an application is not related to privilege level.

Chapter 2: Case Scenario Answers

Case Scenario 1: Evaluating Windows Vista Installation Options

1. Neither. Based on the customer's need to retain existing programs without the ability to reinstall, an in-place upgrade would be the only way. However, based on the edition of Windows Vista he purchased and his existing operating system, only a clean installation is supported.
2. The customer will be asked to purchase Windows Vista Home Premium to perform an in-place upgrade.
3. The customer should download, install, and run the Windows Vista Upgrade Advisor to test the system for compatibility.

Case Scenario 2: Disk Partitioning

1. Clean installation only.
2. She will be asked to back up her files and settings because a clean installation will replace the contents of the C partition.
3. The customer should download, install, and run the Windows Vista Upgrade Advisor to test the system for compatibility.

Chapter 3: Lesson Review Answers

Lesson 1

1. **Correct Answer: D**
   A. **Incorrect:** Lowering the resolution setting for the graphics adapter will not disable the updated look and feel settings for Windows Vista.

    B. **Incorrect:** Increasing the refresh rate for the display adapter will not disable the updated look and feel settings for Windows Vista.

    C. **Incorrect:** The Windows Aero appearance setting will use the updated user interface features of Windows Vista.

    D. **Correct:** The Windows Standard and Windows Classic options in the Appearance settings will change the desktop settings to appear as they did in previous versions of Windows.

2. **Correct Answer: A**

    A. **Correct:** The Window Color And Appearance dialog box enables the user to change the color of the glass effect.

    B. **Incorrect:** The Desktop Background settings affect the wallpaper used for the desktop but do not allow for changing glass effect colors.

    C. **Incorrect:** Theme settings can be used to change window colors, but they do not allow for modifying the color of glass effects.

    D. **Incorrect:** Display settings are related to the configuring of the display adapter and do not affect the color of glass effects.

Lesson 2

1. **Correct Answer: C**

    A. **Incorrect:** The Bring Gadgets To Front command temporarily makes all gadgets viewable by placing them on top of other open windows. It does not specify that they will always be visible over other windows.

    B. **Incorrect:** The View List Of Running Gadgets command shows a list of running gadgets and does not affect how they appear on the desktop.

    C. **Correct:** When enabled, the Sidebar Is Always On Top Of Other Windows option ensures that all gadgets for Windows Sidebar are always visible, even if another application window might have otherwise covered them.

    D. **Incorrect:** The Restore Gadgets Installed With Windows command installs gadgets that were manually installed from the Windows Sidebar configuration, but it does not affect how they are displayed.

    E. **Incorrect:** The Opacity setting affects the transparency of individual gadget items only and will not control whether they are visible over other windows.

2. **Correct Answer: B**

    A. **Incorrect:** Uninstalling the gadget would remove it from Windows Sidebar, but it would also remove it from the system. When the user wants to add it, he or she will first need to restore all default gadgets that were installed with Windows Vista.

      B. **Correct:** Closing the gadget removes the gadget from the display, but it can still be quickly added back to Windows Sidebar in the future.

      C. **Incorrect**: It is not possible to set the Opacity property of a gadget to 0%.

      D. **Incorrect:** It is not possible to place one gadget over another.

      E. **Incorrect:** Detaching the gadget will not remove it from the desktop.

  3. **Correct Answer: C**

      A. **Incorrect:** Using the All Feeds setting would display all eight feeds in a single Feed Headlines gadget.

      B. **Incorrect:** The Feed Headlines gadget does not provide a method for selecting only certain feeds.

      C. **Correct:** Adding three separate gadgets to the desktop will enable the user to configure each Feed Headlines gadget to monitor a single feed, and it will enable him to view headlines from all three within Windows Sidebar.

      D. **Incorrect:** Using the All Feeds option would display all eight feeds in each of the three Feed Headlines gadgets.

Chapter 3: Case Scenario Answers

Case Scenario 1: Customizing the Windows Vista Desktop

1. The user can access the Display Settings dialog box and increase the resolution of the display. The optimal settings will be based on the capabilities of his video adapter, the capabilities of the monitor, and personal preference.

2. By accessing the Window Color And Appearance dialog box and clicking Show Color Mixer, the user can define the exact color he would like to use.

3. Clicking Theme in the Personalization window enables the user to save and restore sets of display-related settings easily.

Case Scenario 2: Configuring Windows Sidebar

1. The customer can launch Windows Sidebar by accessing the Windows Sidebar properties application. This can be launched directly from the Start menu or by accessing the Windows Sidebar Properties item in Control Panel.

2. She can access the properties of each Weather gadget separately by using the Configuration icon or by right-clicking the gadget and selecting Options.

3. She can add a single Feed Headlines gadget to Windows Sidebar and configure it to display headlines from all feeds.

Chapter 4: Lesson Review Answers

Lesson 1

1. **Correct Answers: C and D**
   A. **Incorrect:** The No Automatic Filtering option effectively disables the Junk E-mail filter.
   B. **Incorrect:** Setting the Junk E-mail filter to High removes most junk e-mail, but it does not limit accepted messages to only those from senders on the Safe Senders List.
   C. **Correct:** The Safe List Only option specifies that only the e-mail addresses that are configured on the Safe Senders List are received in the Inbox.
   D. **Correct:** The customer should add the e-mail addresses from which she wants to receive messages to the Safe Senders List.
   E. **Incorrect:** The potential number of junk e-mail senders is very large, and adding all of them to the Blocked Senders List is impractical.
   F. **Incorrect:** Blocking top-level domains is done primarily to prevent junk e-mail that originates in specific countries. It does not restrict the receipt of messages to only those from specified senders.

2. **Correct Answers: B and D**
   A. **Incorrect:** Having children subscribe to the father's calendar enables them to view his appointments but not vice versa.
   B. **Correct:** Storing each child's calendar in a shared folder makes them accessible to all users.
   C. **Incorrect:** Publishing the parent's calendar does not automatically add the children's appointments to it.
   D. **Correct:** The father can subscribe to calendars that are located in a shared location to add their appointments automatically to his calendar.

3. **Correct Answers: D and E**
   A. **Incorrect:** A meeting cannot be created with a blank name.
   B. **Incorrect:** Using a strong password does not prevent other people on the network from seeing the meeting.
   C. **Incorrect:** The People Near Me settings are used to determine from which types of users meeting requests can be received. It does not affect the creation of a new meeting.
   D. **Correct:** Sending the invitation through e-mail helps ensure that only authorized users are aware of the meeting.
   E. **Correct:** Choosing not to allow others to see the meeting prevents them from automatically discovering it on the network.

Lesson 2

1. Correct Answer: C
    A. **Incorrect:** The user would need to drag images manually for all .jpg files. Therefore, this is not the easiest way to resolve the problem.
    B. **Incorrect**: Adding folders to the gallery does not automatically allow .jpg files to open using Windows Explorer.
    C. **Correct**: Resetting the Windows Photo Gallery file associations restore the ability to double-click .jpg files and have them open automatically.
    D. **Incorrect**: The Set Program Access And Computer Defaults option does not allow for setting the default image viewer application.

2. Correct Answer: A
    A. **Correct:** A setup key must be generated on the Xbox 360 console and then entered into Windows Media Center on the computer running Windows Vista.
    B. **Incorrect**: Setup keys cannot be generated on the computer running Windows Vista.
    C. **Incorrect**: A TV tuner card is not required to access video and audio files. It is required for recording television programs.
    D. **Incorrect**: File association settings do not affect whether the Xbox 360 can communicate with Windows Media Center.

Chapter 4: Case Scenario Answers

Case Scenario 1: Configuring Windows Mail

1. The customer should know the server type for her e-mail provider (POP3 or IMAP), the server address, her logon and user name, and any associated advanced port or authentication settings.

2. The Windows Mail Junk E-mail filter provides several options for the level of filtering. In addition, the user can choose to define safe senders, blocked senders, and restrictions based on the source and encoding of international e-mail.

3. Message rules in Windows Mail can be used to move or copy messages automatically to folders based on the contents of the subject line or other parts of the message.

Case Scenario 2: Working with Windows Media Center

1. To record two television programs at the same time, the computer must be configured with two TV tuner cards.

2. The customer can start the process by generating a setup key on the Xbox 360 console. He can then enter this setup key in Windows Media Center to allow the device to connect over the network.

3. The customer needs to purchase an analog capture device that is compatible with Windows Vista to record analog content.

Chapter 5: Lesson Review Answers

Lesson 1

A. **Correct Answer: B**

    A. **Incorrect:** Because the program does not appear on the desktop or the Windows taskbar, it most likely will not show up on the Applications tab. Additionally, the Applications tab does not provide CPU usage statistics.

    B. **Correct:** The Processes tab lists all of the currently running programs on the computer, along with their CPU usage and other statistics. By sorting the list by the CPU column, you can determine which processes are consuming the most processor time.

    C. **Incorrect:** The Services tab does not show details related to CPU usage.

    D. **Incorrect:** The Performance tab shows only overall statistics such as CPU and memory use. It does not provide details about individual processes.

B. **Correct Answer: D**

    A. **Incorrect:** The Windows Experience Index provides a numerical representation of the system's overall performance. It does not provide details about processes or resource usage.

    B. **Incorrect:** Although the Task Manager Network tab displays statistics related to network use, it does not provide details about which applications or processes are using the network. Additionally, the Processes tab does not include columns related to network use.

    C. **Incorrect:** Although it might be possible to use several different Performance Monitor counters to isolate the source of the issue, this is not the quickest method for identifying which process is using the most network resources.

    D. **Correct:** The Resource Monitor includes a chart that displays details about network use. By expanding the Network section of the display, you can quickly view which processes are sending and receiving the most data.

Lesson 2

1. **Correct Answers: B and D**

    A. **Incorrect:** Windows ReadyBoost is useful for improving performance by using external memory devices, but it cannot be used to control which features run at startup.

    B. **Correct:** Windows Defender Software Explorer enables viewing and disabling startup items.

    C. **Incorrect:** Disk Cleanup can be used to remove unnecessary files, but it does not affect startup items.

    D. **Correct:** The Startup tab of the MSConfig utility enables selecting which items will run automatically when the system is started.

    E. **Incorrect:** The Disk Defragmenter utility can be used to optimize disk performance, but it will not control which items are run at startup.

2. **Correct Answer: C**

    A. **Incorrect:** Because the user has not installed any new software recently, it is unlikely that the slower performance is due to a startup item.

    B. **Incorrect:** Visual effects will not have a large impact on the performance of copying files.

    C. **Correct:** When files are moved and copied frequently, they often become fragmented. Performance can be restored by running the Disk Defragmenter.

    D. **Incorrect:** Because no new software was installed, it's unlikely that a running service is causing the decrease in file system performance.

Chapter 5: Case Scenario Answers

Case Scenario 1: Monitoring Performance

1. The Resource Monitor application provides a graph of network usage. By clicking the Network section, you can see which applications, processes, or services are creating the most network activity.

2. It's likely that new startup items are causing the computer to start up more slowly. You can disable these items by using the System Configuration (MSConfig) tool or by using Windows Defender Software Explorer.

3. You can run the System Performance Data Collector Set to generate a report of overall system activity. This feature is accessed using the Reliability And Performance Monitor console.

Case Scenario 2: Optimizing Performance

1. Attaching an external memory device (such as a USB flash drive) and enabling Windows ReadyBoost will make Windows Vista able to use more physical memory.

2. System responsiveness can be improved by disabling various Visual Effects tab settings for the Windows desktop interface.

3. The Disk Cleanup utility can be used to find unnecessary files that can be removed from the system.

Chapter 6: Lesson Review Answers

Lesson 1

1. **Correct Answers: B and C**

   A. **Incorrect:** Changing the password for a user's own account does not require privilege escalation.

   B. **Correct:** Administrator permissions are generally required to install new device drivers on the computer.

   C. **Correct:** Administrator permissions are generally required to install new software on a computer.

   D. **Incorrect:** Standard user permissions are sufficient for changing user settings such as desktop wallpaper.

2. **Correct Answer: B**

   A. **Incorrect:** An Administrator account will have complete permissions on the system, including the ability to make permanent changes. Therefore, this is not the best choice for temporary users.

   B. **Correct:** The Guest account is designed to provide temporary access to a computer. This account is disabled by default, but you can enable it for use by friends and co-workers as needed.

   C. **Incorrect:** A standard user account will run with a minimal set of permissions, but each account is designed to store separate collections of settings for regular users of the system.

   D. **Incorrect:** Members of the Power Users group have many advanced permissions on the system. Occasional users do not have a need for these permissions.

Lesson 2

1. **Correct Answer: D**

    A. **Incorrect**: The User Account Control: Virtualization File And Registry Write Failures option controls the automatic redirection of write operations for earlier applications.

    B. **Incorrect:** The User Account Control: Admin Approval Mode For The Built-In Administrator Account option affects settings for the default Administrator account only.

    C. **Incorrect:** The User Account Control: Only Elevate Executables That Are Signed And Validated option controls whether applications must be signed by digital certificates to be installed.

    D. **Correct:** When set to Disabled, the User Account Control: Run All Administrators In Admin Approval Mode option effectively disables the functionality of the UAC feature.

2. **Correct Answer: A**

    A. **Correct:** Using an Administrator user account with Admin Approval Mode enabled allows the user to run under minimal permissions and permits privilege escalation without providing credentials.

    B. **Incorrect:** Using an Administrator user account with Admin Approval Mode disabled does not allow the user to run with a minimal set of permissions.

    C. **Incorrect:** Using a standard user account with the behavior of the elevation prompt set to Prompt For Credentials requires the user to provide credentials information to approve privilege escalation.

    D. **Incorrect:** Using a standard user account with the behavior of the elevation prompt set to Automatically Deny Elevation Requests completely prevents the user from performing privilege escalation.

Chapter 6: Case Scenario Answers

Case Scenario 1: Creating User Accounts Based on Customers' Requirements

1. The best option is to create an Administrator account and to use the Admin Approval Mode. This allows the convenience of providing consent (rather than credentials) for approval while still running under a minimal set of permissions.

2. The children should be given standard user accounts to minimize the operations that they can perform on the computer. If they need to perform administrative functions such as installing new software, parents can provide the necessary credentials. This is

often referred to as "over-the-shoulder" mode.

3. Parents can set the privilege level on the Compatibility tab of the Properties dialog box of a program or shortcut. They can also right-click the program or shortcut and select Run As Administrator whenever it is necessary.

Case Scenario 2: Configuring UAC Settings Based on Customers' Requirements

1. To be able to provide consent without providing credentials information, the customer should use an Administrator account. To ensure adequate security, you should verify that Admin Approval Mode is enabled.

2. You use the Local Security Policy console to configure settings related to the behavior of UAC.

3. You should set the User Account Control: Switch To The Secure Desktop When Prompting For Elevation option to Disabled.

Chapter 7: Lesson Review Answers

Lesson 1

1. **Correct Answers: A and C**

    A. **Correct:** If no antivirus product is currently installed on the computer, the Malware Protection section in Windows Security Center will not display in green.

    B. **Incorrect:** If UAC is turned off, this information would be shown in the Other Security Settings section of Windows Security Center.

    C. **Correct:** If Windows Defender is disabled, the Malware Protection section in Windows Security Center will not display in green.

    D. **Incorrect:** Settings related to Windows Firewall are displayed in the Firewall section of Windows Security Center.

    E. **Incorrect:** Settings related to Windows Update are displayed in the Automatic Updating section of Windows Security Center.

2. **Correct Answer: D**

    A. **Incorrect:** The Firewall settings determine whether network access is being filtered but do not identify problems with the configuration of Internet Explorer.

    B. **Incorrect:** The Automatic Updating section pertains to whether Windows Update is configured to download and install updates automatically.

    C. **Incorrect:** The Malware Protection section displays details about virus and spyware protection, but it does not evaluate the security settings in Internet Explorer.

   D. **Correct:** The Other Security Settings section of Windows Security Center includes an item for Internet security settings. This item verifies that the configuration of Internet Explorer is set to recommended security settings.

Chapter 7: Case Scenario Answers

Case Scenario: Troubleshooting Security Issues with Windows Security Center

1. Possible causes of warnings in the Malware Protection section include the lack of an installed antivirus or antimalware product. Other common causes of warnings might include security software that is disabled or outdated.

2. The most likely cause of a warning in the Firewall section is that Windows Firewall is disabled. You can resolve the issue by using the Windows Firewall administration tool to enable the firewall.

3. Warnings appear in the Automatic Updating section if the Windows Update feature is disabled or if Windows Update is not configured to download and install new updates automatically.

Chapter 8: Lesson Review Answers

Lesson 1

1. **Correct Answer: D**

   A. **Incorrect:** The High setting does not allow for specifying which types of content to filter. It also does not allow unrated content to be accessed.

   B. **Incorrect:** The Medium setting does not allow for specifying which types of content to filter, as it includes a default set of options. It also does not allow for access to unrated content.

   C. **Incorrect:** The None setting effectively disables automatic Web content blocking.

   D. **Correct:** The Custom option allows the father to specify which types of content should be blocked. It also includes an option for disallowing unrated content.

2. **Correct Answer: C and E**

   A. **Incorrect:** Allowing unrated games does not meet the Parental Controls requirements.

   B. **Incorrect:** Blocking unrated games does not meet the Parental Controls requirements.

   C. **Correct:** Choosing the Everyone 10+ level applies the appropriate setting for all games that are not explicitly allowed or blocked.

   D. **Incorrect:** Blocking violent content will not necessarily block all types of objectionable content.

   E. **Correct:** The Always Allow option overrides the standard game rating restrictions and allows the child to play the game regardless of other Parental Controls settings.

Lesson 2

1. **Correct Answer: C**

   A. **Incorrect:** Disabling Protected Mode does not automatically change browser preferences such as those related to handling ActiveX controls.

   B. **Incorrect:** Changing security settings for the Internet zone applies those options to all URLs that are not included in any of the other zones. This would significantly reduce overall security.

   C. **Correct:** The company's Web servers are automatically included in the Local Intranet security zone. Changing the configuration options for this zone allows users to automatically have the appropriate settings for all of these servers.

   D. **Incorrect:** Although this method would meet the requirements, it would require significant effort. For example, if the company has many different Web servers, all of their respective URLs would have to be entered into the Trusted Sites zone on each computer running Windows Vista.

2. **Correct Answer: D**

   A. **Incorrect:** The Phishing Filter does not directly affect the settings for maintaining cookies.

   B. **Incorrect:** Changing the privacy setting would reduce overall security and would not necessarily delete all existing cookies.

   C. **Incorrect:** Changing the privacy setting would reduce overall security and would not necessarily delete all existing cookies.

   D. **Correct:** The Delete Browsing History command allows for removing all cookies that have been downloaded to the computer. It also allows keeping all current security settings at their recommended values.

Chapter 8: Case Scenario Answers

Case Scenario 1: Using Parent Controls

1. The mother should be set up with an Administrator account, and her son should be given a standard user account.
2. The mother should choose a game rating system and then specify which ratings are allowed for her son.
3. The easiest method of filtering Web content is to choose the High, Medium, or Custom option for Web sites. She can also choose to block or allow access to only specific Web sites.

Case Scenario 2: Configuring Web Browser Security

1. The purpose of the Phishing Filter is to automatically verify Web sites against a known list of malicious URLs.
2. Internet Explorer automatically verifies security certificates and enables HTTPS connections when requested by Web sites. The user should look for the lock icon next to the address to ensure that security is enabled.
3. There are several ways to reset configuration settings to their default values. Commands are available on the Security, Privacy, and Advanced tabs of the Internet Options dialog box. Additionally, you can choose to reset all Internet Explorer options to their defaults on the Advanced tab.

Chapter 9: Lesson Review Answers

Lesson 1

1. **Correct Answer: C**
   A. **Incorrect:** The IP address is probably configured properly because the user can access other computers on the local network.
   B. **Incorrect:** The subnet mask is probably configured properly because the user can access other computers on the local network.

   C. **Correct:** Because the customer cannot communicate with computers or devices outside of the local network, it is most likely that the default gateway address is incorrect or missing.

   D. **Incorrect:** The name of the network will not affect connectivity.

2. **Correct Answer: A**

   A. **Correct:** DHCP is designed to assign network addresses and related information automatically to computers on the network.

   B. **Incorrect:** DNS is used to resolve network names to IP addresses but does not help with automatically assigning network information.

   C. **Incorrect:** The PING utility is used to verify network connectivity between computers and cannot be used to assign IP addresses automatically to new computers.

   D. **Incorrect:** The IPCONFIG command provides information about the current network configuration of a connection but cannot be used to assign IP addresses automatically to new computers.

Lesson 2

1. **Correct Answer: D**

   A. **Incorrect:** Because the computer is able to connect to wireless networks, reinstalling the drivers will not help resolve the problem.

   B. **Incorrect:** The wireless network adapter is already enabled because it is able to connect to wireless networks.

   C. **Incorrect:** It is not possible to change the preferred connection order for wireless networks using the Network Map view.

   D. **Correct:** The Manage Wireless Networks option enables users to configure the preferred order for the connection of networks. It is likely that the undesired wireless network at the customer's office is higher in the list than the desired one.

2. **Correct Answers: A and D**

   A. **Correct:** Wireless signal strength is shown in the properties of a wireless network connection.

   B. **Incorrect:** The network map does not show the strength of a wireless network connection.

   C. **Incorrect:** The Set Up A Connection Option does not include details related to the strengths of available wireless networks.

   D. **Correct:** The system tray icon for a wireless network connection can show signal strength information.

Chapter 9: Case Scenario Answers

Case Scenario 1: Adding a New Computer to a Network

1. Because there are no other computers on the network, and based on the subnet mask, any valid address should begin with 10.10.0. The last portion of the TCP/IP address can be any number between 2 and 254 (inclusive), except for 120 (because it is in use by another computer). Note that the .1 address is reserved for the default gateway.

2. The computer should be configured to use the same subnet mask as the other computer: 255.255.255.0. This value places both computers on the same network and allows them to communicate with each other and with the default gateway.

3. Open the Network And Sharing Center and click View Status next to the item for the wired network connections. Click Properties again. Then, select the item for the TCP/IPv4 protocol and click Properties. Choose to assign the appropriate values and provide the relevant information manually.

4. DHCP can be used to assign and manage TCP/IP network addresses automatically. The customer might be able to enable the DHCP function of an existing router, or he might need to purchase a new device that provides this functionality. After that is done, he should configure both computers to use dynamically assigned IP addresses.

Case Scenario 2: Managing Wireless Network Connections

1. When a new wireless network connection is created, the user will be prompted to choose whether she wants to save the network information. If she chooses not to save the information, she will be prompted for security details whenever she connects to the network.

2. The Manage Wireless Networks option in the Network And Sharing Center enables the user to set the order of preference for various wireless networks on the list.

3. To enable network profiles to be managed separately for different users, in the Manage Wireless Networks section of the Network And Sharing Center, she should click Profile Types. She should select the Use All-User And Per-User Profiles option. Once enabled, new network connections can be created only for use by a particular user account.

Chapter 10: Lesson Review Answers

Lesson 1

1. **Correct Answer: B**
    A. **Incorrect:** Although the file sharing option could be used to meet the technical requirements, it is not the simplest method of doing so.

   B. **Correct:** The simplest method of providing anonymous access to multiple users is to enable Public folder sharing.

   C. **Incorrect:** Password-protected sharing should remain disabled because the customer does not want users to have to provide logon information.

   D. **Incorrect:** Media library sharing is primarily used to provide photos, music, and video files to compatible devices.

2. **Correct Answer: C**

   A. **Incorrect:** Disabling network discovery would prevent the computer from automatically finding other computers.

   B. **Incorrect:** Setting the network location to Public Place automatically disables the network discovery feature.

   C. **Correct:** The process of network discovery is often fastest when all computers are configured to use the same workgroup.

   D. **Incorrect:** The names of the computers do not affect the speed of network discovery.

   E. **Incorrect:** Because network discovery can eventually find all of the other computers in the environment, it is unlikely that Windows Firewall is causing the problem.

3. **Correct Answer: C**

   A. **Incorrect:** Files stored in the Public folder are not directly accessible to the Xbox 360, and other users on the network are able to access the files.

   B. **Incorrect:** Password-protected sharing does not prevent users with the proper credentials from accessing the files over the network.

   C. **Correct**: The purpose of the media library sharing functionality is to enable streaming devices to access media files such as photos, music, and videos. The customer can configure which devices are allowed to access the media library in the configuration settings.

   D. **Incorrect**: The Xbox 360 cannot directly access a file share, and this method would require additional effort to configure so that other users will not have access to the files.

Lesson 2

1. **Correct Answer: D**

   A. **Incorrect:** The Public folder settings specify the permissions that users have when accessing files, but it does not force them to provide logon information.

   B. **Incorrect:** The status of the Network Discovery feature does not affect whether users are prompted for logon information.

   C. **Incorrect:** Changing passwords on the local computer does not cause users to be prompted for logon information when connecting to the Public folder.

   D.   **Correct:** Enabling Password Protected Sharing requires users to provide logon
        information for the local computer before accessing resources stored in the Public
        folder.

2.   **Correct Answer: B**

   A.   **Incorrect:** Because Home01 can see other computers, Network Discovery appears
        to be enabled on this computer.

   B.   **Correct:** Because Home04 is the only computer that is not accessible to the others,
        it is likely that Network Discovery is disabled on this computer.

   C.   **Incorrect:** Because Home01 can see other computers, it is likely that Windows
        Firewall is properly configured on this computer.

   D.   **Incorrect:** A private network connection enables Network Discovery by default.

Chapter 10: Case Scenario Answers

Case Scenario 1: Choosing Folder Sharing Options

1.   The technical requirements for the solution suggest that you should enable the File Shar-
     ing and Password Protected Sharing options. Enabling Network Discovery can also be
     helpful for finding other computers on the network.

2.   To simplify the discovery of network resources, all computers should be assigned to the
     same workgroup.

3.   The customer needs to define at least two different local user accounts on her computer.
     She should assign permissions for adding and changing files to one user account and
     only Reader permissions for the other account. Users should be provided the appropri-
     ate logon name and password based on the security requirements.

Case Scenario 2: Working with Public Folder Sharing

1.   You should enable Public Folder Sharing and turn off Password Protected Sharing to
     meet the customer's requirements. Additionally, enabling Network Discovery helps
     other users find the shared resources.

2.   The customer should choose the Public folder sharing option Turn On Sharing So Any-
     one With Network Access Can Open Files.

3.   The Media Sharing option in the Network and Sharing Center provides the option to
     enable devices such as a compatible game console to stream media files over the net-
     work. The process involves approving which devices have access to the data.

Chapter 11: Lesson Review Answers

Lesson 1

1. Correct Answer: A, C, and E

    A. **Correct:** An analog modem that can send faxes is required to transmit the document.

    B. **Incorrect:** A printer is only required to print hard copies of received faxes. Because the customer only wants to view the documents, a printer is not required.

    C. **Correct:** A scanner is required to convert physical pages into a digital format that can be sent to fax devices.

    D. **Incorrect:** Fax transmissions do not require a network connection.

    E. **Correct:** An analog phone line is required for sending fax documents. The line should be connected to the modem.

2. Correct Answer: C and E

    A. **Incorrect:** One shared printer device is sufficient to allow multiple network users to access the printer.

    B. **Incorrect:** This option could potentially reduce performance by storing copies of all printed documents on the local computer.

    C. **Correct:** Rendering print jobs on the client computer minimizes the performance impacts to the local system.

    D. **Incorrect:** Printing directly to the printer generally does not increase performance for clients or for the computer that is working as the print server.

    E. **Correct:** Users on each client computer should choose to add the shared printer as a network printer.

Lesson 2

1. Correct Answer: C

    A. **Incorrect:** Because the mobile device is connected using a USB connection, Bluetooth capabilities are not required.

    B. **Incorrect:** The device is connected through USB, so network settings do not affect Windows Sync Center options.

    C. **Correct:** The Windows Mobile Device Center software is designed to add functionality for connecting with devices based on the Windows Mobile operating system.

    D. **Incorrect:** Sync conflicts are caused by issues with coordinating data between multiple locations. Because a sync partnership has not yet been created, this does not help identify the problem.

2. **Correct Answer: B**

   A. **Incorrect:** The security permissions are automatically configured for the local copy of offline files. Changing these settings does not increase security.

   B. **Correct:** By default, offline files are stored in an unencrypted format. By encrypting the files, you can prevent them from being used by unauthorized individuals.

   C. **Incorrect:** The method of synchronization (one-way or two-way) does not directly affect security. Also, you need to be able to make modifications to files in both locations.

   D. **Incorrect:** Permissions on the shared folder only affect which users can connect to the data. It does not affect the security of the offline copies of the files.

   E. **Incorrect:** Windows Firewall is used to determine which network traffic is allowed to or from the computer. This does not affect the storage of the offline files.

Chapter 11: Case Scenario Answers

Case Scenario 1: Managing Mobile Devices

1. The customer should download and install the Windows Mobile Device Center application. This provides options for synchronizing data.

2. Windows Sync Center allows the customer to create sync partnerships that define which types of information are transferred between the systems. She can also specify whether the relationships should be one-way or two-way.

3. The Presentation Settings feature in Windows Mobility Center allows users to specify temporary options such as alternate desktop backgrounds and sounds settings.

Case Scenario 2: Configuring Media Devices and Features

1. The customer would install the printer on one of the computers running Windows Vista and then choose to share it. Other users can then add the printer as a network printer.

2. The minimum requirement is the presence of an analog modem that has fax capabilities and access to an analog phone line. A scanner allows for importing paper documents, and a printer provides the ability to generate hard copies of received fax messages.

Chapter 12: Lesson Review Answers

Lesson 1

1. **Correct Answers: B and C**

    A. **Incorrect:** System Restore rolls back the configuration of a computer to its previous state. This does not meet the requirements because it makes permanent changes to the system configuration.

    B. **Correct:** Safe Mode starts Windows Vista with a minimum set of device drivers and services. It is likely to work because Windows Vista does not load the driver for the new display adapter.

    C. **Correct:** Safe Mode With Networking starts Windows Vista with a minimum set of device drivers and services and adds support for connecting to a network. It is likely to work because Windows Vista does not load the driver for the new display adapter.

    D. **Incorrect:** The Memory Diagnostics Tool is designed only to analyze the physical memory on the computer. It does not allow for further troubleshooting of the display adapter problem and does not resolve the boot problem.

    E. **Incorrect:** The Last Known Good Configuration looks for an earlier collection of configuration settings for the computer. This does not meet the requirements because it makes permanent changes to the system configuration.

2. **Correct Answer: D**

    A. **Incorrect:** Safe Mode is not accessible because you cannot access the startup menu.

    B. **Incorrect:** Safe Mode With Networking is not accessible because you cannot access the startup menu.

    C. **Incorrect:** To load the Last Known Good Configuration, the startup menu must be accessible.

    D. **Correct:** You can fix many boot-related problems by starting from the Windows Vista installation media and then choosing the Repair option.

3. **Correct Answer: A**

   A. **Correct:** Creating a new restore point before you install the program enables you to roll back the computer easily to its previous configuration in case the automatic uninstaller fails to work.

   B. **Incorrect:** Creating a new restore point after you install the program does not enable you to revert to the configuration just before you installed it.

   C. **Incorrect:** You use the selective startup settings primarily to troubleshoot startup problems. They do not directly affect the installation or removal of a new application.

   D. **Incorrect:** Changing Registry settings for the computer does not affect the way in which the program is installed and does not provide a simple way to remove the program if problems occur.

Lesson 2

1. **Correct Answer: C**

   A. **Incorrect:** Removing the program prevents it from doing damage to the system, but it does not provide an easy way to reenable it.

   B. **Incorrect:** Ignoring the item allows the program to make potentially unwanted changes to the computer.

   C. **Correct:** Placing the program in quarantine prevents it from making unwanted changes to the system but enalbes you to readd it easily if the program is required.

   D. **Incorrect:** Allowing the program to run might cause unwanted changes on the computer.

2. **Correct Answer: D**

   A. **Incorrect:** Resetting Internet Explorer's settings changes all settings back to their initial values.

   B. **Incorrect:** Deleting the browsing history removes temporary files but does not remove items such as add-ons.

   C. **Incorrect:** Because the utility was originally designed for use with Internet Explorer, it is unlikely to be found by Windows Defender.

   D. **Correct:** The Manage Add-Ons dialog box provides an easy way to enable or disable items such as toolbar add-ons.

Chapter 12: Case Scenario Answers

Case Scenario 1: Diagnosing and Troubleshooting Startup Problems

1. You should choose to boot the computer with the Safe Mode With Networking option. This loads a minimal set of drivers and still allows access to the network.

2. You should run the Windows Memory Diagnostics Tool from the Windows Vista boot menu. Because the user can access the Advanced Boot Options screen, he should also be able to select this option.

3. You can enable boot logging from the Advanced Startup Options menu. You can then boot the computer in Safe Mode (assuming that is successful) or use the Windows Vista installation media to access a command prompt and view the file.

Case Scenario 2: Working with Windows Defender

1. To ensure that Windows Defender automatically downloads new definitions, she should verify that the Windows Update feature is properly configured. Additionally, she should verify that Windows Defender is configured to download new definitions automatically prior to performing a regular scan.

2. Windows Defender on each of the computers should be configured to use an advanced membership to the Microsoft SpyNet community to be notified of potential malware that has not yet been classified.

3. She can use the History option in Windows Defender to view previous malware removals.

Chapter 13: Lesson Review Answers

Lesson 1

1. **Correct Answer: B**

   A. **Incorrect:** The Complete PC backup feature does not allow for storing backups to a network location.

   B. **Correct:** Creating a backup job to save files to a network location is the easiest way to meet the requirements.

   C. **Incorrect:** The System Restore feature does not offer a method for storing data remotely.

   D. **Incorrect:** Although storing files to an external hard disk is an option, this method is not the easiest way to meet the requirements.

   E. **Incorrect:** Creating a job to copy files over the network might work, but it involves significantly more effort to set up and manage.

2. **Correct Answer: C**

   A. **Incorrect:** Restoring the latest version might not revert to the version of files the user requires. For example, the changes might have been made prior to the creation of the latest stored version of the file.

   B. **Incorrect:** Restoring the first previous version might not revert to the version of files the user requires. For example, he might lose a large amount of work that was performed on the files since this version was created.

   C. **Correct:** By copying several previous versions of the folder to another location, the user can determine which file versions he wants to keep.

   D. **Incorrect:** Opening the most recent previous version might not include the desired versions of the files.

3. **Correct Answer: D**

   A. **Incorrect:** Restore points are unrelated to restoring data from a backup created on another computer.

   B. **Incorrect:** The Restore Computer command is used to restore an entire computer using a Complete PC backup image.

   C. **Incorrect:** The Back Up Files command is useful only for creating new backups.

   D. **Correct:** The Advanced Restore command enabless you to restore data from a backup that was created on another computer.

Lesson 2

1. **Correct Answer: A**

   A. **Correct:** The System Recovery menu includes options for performing a Windows Complete PC restore. You can access this option by booting from the Windows Vista installation media and choosing the Repair option.

   B. **Incorrect:** Manually reinstalling the operating system requires the user to reconfigure the operating system. Therefore, this method would not be the fastest option.

   C. **Incorrect:** The new hard disk does not yet contain an operating system, so you will be unable to boot the computer into Windows Vista.

   D. **Incorrect:** The new hard disk does not yet contain an operating system, so you will be unable to boot the computer into Windows Vista.

2. **Correct Answers: A and C**

   A. **Correct:** A monthly Complete PC backup provides a fairly current copy of the system configuration, operating system files, and related data. To save disk space, the customer can manually delete prior Complete PC backups before new ones are made.

B. **Incorrect:** Monthly file-based backups are not frequent enough to protect against the loss of the user's important files.

C. **Correct:** Performing a nightly full backup provides reasonable protection against data loss.

D. **Incorrect:** The customer has limited disk space, and the process of creating a Complete PC backup every evening is probably not necessary.

Chapter 13: Case Scenario Answers

Case Scenario 1: Evaluating Restore Options

1. Because a Complete PC backup is available, you should launch the Windows Complete PC restore process by booting from the Windows Vista installation media and choosing the Repair option. Using this method, you can avoid reinstalling and reconfiguring the numerous applications that the customer installed.

2. After performing a Complete PC restore, the customer can use the Advanced Restore link in the Backup and Restore Center. This enables him to choose a backup set from which to recover data.

3. The customer should verify that System Protection is enabled and that he is performing regular backups. Each of these operations stores previous versions of files that have been recently modified.

Case Scenario 2: Evaluating Restore Options

1. The customer should create and schedule a backup job on each of the computers in her small-business environment.

2. Because the customer would like to store all backup files centrally, the best option is to use a network share on one of the computers as the destination. She can schedule the backups on each computer to run at different times to minimize the load placed on this computer.

3. The Complete PC backup enables the customer to make a backup that contains operating system files, applications, and user data. In the case of a hard disk failure, the failed drive should be replaced. Then, the customer can boot the computer using her Windows Vista installation media. She should choose the Repair option and then launch the Windows Complete PC restore process from the System Recovery menu.

4. Both the Backup Status and Configuration utility and the Backup and Restore Center can provide information about the date and time of the last backup that was performed on the computer.

Glossary

Activity reports A Parental Controls feature that allows parents to view information about their child's activity on the computer. Details include a list of visited Web sites, the amount of time spent on the computer, and which programs were used.

ad hoc wireless network A wireless network created directly between computers without the need for a wireless access point.

Admin Approval Mode Configured settings for User Account Control (UAC) that minimize the effect permissions of an Administrator user account while allowing for privilege escalation.

Advanced Boot Options A troubleshooting menu that is available during the Windows Vista boot process. The menu might show up automatically if problems were detected, or it can usually be accessed by pressing F8 before the boot process begins.

Advanced Restore An option in the Backup and Restore Center that enables restoring backups that were created on another computer.

Backup and Restore Center A Windows Vista utility that enables creating file-based backups and Complete PC backups.

backup catalogs Files that are used to describe the contents of a backup set or collection of backup files. Catalog files make the process of accessing data stored in backup files much quicker.

backup files (folder) Folders that contain the contents generated when performing file-based backups in Windows Vista.

backup set (folder) A collection of backup files for a computer. A backup set generally includes a full backup and might also include additional collections of backup files that contain changes that were made since the full backup.

basic input/output system (BIOS) The firmware code run by an IBM-compatible PC when first powered on.

Bluetooth A personal wireless standard for connecting devices. Bluetooth connections require a transmitter and receiver, and can be secured using a passcode or passkey.

boot logging An advanced Windows boot option that instructs the boot process to create text file called Ntbtlog.txt in the computer's Windows directory. This option is useful for identifying the drivers or applications that are preventing a successful system startup.

Certificates A security mechanism by which a trusted third party can certify whether a particular Web site is owned by the organization it claims to be.

clean installation An installation in which the current version of Windows, including all of the files, settings, and programs, is automatically replaced.

codec Short for compressor/decompressor, a codec is software for viewing and creating media created in a variety of different formats.

Compact Flash card A memory storage standard that is common on mobile devices such as PDAs, music players, and phones.

Complete PC backup A Windows Vista backup that contains all of the contents of the system drive, including operating system files, applications, and user data.

Complete PC restore The process of recovering a computer running Windows Vista by using a Complete PC backup. The restore process recovers all contents of the system drive, including operating system files, applications, and user data.

computer description   A text-based description of a computer that can be viewed by remote computers over the network. Useful descriptions often include details about the purpose of the computer, its primary user, or its physical location.

computer name   The name by which a computer can be accessed over the network.

consent   A privilege escalation request that allows a user to approve the action without providing credentials.

Cookies   A method that is used to retain user identity and preference settings between HTTP requests. Cookies can be blocked using the Privacy tab of the Internet Options dialog box in Internet Explorer 7.

credentials   Logon information (including a user name and password) that is used for verifying the identity of a user.

Data Collector Sets   Combinations of settings that specify which information should be collected for later analysis. Data Collector Sets can be managed from within the Performance and Reliability Monitor.

default gateway   A TCP/IP address to which all communications that are destined for a nonlocal subnet are sent.

Desktop theme   A set of Windows desktop configuration settings that can be loaded or saved for simplified management.

Domain Name System (DNS)   A network-based standard for resolving friendly hierarchical network names to TCP/IP addresses.

Dynamic Host Configuration Protocol (DHCP)   A network protocol that is used to provide IP address information and related details including a subnet mask, default gateway, and DNS server addresses automatically.

elevation prompt   A standard user interface dialog box that prompts the user for approval of permissions escalation. Depending on security settings, the user might be required to provide consent or credentials.

Entertainment Software Rating Board (ESRB)   A North American organization that evaluates game and entertainment software and provides age-based ratings suggestions.

Event Viewer   A utility that is used for viewing events that are stored in Windows Event logs.

Event Viewer   A graphical application that is designed for reviewing messages that are stored in the Windows event logs.

Feed Headlines   A gadget for Windows Sidebar that can be configured to show RSS feed headlines on the desktop.

file associations   Windows system settings that define which file types are associated with which programs.

Flip 3D   A feature of the Windows Aero user interface that allows users to see live window previews in a stacked, 3-D arrangement. Access it by using the Windows Key+Tab key combination.

gadgets   Small applications or utilities that are designed for use from within Windows Sidebar. Windows Vista ships with numerous gadgets, including Clock, CPU Meter, Feed Headlines, Calendar, Notes, and Stocks. New gadgets can also be downloaded and installed from various sources.

Game rating systems   A method that allows independent, third-party organizations to evaluate game and entertainment content and provide ratings. The Windows Vista Parental Controls feature provides support for several worldwide standards.

Game restrictions   A Parental Control feature that allows parents to determine the acceptable ratings for games that their children can play. This feature can also be used to allow or block specific game titles.

hard disk, external   A device that contains hard disk–based storage. External hard disks are typically connected to a computer through a USB or FireWire connection.

Hypertext Transfer Protocol (HTTP) The primary TCP/IP–based protocol used for accessing Web sites.

Hypertext Transfer Protocol Secure (HTTPS) A secure version of the HTTP protocol that is used to access Web sites. The protocol supports the use of encryption and certificates to protect sensitive data.

inbound filter A Windows Firewall rule that determines which applications on a computer can be accessed from other computers in the environment.

Infrared Data Association (IrDA) A communications standard that allows for transferring information between computers and other devices. It uses infrared waves that must have a clear line of sight between the transmitter and receiver.

in-place upgrade An installation in which you can keep the programs, files, and settings from the current version of Windows.

Internet Message Access Protocol (IMAP) A protocol that enables downloading and managing e-mail messages. It provides several enhancements over POP3 and is supported by Windows Mail.

Internet Protocol v4 (IPv4) The standard version of the IP standard that is used on the Internet and in local area networks.

Internet Protocol v6 (IPv6) A newer version of the IP standard that provides for a larger namespace, increased performance, improved security, and other features.

IP address The network address of a computer that is configured to use TCP/IP. IP addresses should be unique within a network.

Last Known Good Configuration An advanced Windows boot option that rolls the computer back to its configuration during the last successful boot of the operating system. In some cases, this can result in system changes that might require further troubleshooting.

Legacy hardware A term that applies to older hardware that generally is not Plug and Play enabled.

local area network (LAN) A network that is usually defined within one building or location. The boundaries of a LAN are typically managed by a single individual or by an organization.

Live taskbar previews A feature of the Windows Aero user interface that displays a live thumbnail preview of the contents of an application window when the mouse is hovered over the item in the taskbar.

Local Security Policy An administrative tool that enables users to configure computer policy settings such as the behavior of User Account Control (UAC).

malware Malicious software that can cause a wide variety of system problems, including reduced performance, reliability issues, and data loss. This term generally includes such products as adware, spyware, viruses, and Trojans.

media library sharing A Windows Vista feature that is designed to provide photos, music, and video files to other Windows computers and compatible media devices.

Mobile device A piece of handheld equipment such as a portable music or video player, PDA, mobile phone, or Windows Mobile device that works on its own but can also connect to a computer. Many of these devices can sync information with Windows.

network discovery A Windows Vista networking feature that enables finding computers that are located on the network.

network locations A network connection setting that enables users to specify whether they are connected to a secure environment (for example, home or work) or to a public place.

Network News Transfer Protocol (NNTP) The protocol used by news servers to enable users to view and post messages. It is supported by Windows Mail.

outbound filter   A Windows Firewall setting that determines which applications and services on the local computer are able to communicate with other computers over the network.

Parental Controls   A Windows Vista feature that allows parents to place restrictions on the types of activities that their children can perform on the computer. Restrictions include time limits, configuring allowed games and applications, and preventing access to Web sites with inappropriate content.

password-protected sharing   An option in the Network and Sharing Center that can be used to require users to provide logon and password information before accessing shared resources such as files, folders, and printers.

Performance Monitor   A utility that enables viewing performance statistics. Hundreds of statistics are included with Windows Vista, and new applications can add more.

permissions   Security settings that define which users can connect to a particular resource (such as a file or a folder) and what actions they can perform (such as reading or modifying data).

Personal digital assistant (PDA)   A mobile device that can perform functions such as managing contacts and editing documents. Capabilities vary greatly between different types of devices.

Phishing   The act of trying to trick users into providing sensitive information such as passwords or financial data. Phishing attempts usually take the form of a Web site that is designed to appear like that of an official organization (such as a bank), but that actually records transmitted information for fraudulent use.

Phishing Filter   An Internet Explorer feature that allows the Web browser to automatically check if a site is a known phishing site. This feature also allows for reporting suspected phishing sites to Microsoft.

Pop-Up Blocker   An Internet Explorer feature that allows for automatically blocking unwanted browser windows.

Post Office Protocol (POP3)   The most common protocol that is used to download and manage e-mail messages. It is supported by Windows Mail.

Previous Versions   A feature that allows users to access earlier copies of their data files quickly and easily. Previous versions are based on backups or the creation of restore points.

printer sharing   A method by which computers running Windows Vista can enable remote computers to send print jobs over the network for output to a locally attached print device.

privilege escalation   The process by which a user temporarily increases the security permissions for a particular program or task to function.

Problem Reports and Solutions   A Windows Vista feature that allows for automatically sending application and operating system error reports to Microsoft. The tool also provides direct links to downloads that can resolve common problems.

Protected Mode, Internet Explorer   A security feature that is available to Internet Explorer 7 users in Windows Vista. Protected Mode prevents Internet applications from being able to access sensitive areas of the system, such as the file system.

Public folder   A special Windows Vista folder that is designed to enable simplified file sharing.

registry   A central database that stores operating system, application, and user settings in Windows. You can access and modify the Registry using the Registry Editor (RegEdit) tool.

Registry Editor (RegEdit)   A graphical utility that you can use to view and modify Windows Registry settings.

Reliability Monitor A Windows Vista utility that shows details about actions that affect system reliability. Details include operating system crashes and the installation of new updates and software.

Repair command prompt A special command prompt that you access through the Windows Vista Repair process. It allows the user to perform basic file system and related tasks for troubleshooting an installation of Windows Vista.

Resource Monitor A Windows Vista utility that enables monitoring CPU, memory, disk, and network resources, along with which processes are using each.

restore point A backup of important system settings and data files based on the Windows Vista System Protection feature.

restore points Point-in-time backups of the Windows Vista system configuration that can be used by the System Restore feature to revert to an earlier configuration.

RSS A standard for providing access to content on the Internet. The Feed Headlines gadget for Windows Sidebar is able to display RSS feed headlines on the desktop.

Safe Mode A special Windows startup mode that is designed for troubleshooting boot-related problems. When booting in Safe Mode, only a minimal set of drivers and services is loaded.

Scanner A device that allows users to make a digital copy of a paper document or photo.

Secure Digital (SD) card A removable memory card using a storage standard that is common on mobile devices such as PDAs, music players, and phones.

Security zones An Internet Explorer feature that allows for setting different security options based on the source of a Web site. For example, local intranet Web sites can have different settings from those that are located on the public Internet.

Selective Startup An option in the System Configuration (MSConfig) utility that enables users to specify which settings should be used during the next reboot of the computer.

Services Programs that are generally designed to run without requiring a user logon or user interaction.

Service Set Identifier (SSID) The name of a wireless network that is usually broadcast from a wireless access point. SSID broadcasts can be disabled.

shadow copy A Windows Vista file system feature that enables the operating system to back up files that are in use while the backup is running.

Shared folder A folder that has been configured to be accessible over the network. A shared folder includes permissions specifying which users can access the files.

Simple Mail Transfer Protocol (SMTP) A protocol for sending e-mail messages over the Internet. It is supported by Windows Mail.

Site reviews A method by which Web site administrators and end users can submit feedback related to potentially incorrectly categorized Web sites. The site can be accessed directly or through the use of the Parental Controls Web Restrictions dialog box.

Startup Repair A feature that automatically attempts to diagnose and resolve problems that are keeping Windows Vista from properly booting. This option is available when starting from the Windows Vista installation media and choosing the Repair option.

subnet mask A TCP/IP setting that helps determine which network addresses are located on the same local network.

System Configuration (MSConfig) tool A Windows Vista utility that can be used to manage startup items and to perform troubleshooting.

System Information (MSInfo) tool A Windows Vista utility that provides a way to view and save hardware and software configuration details.

System Protection   An operating system feature that enables the manual or automatic creation of restore points for use by the System Restore feature.

System Restore   A Windows Vista feature that enables rollback of the configuration of a computer to a previous point in time.

Task Manager   A Windows Vista utility that enables monitoring performance as well as running applications, processes, and services.

Time Limits (Parental Controls)   A Parental Controls feature that allows parents to specify the times during which children can log on to and use their computer.

Trusted device   A mobile device that is considered to be secure by its owners and users. Examples include mobile phones and mobile devices such as PDAs.

TV tuner   Enables applications such as Windows Media Center to record live television programming. Tuners can support analog, digital, or both types of broadcasts.

Universal Naming Convention (UNC)   A standard naming method designed for accessing computer resources over the network. A UNC path includes the name of the computer and a path to the shared resource (for example, \\Computer01\SharedFolder).

User Account Control (UAC)   A security feature in Windows Vista that allows users to run with minimal privileges while supporting earlier applications that require elevated privileges.

Web restrictions   A Parental Controls feature that allows parents to determine which types of Web sites their children can access.

Wi-Fi Protected Access (WPA)   A wireless security protocol that provides a strong level of encryption for wireless network connections.

Windows Aero   New user interface features in Windows Vista that include transparency effects and the ability to navigate open windows using a video adapter's 3-D effects.

Windows Complete PC restore   A System Recovery option that is available when booting Windows Vista from the installation media and choosing the Repair command.

Windows Defender   A security program that can scan for and remove malware. Windows Defender also includes features for managing startup items and running processes.

Windows Defender Software Explorer   A feature in Windows Defender that enables viewing and managing startup items.

Windows Device Driver Model (WDDM)   A specification for Windows Vista graphics drivers that helps ensure compatibility, reliability, and performance.

Windows Error Recovery   A feature that automatically presents the user with boot options in the event of an unsuccessful startup. Options include the ability to start Windows normally or to start up in Safe Mode.

Windows event logs   An operating system feature that enables programs and services to write messages to a central system database. These messages can be reviewed using the Event Viewer application.

Windows Experience Index   A benchmark that assesses the performance of a computer's CPU, memory, disk, and graphics performance.

Windows Firewall   A network security feature in Windows Vista that enables users to restrict the types of traffic that are allowed.

Windows Firewall with Advanced Security   A Windows Vista management tool that enables users to create advanced rules that control the behavior of Windows Firewall.

Windows Media Center   A Windows Vista feature that allows users to watch and record live television programs. This feature requires the use of a TV tuner card.

Windows Media Center Extender A device that is able to connect to and display audio and video content from a computer that is running Windows Media Center. An example is the Xbox 360 console.

Windows Memory Diagnostics A Windows Vista utility that is designed for testing the physical memory installed on the computer. The utility runs outside of the Windows Vista operating system and can be selected during the startup process.

Windows Mobile (OS) Microsoft's standard operating system for small mobile devices such as PDAs and phones.

Windows Mobile Device Center A downloadable utility that allows the managing and synchronizing of data between Windows Vista and a compatible device.

Windows Mobility Center A standard Windows Vista feature that provides the most commonly accessed features on notebook computers in a consistent way.

Windows ReadyBoost A Windows Vista feature that enables the use of external memory devices (such as USB flash drives and memory cards) to improve system performance.

Windows security alerts An icon and notifications that are displayed in the system tray that are designed to alert users about potential security configuration issues.

Windows Security Center A Windows utility that enables users to obtain an overview about the configuration of various security features and settings.

Windows Sidebar A Windows Vista desktop component that allows for displaying numerous small applets called gadgets. Windows Sidebar can be enabled or disabled, and users can easily add and remove gadgets based on their preferences.

Windows Sync Center A Windows Vista application that allows users to synchronize data between computers and mobile devices.

Windows Update A Windows Vista feature that enables automatic download and installation of updates from Microsoft.

Windows Vista editions Windows Vista versions that include different combinations of features and options. The consumer-focused editions include Windows Vista Home Basic, Windows Vista Home Premium, Windows Vista Business, and Windows Vista Ultimate.

Windows Vista Upgrade Advisor A free utility that can be downloaded and installed to assess whether a current computer is upgradable to Windows Vista. The utility examines installed hardware and software.

Windows Vista Upgrade Advisor A free utility that can be downloaded and installed to assess whether a current computer can be upgraded to Windows Vista. The utility examines installed hardware and software.

Windows Vista Web Filter A Parental Controls feature that allows parents to determine which types of Web sites their children can access.

Wired Equivalent Privacy (WEP) A wireless security protocol that enables wireless traffic encryption. WEP has known security vulnerabilities.

workgroup name A name that is usually set to the same value for related computers in a network environment.

Index

Windows Vista™ Resources for Administrators

Windows Vista Administrator's Pocket Consultant
William Stanek
ISBN 9780735622968

Portable and precise, this pocket-sized guide delivers immediate answers for the day-to-day administration of Windows Vista. Featuring easy-to-scan tables, step-by-step instructions, and handy lists, this book offers the straightforward information you need to solve problems and get the job done—whether you're at your desk or in the field!

Windows Vista Resource Kit
Mitch Tulloch, Tony Northrup, Jerry Honeycutt, Ed Wilson, Ralph Ramos, and the Windows Vista Team
ISBN 9780735622838

Get the definitive reference for deploying, configuring, and supporting Windows Vista—from the experts who know the technology best. This guide offers in-depth, comprehensive technical guidance on automating deployment; implementing security enhancements; administering group policy, files folders, and programs; and troubleshooting. Includes an essential toolkit of resources on DVD.

MCTS Self-Paced Training Kit (Exam 70-620): Configuring Windows Vista Client
Ian McLean and Orin Thomas
ISBN 9780735623903

Get in-depth preparation plus practice for Exam 70-620, the required exam for the new Microsoft Certified Technology Specialist (MCTS): Windows Vista Client certification. This 2-in-1 kit focuses on installing client software and configuring system settings, security features, network connectivity, media applications, and mobile devices. Ace your exam prep—and build real-world job skills—with lessons, practice tests, evaluation software, and more.

MCITP Self-Paced Training Kit (Exam 70-622): Installing, Maintaining, Supporting, and Troubleshooting Applications on the Windows Vista Client – Enterprise
Tony Northrup and J.C. Mackin
ISBN 9780735624085

Maximize your performance on Exam 70-622, the required exam for the new Microsoft® Certified IT Professional (MCITP): Enterprise Support Technician certification. Comprehensive and in-depth, this 2-in-1 kit covers managing security, configuring networking, and optimizing performance for Windows Vista clients in an enterprise environment. Ace your exam prep—and build real-world job skills—with lessons, practice tests, evaluation software, and more.

MCITP Self-Paced Training Kit (Exam 70-623): Installing, Maintaining, Supporting, and Troubleshooting Applications on the Windows Vista Client – Consumer
Anil Desai with Chris McCain of GrandMasters
ISBN 9780735624238

Get the 2-in-1 training kit for Exam 70-623, the required exam for the new Microsoft Certified IT Professional (MCITP): Consumer Support Technician certification. This comprehensive kit focuses on supporting Windows Vista clients for consumer PCs and devices, including configuring security settings, networking, troubleshooting, and removing malware. Ace your exam prep—and build real-world job skills—with lessons, practice tests, evaluation software, and more.

See more resources at **microsoft.com/mspress**
and **microsoft.com/learning**

System Requirements

The lessons and practice exercises require access to a computer that is running Windows Vista Home Premium or Windows Vista Ultimate. You should use a test computer on which you can make configuration changes in order to complete the steps of the practice exercise. Some practice exercises have additional requirements, such as an Internet connection or access to specific peripherals. Alternatively, you can complete most practice exercises using a virtual machine instead of a dedicated physical computer.

Hardware Requirements

Your computer should meet the following recommended hardware specifications:

- Personal computer with a 1-GHz or faster processor
- 1 GB of RAM
- 40 GB hard disk with at least 15 GB available
- DVD-ROM drive
- Direct X capable graphics card with 32 MB of graphics memory
- Keyboard and Microsoft mouse or compatible pointing device

Software Requirements

The following software is required to complete the practice exercises:

- Windows Vista Home Premium or Ultimate edition.
- To create a virtual machine within Windows, you can use Microsoft Virtual PC 2007, a free product that is available at *http://www.microsoft.com/windows/downloads/virtualpc /default.mspx*.

What do you think of this book?

We want to hear from you!

Do you have a few minutes to participate in a brief online survey?

Microsoft is interested in hearing your feedback so we can continually improve our books and learning resources for you.

To participate in our survey, please visit:

www.microsoft.com/learning/booksurvey/

...and enter this book's ISBN-10 number (appears above barcode on back cover*).
As a thank-you to survey participants in the United States and Canada, each month we'll randomly select five respondents to win one of five $100 gift certificates from a leading online merchant. At the conclusion of the survey, you can enter the drawing by providing your e-mail address, which will be used for prize notification only.

Thanks in advance for your input. Your opinion counts!

*Where to find the ISBN-10 on back cover

ISBN-13: 000-0-0000-0000-0
ISBN-10: 0-0000-0000-0

Example only. Each book has unique ISBN.

Microsoft®
Press